ISBN 978-1-333-68756-4
PIBN 10535776

This book is a reproduction of an important historical work. Forgotten Books uses
state-of-the-art technology to digitally reconstruct the work, preserving the original format
whilst repairing imperfections present in the aged copy. In rare cases, an imperfection in
the original, such as a blemish or missing page, may be replicated in our edition. We do,
however, repair the vast majority of imperfections successfully; any imperfections that
remain are intentionally left to preserve the state of such historical works.

1 MONTH OF
FREE
READING

at

www.ForgottenBooks.com

By purchasing this book you are eligible for one month membership to ForgottenBooks.com, giving you unlimited access to our entire collection of over 1,000,000 titles via our web site and mobile apps.

To claim your free month visit:
www.forgottenbooks.com/free535776

THE CAT AND HAWK. p. 97.

SKETCHES AND ANECDOTES

OF

ANIMAL LIFE.

BY

THE REV. J. G. WOOD, M.A., F.L.S., ETC.,

AUTHOR OF THE

"ILLUSTRATED NATURAL HISTORY," "BEES," ETC., ETC.

WITH ILLUSTRATIONS BY HARRISON WEIR.

LONDON :

G. ROUTLEDGE AND CO., FARRINGDON STREET.

NEW YORK : 18, BEEKMAN STREET.

1854.

LONDON :

PRINTED BY WOODFALL AND KINDER,

ANGEL COURT, SKINNER STREET.

PREFACE.

DURING the progress of a former work, the "Illustrated Natural History," it was found that the very numerous engravings consumed so much space, that the history of each animal was necessarily reduced to the smallest possible compass.

In order, therefore, to compensate in some degree for that deficiency, a portion of those sketches and anecdotes which were originally intended to have been inserted in the first work, have been brought together in a separate volume.

Even in these pages, which are devoted exclusively to the history of animals, space has failed; and it has been found necessary to postpone several quadrupeds, such as the elephant, rhinoceros, hippopotamus, and many others, to another occasion. It had been intended to include, at least, the whole of the mammalia in this volume; but its limit was unexpectedly reached before the "Sketches" were concluded.

MERTON COLLEGE,
April 7, 1854.

ANECDOTES

OF

ANIMAL LIFE.

"And the Lord God formed man out of the dust of
the ground, and breathed into his nostrils the breath
of life, and man became a living soul." This is related of man alone. Although all other living creatures were also formed out of the dust of the earth,
and endued with the mysterious power of life, yet it
is told of man only, that God himself breathed into
his nostrils the breath of life, and that, in consequence, man became a living soul; that is, that in
the material body of man was implanted, in some
mysterious way, a soul emanating from Divinity itself,
and superior to the life-principle of the inferior animals, inasmuch as it partook of the eternity of its
divine Author. Man became a *living* soul, as distinguished from the beasts that perish.

Here, then, is the great difference between man and
beast. Man is essentially a *soul*, a living soul, that
shall be to all eternity; whose earthly habitation, the
body, partakes of the nature of brute beasts in all
things, excepting that, whereas the bodies of brute
beasts, when the breath of life has departed out of
their nostrils, turn again to their earth, and never take
again the form that had seen corruption, the body of
man attains to such a participation in the nature of
its heavenly inhabitant, that when the last day shall

B

end time, and eternity shall begin, it will also partake in the resurrection.

We will still further pursue the revelations given to us in Holy Writ. " To every beast of the earth, and to every fowl of the air, and to everything that creepeth upon the earth, wherein there is life, I have given every green herb for meat." The spirit of life that exists in living animals renders them far superior to those creatures that increase and grow without possessing life, by which, in this case, we must understand the power of voluntary motion. All living animals had, therefore, power given them over things inanimate; they had their dwelling on the inanimate ground, or pursued their course through the inanimate air, while every green herb was subject to them. Now, while power is given to all living creatures, man of course included, over every green herb of the field, we find that a still superior power is given to man. "Let him have dominion over the fish of the sea, and over the fowl of the air, and over the cattle, and over all the earth, and over every creeping thing that creepeth upon the earth." There must, therefore, be something in man as superior to the beasts of the field as their living principle is superior to that of the herbs of the ground. This something is the eternal soul.

· Every living creature that draws the breath of life has implanted in it a certain power called Instinct. To instinct may be referred the impulse that causes animals to seek those places where their food is most abundant. The lion, for example, is led by the force of his instinct to prowl over the deserts, or lie in wait among the bushes, where he may strike down the unwary antelope, who, in obedience to its own instinct, comes thither to devour the green herbage. The spotted jaguar seeks the gnarled branches of large trees, and remains concealed among the variegated foliage of its native country, while the puma stretches its tawny length upon a branch almost exactly similar to its fur in colour; so that each of these creatures is enabled to capture other animals, whose activity would certainly carry them out of their enemy's reach, had not an over-ruling instinct caused them to assimilate themselves with the substances around, that their prey may inadvertently wander near them. The huge snakes that inhabit the tro-·pical forests hang suspended from the branches, and so closely resemble the creepers that are flung from branch to branch in wild profusion, that the passing stag, buffalo, or puma (if accounts may be relied upon), walks unsuspectingly into the very jaws of the expec-tant serpent.

Such food-procuring instincts are imitated by man, especially when he endeavours to secure any living animal. In imitation of the above-mentioned instinct, the Chinese becomes a successful hunter of water-fowl. After the surface of a sheet of water has been covered with empty gourds, the water-fowl, although at first alarmed, afterwards become accustomed to the floating gourds, and at last actually polish their beaks upon them. The hunter, then, after placing a similar gourd on his head, wades gently into the water, and quickly gains the very centre of the flock of wild fowl. When he has approached sufficiently near any particularly fine bird, he seizes it by the legs, draws it under water, and fastens it to his girdle, where it soon perishes without alarming its companions in the least. In this, man only copies the brutish instinct, and identifies himself with sur-rounding objects, in order to obtain those animals which, from their superior activity, would otherwise make their escape.

Other animals there are which not only avoid frightening their expected prey, but actually entice it to them. Such is the fishing frog (*Lophius piscatorius*), which, after concealing itself in the mud, agitates certain appendages on its head, which by their motion delude inexperienced fish into the idea that they can

make an excellent meal of some very lively worms.
They therefore make an open-mouthed bolt at the supposed worms, and are immediately engulphed in the
enormous jaws of the concealed *Lophius*. So, when,
according to Dr. Johnson's cynical definition, a fool
places himself at one end of a stick, with a worm
dangling from the other, he need not flatter himself
that he is exercising a power which does not belong to
the lower animals—the greatest distinction being probably in the success.

Again, when an enthusiastic sportsman takes the
field on the first of September, accompanied by all
his paraphernalia of dogs, guns, shot-belts, powder-
flasks, &c., &c., he is but exercising a power common to him as to one of the fishes, that of bringing
down a distant prey with a missile. I of course
allude to the chætodon, a beautifully marked fish,
with a beak something like a flageolet, through which
it can aim a drop of water so correctly as to bring
down a fly with certainty at the distance of several
feet.

The African savage finding himself annoyed by
the predacious habits of the lion, or the obstinate
ferocity of the rhinoceros, digs a pitfall, covering the
surface with a treacherous layer of thin twigs and
tempting grass, into which the obnoxious quadruped
is decoyed, and on reaching the bottom impales himself on a sharp spike placed ready to receive him.
Yet, even here, the reasoning operations of man are
anticipated by the instinctive capacities of an insect.
The larva of the ant-lion (*Myrmeleon formicarius*) digs a
pitfall in the loose sand, into which any insect venturing to approach too near the edge is sure to fall, and
is received, not upon a sharp stake, but in the extended
jaws of the ravenous ant-lion at the bottom of his den,
who after sucking all the juices of his victim, throws
away the shrivelled body, and prepares himself for
another.

While, however, similarity of colour is used by

many animals as a means of procuring food, it is by many others made to contribute to their preservation, by deceiving the eyes of those who would otherwise have destroyed them. The elephant, for example, lives among the thorny brakes of its native land, and is so similar in colour to the plants which it haunts, that in spite of its huge bulk, a practised eye is required to discern it. We are told by several authors, that a large herd of elephants can inhabit a comparatively small thorn brake without being seen. Again, the gigantic giraffe, whose long towering neck and spotted hide would appear to render it conspicuous at any distance, is frequently passed by, because the hunter has mistaken it for the trunk of a tree. The giraffe lives among tall, straight trees, and feeds upon their lower branches. Harris remarks of the first giraffe that he had ever seen wild in its native land, "An object which had repeatedly attracted my eye, but which I had as often persuaded myself was nothing more than the branchless stump of a withered tree, suddenly shifted its position, and the next moment I distinctly perceived that singular form of which the apparition had oft times visited my slumbers, but upon whose reality I now gazed for the first time."

When creatures so gigantic as the elephant and giraffe can successfully conceal themselves from the attacks of their enemies by living among objects that resemble themselves in colour, we need not wonder if smaller animals do the same. The Alpine hare, for example, and the ptarmigan, find their safety in the brilliant white coat which assimilates with the snows of winter, while the brown coat which they wear in the summer time so resembles the wastes on which they live, that they are scarcely to be seen even by those who know where and how to look for them, while to the inexperienced eye they are altogether invisible.

This peculiar instinct is largely exemplified in the

insect world. Many insects which are considered as exceedingly rare, are, in fact, comparatively common; but on account of their colours assimilating so nearly with the substances on which they live, they escape the observation of the too eager entomologist. Every one must have noticed how the tortoiseshell butterfly always settles on bright red flowers, and is constantly resting on red bricks, or on a patch of red sand. The geometrical caterpillars stretch their bodies from twigs of trees in such a way that they exactly resemble dead broken branches. I have had hundreds of these caterpillars in confinement, and have frequently seen strangers examine the branches of my insect menagerie for some time without being able to see a single caterpillar. The grasshopper is scarcely to be distinguished from the green herbage among which it lives. The pill-beetle when alarmed draws its legs up to its body, and rolls itself in the dusty roads, where it lies motionless as a dusty pebble, for which it is usually taken. Perhaps a more curious example of the working of this instinct is found in the volucella, a large dipterous insect, which in its larval state lives in the nests of the humble bees. So close is the resemblance between the volucella and a humble-bee, that it walks unsuspected into the nest, lays its eggs, and makes its escape from the castle of those insects whose stings would speedily end its existence, were it not protected by the similarity of its body to those of its enemies. So the North American savage paints his body until all resemblance to man is almost obliterated, so that he can lie unobserved while his enemies are searching for him; and so does he, imitating by his reason the instinct of the volucella, clothe himself in the skin of a slaughtered bison, and unsuspectedly deal destruction among those powerful animals who, if they had not been deceived by his resemblance to themselves, would speedily trample him to pieces.

Although the reason of man leads him to imitate

the instincts of these animals, yet there is one great difference between his imitation and their instinct. Man does so with the intention of producing a certain effect, while the animals whom he imitates only obey a powerful desire implanted in themselves which they cannot resist or change. The boa, for example, would never learn to attack its prey as does the lophius ; nor would the ant-lion learn to hide upon branches like the puma. Indeed, in many cases, we are warranted in supposing that animals obey their instinct unconscious of its effect. It is not likely that the lophius has the least idea that small fish are fond of worms, or that the appendages on its head, which it has never seen, bear any resemblance to worms, or are intended to decoy its prey. It only obeys the impulse of that instinct which leads it to act in the manner which has been already related, without at all referring the effect to the cause. Neither do we suppose that the volucella knows that its body bears any resemblance to that of the humble-bee ; in all likelihood it is not even aware that it runs any risk in its invasion of the humble-bees' nest. It only yields to the overpowering instinct which leads it to enter the nest, and there to deposit its eggs. Nor has it any knowledge of the fact that when hatched, those eggs will become larvæ, who will find themselves at once amid their proper food. So, when the eider duck tears the down from her body, and lines her nest with it, we need not think that she does so from any foresight respecting the future wants of her offspring, but only because her natural instinct teaches her so to do.

Man, however, in imitating these instincts, does so with a definite purpose, and aiming at a definite end. Does he wade, concealing his head in a hollow gourd, while his body is submerged under the water, or does he wrap himself in the hide of a bison, it is, in the one case, to obtain possession of those creatures whose superior activity would otherwise carry them out of his reach, or to destroy with impunity those animals whose bodily powers are far superior to his own. When an angler visits the waters, armed with his rod and line, he does so because he has noticed that fish are attracted by worms; and he, therefore, conceals in his worm an instrument calculated to retain the fish. When the sportsman levels his gun at a bird, he does so in the knowledge that certain substances which he has placed in his gun will so operate, that part of them will be driven with sufficient violence against the bird to maim it, and bring it within his reach. Now, the chætodon, probably, knows not that the drop of water held within its jaws can so operate upon a fly as to destroy its powers of flight, and cause it to fall into the water; nor does it by practice obtain its powers of striking the object aimed at. The first fly ever shot at was struck with as great certainty as the last; it could not miss without acting against its instinct; while the human marksman requires much practice to enable him to strike the object at which he aims.

In the same way the ant-lion digs its pitfall, not because it has any ultimate idea of ensnaring prey, but because the instinct existing within it forces it to do so. But when the man digs a pitfall, he does so in opposition to his instinct, which rather teaches him to lie on his back and do nothing at all. He digs the earth, removes the mould taken from the pit, lest the sharp eyes of his expected prey should see it; he spreads branches over the mouth of the pit, which he knows will not sustain the weight of the animal whom he afterwards decoys to the spot; and, lastly, plants a sharpened stake at the bottom, which he knows will pierce his prey when it has been captured, and thereby enable him to remove it with safety.

Again, the beaver is well known to construct dams across rivers, by which the course of the stream is retarded, and a sufficient depth of water obtained for its purposes. Yet we cannot think that the beaver acts thus from any foreknowledge of the effect that will be produced by this act, because it is found that, when beavers are in captivity, they are constantly building dams with any material that they can find, and appear perfectly satisfied with their labours, even where there is no water at all. A beaver kept in a room was in the habit of collecting the hearth-brush, fire-irons, footstools, &c., and with them erecting a barricade across the corner of the room, within which he sat, apparently as fully convinced of the importance of his work as the Parisian insurgents were of their stronger barricades.

Each animal, then, obeys its own instinct, without taking up that of another, while man is able to take advantage of the instinct of any creature placed in subjection to him, and to use it for his own purposes. Not that man is without instinct; it is instinct which induces the new-born child to seek its mother's breast, or which teaches it to cry when it feels uneasiness. In farther advanced life, although reason has gained the dominion, instinct still holds a partial and salutary sway. There are times when instinct acts as a preservative, where reason would be useless. Among such instances may be noticed the rapid closing of the eyes when menaced by any danger, or the sudden effort made by one who slips over a precipice. In the latter case, it has more than once been recorded, that the adventurer has found himself lying safely on the summit of the precipice, without the slightest recollection of the manner in which he got there, thereby showing that the instinctive force had acted, while the rational powers were, for the time, in abeyance. While, then, both man and beasts possess instinct, one great difference between them lies in this, that beasts implicitly obey, and are entirely ruled, by their instinct, while man has made his instinct subservient to his reason. Now, while we allow that man is endowed with instinct, we must not deny that beasts possess some share of reason. It is but a small share, confined in its limits, and abbreviated in extent, but it is yet reason.

As this volume is not intended to be a treatise on metaphysics, but is merely written to exhibit the instinctive and reasoning powers of animals, I shall not now discuss the difficult and complex question of the effect of the soul upon reason, but will merely observe that the preceding remarks may be summed up in the following brief manner :—

All living creatures possess instinct.

Some also possess a share of reason.

Man possesses instinct, reason, and a soul.

The reasoning powers are particularly exemplified in the cases of domesticated animals, who learn, by their reason, to overcome their instinct. The natural instinct of a cat or dog when left alone in a room where provisions are laid on the table, is to satisfy their hunger by eating the food that lies before them, but their reasoning powers tell them that if they do so their master will certainly punish them : they, therefore, by the exercise of their reason, subdue their instinct. The same may be said of every case where animals diverge from the general rules, and alter their plan of operation to suit circumstances. All birds, when they build their nests, build them according to a plan which rules in each species, so that any one acquainted with practical ornithology, will, at once, on being shown a nest, not only tell the name of the bird that built it, but can also name the locality where it was found. As long as the bird follows the general plan, it works by instinct, but if it departs from that plan, then it may be said to work by reason.

Again, we are told by credible observers, that when an Egyptian dog wishes to drink at the Nile, he goes some way up the river, and howls for some time. The crocodiles, being attracted by the sound, immediately crowd to the place, while the dog hastily runs to the part which the crocodiles have left, and drinks in safety. Precisely the same account is given of the

Indian dogs, who resort to the same ruse when they wish to cross the rivers. Now, if a dog always howled before it drank, or before it took to the water, we should say that it was acting under the influence of instinct; but we know that English dogs do not hesitate to drink at the river side, or to plunge into them without the preliminary of howling. We must, therefore, allow that the Egyptian and Indian dogs act from the impulse of reason, not of instinct.

There have been many works professing to treat of the " instincts " of animals, but, in almost every case, the title is a wrong one. The strictly scientific naturalist is the man who really studies the instincts exhibited by animals, while the general observer usually remarks the reason exhibited by various creatures. Such works, therefore, should be entitled " reason " of animals rather than " instinct." Few but naturalists care about the instincts of living creatures, but every one is interested by the manner in which animals reason. This work is intended not for the scientific naturalist, but for those who, although they may not be enabled to tell the scientific name of an animal, and are content to use the common names of hedgehog or cockatoo in preference to " Erinaceus Europæus," or " Plyctolophus galeritus," yet are interested in the wonderful works of that God who made these creatures as well as themselves, and whose superior mental powers can receive gratification from contemplating the implanted instincts and reason of those creatures placed in subjection under them.

There is also another object. The mind of man is always endeavouring to attain greater and more perfect knowledge of things invisible. Now, if we examine the plans of a building, and see the working of the whole from the time that the foundation stone was laid to the time when the last blow is struck, we attain to some idea of the working of the mind of the architect who built it. Again, supposing that we had before us a painting by some mighty master, our admiration of it is much increased if we also have presented to us the first rude sketches on which he built the perfect master-piece. We see how one idea is carried out and improved upon, and how another is rejected as unsuitable to the unity of the piece ; so that we, as it were, follow the progress of the artist's mind through the medium of his works. So, if we lay before us the works of God, if we contemplate the vast edifice reared by the Great Architect of the Universe, we see how every part of it was placed in just and due order, until the building was completed, by man its copestone. And again, if we desire fully to understand the nature—that is, the physical nature—of man, we must first study the structure, instincts, and habits of the lower parts of creation, which are thus to us, as it were, the sketches leading to the completion of the great work itself. Thus by following the works of the Almighty through their several stages, we are enabled to gain one more step towards the knowledge of God himself.

With regard to the arrangement of the following anecdotes, I have found great difficulty. My first idea was to class them according to the principle developed in them. For example, if that plan had been carried out, every instance of love for young would have been placed together. The difficulty of reference to any particular animal was so great an objection to this arrangement, that it was rejected. At last, I have determined, that as these anecdotes were intended as a companion to the " Illustrated Natural History," the order of that work should be followed, not, perhaps, literally, but, at all events, in the greater divisions. I have, therefore, commenced with the monkey tribe, in defiance of the popular opinion, which appears to demand the lion as the only animal fit to head a Natural History. The monkeys, however, occupy the first place in the British Museum, and, therefore, may here take precedence of the lion.

MONKEYS.

OF all the inferior animals, the monkey tribe approach nearest to the structure of man. Yet this apparent resemblance is mostly in externals, and lessens as we examine into the anatomy of the creature. Our general idea of a monkey is that of an animal sitting or walking upright, and capable of using its hands with as much dexterity as ourselves. This idea is prevalent because so few have seen monkeys in their native state; those whose acquaintance we make being generally instructed to behave in a much more precise manner than is adopted by their relations in their native woods. The erect posture is not at all characteristic of monkeys, for when upon level ground, they always walk upon their hands and feet at the same time, and seldom assume the erect attitude, unless they support themselves by their hands. Any one may see this by paying a visit to the spacious cage at the Regent's Park Zoological Gardens, where they will see that the monkeys scarcely ever assume the erect posture, unless they are clinging to the branches, or to the sides of their cage. The structure of the skeleton is such that the erect posture can only be maintained with considerable effort. The head, too, is set on the neck in quite a different manner from the human head. The head of the monkey is, like that of the quadrupeds, set on very far back, forcing nearly the whole of the face forward and downward.

The monkeys possess a very large share of sagacity, and have the power of acting in concert with each other to an extent that renders them very dangerous as bodies, although comparatively insignificant as individuals. They make regularly-organised descents upon orchards and other cultivated grounds, and contrive

to do an incredible amount of mischief in a very short
time.   It is said that they will silently strip the trees
of their fruit, and convey their ill-gotten spoils into
their own domains by passing it from hand to hand
along the line of monkeys, which have arranged themselves at regular distances from the forest to the or-
chard. This, however, is scarcely authenticated enough
to be admitted without further proof.

They seem devoted to mischief, and apparently
undertake a mischievous task purely from a love of
mischief itself without the hope of gaining anything,
and frequently even when they are perfectly certain of
being punished for it.   My readers will doubtless remember the exploits of that monkey whose numerous
tricks are related by Basil Hall in his Fragments.
The cunning animal would wait at the hatchway with
a handspike in his hands until he heard some one
mounting the steps, when he would let the handspike
drop clattering down the ladder, and immediately take
to his heels.   The aggrieved party below, on finding
his shins considerably scarified by the falling handspike, naturally enough vowed vengeance against
Jaeko, who would sit in the rigging alternately
screaming with delight at his successful bit of mischief, and chattering with fear at the punishment
which he knew would inevitably follow.

These tricks he would constantly play until even the
forbearance of the sailors would be exhausted, and
Jaeko was submitted to court-martial, tried, and condemned to suffer certain lashes.   This he resented
greatly, and on more than one occasion bit several of the
sailors rather severely. The captain accordingly issued
his mandate that the monkey should be thrown overboard, but the sailors, unwilling to lose their favourite,
consulted with the assistant surgeon, who by depriving the monkey of his sharp teeth, rendered him quite
harmless.   Indeed, it would have gone to the sailors'
hearts to lose him, as he was instructed to play most
of his tricks on the marines, between which body of

THE MONKEY AND THE NUTS.   p. 15.

...the sailors there is always a feud. The un-
...animal at last lost his life by his love of
... for on seeing the doctor very busily making
... pills, he naturally thought he must value the
...one at which he was working so hard. Accord-
...directly the doctor's back was turned, he pounced
... entire mass of pills, and cramming them into
...uch, scudded off to the mast head, where he
...ptured just as he had swallowed the last por...
... the stolen property. He had abstracted enough
...l pills to dose the whole ship's company, and
...rse, his constitution was not proof against the
... In spite of every remedy, he died in a short
...fter he had swallowed the fatal pills.

...nay appear singular that so small an animal
...stow away so much in his cheeks; but the
...lity of a monkey's pouches is almost as in-
...hi... as the ... of a dragon-fly or a school-
...I have ... ... endeavoured to fill the
... of a monkey in ... ... but have never
... ... A friend of mine, how-
... ... in the
... ... a
... full of ... ... seeing
...the animal ... ...
... could contain no ...
...ging to ... to insert ...
...lled receptacle, it turned out ...
...nto its hands. Immediately it ...
... other monkeys, who had been ...
...ng the appropriation of so many ...
...eant a member of their society, and ...
...the hands that endeavoured to snatch ...
...fortunate little monkey's property. ...
... creature made its way to a shelf, ...
...ded, and covered it with its two hands. This
...tainly guarded the nuts from the depredations
...rounding monkeys, but effectually prevented the
...rance of any of them to the mouth of their

men and the sailors there is always a feud. The unfortunate animal at last lost his life by his love of mischief; for on seeing the doctor very busily making calomel pills, he naturally thought he must value the substance at which he was working so hard. Accordingly, directly the doctor's back was turned. he pounced on the entire mass of pills, and cramming them into his pouch, scudded off to the mast head, where he was captured just as he had swallowed the last portion of the stolen property. He had abstracted enough calomel pills to dose the whole ship's company, and of course, his constitution was not proof against the poison. In spite of every remedy, he died in a short time after he had swallowed the fatal pills.

It may appear singular that so small an animal could stow away so much in his cheeks; but the capability of a monkey's pouches is almost as inscrutable as the appetite of a dragon-fly or a schoolboy. I have more than once endeavoured to fill the pouches of a monkey to overflowing, but have never yet succeeded in so doing. A friend of mine, however, by selecting one of the smallest monkeys in the cage at the Zoological Gardens, and purchasing a large bag full of enormous nuts, did succeed in giving the little animal such a number of nuts that its pouches could contain no more. At last, after endeavouring in vain to insert another nut into the over-filled receptacles, it turned out the entire contents into its hands. Immediately it was surrounded by the other monkeys, who had been indignantly watching the appropriation of so many nuts by so insignificant a member of their society, and numerous were the hands that endeavoured to snatch some of the unfortunate little monkey's property. The persecuted creature made its way to a shelf, deposited its burden, and covered it with its two hands. This ruse certainly guarded the nuts from the depredations of surrounding monkeys, but effectually prevented the conveyance of any of them to the mouth of their legitimate owner, as the moment that one of the hands were lifted off, half a dozen paws were instantly thrust forth, and the unfortunate little monkey, suffering as many human creatures do from à superabundance of wealth for which all its relations were persecuting it, was forced to replace its hand, and content itself with showing its teeth, and chattering vigorously at its assailants. Suddenly a bright thought struck it. It pushed all the nuts up into a corner, watched an opportunity when its persecutors were not on their guard, suddenly turned round and sat on them. Then looking with an air of triumphant defiance at the baffled fortune hunters, it drew the nuts one by one from beneath its person, and cracked them with great composure and dignity.

A baboon has been known to cram into its cheek pouches a lady's purse, gloves, and handkerchief, of course with no other object in the world than mischief; as a monkey is an excellent judge of what is good to eat, and is not at all likely to be deceived into the idea that a purse, gloves, and handkerchief are eatable, however delicately scented the latter may be.

When monkeys are in captivity they always endeavour to be noticed by visitors, partly for vanity's sake, and partly because they hope for certain donations of nuts, apples, and other dainties. Their jealousy is easily excited, and knows no bounds if they imagine that their rival is getting more than his fair share of the good things. I was once a witness to a most absurd scene of jealousy.

A few years ago, one of Wombwell's well-known collections visited Oxford, and, as usual, exhibited a large allowance of monkeys. These little animals, exercised all their ingenuity in attracting the notice of the visitors in order to obtain some of the nuts, cakes, &c., which they saw the elephant receiving. One particularly lively monkey had attained to considerable eminence in his art, and used to monopolise no small portion of the various delica-

cies. Suddenly he failed to procure his usual supplies, and saw, with great indignation, that most of
the visitors, particularly the ladies, had turned their
attentions to the next cage. This, of course, excited
his jealousy and curiosity, and he exercised all his
endeavours to discover the cause of his desertion. At
length, by dint of great perseverance, he contrived to
poke out a knot in the board which divided their par-
titions, and, on looking through, discovered that the
inhabitant of the adjoining tenement had lately been
blessed with a baby. That unfortunate baby-monkey
instantly became the object of his unremitting perse-
cution. He watched it through his knot hole; he put
his hand round the corner, and tried to pinch the poor
little animal; he picked the keeper's pocket of the
food that ought to have gone to the rival; and, in
fact, spent his time in devising new annoyances. The
mother all this time was perfectly acquainted with the
evil designs of her neighbour, and carefully kept her
baby away from the dangerous corner where the monkey's hand was continually intruding itself. In a short
time the little one was suffered to go about by itself,
and its untiring enemy redoubled his exertions.

At last his time of revenge arrived. One day he was
observed to pay more attention than usual to his peep-
hole, and after long and patient watching, he was seen
to commence that peculiar vibrating movement which
generally prefaces a monkey's mischief. Suddenly his
eye was withdrawn from the knot-hole, his hand thrust
through like lightning. and withdrawn, bringing with
it the tail of the unfortunate little monkey on the
other side of the partition. He fixed his feet firmly
on each side of the knot-hole, and tugged away at his
rival's tail, alternately screaming with delight, and
chattering with fear at the punishment which he well
knew would follow. The poor baby-monkey, on being
assaulted in such an unexpected manner, set up a
most heart-rending outcry, on hearing which, its mother flew to its assistance, and seeing her offspring

c

apparently fastened to the wall, seized it by its arms,
and pulled with all her might in order to release it.
The aggressor chattered, the mother remonstrated,
and the baby screamed, until the outcry drew the attention of a keeper, at whose approach the aggressor
loosed his hold of his victim's tail, and crouched into
the farthest corner of his cage, where he displayed
exceeding ingenuity in avoiding the cuts of the keeper's
whip.

It was fair time at Oxford, and Wombwell's was, of
course, a great attraction, and the monkeys, as usual,
were much appreciated by the visitors. Among the
spectators was a boy of about twelve or thirteen, who
had deemed it necessary to pay due honour to the
fair by appearing in a new cap. He, among others,
had been attracted by the ludicrous antics of a cage
full of monkeys, and in his delight at their wit and
activity he approached too near the wires. Instantly
the ready hand of a monkey seized his much-prized
cap, dragged it through the bars, and held it in
triumph for the inspection of the other inhabitants of
the cage. The keeper immediately came to the rescue,
but the monkey, who appeared to be perfectly acquainted with the length of the keeper's whip and
arm, retreated to the further corner of the cage,
twisted the crown of the cap up like a rope, bit a
great circular piece out, and flung it at the former
owner. This process was continued until he had
disposed of the entire cap, with the exception of the
leather shade. This made him very angry, and he
danced about the cage in great indignation, biting
and tearing at it without the slightest effect. At last
he seemed to consider it a hopeless business, and
consoled himself with using it as a missile against
the spectators who were watching his proceedings.

It is very amusing to give a monkey something
which he does not quite understand. The air of
supreme wisdom and indifference, with which he at
first views it, soon yields to the spirit of curiosity so

deeply seated in monkeys as well as in men ; and he examines it with cautious fear ; but soon either declines meddling with it altogether, or else despises it as a weak invention of the enemy. There are always some monkeys kept in the Botanical Gardens at Oxford, and these creatures afford a never-failing fund of amusement to those who walk in the gardens. Every one goes to look at the monkeys ; some tease them by poking them with sticks, pelting them with small stones, or, what seems to irritate them more than anything else, by grinning at them—an art which some of the undergraduates possess in great perfection. The monkeys are particularly fond of the leaves that are blown within their reach, and appreciate them almost as much as they do orange-peel.

A few days before these lines were written, a great humble-bee that had maimed itself was pushed into the monkeys' cage. Of course it set up a tremendous buzzing, which immediately drew the attention of the monkeys. They were evidently completely upset by the entrance of such an unwonted intruder. Banquo's ghost himself could not have caused more dismay than did the great humble-bee among the monkeys. They approached it with great care, always dashing up the sides of the cage at every fresh ebullition of the humble-bee, and looking down at it with intense horror. At last one of them, after considering the matter, picked up a piece of paper that, among other objects, had been inserted into their cage, and with a dexterity that a grocer might have envied, twisted it up into a sugar-loaf form. He then approached the humble-bee, which was lying on its back, spinning round and round, and making an extraordinary hubbub, swept it into the paper receptacle, twisted it up with astonishing rapidity, and patted and rolled it about until the hums of the enclosed bee were most effectually stopped by being mashed into a pulp. When this end had been attained, the monkey took up the paper containing the triturated bee, and flung it through the railings with all its strength.

The same monkeys were also particularly perplexed by a snail that had made its way into their cage. They seldom ventured to put their fingers near it, but when it began to crawl, and waved its head and horns in the air, the temptation was irresistible ; and they accordingly just pushed it with the tips of their fingers.   On feeling the cold slimy surface of the snail, and seeing it retreat within its shell, they looked with the most ludicrous dismay, first at the ends of their fingers, and then at the retreating snail.

A monkey is a sufficiently amusing animal to keep, but not at all a safe one, for, if it should chance to gain its liberty, nothing can be considered safe from its attacks.   Even when safely confined in a cage it will continue to perpetrate sundry mischievous acts. I once saw the keeper at the Zoological Gardens feeding the monkeys with slices of turnip and carrot. After he had fed one set of monkeys, he turned round to feed the others.   Scarcely had he moved, when a paw was protruded from one of the cages, and busily occupied in ransacking the keeper's pockets.   However, the keeper was accustomed to such tricks, and had placed in his pocket, entire turnips and carrots, which the monkey could not draw between the bars. The smaller monkeys are particularly fond of insects, especially beetles, and will devour large quantities of them.   Let no entomologist venture to keep a monkey, but take warning by a disastrous affair that took place in the museum of an enthusiastic naturalist.

He had been for some time amassing the insect pro- ductions of the country, and had brought together a large collection of insects, particularly beetles.   One day he left open a valuable work containing coloured figures of beetles, by which he had been making out the species. A small monkey which he had in confine- ment escaped from its prison, and in course of its peregrinations, in which it indulged in regaining its liberty, unfortunately entered the room where the beetles were kept. Of course such a prize was not to be withstood. There were two opportunities presented to it here, each of them attractive to a monkey, but when conjoined perfectly irresistible. First, there was a splendid chance of doing considerable mischief, and secondly, there were several hundred beetles lying helpless before it. So the monkey immediately commenced operations. When the naturalist re-entered his room, his horror was very great to find that the monkey had pinched out all the figures of beetles from the book and eaten them, paying a compliment to the draughtsman not inferior to that which the birds paid to the painted grapes of Zeuxis.

This was not the worst of the misfortune, for the little insatiable animal had also eaten all the impaled beetles in the boxes. The irate entomologist immediately went in search of the robber, fulminating all kinds of threats against the ruthless destroyer of his museum, but his anger was soon changed into pity on seeing the miserable state of the poor monkey. The unfortunate animal in robbing the cabinet had been in such haste, for fear of detection, that with the beetles he had also swallowed all the pins on which they were impaled. Of course, no powers of digestion could overcome such a dinner as this, and the poor creature died next day in great agonies, a victim to natural history.

There is always a deadly feud between the parrots and monkeys in their native lands, the subject of dispute being the parrots' tails. In general, monkeys appear to have a great objection to a tail being worn by any one but themselves, and never lose an opportunity of giving the tail of a companion a sly pull. The curly tail of a pig always appeared to excite great indignation in the mind of one monkey, who lived on board the same vessel with it. As the pig ran about the deck, the monkey, immediately taking

umbrage at the pig venturing to wear a curly tail contrary to the fashion of his own, which was straight,
used to run after him, and hold on by the pig's tail,
tugging at it with all his might to drag it straight in
uniformity with his own. Were we Pythagoreans, we
should pronounce that the soul of Paul of Russia had
transmigrated into the monkey.

The monkeys pull the parrots' tails for a very different purpose. They like to suck the soft juicy end
of the quills, and are in consequence always stealing
after the unfortunate parrots. Even in captivity they
retain the same eager desire for parrots' tails, and if a
monkey and parrot are in the same room the monkey
is constantly hovering round the cage watching his
opportunity to thrust his paw through the wires and
take a pull at the feathers. The parrot exhibits her
sagacity by keeping her face always towards the
monkey, and making a peck with her sharp bill at his
outstretched hand, so that at a short distance the
parrot appears to be continually bowing to the monkey
with the greatest and most formal politeness.

Mr. Bennett, in his "Wanderings," gives a very
interesting account of a monkey which lived on board
with him. It struck up a great friendship for a little
Papuan girl, and would share its biscuit with her in
the most loving way. Among its peculiarities it had
a great hankering for a piece of soap possessed by
Mr. Bennett, and would constantly endeavour to steal
it when he was not watching it. On one occasion he
pretended not to see it, and permitted the monkey to
take the soap, and walk half across the cabin with its
prize. On speaking to it the monkey went back and
quietly replaced the soap where it had found it. This
monkey was a Siamang, and probably inherited the
wish for soap from his parents, for the Siamangs are
very careful of the cleanliness of their children, and
wash them with great assiduity.

It is related of a monkey who lived on board ship
where there were also some pigs, that he was the

plague of their life. No sooner did a pig venture to take a walk than the monkey slid down some rope, and mounting on his back, forced his unwilling steed to carry him about the deck. A stranger steed than this was used by the monkeys at the Zoological Gardens, who pressed into their service an armadillo, who lived in a burrow at the bottom of the monkey-cage, and who never ventured out of his hole without having to carry one or more monkeys across the yard.

The same strange fellowship took place in one of Wombwell's caravans. In the same cage were eight or ten monkeys of various sizes, an armadillo, and a hedgehog. The latter animal was, on account of his spikes, evidently considered by the monkeys as an unpleasant companion who must be let alone, but the armadillo spent quite a different life. Its usual place of rest was in a corner, but no sooner had it settled itself quietly for a nap, than the largest monkey came gravely and seated himself on the armadillo's back, and surveyed the scene with a most solemn and self-satisfied air. Presently another monkey came and took a seat by the first, and then a third added himself to the load, until in a very short time the unfortunate armadillo was quite hidden under a pile of monkeys. Not that it seemed to trouble itself much about its riders, for it trotted about with the greatest unconcern, evidently caring little whether a monkey were sitting on its back or not.

The desire for equitation seems to be naturally implanted in the monkey mind. Not long ago, a gentleman who rather prided himself on a very fine stud of hunters, found that the horses did not appear properly refreshed by their nightly rest. One of the grooms, on being desired to keep a strict watch, discovered that a tame monkey belonging to the house was accustomed to ride on the horses' backs almost all night, preventing them from taking sufficient rest. His master, on discovering his penchant for riding, and being averse to killing the monkey on account of his horsemanship, succeeded in curing him effectually of his love for horses. The next time that the hounds met, he had the monkey put into a full hunting suit and secured by a strap to the saddle of his most spirited hunter, and took him away to the meet. When the fox was found the horse pricked up his ears at the well-known sound, and started off at once. The chase happened to be a particularly long and severe one, the monkey of course from his light weight being far ahead of the legitimate huntsmen. A country-man, who was coming from the direction which the fox had taken, was interrogated by some of the sports-men who had been thrown out as to the position of the hunt, and told them that the fox was looking tired, but that none of the huntsmen was near, except a little gentleman in a yellow jacket, who took his leaps beautifully. Sure enough, Master Jacko was in at the death, but did not by any means appreciate the honour. After the fox had been killed, there was a long ride home again, by the end of which time the monkey seemed thoroughly wearied out. After the experience that he had of a day's hunting he was never known to mount a horse again.

A pony of my acquaintance was celebrated for his talent at throwing every one who tried to mount him, his principal manoeuvre being a rapid twist to his right as he descended from a rear, and then a sudden jump to the left directly his feet touched the ground. I never saw him beaten except on two occasions. On one occasion his rider was a monkey, who stuck so firmly with all his four hands to the saddle that the pony could not even shake him; and the rider on the second occasion was a very long-legged butcher's lad, who contrived to hitch his feet together under the pony's belly, and by squeezing him whenever he attempted to rear completely mas-tered him.

It is rather remarkable that there are very few

THE MONKEY CURED OF RIDING.   p. 24.

animals who will live together without quarrelling. I do not allude to animals of different species, as they could hardly be expected to be in constant contact with each other without some disagreements. Of course the "happy (?) families" exhibited in various parts of London are exceptions to this rule, but they are only examples of the success of the training employed in forcing animals so incongruous to live in the same cage in perfect harmony. The cats and owls, for example, sit and doze away the hours, perfectly heedless of their natural prey the rats, mice, and small birds, which not only run or hop about devoid of all fear, but actually on a cold day may be seen nestling in the warm fur of the cat, or the soft feathers of the owl.

Animals, however, belonging to the same species, nearly always quarrel when in captivity, at all events until the question of supremacy is completely settled. Such being the case, it can hardly be expected that monkeys should be exempt from the rule. Whenever a number of monkeys are confined in one place, even though it be a large and spacious apartment, there is a constant bullying going on which forcibly reminds one of Oriental governments. The biggest monkey beats, bites, or robs the second biggest monkey. He revenges himself by beating, biting, and robbing monkey number three, who in his turn solaces himself by bullying number four, and so on down to the smallest and weakest monkey, who is so harassed by all the others, that if any one monkey makes a demonstration at any other monkey, it scuds up the side of the cage, and squeezes itself into a corner, squeaking piteously in anticipation of future sufferings.

There was a significant phrase in very general use some time ago. Crouched into the very smallest space into which a human being could be supposed to be compressed, and striving to hide his countenance behind two dictionaries and a gradus placed

fortress-wise at the top of his desk, sits a boy endeavouring to eat an apple during those "graver hours
that bring constraint." As well might the Chinese
trust to their pasteboard armour against the European musket ball, as the unfortunate boy endeavour
to shield his delinquencies from the fire of the master's eye behind his paper fortification. The very
presence of the battlements proves that there is an
enemy to be guarded against; so, by a brisk flanking
movement, he sweeps the glacis, *i. e.* the desk, and
intercepts the enemy in the very act of foraging on
forbidden ground. So he immediately issues a summons : "Appelquit, come here," and as the poor
boy obeys the summons, he adds in a very deliberate
tone, and with a nod at every second word, "I have
a crow to pluck with you." And the crow is accordingly plucked; an operation, which, if we may judge
from the demeanour of the culprit, who is supposed to assist in the crow-plucking, is of a nature
anything but agreeable, and has the effect of causing
him to choose a seat with great circumspection when
it is completed.

Now, from whence did this phrase "plucking a crow"
originate? Surely from the conduct of a monkey.
The animal in question was accustomed to reside at
the end of a chain, whose other extremity was attached to an iron ring passing round a tall pole, up
and down which it easily played, so that the monkey
might amuse himself by climbing up and down the
pole. Of course there was at the summit of the pole
what sailors call a "truck," i. e. a cheese-shaped piece
of wood, which prevented the monkey from drawing
the ring over the top of the pole; and on this
truck, the monkey usually sat. His daily food was
always supplied in a pan placed near the foot of the
pole. A colony of crows soon discovered the constant supply of food, and as they could fly faster than
the rightful owner could slide down the pole, they
generally carried off the greater part of the provisions

before he reached the pan. This state of things continued for some time, until, at last, the poor monkey became quite desperate; and, after long deliberation, hit upon a plan for keeping his dinner to himself.

One day, the pan was put down as usual, and the crows as usual commenced an attack. The monkey thereupon began to slide down the pole by slow degrees, as if he were very ill. When he reached the ground, he commenced rolling about as if in great agony, taking great care to get nearer to the pan at each struggle. When, at last, he succeeded in reaching it, he lay down as if he were completely worn out. By this time, only one solitary morsel was left in the dish, round which the crows were circling, partly in fear, partly in hope. Emboldened by the quiet demeanour of the monkey, one crow, more daring or more hungry than the rest, made a bold dash at the plate. Scarcely had its beak reached the coveted prize, when the arm of the monkey was stretched out with a swiftness that the bird had by no means calculated on, the crow seized by the neck, and the monkey completely restored to health. Still grasping the crow by the neck, its captor deliberately ascended the pole, and took his accustomed seat. Placing the offending bird between his knees, and chattering defiance at his winged foes, whose notes of exultation were now changed to screams of terror, he slowly and carefully plucked the bird, feather by feather, until it was entirely stripped. After grinning and chattering at the unfortunate bird for a few minutes longer, he flung it high into the air among its screaming comrades. Of course, the denuded crow fell to the ground with a violence that immediately put an end to the small amount of vitality that had survived the plucking process. Ever after this incident, the monkey was permitted to enjoy his dinner in peace and quietness.

Non-zoological parents have often confessed themselves unable to distinguish between their mischievous offspring and the monkey tribe. Perhaps their perplexities might be increased if they knew how similar the rule of a large school is to that of a large monkey cage. In each there is one tyrant who bullies everybody, and one weakling who is bullied by everybody. In each, the members are always on the look-out to play each other practical jokes, and it is impossible to say whether monkeys or schoolboys rejoice most at the success of a joke played at the expense of some one else. Then both monkeys and schoolboys have an unlimited capacity for apples, nuts, cakes, and other irregular articles of food, while if a little one gets an apple, a big one takes it away, whether boy or monkey. Moreover, both boys and monkeys display the same semi-contemptuous fear of their master, and while exhibiting the demurest of deportments while his eye is upon them, never neglect an opportunity of taking a sly grin when his back is turned. Sometimes one of the monkeys takes a particular spite against another, and is constantly persecuting it on grounds quite as trifling as the causes of offence given by the Æsopian lamb to the wolf. I lately saw a rather amusing example of a persecuting monkey receiving his deserts.

The monkey in question had a great objection to another in the same cage—of course a smaller one—and was always looking out for some pretext to worry it. Soon the small monkey, being enticed by a piece of apple, ventured within arm's length of its persecutor, who instantly plunged at it, tumbled it on the ground, and bit it in the neck. It then grasped the poor little creature's tail, and ran up to the roof of the cage, when it transferred the end of the victim's tail to its mouth, and swung it backwards and forwards, of course biting the poor animal's tail most severely. The little monkey naturally made an extraordinary outcry, which reached the ears of the keeper, who left his work and proceeded towards the cage. " I 've been watching you," said the keeper ; whereupon the big monkey let go the little monkey's tail, and tried

to look as if he were some one else. The keeper
opened the door and entered the cage, the monkey
sitting quite still, but watching him out of the corner
of his eyes. Presently the keeper produced a whip,
and made one step to the corner where the delinquent was sitting, when the monkey was everywhere at
once, hoping to elude the whip. Just, however, as he
made a great spring, the whip descended upon him
in mid air, whereat he uttered a doleful howl, and
dashed into a corner. Down came the whip again,
and away went the monkey, still followed by the whip,
until at last he coiled himself up very small, packed
himself into a corner, and contented himself with squeaking at each cut. In the meanwhile, all the other monkeys had clung in a knot to the rails, except one, who
had chosen a capital plan to avoid a chance stroke of
the whip; for at the beginning of the chastisement
he had jumped on the keeper's back, and stuck there
firmly, nor was he dislodged without some difficulty.

There have been many tales of the combination of
monkeys armed with sticks, who have made war or
resisted their enemies with great effect. This is not
true, as it has been satisfactorily ascertained that in
their native state, these animals have no idea of weapons, and that the sticks, &c., said to be thrown at
travellers as they pass under the branches of trees,
are merely the dead branches broken off, as with the
mischievousness of their tribe they pass along the
tops of the trees to watch the proceedings of the
intruders below.* They can, however, be taught to
use a stick, and to use it well. Some time ago, two
Italians were the joint proprietors of an organ and a
monkey, the latter animal attracting the spectators'
sympathies to a great extent. During one of their
exhibitions a dog flew at the little monkey, and of
course excited the indignation not only of its owners,
but of the bystanders. Words ran high on both

* Perhaps the smaller monkeys may do so, the large ones
do not.

sides, and at last it was agreed that the dog and monkey should fight it out, the monkey in consideration of his inferior size, to be allowed a stick.

A suitable staff was accordingly prepared, and the monkey instructed in the part he was to play, in the following manner. One of the Italians went on all fours barking like a dog, while the other got on his back, grasped his hair, and beat him about the head with the stick. The monkey looked on with great gravity, and when the instruction was over, received the stick with the air of a man who knew his work, and meant to do it. Preliminaries being settled, the dog flew at the monkey with open mouth. The monkey immediately leaped on his back, and grasping the dog's ear, paid away at his head with such good will, that his adversary speedily gave in. The monkey, however, was not content with a mere victory, but continued pounding at the dog's head until he left him senseless on the ground.

These various tricks belong only to the smaller monkeys, the larger ones being exceedingly savage and morose as they grow old, although they are gentle, and affectionate enough when young, and may be taught sundry tricks. Even the savage orang-outang* is a very gentle creature during its youth. Many of my readers may remember the young orang-outang at the Zoological Gardens, and its quiet manners. It used to take walks in the garden leaning on its keeper's arm, or sometimes accompanied by a lady. Yet had it lived to its full growth, this creature would most assuredly have sunk into a savage, ferocious, and unapproachable animal.

The docility of this animal when young is well shown in the description of a tame orang named Tuan, in the possession of Dr. Yvan, a French traveller. He was about three years old when first presented to Dr. Yvan, and about as tall as a child of the same age. When he was first introduced to his cell, he collected all the linen he could lay his hands

* *Simia Satyrus.*

upon, carried it into his room, and covered the walls with it. Having completed these arrangements, he took a napkin, rolled himself up in it, and took formal possession of his new home. He was very fond of clothing himself, for what reason it is difficult to say. Cold could not have been the cause, for the temperature of the tropics is more likely to induce one to throw off clothes than to put them on. Everything of a textile nature was heaped upon his shoulders and head, even to the carpet of his room.

His disposition was not unlike that of a spoiled child, agreeable and gentle as long as he had his own way, but pettish and irritable if he were opposed or contradicted. " One day," writes Dr. Yvan, " I took from him a mango he had stolen; at first he tried to get it back, but being unable to do so, he uttered plaintive cries, thrusting out his lips like a pouting child. Finding that this pettishness had not the success he anticipated, he threw himself flat on his face, struck the ground with his fist, screamed, cried, and howled, for more than half an hour; at last I felt that I was acting contrary to my duty in refusing the fruit he desired. For, in opposition to God's will, I was seeking to bend to the exigences of our civilisation the independent nature which He had sent into the world amidst virgin forests, in order that it should obey its instinct and satisfy all its passions. I approached my ward, calling him by the most endearing names, and offered him the mango. As soon as it was within his reach, he clutched it with violence, and threw it at my head.

" There was something so human in this action, something so evil in the expression of his rage, that I had no hesitation that day in classing Tuan among our own species, he reminded me so much of certain children of my acquaintance. But since then I have learned better, he was only on rare occasions peevish and naughty." The doctor's experience of children must have been rather unpleasant—we will hope that few children of our own country have come in his way. This pouting of the lips seems to be the common habit of the orang when displeased or perplexed.

At table the orang behaved himself very well after a few lessons. At first he used to stretch his long arms over the table, and snatch at everything that pleased him, and when admonished by a box on the ear that his deportment was not quite so perfect as that of the celebrated Mr. Turveydrop, he guarded his face with one hand, while he extended the other towards the dish. A rap on the offending hand from the handle of a knife taught him that although his face might be shielded, his hands were equally assailable, and afterwards he waited to be helped. When a plate of soup was first presented to him, he exhibited little less distress than the stork in the fable under similar circumstances. He got on the table and tried to lap it up, and finding this process very slow, he returned to his chair, and lifting up his plate, tried to drink out of it. Of course he then spilled the soup over his breast. Taught by these failures, he soon learned the use of a spoon, and ever after made use of it with great address.

On board ship he became quite one of the crew, having, like the men, his spoon and tin basin, which he used to take with him in the morning and get filled with coffee, after which, he would take his breakfast with the crew.

He did not, however, confine himself to coffee, but became a perfect connoisseur in wines. He had once a glass half full of claret, and another half full of champagne given him. In order to make sure of the best, he took them both, one in each hand : a bystander then endeavoured to take away the glass containing the champagne. The monkey was too sharp for him, for he instantly poured the champagne into the claret glass, and then held out the empty glass to the person who had offered to take it away. Another time, as he was amusing himself among the ropes of the ship, he was called down to partake of a glass of beer. Now beer was a very favourite beverage with Tuan, but swinging in the ropes was also a very favourite amusement, and he had not the smallest intention of substituting the one for the other until he was sure of gaining by the exchange. So he stayed among the ropes for some time, looking earnestly at the liquid, evidently half suspecting that it was not beer. So he laid hold of a loose rope, lowered the end of it into the tumbler, drew it up again, and sucked the moistened end. Having thus satisfied himself that the proffered beverage really *was* beer, he descended at once.

Like almost all the large apes, Tuan held the smaller monkeys in supreme contempt, and would even prefer the company of a dog or a sheep to that of the other monkeys on board. No animal was suffered to enter his cage, and one day he caught and plucked an unfortunate pigeon that had entered his domains. His principal playfellows were the Tagal girls, and his principal employment mango stealing, in which act he was quite an adept. He had some notion of property, for when the mangoes on which he was fed were placed on board, he could be trusted to go into the place where they were stowed away together with fruits belonging to the officers, the only precaution necessary being to point out his own bunches of mangoes. These he would consider his own, and never offered to touch the others until his own were gone, when he devoted his energies to stealing those that remained. In that case his whole demeanour altered. As long as he had mangoes of his own in the cabin, he used to go in boldly, but when his own had been exhausted, and he was attempting to steal, he used to crawl in very slowly and stealthily, and after having committed the theft, would run away as fast as he could.

Dr. Yvan utterly denies that orangs have ever

D

learned to smoke, and denounces all pictures representing them so doing as " stereotyped lies."

BATS.

MANY of my readers are, doubtless, acquainted with
Paget's humorous, and, withal, instructive work, " The
Hope of the Katzekopfs of Katzenellenbogen," and
will recollect the fate of the self-willed hero of the
tale, how that he defied the power of his fairy god-
mother, and how he endeavoured to wrest the magic
wand from her hand, and the disastrous consequences
that followed.   How the fairy shot through the keyhole of the door, carrying her wand with her, and
how, when the wilful prince refused to loose his hold
of the top of the wand when ordered, found that he
was unable to do so when he wished—the wand exercising a power similar to that produced by the inno-
cent-looking cylinders suspended to a galvanic battery
—and how he found the wand slowly but surely passing through the keyhole, dragging his fingers with it,
which elongated like wire as they reached the narrow
aperture, and how his whole body afterwards followed,
and was rolled up into a highly elastic football by the
incensed fairy.
   Now, if you were to attach to the end of the fairy's
wand the limbs of a mouse instead of a prince, and
draw them through a piece of lady's perforated card
as far as the shoulder, and afterwards to place the
elongated limbs under Nasmyth's steam hammer, in
order to flatten out the skin, you would get a very
decent imitation of a bat.
   There are many species of bats spread over the
greater part of the globe, of which about twenty-three
are known to inhabit England.   The most common
of these, are the common bat (*Scotophilus murinus*), a
name that may be translated " Mouse-coloured Lover-
of-Darkness—and the common long-eared bat, whose

scientific name (*Plecotus communis*) means " the common Folded-ears." The latter of these creatures is the most beautiful of all our British bats, owing its beauty to its enormous semi-transparent ears, which are constantly in motion, and thrown into the most elegant curves. This creature is easily tamed, and has been known to be so far domesticated, as to live in the room with a family, and take flies from the hand. It would also take a fly from between the lips of any of the family, and was so familiar with its friends, that if any of them made a humming noise with the lips in imitation of a fly, the bat would immediately settle on its friend's cheek and search about his lips for the expected prey.

Some interesting accounts of the habits of the British bats have been given by various persons who have had them in captivity. The manner of feeding and seizing their prey differs in the various species. The British bats are entirely insectivorous, although they will feed upon raw meat when in confinement. The great bat (*Noctulinia altivolans*) pounces on its food just as a dog snaps at a piece of meat, while the pipistrelle (*Scotophilus murinus*) directly a fly comes within range of its wings, strikes it down with a sharp blow, and falls down upon it, cowering over it with its wings like the Nameless Horror, Zanoni's fearful Dweller of the Threshold, and putting its head under its wings, soon secures its imprisoned prey. This same bat has been frequently found saving itself the trouble of hunting after flies, by getting into larders, and making a meal upon the meat which it found there. A Great bat, or *Noctule*, when in confinement, would not touch flies, but devoured chopped raw meat with avidity, the only insect it would eat being the common cockchafer, and the greater part of even that insect was rejected. The same bat was fortunately possessed of a baby, and exhibited, or rather did *not* exhibit the method of nursing its offspring. In this duty, the flexible membrane of the wings was called into play, and turned to a rather unexpected use. The young bat was completely enveloped in the folds of its mother's wings, which were thus converted into a warm and soft cradle, which not only possessed the advantage of warmth, but also kept the young from falling out of it. So tightly did the mother bat wrap up her young one, that it could not be seen at all. It does not exactly agree with our notions of infant nurture that a mother should hang head downwards while she held her young to her breast, yet this was the position usually occupied by the bat. This is, however, the usual attitude of bats when at rest. The claws on their hinder feet are very sharp and curved, and it is by means of these claws that the bat suspends itself. When the long-eared bat is at rest, it presents a most singular appearance, for it folds its large ears under its arms, wraps the wings closely round its body, and hangs from its hind feet. There is an internal membrane in the ear, called the tragus, and this is fully exposed when the ears are turned back, so that the bat appears to possess narrow pointed ears instead of the enormous organs with which it is in reality furnished.

The bat above-mentioned was very particular about her personal appearance, and used to spend much time in combing herself with her hind feet. She was as careful of the parting of her hair as any lady might be expected to be, and made a beautifully straight line from the head along the back, as far as the tail. The young of the bat is blind, like the young of several other animals, and remains with its eyes closed for more than a week. Even from the first day of its life the little bat is enabled to cling firmly with its hind claws to its mother's fur, or even to any rough surface. The common bat can use its tail both for climbing and for walking on a flat surface.

All the bats are nocturnal, or rather, crepuscular in their habits, not venturing from their place of concealment until the dusk begins to come on. Then they may be seen plentifully in the air darting after the various flies and other insects that come out in the evening, and displaying a command of wing but little inferior to that of the swallow, although their manner of flight is very different. Like the owls, when they make a mistake, and get out into the blaze of daylight, they are quite bewildered, and fly about in the most vague and perplexed manner. Not very long since, I was walking in Oxford, about noon, when I saw a long-eared bat come flying up the street, sometimes turning back, and then going forward again, evidently completely out of its element. At last it came straight over my head. I almost instinctively leaped up, and struck at it with a whalebone switch, not imagining that it could be hit. To my very great astonishment, the stick met with a resistance, and the bat came to the ground, literally cut in two, lengthwise, as clean as a knife would have done it. I picked up the pieces and carried it home, but the small parasites that issued from its skin were so numerous, that it was soon ejected. It was rather remarkable that not a drop of blood was spilled. That same whalebone switch must have been enchanted, for it once killed a fine oak-egger moth in much the same way, driving it high into the air without the least damage, the point of the cane having struck it below, exactly in the centre of the thorax.

Although the bats of England are insectivorous, those of other countries vary in their food, some, as the kalongs, being fruit-eaters, while others, the vampires, live upon the blood of animals. The Javanese kalong is an enormous creature, measuring five feet in the spread of the wings. Now, bats are very voracious: a bat weighing only ten drachms frequently eating food to the weight of half an ounce at a single meal. The amount of food, therefore, that is required by these great kalongs must be correspondingly large. Accordingly we find that the natives of those places where they live are forced to protect their fruits with bamboo baskets, just as gardeners in this country secure their grapes by tying them in a bag. The teeth of these bats are so powerful that they not only devour the ordinary fruits, but even contrive to gnaw through the cocoa-nut. During the day, the kalongs hang from the branches of trees suspended by their hind feet, which retain such a hold on the branch, that if they are shot while thus at rest they do not fall, but still remain suspended. I have known a similar instance of this power of the claws to sustain an animal after its death. A common creeper (*Certhia familiaris*) was running round the trunk of a tree in its usual spiral course, when it was suddenly arrested by a charge of shot which killed it instantly. The little bird, however, did not fall, but still remained holding on to the rough bark with its long sharp claws. The whole body fell backward, and its beautiful head hung down, but the claws had taken so firm a hold, that when I climbed up to the place where it was hanging, it required some little force to detach it from the bark.

The vampire* affords a great contrast to the kalong. The blood-sucking propensities of this creature are well known, perhaps too well known, for accounts of men who have lost their lives by the wound inflicted by the vampire are not uncommon, but are in all probability untrue. These bats appear to be very fastidions in their tastes, affecting one person, while they will not have anything to do with another. Mr. Waterton laments bitterly, that while happier people were bitten by the vampire close to him, and lost plenty of blood, he was so unfortunate as to escape without one single bite. Man, however, is not so often a victim to this winged leech as cattle. These, especially horses and mules, are bitten either on the shoulder or at the tip of the ear. The bat is probably led to choose the shoulder because this animal cannot beat it away with its tail or push it off with its nose; and the ears are of course bitten because there the blood runs so

* *Vampirus spectrum.*

freely. The people say that the horses are more injured by the inflammation caused by the pressure of the saddle on the wounded part than by the actual loss of blood, although that is far from inconsiderable, as the rapacious vampire is not content with sucking its fill, but when full disgorges, and again begins sucking. Ten or twelve ounces of blood are thus frequently lost. Waterton mentions an instance of domestic fowls being killed by bats.

The usual colour of bats closely resembles that of the common mouse; but two examples are said to have been known of bats being of a bright *scarlet*. In both instances they were entombed in living wood—one being secluded in a cherry tree, and the other in a pear tree—and in both instances the person who discovered them let them go under the impression that they were not inhabitants of this world. One of these singular animals was found in Cheshire, and the other in Selkirkshire. The cavity where these prisoners had been confined was perfectly smooth in the interior, and afforded no perceptible aperture through which the bat could have drawn either air or nourishment.* Of course the reader will perceive the singular analogy between these bats and the toads that have been discovered by workmen deeply imbedded in the recesses of a large stone, and apparently happy in their seclusion. There have also been instances of toads having been found imprisoned in the trunks of trees, exactly as were these bats. A bird's-nest well furnished with eggs was once found in the centre of an apparently solid log of wood.

The nursing habits of the bat have been already described. One habit, however, was omitted, that the female bat can not only carry her young one about with her while at home, and rock it in the cradle of her wings, but can also fly about with the young bat still hanging to her body. This it does by means of the hind feet, which grasp the parent firmly on each

* Many naturalists doubt both the stories.

side, so that while the mother bat is flying in the
usual position, her young one is hanging upside down
suspended from her fur, the two together presenting a
most extraordinary appearance.

LION.*

OUR histories and descriptions of lions may be divided
into 1, the marvellous; 2, the matter-of-fact; and 3, the
imaginative.   Let it then be the aim of the following
pages to combine these several qualities, and so to temper one with the other, that the marvellous may not
overpass the bounds of truth, that the matter-of-fact
may not degenerate into dryness, and that the imaginative may not wander too unrestrainedly.

Firstly, then, for the necessarily dry details, which
must as necessarily be overcome before entering on
the more interesting description, as the shell must be
broken before the kernel can be obtained; for as the
shell acts as a preservation to the kernel, and yet is in
itself hard and difficult to be broken, so the statistical
details which encompass every branch of science, at
the same time that they act as guardians to that
science, which is as it were inclosed by them, do not
yield up their guarded fruit until they are themselves
overcome.

At the head of the beasts of prey are placed the
cat-tribe, on account of the perfection of their form,
their beauty, and their exceeding activity; and at
their head stands that beast which excels in all these
characteristics, the noble Lion.   A few words respecting the extensive and beautiful family to which the
lion belongs will be pardoned here.   The *Felidæ* are
mostly nocturnal animals, seeking their prey by night,
and lying concealed in their dens during the day.   In
order to adapt their vision to the darkness of night, the

---

* *Leo barbarus.*

pupil of the eye is capable of very great enlargement, so as to take in every ray of light however dim. To give it a greater power of dilatation, in many of the smaller *felidæ*, the pupil of the eye opens in a slit-like form, which is constantly changing its shape and size, as any one may see by examining the eyes of an ordinary cat. The teeth are arranged in a manner beautifully adapted to the predatory life which they lead. All the teeth are sharp—the canine teeth being curiously long and pointed. This structure causes the peculiar pecking-like motion with which the *Felidæ* eat their food, because they have no flat grinder teeth between which the food can be ground as in a mill, the sharp teeth with which they are furnished only acting as the teeth of a carding machine, and tearing the food into strips. The size of the canine teeth is very deceptive. No one who has not seen the canine teeth of a full-grown lion taken out of their sockets can have any idea of their real size. They form a good handful, and are extremely heavy, leading those who see them for the first time to mistake them for small elephant or walrus tusks.

The long stiff bristles on each side of the mouth, called whiskers, are each joined at their base to a large nerve, and consequently become delicate organs of touch, whose probable use is to indicate to the animal any obstacle which the darkness of night might render invisible, and which, if agitated, might rouse the wary animals whom it was attempting to approach by stealth. Some think that the whiskers serve as gauges to ascertain the width of any aperture through which the animal wishes to pass.

The powerful limbs are furnished at their extremities with sharp curved claws, used in striking down, securing, and rending their prey. These would be useless if they were not constantly kept sharp; and in order to keep them from contact with the ground when the animal is walking, each can be retracted within a sheath. This movement is managed by two

elastic tendons, which contract or relax, according as
the limb is extended or suffered to remain in its ordinary position. When the animal strikes out with its
paw to secure its prey, the tendon is shortened by the
contraction of the muscles, and throws out all the
claws. This action is admirably expressed in one of
the Nineveh sculptures, delineating a struggle between
a lion and a bull. As usual in these sculptures, the
claws are rather exaggerated; but the action of the
lion, who, with one paw on the bull's head, is aiming
a tremendous blow with the other, is extremely spirited, and, making allowances for unskilful drawing,
very exact. Many of the *felidæ* can ascend trees by
means of their claws; but of this power the lion is
destitute.

It is rather a characteristic fact, that although the
present race of men are prodigiously sceptical in
everything that militates at all against their own pre-
conceived ideas, and refuse to believe anything that
themselves have not seen, a former generation placed
too implicit a credence in the accounts of men who
had visited other countries, and thereby strongly
tempted them to declare that they had seen all kinds
of marvels which they knew their stay-at-home friends
thought they ought to have seen. There was scarcely a
traveller who had not a personal acquaintance with
Prester John, or had not witnessed a terrific combat
between a lion and a unicorn, faithfully narrating how
the lion cunningly got in front of a tree, behind
which he jumped just as his foe charged at him,
thereby causing the unicorn to strike his horn deep
into the tree. Then he tells how the lion calmly
walked up to his impotent foe, and deliberately ate
him up, much in the same way that certain savages
eat criminals in the present day, viz. by tying them to
a post, and cutting off the delicate pieces with oyster
shells.

Is the traveller an artist? he thinks it necessary to "depict ye representation" of the various

beasts he sees, and accordingly puts his rhinoceros into a full suit of plate armour, carefully marking the rivets and joint bosses, and screwing on a supplementary horn wherever he finds room.   Does he depict a hyæna—he adorns its countenance with a fascinating smile, supposed to be indicative of the laughter wherewith it beguiles its prey to the scene of imagined joviality, and then devours them with the triple row of wedge-shaped teeth, with which its jaws are duly furnished, after piercing them to the heart with a spike from the extremity of its tail.   Then, there are some animals which he has not seen, but which he thinks he ought to have seen—so he draws them too; and it is difficult to say which is the more extraordinary work, the drawing on the paper, or the drawing on his imagination.

An acquaintance with the appearance of the satyr, he knows well will be expected of him—so he draws a satyr accordingly.   First, he goes to the pantomime, and takes from thence Pantaloon, whom he puts on all fours.   He then substitutes vulture's claws for his feet, and lion's paws for his hands.   He then goes to the nearest wool-combers, and takes an armful of wool, with which he decorates each joint, and fringes the ears.   He then draws an accurate portrait of the creature, and calleth it a satyr.   So his readers are perfectly satisfied, and inspect the portrait of a satyr with no small edification—and are thankful that they never saw such things.

Then there is the phœnix, upon whom the traveller came just as the resuscitated bird sprang rejoicing from the ashes, and succeeded in rescuing part of a feather, and a piece of half-burnt cedar, from the flames, both of which relics he brings home, together with the Tartar lamb, and a branch of the upas tree, which relics he exhibits with great complacency during his lifetime, and at his death bequeaths to form the foundation of a museum.

Heu prisca fides! In those happy days no one

would have ventured to contradict a traveller in his assertion that he had eaten unicorn steaks, or slain a griffin with naked hands. Now a man is laughed at if he relates the circumstances attending a meal made upon slices of meat cut from a living cow, or narrates the stirring incidents and dangers attending a lion hunt.

Let me here give an account of the sagacity of a lion as recounted by one of those ancient writers to whom I have alluded. The writer in question, Topsell, is so quaint in his language, so remarkable in his reflections, and so delightfully simple in his credulity, that I purpose affording my readers the pleasure of perusing some of his ideas concerning various animals of which the following pages will treat. The work, an enormously large one, is copiously illustrated with the most mirth-provoking drawings, executed with considerable spirit, but designed with more imagination than veracity.

" In Pangius, a mountain of Thracia, there was a lionesse which had whelpes in her den, the which den was obserued by a Beare, the which Beare on a day finding the den vnfortified, both by the absence of the Lion and the Lionesse, entred into the same and slew the Lion's whelpes, afterward went away, and fearing a reuenge, for her better securitie against the Lion's rage, climbed vp into a tree, and there sat as in a sure castle of defence; at length the lion and lionesse returned both home, and finding their little ones dead in their owne blond, according to naturall affection fell both exceeding sorrowfull to see them so slaughtered whom they both loued; but smelling out by the foote the murderer, followed with rage vp and downe vntil they came to the tree, whereinto the Beare was ascended, and seeing her, looked both of them gastly upon her, oftentimes assaying to get into the tree, but all in vain, for nature which adorned them with singular strength and nimblenesse, yet had not endued them with power of climbing, so that the tree hindring them from reuenge, gaue vnto them further occasion of mourning, and vnto the Beare to reioyce at her owne crueltie, and deride their sorrow.

" Then the male forsook the female, leaning her to watch the tree, and he like a mournfull father for the losse of his children, wandred vp and downe the mountaine, making great moane and sorrow, till at the last he saw a Carpenter hewing wood, who seeing the lion comming towards him, let fall his Axe for feare, but the lion came very louingly towards him, fawning gently vpon his breast with his fore feete, and licking his face with his tongue; which gentlenesse of the lion the man perceauing, he was much astonished, and being more and more embraced, and fawned on by the Lion, he followed him, leauing his Axe behind him which he had let fall, which the Lion perceauing went backe, and made signes with his foote to the Carpenter that he should take it vp; but the Lion perceauing that the man did not vnderstand his signes, hee brought it himselfe in his mouth, and deliuered it vnto him, and so led him into his caue, where his yongue whelpes lay all embrewed in their owne bloude, and then led him where the Lionesse did watch the Beare; she therefore seeing them both comming, as one that knew her husband's purpose, did signifie vnto the man he should consider of the miserable slaughter of her yongue whelpes, and showing him by signes that he should looke vp into the tree, where the Beare was, which when the man saw, he coniectured that the Beare had done some grieuous iniurie vnto them; he therefore tooke his Ax, and hewed downe the tree by the rootes, which being so cut, the Beare tumbled downe headlong, which the two furious Beastes seeing, they toar her all to peeces. And afterwards the lion conducted the man vnto the place and worke, where he first met him, and there left him, without doing the least violence or harme vnto him."

Perhaps some may be glad to know the reason why

beasts wag their tails. The rationale of this process is
given at full length by the same author. "The back-
bone of some such beasts is hollow, and containeth
in it marrow, which reacheth to the taile, and, therefore, there is in the taile a kinde of animall motion
and power, for which cause, when the beaste seeth
one of his acquaintance, he waggeth his taile by way
of salutation, for the same reason that men shake
hands, for that part is the readiest and nimblest
member of his body, but bulls and lions are con-
strained to the wagging of their tailes, for the same
reason that angry men are light fingered, and apt to
strike, for when they cannot have sufficient power to
renenge, they either speake if they be men, or else
barke if they be dogges, or smite their sides with
their tailes if they be lions; by that means vttering
the furie of their rage to the ease of nature, which
they cannot to the full desire of revenge."

It has been the custom for naturalists to speak of
the lion as a solitary animal, living by himself, or, at
all events, only permitting the society of his wife and
family for the time being, and violently assaulting
every other lion that happens to come near him. All
beasts are said to fly from his neighbourhood, except
the jackal, who was said to be retained as a kind of
messenger, or confidential servant, who might be
trusted to look out for prey, and help to catch it for his
master, who, after he had eaten as much as he possibly could, and given his family the remainder, gene-
rously suffered the jackal to pick the bones. Many
were the poetical similes brought to bear upon un-
sociable monarchs, who were compared to the kingly
lion, suffering none to approach his royal person.
Now Cumming, to whose intrepid exertions and faithful accounts of the various animals seen by him in
their native wilds, science is so much indebted, repeatedly saw three or four lions very amicably hunting
together, without the slightest desire to wage a civil
war, while, on one occasion, six full-grown lions were

seen drinking at a fountain. Moreover, if the lion is feasting on a large carcass, numbers of hyænas, jackals, &c., do not hesitate to play their part in the demolition of the feast. They do not appear to stand in much fear of the lion, but, of course, move out of his way if he makes a step in their direction. A very spirited illustration of this habit was seen when the hunter had shot three rhinoceroses near a fountain. It was his custom, when desirous of watching for lions, to dig a hole in the ground near the water, where he stowed his blankets and pillows, and ranged a goodly supply of guns, whose contents were intended to make a speedy acquaintance with the internal anatomy of the lion, or other animals who should come and drink at the fountain. Soon after nightfall, on looking towards the place where the carcasses of the rhinoceroses were lying, he saw that there were many large animals, whom his servant took to be zebras, capering about the spot. These creatures turned out to be six lions, twelve or fifteen hyenas, and a large number of jackals, all of which were devouring the recently-slain animals. The lions feasted quietly enough, calm, and trusting in their strength, but the lesser animals quarreled incessantly, snarling and growling over each mouthful. This busy scene continued for some time, until a lioness discovered the lurking foes, and as she came round with no very amicable intentions, she was obliged to digest one of those leaden pills that look, in their canvas jackets, like tennis balls in miniature. On handling a few of these balls, which were exhibited in the South African collection, one ceases to wonder at the magical effect of a single shot in rolling over a large animal, even when the wound is not mortal. This rough salute, of course, immediately broke up the festive party.

Sydney Smith, in one of his witty papers, refers to the supposed solitary habits of lions, and remarks that if they only could learn to act iu concert, no animals, not even man, could oppose them. Now it has been proved that not only are lions not solitary animals, but that they live and hunt peaceably together. Moreover, an incident that occurred at the encampment of Mr. Cumming, shows that lions can also act in concert, and play into one another's hands. The morning on which that event occurred had been stormy and cold, so that the hunter had not left his waggon at his usual hour. The oxen were, as usual, near the waggons, under the protection of the Hottentots. These guards, however, on hearing the cry of a honey-bird, set off, according to the manner of Hottentots, in quest of the honey, leaving the oxen unguarded. In so deserting their post, although they might, for the time, escape the observation of their master, they were closely watched by two pair of gleaming, hungry eyes. While the hunter was reclining in his waggon, consoling himself with a book, he was rather startled by hearing the entire herd trot by in front of the waggons, as if they were driven sharply. The driver soon became apparent in the person of a lioness, who was following behind at a few yards' distance, and on looking a little farther, her mate, a venerable shaggy-maned lion, was seen quietly waiting just in front of them, and was evidently placed there for the purpose of springing upon the oxen directly his spouse had scattered them by a charge from the rear. There can be no doubt but that this was a preconcerted plot between the two lions, who must have arranged the whole matter beforehand, and have taken advantage of the departure of the Hottentots with no less skill than cunning. It is said that lions frequently employ this *ruse* to scatter herds of wild buffaloes, so that both may be able to fall on one devoted buffalo, whose strength and courage would, if he were assailed by a single lion, make him a most formidable antagonist.

Lions seldom choose to attack mankind, unless they are very hungry, or unless they are first assaulted. When, however, they have once tasted human blood, they are said to prefer it to any other food, and will seek their prey in the most determined manner. Such lions are significantly called by the natives "man-eaters." As an example of the resolute manner in which a hungry "man-eater" will attack a human being, the account of Cumming will suffice :—

"After supper, three of my men returned before their comrades, and lay down; these were John Stofolus, Hendrick, and Ruyter. In a few minutes an ox came out by the gate of the kraal and walked round the back of it. Hendrick got up and drove him in again, and then went back to his fire-side and lay down; Hendrick and Ruyter lay on one side of the fire under one blanket, and John Stofolus lay on the other. At this moment I was sitting taking some barley broth. Our fire was very small, and the night was pitch-dark and windy. Owing to our proximity to the native village, the wood was very scarce, the Bakalahari having burnt it all in their fires.

"Suddenly the appalling and murderous voice of an angry bloodthirsty lion burst upon my ear within a few yards of us, followed by the shrieking of the Hottentots. Again and again the murderous roar of attack was repeated. We heard John and Ruyter shriek, 'The lion! the lion!' still for a few minutes we thought he was chasing one of the dogs round the kraal; but the next instant John Stofolus rushed into the midst of us, almost speechless with fear and terror, his eyes bursting from their sockets, and shrieked out, 'The lion; the lion! he has got Hendrick; he dragged him away from the fire beside me; I struck him with the burning brands upon his head; but he would not let go his hold. Hendrick is dead! Oh God! Hendrick is dead! Let us take fire and seek him.' The rest of my people rushed about shrieking and yelling as if they were mad. I was at once angry with them for their folly, and told them if they did not stand still and keep quiet the lion would have another of us, and that very likely there was a troop of them. I ordered the dogs, which were nearly all

E

fast, to be made loose, and the fire to be increased as
far as could be. I then shouted Hendrick's name,
but all was still. I told my men that Hendrick was
dead, and that a regiment of soldiers could not now
help him, and hunting my dogs forward, I had everything brought within the cattle-kraal, when we lighted
our fire and closed the entrance as well as we could.

" My terrified people sat round the fire with guns
in their hands till the day broke, still fancying that
every moment the lion would return and spring again
into the midst of us. When the dogs were first let
go, the stupid brutes, as dogs often prove when most
required, instead of going at the lion, rushed fiercely
on one another, and fought desperately for some
minutes. After this they got his scent, and going at
him, disclosed to us his position; they kept up a continual barking till the day dawned, the lion occasionally springing after them, and driving them in
upon the kraal. The horrible monster lay all night
within forty yards of us, consuming the wretched man
whom he had chosen for his prey. He had dragged
him into a little hollow at the back of the thick bush,
beside which the fire was kindled, and there he remained till the day dawned, careless of our proximity.

" It appeared that when the unfortunate Hendrick
rose to drive in the ox the lion had watched him to
the fire-side, and he had scarcely lain down when the
brute sprang on him and Ruyter (for both lay under
one blanket) with his appalling murderous roar, and
roaring as he lay, grappled him with his fearful claws,
and kept biting him on the breast and shoulder, all
the while feeling for his neck, having got hold of
which, he at once dragged him away backwards round
the back into the dense shade.

"As the lion lay on the unfortunate man he faintly
cried out, 'Help me; help me, oh God! men, help me!'
After which the fearful beast got a hold of his neck,
and then all was still, except that his comrades heard
the bones of his neck cracking between the teeth of

the lion. John Stofolus had lain with his back to the fire on the opposite side, and, on hearing the lion, he sprang up, and seizing a large flaming brand, he had belaboured him on the head with the burning wood; but the brute did not take any notice of him. The bushman had a narrow escape; he was not altogether scatheless, the lion having inflicted two gashes in his seat with his claws."

It may be satisfactory to those who read the above passage to know that the lion had no more opportunities of exercising his man-eating propensities, for at the morrow's dawn the death of his servant was revenged by Mr. Cumming, who traced the lion to his lair, and there shot him. By the way, it is rather amusing to mark the contrast between the descriptions of lion-shooting in Cumming's book, and in the works of other authors. Perhaps the narrative of the lively and verbose Vaillant is as complete a contrast as can be found. Mr. Cumming goes out in the morning, " bowls over" a lion before breakfast, and jots the event down among the daily occurrences of desert life. M. Vaillant visits a horde of Hottentots, and excited by their complaints of a lion and lioness that had taken up their residence in a small coppice, magnanimously determines to attack the enemy. So, taking with him the whole of the Hottentot tribe, he visits the coppice, and matures his plans. As neither the Hottentots nor himself had the smallest intention of entering the coppice, they drove a herd of oxen into it. The lions, being disturbed, began to roar in a manner which, according to our Homeric author, was not less tremendous than the shock of two armies. After some time, Vaillant records with great glorification, the death of the lioness, which, however, he did not shoot himself, as she fell by the hand of one of his attendants. Having thus settled the lioness, he was naturally encouraged to try to shoot her mate. So he recommenced his plan of driving oxen into the wood, and worked hard all day to drive out the lion

towards his band of marksmen.   At sunset, however,
he wisely considered that the attack might become
dangerous, and accordingly postponed proceedings
until the morning. As might have been expected, when
he came to renew the attack on the following morning, the coppice was empty. The Hottentots might
have been set free from both their foes if Mr. Cumming had been by, nor would he have required the
help of all the tribe.   Indeed, he held the native
courage in most supreme contempt, especially since
the time when he saw one lion put to flight two hundred
and sixty armed men.   The savages appear to hold a
lion in the same estimation that Waverley's pistol
was held by the mob.   It certainly may only kill one
man, but then each might be that one, so they prudently all ran away.

Every one has heard of Androcles—you will please
to call him Andrŏcles—and his lion-companion ; how
the persecuted slave, escaping from his master, hid
himself in a desert cave ; and how the cave turned
out to be the castle of a lion, who, instead of eating
his guest, made him his surgeon in ordinary, and
gave him a plentiful board and a dry lodging.   Then
every one knows the catastrophe of the story, how
the slave, being recaptured, was condemned, according to the civilised law of Rome, to fight unarmed
with lions ; and how his antagonist proved to be his
ancient host, who had been captured nearly at the
same time as himself, and who, being freed by the
unanimous voice of the Roman people, lived with
Androcles, and spent the remainder of his life in a
quiet and gentlemanly manner, without having to
work for his living.

Now, although in these days we do not meet
people walking about accompanied by lions, such a
circumstance not having taken place since the days
of Nero; yet lions do live on most comfortable
and even affectionate terms with those to whom
they are accustomed, suffering them to take liber-

ties which most domestic cats would resent. I have seen a keeper knock a lion down, and then drag him about the cage by his ears, or pull his tail with exceeding violence, and, in fact, offer him all manner of insults, to which the lion only answered by a self-satisfied kind of a purr. While examining the beautiful animals with whom he was playing such tricks, I asked the keeper if he would cut off a piece of the lion's mane for my inspection. I was rather horrified to see him take hold of the mane and actually pull out a respectably-sized bunch of hair, of which the lion took not the slightest notice. Two more good-natured affectionate animals cannot be conceived than those inhabiting the cage; and many were the wishes expressed by the spectators to have them as pets. There was a very small boy, who was accustomed to go into the den, and who seemed to consider the lions as his natural playfellows, pushing them down, and sitting on them without any ceremony. Contrary to the habits of most of the *Felidæ*, these two gentle lions did not make any disturbance while feeding, but took their allowance (and a very small allowance it appeared) as quietly as a well-trained dog. One was fed a few minutes before the other; but the unfed one did not make a fuss, as might have been expected, but waited quietly for his turn. The other animals were not nearly so patient, for on the first sniff of a piece of meat carried by a man along the front of the cages, the tigers, leopards, wolves, and hyena, began a great outcry, and were not to be pacified until they had each received their food.

During part of the day, the two pet lions were engaged in a regular game of bo-peep with a young woman belonging to the establishment; and they sprang and danced about with such agility that it was impossible not to wish them a larger cage for the exercise of their limbs. No lion in a cage can give an idea of the majestic deportment of the animal when in its own country, walking free and at large, real "monarch of all he surveys," for between the lion and the elephant and rhinoceros a kind of mutual compact seems to take place, that neither shall meddle with the other. No one has seen the lion to such perfection as Gordon Cumming, whose book is so well and so deservedly known, that I must first apologize for quoting from it at all, and secondly, that I extract so little. Let it be therefore understood, that all who wish to obtain an insight into the habits of this magnificent animal, as he wanders free and unconstrained through his native wastes, are recommended to obtain Mr. Gordon Cumming's work, and read it carefully. There is no one who has seen so much of the lion as has Mr. Cumming, for there is no one who has dared so much in the pursuit. Not the least valuable part of his work is the journal-like form of its pages, which, while they do not aim at florid description, impress their truth more firmly by their simplicity. The work carries the evidence of its truthfulness in its front, and to none is its accuracy so evident as to naturalists, for although many who are ignorant of natural history, or who only possess a sufficient smattering to make them conceited at their attainments, have been pleased to sneer at statements made in that work, the sneer proceeds from ignorance and not from knowledge.

It is a curious fact, that a good naturalist will often, from the very extent of his knowledge and the diffidence which extended knowledge on an unlimited subject always produces, be more likely to give credence to a strange fact than one whose knowledge of the subject is very limited indeed. One anecdote in particular that he related roused the incredulity of innumerable individuals, who suggested that Mr. Cumming had employed the long bow instead of the rifle. Those who are acquainted with his work will recollect that he mentions the rather curious fact of a snake spitting poison. "A horrid snake, which Kleinboy had tried to kill with his loading-rod, flew up at my eye, and spat poison in it; immediately I washed it out at the fountain. I endured great pain all night, the next day the eye came all right." Now this statement drew down a storm of incredulous laughter at the individual who ventured to assert anything so palpably false. The incredulous, however, were not aware that in that very part of Africa there does exist a venomous serpent, one of the Najas, which really ejects its poison precisely in the manner described. Another proof of his accuracy in describing events as they really happened is, that he has ventured to accuse the lion of occasional cowardice.

The cubs of the lion are pretty playful things. Their weight is very great in proportion to their size, and they are stronger than their appearance warrants, so that a playful pat of their paw is far from agreeable. Few people have any conception of the power of a lion's paw. The dissection of the muscles of the fore-arm of the lion gives some idea of the strength that once reposed in those knotty cords, but the force of the blow can only be judged from its effects. It is well known that a stroke from the paw of a lion will fracture a man's skull, or dash even a large beast to the ground; but its real strength is perhaps better exhibited when the animal does not wish to use violence, than when it is excited by rage or hunger. A full grown lioness is a large animal, and more than proportionately heavy; yet I once saw a lion, with the very slightest imaginable wave of his paw, dash his mate from the corner of the cage, where she was rearing against the bars, and send her sprawling on her back as if she had been a little lamb.

Among the many noble animals which adorned Van Amburgh's collection of wild beasts, there were two, a lion and a tiger, who had been lately placed in the same den, as it was hoped that an intimacy might commence between them. However the plan might have succeeded eventually, at the time when I saw them they were by no means on friendly terms with each other, and neither would let the other approach without a growl and a scratch. On one of these occasions, the lion struck its claws so deeply into the tiger's foot, that a large piece of the flesh was cut completely out of the upper part of the foot, and the movements of the bones were visible. The tiger did not seem to trouble himself much about it, and certainly did not seem half so discomposed as those who witnessed the accident.

When the animals belonging to the cat-tribe have seized their prey, they often lie quietly for some time before they begin to devour it, just as a cat may be observed to do with a newly caught mouse. This quietude, however, vanishes directly the captured animal begins to move. It is therefore possible for a man, who has been struck down by a lion, either to kill the animal, or to make his escape. The courageous conduct of Captain Woodhouse, when lying under the claws of an enraged lion, is too well known for me to do more than refer to it. The captain had been hunting a lion, and had been knocked down by the infuriated animal. He had the presence of mind to remain quite still even when the lion was crunching one of his arms. The lion, finding his victim offered no resistance, let go his arm and lay down with his paws upon the captain's breast. In this position they remained until the friends of the fallen man arrived, when a ball laid the lion prostrate by the side of his intended victim. If Captain Woodhouse had attempted to make the least resistance, he would inevitably have been killed. Even as it was, he unthinkingly raised his hand once, when the lion immediately seized his arm in his mouth, and again began crunching it, fracturing the bone in a fresh place. The fact is, that the lion, as well as the other *Felidæ*, is very suspicious, and possesses a strong spice of cowardice among his undoubted valour. Sometimes, too, he seizes upon a man in the impulse of sudden fear, if he comes upon him unexpectedly.

There have been several instances known where a lion has pounced upon a man evidently urged by fear, and when the man has remained passive under his attack the lion has left him uninjured, except by fright.

It is well known that the human voice has a great effect upon all animals. This is not so much the case when the voice is raised in loud shouts, as when it is used in articulating words, the very sound of which appears to terrify even the most savage beasts. A lioness is at all times fiercer than a lion, and when wounded she becomes a perfect fury, heeding no obstacles and flying at her assailants with the most indomitable ferocity. Yet Mr. Cumming has recorded an adventure in which even a wounded lioness was checked by the sounds of the human voice. He had shot at a lioness, having at the time only one charge in his rifle. "The ball told badly; the lioness at which I had fired wheeled right round, and came on lashing her tail, showing her teeth, and making that horrid murderous deep growl which an angry lion generally utters. Her comrade hastily retreated. The instant the lioness came on I stood up to my full height, holding my rifle and my arms extended high above my head. This checked her on her course, but on looking round and missing her comrade, and observing Ruyter slowly advancing, she was still more exasperated, and fancying that she was near being surrounded, she made another forward movement, growling terribly. This was a moment of great danger; I felt that my only chance of safety was extreme steadiness, so standing motionless as a rock, with my eyes firmly fixed on her, I called in a clear commanding voice, ' Holloa, old girl! what 's the hurry? Take it easy! Holloa! holloa!' She once more halted and seemed perplexed, looking round for her companion. I then thought it prudent to beat a retreat, which I very slowly did, talking to the lioness all the time. She seemed undecided as to her future movements, and was gazing after me and sniffing the ground when I last beheld her."

It not unfrequently happens that lions, when in captivity, make friends of some smaller animal, and not only forbear from injuring it but even suffer themselves to be bullied by it. I lately saw in one cage a particularly large lion and a particularly small dog. The latter animal evidently considered himself the master of the house, and acting in that capacity, patronised his enormous companion in the most condescending manner. The spectators soon found out the dog's propensities, and amused themselves by pretending to assault the lion, whereupon the little dog—it was a dun-coloured terrier—flew at the assailants with the utmost fury, and barked at them until weary, when he retired to the back of the cage, and sitting down between the lion's huge paws, behind which he was almost entirely concealed, surveyed the scene with a consequential and lordly air. It was once imagined that the lion would suffer no other animals to live in its cage; but now a cage full of lions and leopards is no uncommon event, and I have already mentioned an instance of a lion and tiger inhabiting the same den. Once, a lion chose a very singular associate. Some cruel-minded men wished to witness a combat between a lion and a bear. A large bear was accordingly let down into the lion's den, and immediately flew at his foe. The lion, however, instead of retaliating, received the bear quietly, and took it under his protection, watching with the utmost jealousy every one who approached the cage, and even gave to his strangely found friend the food intended for himself. This latter circumstance is in my opinion the most remarkable trait in the character of this lion, for if there be any occasions on which the savage nature of beasts breaks out it is while they are being fed. Even the domestic cat is not always safe to touch if she has in her mouth a newly caught mouse, very few being sufficiently tame to suffer the prey to be meddled with. Of course I do not include those animals which are mothers, and who, according to their maternal instinct, divide the prey with their young. The only instance in which I ever saw an animal voluntarily divide its food with a friend occurred some years ago, when a kangaroo, on receiving a biscuit, broke it in two pieces and pushed one of them to a companion inhabiting the same cage.

The most fearless, and, in consequence, the most dangerous lions, are those who infest the most uninhabited regions, where they have been accustomed to roam, owning no master; but where they have heard the sound of the human voice, and witnessed the irrevocable progress of man, they seem to own that their master is near, and retreat in terror at the sound of his dreaded voice. Some years since, a new line of caravans was organised over the desert. During the first few journeys lions were met, who knowing no fear, and being accustomed to overcome every animal in their country, boldly sprang upon the caravan, and did no inconsiderable harm to the beasts of burden. In a very short time, however, they learned caution, and carefully kept out of the way. This, by the way, shows that animals must have some method of communicating and spreading information.

I have already stated that in the *Felidæ* the sense of smell is much inferior to that of hearing, It is, comparatively, but little exercised, the creature depending more upon its sight and swiftness than its powers of scent. Sometimes, when it can no longer see its intended prey it brings its olfactory organs into use, as the following anecdote will show. A Hottentot, who was guarding a herd of oxen, was endeavouring to drive his charge into a pool of water enclosed between two ridges of rock. The animals were unwilling to enter, and with good reason, for in the midst of the pool there couched a huge lion. The keeper very naturally took to his heels, and having the presence of mind to recollect that a lion

seldom troubles himself about a man, if he can get
hold of an ox, ran through the herd. The lion, however, who we must suppose was a man-eater, had not
the smallest intention of being put off with beef,
when he had made up his mind for man, and accordingly broke through the herd, and gave chase to the
unfortunate Hottentot.

The man, on finding that the lion was pursuing
him, rushed to a tree, in the trunk of which some
steps had fortunately been cut, and sprang up just
in time to escape from a tremendous spring of
his pursuer. The steps had been cut in the tree
for the sake of reaching a large mass of the nests
of the sociable grosbeak. This bird acts much
on the same principle as the bees and wasps,
making a great number of separate nests, all under
one roof. Behind this building the Hottentot crept,
and after waiting some time for the lion to go away,
put his head round the nests to reconnoitre. To his
great horror, he saw the lion looking up at the tree,
with eyes that, as the man said, flashed fire at him.
The lion did not evince any intention of moving, and
presently laid himself down at the foot of the tree
determined to secure the herdman. For twenty-four
hours the lion kept his watch, but at last, being
parched with thirst, he set off to a spring at some
distance in order to drink. The Hottentot then ventured to descend, and ran as fast as he could to his
house, which was not more than a mile distant, where
he arrived in safety. It was well that he did make
haste, for it was found that after the lion had quenched
his thirst he had returned to the tree, and not finding
the man there, had followed up his track to within a
few hundred yards of his house.

When these animals are in their native state, they
have no opportunities of satisfying their hunger regularly, as they have often to fast for several days after

before they can catch something else. It is, therefore, found necessary, when they are in captivity, occasionally to keep them without food for a day once a week, Sunday being their usual fast day. Water, however, they require regularly, as in their native state they never wander far from their well-known spring, at which they are accustomed to quench their thirst as soon as the sun goes down.

It is not generally known that the carnivorous animals do not subsist entirely upon the flesh of the larger animals, but make insects a large portion of their food. Even the lion is a great consumer of insects, which in his native woods are of a size that renders them very substantial food.

TIGER.*

THERE is rather a dearth of information respecting this beautiful, although ferocious, animal, and it is much to be wished that Mr. Cumming would make India his next hunting-ground, and bring us back from thence as graphic and interesting accounts of the tiger as he has already brought of the lion from Africa.

The tiger is an Asiatic animal, and is found plentifully in Hindostan, where its chase affords magnificent sport to the inhabitants. We have very few accounts of tigers, except from those who have gone to the chase in the usual manner, mounted high on elephants' backs, and enjoying their sport in comparative safety. We want somebody who will trace the tiger to its den, or watch its nocturnal manœuvres, after the fashion of the hunter already mentioned, whose cool matter-of-fact way of treating lions almost borders on the ludicrous. I have before mentioned the incredulity with which many individuals received some of his accounts. The unbelief of these gentlemen who " sat at home at ease " is by no means shared by the

* *Tigris regalis.*

natives among whom he lived, and in whose presence
(when they did not run away) he slaughtered many a
lion and rhinoceros. They look upon him as some
being of another world, and not content with treasur-
ing up stories of the man, who delivered them from
their dreaded foes, or who fed hundreds of them for
days together—a luxury almost beyond the comprehension of those wild tribes—they relate sundry other
tales of him, among the least remarkable of which may
be reckoned the story that he went to sleep one night
in a lion's den, and in the morning shot his host.

The elephants used in hunting mostly stand in
great awe of the tiger until they are thoroughly
trained, as this active animal always aims at seizing
the trunk, which is the most sensitive part of the
elephant. The trunk is, therefore, either raised high
above the head, or kept curled up out of harm's way.
The principal danger of riding an untrained elephant
is, that it is very likely to turn round the moment it sees
the tiger, and run away as fast as it can, which conduct
sometimes deprives its rider of his proper share of the
sport, and sometimes gives him too much of it, as the
infuriated tiger has often been known to leap upon
the elephant's hind quarters, and from thence to make
its way to the howdah where the sportsmen sit. On
feeling the tiger's claws, the elephant usually shakes
itself with such vehemence that the hunters have
great difficulty in keeping their seat, and sometimes
do fall off. On one such occasion a gentleman fell
actually upon the tiger, who was so terrified at the
accident, that he permitted the hunter to escape with
no other injury except the fright and a bruise naturally
produced when two bodies meet together with a certain
momentum.

With the perverted taste common to all partly-
civilized nations, and which vanishes as civilization
proceeds, the Eastern rulers sometimes amuse themselves with tiger and elephant fights. In the following anecdote of one of these performances, it will be

seen that the tiger had hardly fair play, while the idea
of punishing the rider of an elephant by incontinent
vapulation because his beast chose to run away, is
ludicrously Oriental. The story is given in an account
of Cochin China, by Mr. Crawford. " After tea was
served to us we were invited to be present at an elephant and tiger fight, and for this purpose mounted
our elephant, and repaired to the glacis of the fort,
where the combat was to take place. The governor
went out at another gate, and arrived at the place
before us in his palanquin. When the hall broke up
a herald or crier announced the event. With the
exception of this ceremony great propriety and deco-
rum were observed throughout the audience. The
exhibition made by the herald, however, was truly
barbarous. He threw himself backward, projecting
his abdomen, and putting his hands to his side, and
in this absurd attitude uttered several long and loud
yells. The tiger had been exhibited in front of the
hall, and was driven to the spot on a hurdle. A great
concourse of people had assembled to witness the
exhibition. The tiger was secured to a stake by a
rope tied round his loins, about thirty yards long.
The mouth of the unfortunate animal was sewn up,
and his nails pulled out. He was of large size, and
extremely active. No less than forty-six elephants, all
males of great size, were seen drawn out in line. One
at a time was brought to attack the tiger. The first
elephant advanced, to all appearance, with a great
show of courage, and we thought from his determined
look that he would certainly have dispatched his
antagonist in an instant. At the first effort he raised
the tiger upon his tusks and threw him to the distance
of at least twenty feet. Notwithstanding this the
tiger rallied, and sprang upon the elephant's trunk
and head up to the very keeper who was upon the
neck. The elephant took alarm, wheeled about, and
ran off, pursued by the tiger, as far as the rope would
allow him. The fugitive, although not hurt, roared

most piteously, and no effort could bring him back to
the charge.   A little after this we saw a man brought
up to the governor, bound with cords, and dragged
into his presence by two officers.   This was the conductor of the recreant elephant.   A hundred strokes
of the bamboo were ordered to be inflicted on him
upon the spot.   For this purpose he was thrown on
his face upon the ground, and secured by one man
sitting astride upon his neck and shoulders, and by
another sitting upon his feet, a succession of execu-
tioners inflicting the punishment.   When it was over,
two men carried off the sufferer by the head and
heels, apparently quite insensible.   While this outrage
was perpetrating, the governor coolly viewed the
combat of the tiger and elephant, as if nothing else
particular had been going forward.   Ten or twelve
elephants were brought up in succession to attack the
tiger, which was killed at last merely by the astonishing falls he received when tossed off the tusks of the
elephants.   The prodigious strength of these animals
was far beyond anything I could have supposed.
Some of them tossed the tiger to a distance of at least
thirty feet, after he was nearly lifeless, and could offer
no resistance.   We could not reflect, without horror,
that these very individual animals were the same that
have for years executed the sentence of the law upon
the many malefactors condemned to death.   Upon
these occasions one toss, such as I have described, is
always, I am told, sufficient to destroy life."

It is impossible not to admire the courage of the
unfortunate tiger in this inhuman sport, who, although
bound by ropes, that of course restrained the movements of an animal accustomed to perfect freedom of
every limb, his sharp claws cut off, and his mouth
barbarously sewn up, yet continued to attack his foes,
who were furnished with every possible advantage.

Yet, although the tiger exhibited such courage
towards his really formidable enemies, he might have
yielded without a struggle had he been opposed to a

much more insignificant enemy—a common mouse. This may appear an extraordinary statement, but it is carried out by the following anecdote related by Basil Hall. There was a beautiful tiger kept in a cage at Mysore, to whom the officers were indebted for many hours snatched from " Miss Edgeworth's demon, foul *ennui;*" for when they had nothing better to do (which was usually the case), they amused themselves by teasing the tiger.

" But what annoyed him far more than our poking him up with a stick, or tantalising him with shins of beef or legs of mutton, was introducing a mouse into his cage. No fine lady ever exhibited more terror at the sight of a spider than this magnificent royal tiger betrayed on seeing a mouse. Our mischievous plan was to tie the little animal by a string to the end of a long pole, and thrust it close to the tiger's nose. The moment he saw it he leaped to the opposite side; and when the mouse was made to run near him, he jammed himself into a corner, and stood trembling and roaring in such an ecstacy of fear that we were always obliged to desist, from sheer pity to the poor brute. Sometimes we insisted on his passing over the spot where the unconscious little mouse ran backwards and forwards. For a long time, however, we could not get him to move, till at length, I believe by the help of a squib, we obliged him to start; but, instead of pacing leisurely across his den, or making a *détour* to avoid the object of his alarm, he generally took a kind of flying leap, so high as nearly to bring his back in contact with the roof of his cage."

Supposing this animal had been captured in a net, as related of the lion in the fable, would he have suffered the mouse to help him out of the toils? The powerful and unaccountable antipathy related above has its parallel in the case of an orang-outan, who, when a small tortoise was introduced into his cage, retreated to the farthest corner of the den, and stood perfectly transfixed with horror, not daring to take its

F

eyes off the dreadful visitant for a single moment:
Mrs. Lee tells us of a wild tiger actually frightened
away by a simple stratagem. Her brother had just
returned from the tent of a brother officer, when his
servants came running up to him in a state of great
alarm, saying that a tiger was near. Having given the
alarm, they immediately ran away, leaving their master
alone in his garden, rather wishing to see the tiger than
otherwise. In a very short time the tiger actually did
make his appearance, and, stopping short in front of
the officer, began to growl, and then crouched in that
most ominous attitude assumed by a cat when about
to spring on a mouse. This convinced the officer
that he had not escaped the animal's observation, as
he had at first supposed; and on the impulse of the
moment, he took off his big bear-skin grenadier's cap,
and putting it before his face, roared in it, endeavouring with some success to make his roar as different as
possible from that of honest Snug the joiner. The tiger,
naturally astounded at such an uncouth sound proceeding from such an uncouth object, turned tail and
leaped into a thicket. All danger being over, the
servants courageously came to help their master with
drums and torches. Really the tiger's panic is not at
all to be wondered at. We English are proudly pre-
eminent among the nations for an execrable taste in
hats, the officers' foraging cap and the "wide-awake"
being the only exceptions; and among these caps,
that of the grenadier is almost the most absurd, while
as a soldier's cap it is most senseless, its only recommendation being that the wearer is forced to walk
very upright to prevent it from tumbling off. No
wonder, then, that a shapeless mass of black fur suddenly protruded in the tiger's face, and animated with
a rough voice reverberating in its wicker recesses,
should scare away an animal who was not sufficiently
civilised to be accustomed to such monstrosities.

The same writer heard from an eye-witness of the
scene, an anecdote showing that the tiger sometimes

snatches away his prey without springing. A gentleman was proceeding along a narrow, high-banked river, in a covered boat, on the roof of which his principal servant had gone to smoke. He did not long enjoy his quiet and elevated position, for a tiger put its paw out, dragged the man off the roof of the boat as it passed, and carried him away into the jungle.

The tiger, as well as the lion, has often permitted the company of other animals in its cage; and in one instance, after it had made friends with a dog, another was substituted, the precaution having been taken to make the exchange after the tiger had been fed. The second companion was welcomed as warmly as the first, and was permitted to take all kinds of liberties with its enormous friend, who even suffered it to bark at and bite him without displaying the slightest resentment.

It is a great mistake to imagine that the tiger is morose and untameable, as it can be tamed quite as easily as the lion, and displays as much affection for its keeper, if he treats it kindly. Great care, however, must be taken with all these animals, as, even although they are apparently quite tame, their savage nature sometimes breaks out on very slight occasions, even though they had previously endured great provocations without complaint. Such was the case a short time since, when the celebrated "lion queen" at Wombwell's fell a victim to the sudden irritability of the tiger. She had been forced to chastise the tiger for some disobedience of orders, when the animal suddenly turned upon her, grasped her by the throat, and, in a very short time after she was taken out of the cage, she died. Death in this case was probably as much occasioned by fear as by the injuries inflicted by the tiger, as, on examination, no wound was found that would have caused death. In all probability, the tiger had no intention of carrying his revenge so far, but, unconscious of his strength, turned on his assailant in a moment of irritability and bit at her,

with no more intention of killing her than a cat has
when she snaps at the hand that pulls her tail.   The
effects, however, of the pat of a cat's paw, or the snap
of a cat's teeth, are very different from the effects of a
blow from a tiger's talons or the grasp of a tiger's jaws,
although they may be dealt with equally harmless intentions.   The strength of this creature is most
extraordinary, especially when we consider in what a
small compass it is comprised.

Captain Hall has given several very interesting
accounts of fights between the tiger and other animals.
One between a tiger and a buffalo I shall quote entire,
as the description is so spirited that any attempt at
compression would spoil it.

" We were promised a grand day's sport one afternoon, when a buffalo and a tiger were to be pitted
against each other.   The buffalo entered the ring
composedly enough ; but after looking about him,
turned to one side, and rather pettishly, as if he had
felt a little bilious, overturned a vessel of water placed
there expressly for his use.   The tiger refused for
some time to make his appearance, and it was not till
his den was filled with smoke and fire that he sprang
out.   The buffalo charged his enemy in a moment,
and, by one furious push, capsized him right over.
To our great disappointment, the tiger pocketed this
insult in the shabbiest manner possible, and passing
on, leaped furiously at the ropes, with which his feet
became entangled, so that the buffalo was enabled to
punish his antagonist about the   rump most in-
gloriously.   When at length the tiger got loose he
slunk off to a distant part of the area, lay down, and
pretended to be dead.   The boys, however, soon put
him up again, and tried to bring him to the scratch
with squibs and crackers ; and a couple of dozen dogs
being introduced at the same moment, they all set at
him, but only one attempted to take any liberty with
the enraged animal.   This bold dog actually caught
the tiger by the tail, but a slight pat of the mighty

monster's paw crushed the yelping cur as flat as a board. The buffalo, who really seemed anxious to have a fair stand-up fight, now drove the dogs off, and repeatedly poked the tiger with his nose, and even turned him half over several times with his horns.

· "As the gentleman showed no pluck, the rajah requested one of us to step down to give him the *coup-de-grace*. I accordingly loaded a musket which was placed in my hands; but on reaching the area I felt rather unwilling to fire, as I just heard a story of a gentleman who the year before, in firing at one of the animals in the ring by the rajah's directions, not only shot the animal, but also killed an old woman who stood on the other side of the ring, the ball having continued its course after piercing the tiger's head. On my expressing a wish to try, in the first place, the effect of cold iron upon his tough hide, a very sharp-pointed spear was given me, and I tried with my utmost force to pass it through his hide, but in vain. He rose, however, on being pressed by the steel; and, by making a violent effort to clutch my hand, thrust his head fairly through one of the meshes of the net, to my no small dismay. Either the ropes were not very strong or the seizings weak, for they began to break; and in the next minute, as it appeared to me, the infuriated monster might have forced his whole body through. In this emergency I quite forgot all about humanity and old women, and, catching up the musket, placed the muzzle of the piece at the tiger's head, and blew out his brains in a moment."

So much for an actual fight, or rather for an intended fight. On a previous occasion, the matter had nearly taken a serious turn, had it not been for the courage of a boy. A tiger was urged into the netted court by the persuasive effects of a handful of lighted squibs and crackers. On reaching the centre of the ring, he was greatly bewildered by the shoutings, drummings, and shriekings, that resounded on every side, and was greatly put out by the evolutions of

some donkeys within the ring, to whose tails blown
bladders filled with dried peas had been attached.
On finding the door of his cage shut, he flew at a
wooden figure of a man that had been stuck up in the
ring, and twisted its head off in an instant. Discovering the cheat, he first tore the figure to pieces, and
then made a dash at the netting that hung by his
cage, up which he scrambled until his fore-paws were
placed on the roof, and another half-minute would
have found him loose among the assembled crowds.
Fortunately, a brave boy about twelve years of age
had perched himself on the top of the cage; and the
moment the infuriated tiger showed his head above
the ropes, he struck it such a rap on the nose with a
short club which he had in his hand, that the animal
fell back head over heels into the inclosure. After
long badgering, the order was given to put the tiger to
death. One of the native chiefs then armed himself
with a bow and arrows, and discharged arrow after
arrow at him until he was bristling all over like a porcupine. At last the English officers, disgusted at the
lengthened torture, begged leave to try the effect of a
musket bullet, which laid him dead instantaneously,
although several arrows had passed completely through
him without producing any visible effect.

This kind of work was all very pleasant for the bystanders, who could stand by in safety, and watch the
struggles of the combatants within the netted ring;
nor were their nerves at all likely to be tried by such
proceedings. The rajah, however, who got up all these
amusements, determined on trying the nerves of his
English visitors a little more. He accordingly ordered
a ring to be formed, not of net, but of armed men,
within which he, his sons, and his visitors sat. Presently several men led two enormous tigers, only
restrained from springing on the inmates of the ring
by a few slight cords. At a sign from the rajah,
even these impediments were loosened, and the
keepers retired, leaving two tigers at perfect liberty.

within a few feet of the guests. After some time had
elapsed, the tigers were withdrawn, and a few lions
and buffaloes were introduced : when they came too close
the rajah's chair, the guards advanced, so as to put
them outside the ring, until they had driven the beasts
back, when they again retired. The lions and buffaloes were then succeeded by a tiger and a bear, who
were intended to fight in the open court. Neither party
appeared likely to begin the contest, even in spite of
all the kicks and thumps lavished upon the intended
combatants. " Tie them together," cried the rajah.
This brilliant notion was immediately carried into
execution, and the tiger and bear dragged each other
about in fine style. At last the tiger got very angry,
and looked as if he were about to make a dash at the
originator of his bondage. Suddenly changing his
course, he sprang across the court in which these
pranks were being played, and springing in at an open
window, commenced smashing the English furniture,
of which the rajah was exceedingly proud, and which
he had heaped together in a room, rejoicing in his
heart that he had accomplished an English drawing-
room. The tiger would have done more mischief,
had he not been brought up suddenly by the rope, to
the other end of which was attached the bear, who
having been drawn up half-way between the window
and the ground by the weight of the tiger, was dangling outside in the most pitiable manner. The rajah,
however indifferent he might be to his own safety, was
not so callous to the fate of his furniture ; and he accordingly had the tiger secured, and the rope cut by which
poor Bruin was suspended. The tiger was then
dragged off by main force, while the aggrieved bear
slunk off sulkily to his den of his own accord.

LEOPARD.*

" THERE have been so many names devised for this
one beast, that it is grown a difficult thing either to
make a good reconciliation of the authors which are wed
to their several opinions, or else to define it perfectly
and make of him a good methodical history ; yet seeing the greatest variance hath arisen from words, and
that which was avowed at the first for the better ex-
planation and description of it, hath turned to the ob-
scuration and shadowing of the truth, I trust it shall
be a good labour to collect out of every writer that
which is most probable concerning this beast, and in
the end to express the best definition thereof we can
learn out of all."

This is the opinion of an author living three
hundred years ago ; and there has as yet been but
little improvement in this respect.   The leopard,
the panther, the ounce, and the ocelot, were, until
very lately, considered as varieties of one species.
The ocelot and the ounce have for some time been
placed in their proper position in the scale of animated nature ; the only difficulty being between the
panther and the leopard. In this difficulty, the opinion
of the furriers was asked, as they were known to sell
panther skins as well as leopard skins—those of the panther being larger, and the shape of their spots different.
The furriers, however, proved useless allies ; for their so-
called panther skins invariably turned out to belong to
the jaguar. The question is now supposed to be settled :
the leopard and panther being considered as one animal, under the name of *Leopardus varius*, the ounce is
called *Leopardus uncia*, and the ocelot is termed *Leopardus pardalis*.

The leopard, although much smaller than the tiger,
is a most formidable antagonist, and when wounded
is little less to be dreaded than the lion or tiger.

* *Leopardus varius.*

Thus Cumming relates an anecdote of a gentleman who, although armed and accompanied with armed attendants, was very nearly killed by an enraged leopard, and although he did escape with life, yet lost the use of both his arms.

" In about an hour the natives came running to the camp, and said that Orpen was killed by the leopard. On further inquiry, however, I found that he was not really killed, but frightfully torn and bitten about the arms and head. They had rashly taken up the spoor on foot, the dogs following behind them instead of going in advance. The consequence of this was, that they came right upon the leopard before they were aware of him, when Orpen fired and missed him. The leopard then sprang upon his shoulders, and dashed him to the ground, and lay upon him howling and lacerating his hands, arms, and head, most fearfully. Presently the leopard permitted Orpen to rise and come away. Where were the gallant Present and all the natives, that not a man of them hurried to assist the unfortunate Orpen ? According to an established custom among all colonial servants, the instant the leopard sprang, Present discharged his piece in the air, and then dashing it to the ground, be rushed down the bank, and jumped into the river. along which he swam some hundred yards before he would venture on *terra firma*. The natives, though numerous and armed, had likewise fled in another direction."

There is but little difference in the courage of natives, whether African or Indian, each being always willing to run away at the approach of a wild beast. If a traveller is passing through an Indian forest, and the roar of a tiger is heard near, the hearers immediately throw down the palanquin, change their usual monotonous grunt into an unearthly screaming, and scatter off in every direction, leaving their master to his fate. After the danger is past, they come back again, and if the tiger has not eaten the traveller, they pick him up and

proceed with their journey. Now, an equal number of
European servants would have proceeded calmly on
their course until the tiger came in sight, when they
would either have driven him off, or resisted his
attack; but the idea of abandoning their master
would never have entered their heads. This cowardice is partly occasioned by the Indian character, and
partly by the constant terror in which they have
always held these creatures. Many a European has
attacked a tiger merely through his ignorance of the
real power of the creature; whereas, had he known
the strength and agility of the enemy he was provoking, he would have considered the matter first.
Certainly, in the matter of such acquaintances as
tigers, leopards, and other similar creatures, familiarity does *not* breed contempt.

So Captain Hall tells us that, when he first landed
through the surf, he thought it capital fun; when he
had made several passages, he looked rather seriously
on the matter; but when he was thoroughly accustomed to the surf, he had great doubts of getting
through at all. A year or two ago a pleasure boat
was on the sea, ruled by an old sailor. The sky began
to look suspicious, and he took in most of his sail.
Presently another boat came dancing along, heeling
almost gunwale under at every blast of wind. The
old sailor looked after the vessel for a minute, and
then muttered to himself, "They fears nothin'—'cos
they *knows* nothin'." I recollect extracting very much
the same opinion from the sailors on board a steamer.
It was the regular cockney voyage from Ramsgate to
Dover, and when we set out there was nothing but a
gentle breeze. This continued for some time, until
we got round the Foreland, when a regular gale rose,
and the waves rose accordingly. The steamer was a
little vessel, and danced about in splendid style, the
waves sweeping the entire deck. This was grand fun
for my sister and myself, and we packed ourselves in
the bows to get more of a pitch. The captain was of

a very different opinion; and as we left the boat at
Dover, he muttered something to the effect that whatever *we* might have thought of it, he did not expect
to have got safe into harbour.

So with the wild beasts. A man who has only seen
a lion or tiger in a show, opposes himself to a lion or
tiger in a wood with all the confidence in life, and
not unfrequently succeeds in destroying it, merely
from the courage given by an ignorance of danger.

There is a curious fact, which may be mentioned in
connection with this subject. However long Europeans may reside in the hot countries, although they
may become hardened to the sight of wild beasts,
they never quite overcome their fear of snakes. Yet
the natives, who fly in such fear from animals that
inflict wounds which may be healed, pass with the
greatest indifference by the most deadly serpents, a
scratch from whose fangs results in certain death.

The leopards that we see tamed in cages are
either born in the menageries or are taken in a
kind of magnified mouse-trap. Of course when
the creature finds itself imprisoned, it makes a
great disturbance, and soon lets its captors know
that somebody is in their trap. It is comparatively easy to get a leopard into a trap, but getting
him out again is not quite so simple a matter. The
hunters generally manage this rather delicate business
by opening certain apertures in the boarded roof,
through which they let down slip-nooses, and gradually imprison all his legs. This part of the operation
completed, the door of the trap is opened, and another
cord thrown round his neck in spite of all his howl-
ings and kickings. He is then dragged out of the
cage, a strong muzzle fastened on his head, and thus
disarmed, is completely at the mercy of his enemies.
Leopards taken in this way are generally reserved for
the amusement of their conquerors. They, having
greater knowledge of the habits of the leopard, refrain
from confining it in a narrow den, but fasten it to a

post by means of a rope, the other end of which is attached to a kind of collar round the creature's loins, just as we see them represented in the Pompeian paintings. In this state of semi-confinement, the leopard is enabled to display his wonderful agility and gracefulness of action with scarcely any impediment. A leopard thus confined was seen by Lichtenstein, a South African traveller, and the beauty of the animal, together with his graceful movements, moved the traveller to rouse the animal to fresh energies by pelting him with stones and otherwise insulting him. Wishing to see in safety the manner in which a leopard would conduct itself when attacked, he sent for some dogs. Just as they were arriving, the leopard, being in a desperate passion, made such a violent spring at his tormentors that the chain broke and left him at perfect liberty. Off set Lichtenstein pursued by the leopard, who made a tremendous spring at him. Probably from the weight of that part of the chain that was still attached to him, the leopard sprang short, and before another spring could be made, was seized by the dogs, who dashed at his throat and ears. One dog fell an immediate victim, being killed by one bite on the head, but the others attacked the leopard with such violence, and bit his throat with such success, that they soon killed him.

The leopard is generally tamed without difficulty, and appears more sportive than any other animal of the same family. There are several young leopards now in the Zoological Gardens, whose movements among the branches of the tree that is placed in their cage are most graceful. They spring about with such rapidity that the eye can hardly follow their figures. Suddenly one of them appears to be tired, and crouches in some strange position, usually lying flat along a branch, or packed into a forked branch, where it lies very quietly until one of its companions comes unsuspectingly by, when it springs up, gives its friend a pat, and dashes off with more energy than ever. In another menagerie where several animals were kept in one cage, the leopards evidently considered that the great object of the black tip of the lion's tail was to afford them amusement. This being their opinion, they acted up to it, and that unfortunate lion could not even wag the end of his tail without a leopard pouncing upon it. Even when he got up and walked up and down his cage, keeping his tail perpendicularly in the air to get it out of the way of his tormentors, one leopard jumped up on a shelf near the top of the cage, and hit the lion's tail a hard pat.every time he passed under the shelf.

Any account of tame leopards would be imperfect without a reference to the noted leopard Saï. This interesting animal was so completely tamed that it was suffered to roam about the house unwatched, its favourite position being under a sofa, the only indications of his presence being a protruding paw, or an occasional peep from behind the cover. Strangers were naturally rather astonished when they saw so powerful an animal at liberty, especially as the leopard appeared to have gained entrance from the woods, and hidden himself for no good purpose. Saï was a very affectionate creature, and could not bear being separated from his master. One day after the governor (his master) had been engaged for many hours at a conference, he returned to his own room and began to write. He presently heard Saï coming up stairs, and on seeing the animal make a great spring upon him, gave himself up for lost. The leopard only meant to show his joy at again finding his master, whom he had not been able to see all day on account of the crowd, and by rubbing his cheek against his master's head, endeavoured to show his affection. He was full of play, and was by no means averse to a practical joke, such as knocking over his attendant while sleeping, or jumping on the back of a prah-prah woman, as she was stooping down to clean the floor with her little broom. The poor woman was of course in a

terrible fright, never doubting that she was intended
to form a dinner for the leopard. Saï had no such
intention, 'but stood there in great glee, waving his
tail about, while the poor woman, not daring to stir,
screamed piteously. The servants came to see what
was the matter, but on seeing the state of affairs, they
set off as fast as they could, leaving the poor prah-
prah woman to her fate. So she screamed, and the
leopard wagged his tail, until the governor came and
released her. So perfectly tamed was this animal,
that the children used to fight with it for the possession of one of the windows, at which the leopard was
accustomed to stand with his chin resting between his
forepaws on the sill. On several occasions, the children, finding him in their way, combined their forces
and pulled him down by the tail.

Saï was passionately fond of lavender water, a predilection discovered accidentally. While his master
was pouring some lavender water on his handkerchief, Saï, who was sitting as usual with his head
resting on his master's shoulder, tore the handkerchief out of his hands, and continued rolling over it,
until it was reduced to fragments. Before his social
qualities were known, he escaped from the yard where
he was kept, and rushed round the ramparts, scattering consternation in his course. The castle gates were
closed, the officers who had doors shut them, and the
sentinels who had none, ran away, and there was a
terrible disturbance until the playful creature had
wearied himself with his scamper, when he lay down
under a gun-carriage, and suffered himself to be led
away to his proper quarters. His life terminated in
England in a rather curious way. Saï was sent to England, and we are told that, when he reached the ship,
he was completely cowed and subdued, for his cage
had been placed in a canoe, the crew of which were
so frightened when he moved, that they contrived to
upset the whole affair, and poor Saï got a thorough
ducking. Moreover he seemed to suffer from sea-sick-

ness, and certainly did suffer from the wet state of his cage, for no one dared open it or attempt to wipe it out. So he lay curled up in a corner, and did not stir until he heard the voice of his mistress. At the well-known sounds he immediately sprang up, danced about his cage, rolled backwards and forwards, and howl'ed tremendously from pure joy. After that time he got on very well until the ship was boarded by pirates, who took away almost all their provisions, so that Saï must have starved had it not been for a large number of parrots on board, among whom there was a great mortality. One parrot per diem was his sub-sistence—hardly enough to keep him from starving; and his sensations being very like those of our friend Oliver, when depicted as asking for more, he devoured his food so ravenously, that he swallowed the feathers together with the bird. This naturally made him ill, but he recovered after a copious exhibition of calomel. During the voyage, he was taught to keep his claws to himself by a very simple process. His love for laven-der water has already been recorded. His mistress was accustomed to give him a daily allowance of a little lavender water in a paper dish. He was so eager to obtain this boon, that he used to strike at the dish with his claws; but when he found that the perfume was withheld until he had drawn in his claws, he soon learned to put out his foot while his claws were withdrawn. On his arrival in Eng-land, he was presented to the Duchess of York, who had him kept at Exeter Change, the former residence of the wild beasts, until he could be taken to his home. One morning, his new mistress called to see him, and played with him, when he appeared to be in his usual health; but at evening, when the coachman called for him, he was found dead. His disease was supposed to be that to which most exotic animals are subject when they arrive in our damp cold climate, inflammation of the lungs.

Not long since I was at Wombwell's collection, and

wondered how the animals could be transferred to
their separate dens. There was one particularly
ferocious-looking black leopard, who had changed its
residence during the night, and had on, indeed, a
muzzle and chain. As during my boyish days I
had often tried unsuccessfully to muzzle the cat, I
inquired from the keeper how he managed such
animals as the leopard. The method was as follows.
A ladder was laid upon the animal, through which,
after turning on its back, it thrust its legs. A pitchfork was then placed upon its neck, and the points
fixed firmly into the ground. The leopard was then
helpless, for several men added their weight to the
ladder, while the man with the pitchfork took great
care of its head. The muzzle was then put on with
perfect ease, and the animal shifted to another den.

I will conclude this account of the leopard with
Topsell's description of the method by which the
leopard obtains its prey. I may observe that the
jaguar is much more given to monkey-eating than the
leopard, and it is not at all improbable that Topsell
has confused accounts of the two animals. " They
ravin upon flesh both birds and beasts, for which
cause they hide themselves in trees, usually in mountains, where they are not very swift of foot, and therefore they give themselves to take apes, which they
attain by this policy; when they see the apes they
make after them, who at their first approaching climb
up into the tops of trees, and there sit to avoid the
panther's teeth, for she is not able to follow them so
high; but yet she is more cunning than the apes, and
therefore deviseth more shifts to take them, that
where nature hath denied her bodily power there she
might supply that want by the gifts of the minde.
Forth therefore she goeth, and under the tree where
the apes are lodged she lyeth down as though she
were dead, stretching out her limbs and restraining
her breath, shutting her eyes, and shewing altogether
tokens of expiration. The apes that sit on the top

of the tree behold from on high the behaviour of their adversary, and because all of them wish her dead, the more easily believe that which they so much desire, and yet dare not descend to make tryal. Then to end their doubts they choose out from among them all whom they think to be of the best courage, him they send down as it were for an espy to certifie all the residue, forth then he goeth with a thousand fears in his minde, and leapeth from bough to bough in no great haste (for dread of an ill bargain), yet being come down dareth not come nigh, but having taken a view of the counterfeit and repressed his own fear returneth back again. After a little space he descendeth a second time and cometh nearer the panther than before, but returneth without touching him. Then he descendeth the third time, looking into his eyes, and maketh trial whether he draweth breath or no, but the panther keepeth both breath and limbs immoveable, by that means emboldning the apes to their own destruction, for the spie ape sitteth down beside the panther and stirreth not; now when those which are above in the tree see how their intelligencer abideth continually beside their adversary without harm, they gather their spirits together and descend in great multitudes, running about the panther, first of all going upon him and afterwards leaping with great joy and exultation, mocking their adversary with all their apish toys and testifying their joy for her supposed death. And in this sort the panther suffereth them to continue a great season till she perceiveth they are thoroughly wearied, and then upon a sudden she leapeth up alive again, taking some of them in his claws, destroying and killing them with his teeth and nails, till he have prepared for himself a rich dinner out of his adversaries' flesh. And like as Ulysses endured all the contumelies and reproaches of both his maids and wives' suitors, until he had a just occasion given him of revenge, so doth the panther the disdainful dealings of the

G

apes; whereupon came the proverb, 'Pardi mortem dissimulat; Thanaton pardaleos hypocrinetai,' against a cunning dissembling fellow, such an one as Brutus was, who counterfeated madness that he might get the Empire."

JAGUAR.*

THE animals already mentioned belong to the Old World, but there are two of the same family inhabiting America particularly worthy of notice. These are the jaguar and the puma. The jaguar is very like the leopard, but is considerably larger, and may be easily distinguished from that animal by the appearance of the spots, which are larger than those of the leopard, and are composed of a black spot surrounded by several others. There is also a black streak across the chest.

It feeds principally on monkeys, and possesses such activity that it can often catch them in a fair chase among the branches. In consequence, the monkeys hold it in supreme terror, and take to flight the moment they hear its cry. We may suppose that the monkeys have not so much intellect as has been supposed, or no jaguar would be able to attack them. As an example of the superiority of man over the beasts, we may cite the well-known example of the man who met a jaguar in his path. He looked at the jaguar, and the jaguar looked at him, but after a short time, a sudden impulse seized him, and he took off his wide-trimmed hat, and bowing low to the animal, wished him a very good morning. The jaguar looked very much astonished, turned round, and walked away. An analogous anecdote is related of a tiger who met an Indian servant, and, on the man's request to let him pass, as he was on important business, walked off and left the path free.

The jaguar's mode of killing its prey differs from

* Leopardus Onca.

that of the other *Felidæ.* The usual method is
to kill it either by a severe blow, or by tearing open
the victim's throat. The jaguar takes quite another
course. He springs upon the back of his prey, and
placing one paw on the back of the unfortunate
animal's head and another on its mouth, gives the
head a sudden twist, which instantly dislocates the
neck. Like most wild animals, the jaguar would
rather avoid man than attack him, except when
pressed with hunger, at which time it is exceedingly dangerous. There is a very interesting story
respecting the perseverance of this animal in obtaining its food. The inhabitants of a log-hut in the
western States of America had gone out, having
closed the door of their hut, in which a piece of
freshly-killed venison was hanging. Near the top
of the hut a small aperture was left in the gable,
for the purpose of admitting light and air. This
aperture was so high that when the settlers, a man
and his wife, left the hut, they did not think that
there was any necessity for closing it. A hungry
jaguar happened to come by, and sniffed out the
meat. So he contrived to scramble up the end of the
hut, and to jump in at the aperture. He then made
his way to the venison, and commenced making a
repast on it. The return of the owners disturbed
him, and he took his departure. The man, discovering what had happened, took away the venison,
imagining that, as the cause of the visitation was removed, the jaguar would not trouble himself to come
back. That night, he was obliged to leave that part of
the country and go to a distance, leaving his wife to
take care of the hut. The man was mistaken in his
supposition, that when the venison was gone the
jaguar would not enter the house, for when evening
came, the jaguar came too, and scrambled in at the
open gable as before. The poor woman was of course
in a great fright, as she had no means of protecting
herself. At last, by screaming with all her might,

and making every noise she could think of, she succeeded in frightening the animal away for a time, but
she knew well that he would come again soon, and
searched for some method of protection.   Just as she
heard the jaguar again climbing up the house, she
bethought herself of a great store-chest, fastening with
a spring, into which she got, and pulled down the lid,
keeping her fingers between the lid and the side of
the chest, lest she should be suffocated for want of air.

Very soon the jaguar came into the room, and
before long discovered her hiding place.   He tried to
push his head into the chest, but could not raise the
lid, nor could his paws obtain entrance.   Presently
he discovered her fingers, and began to lick them with
his rough tongue.   They soon began to bleed, but
she dared not move them lest the spring-lock of the
chest should close.   Not being able to do any good at
the side of the box, he jumped upon the lid, and by
his weight broke the poor woman's fingers.   For a
long time he continued these efforts, smelling round
the chest, trying to force it open, licking the protruding fingers, and leaping on and off, but at last,
finding all his endeavours useless, he went away.
His intended victim dared not leave the chest until
daybreak, when she ran as fast as she could to her
nearest neighbours, where she procured help.   On
her husband's return he searched for the jaguar, and
found a pair, together with their cubs, in the forest
close to the house, and destroyed them all.

It is a cowardly animal, and fears to attack any one
who may possibly retaliate.   Waterton made the acquaintance of a jaguar in rather a curious manner.
He had contrived to get the skin of his feet so scorched
by the sun that at night they were covered with blisters,
and he was unable to sleep.   While tossing restlessly
in his hammock a jaguar came and looked at his
party, but evidently considered them rather too strong
for him.   He was unwilling to leave them, and kept
hovering about them all night, sometimes coming

within the glare of the fire, and sitting on his haunches hke a cat, and sometimes walking round the spot where Mr. Waterton's hammock was slung, but always keeping at a respectful distance.

Perhaps he did not consider the travel-hardened, sun-dried traveller in the hammock so tempting as another jaguar found some priests. The animal had contrived to get into the church of Santa Fé, and as we may suppose he found nothing there but church mice, whose leanness is proverbial, he was naturally disposed to look out for something more substantial. Accordingly, a decidedly substantial padre did enter the church, and was immediately killed by the jaguar. His absence causing some suspicion, a coadjutor went into the church to look after him, but was as unaccountably delayed as his predecessor. After some time another padre went in search of the missing two, and was instantly apprised of the cause of his predecessors' absence by the appearance of the jaguar, who sprang at him also. The animal, however, had become lazy after his former exertion, and had probably made a meal on the bodies of the two unfortunate men whom he had killed, so that, by dodging about from pillar to pillar, the third padre succeeded in making his escape. No one could be found who was willing to enter the fatal building, so the people unroofed a corner of the church, and shot the jaguar without difficulty.

The jaguar is possessed of a discriminating palate, and devours great numbers of turtles. Tortoises, turtles, and all that race, are popularly supposed to be impregnable to all but mankind and the boa constrictor. According to Sidney Smith, man catches them and roasts them, while the boa constrictor swallows them, shell and all, and consumes them slowly in the interior, as Chancery does a large estate. There is, however, another enemy with whom they have to contend. Impervious as the turtle's shell may be, and safely as he may draw in his head, yet the jaguar

is more than a match for him. The eggs of the turtle
are laid in the sand. Therefore the jaguar comes to
the sand too, and when he sees a turtle fairly away
from the water, he rushes at it, and cleverly turns it
on its back. Having thus rendered the creature help
less, the jaguar contrives to insinuate his paw between
the shells, and scrapes out the whole of the interior,
cutting away the muscles as if they had been severed
with a knife. Then, when he has finished the turtle,
he takes a turn at the eggs, scratching them out of the
sandy pit where the mother had placed them. But
the jaguar does not waste his strength merely upon
turtles or turtles' eggs, but even attacks the horses
which run wild in many parts of America, and is
strong enough not only to kill them, but even to drag
them away for a considerable distance. A single
jaguar has been known to swim across one of the
broad American rivers, seize a dead horse that had
been laid down as a bait, drag it to the river's edge,
swim across with it in his mouth, and afterwards
carry it up the opposite bank and away into the
woods.

We have already seen how the jaguar prefers two
courses for dinner, turtle and venison; it only remains
that he should rival the civilisation of man by adding
a third course, namely, fish. Now the jaguar being of
a discriminating palate, does prefer a fish course now
and then, and accordingly goes to the places where
fish live, i. e. to the rivers. There he waits in the
shallow waters, remaining quite motionless, until a
tolerably-sized fish passes by, when a sharp blow of
his ever-ready paw sweeps the fish out of its native
element and leaves it floundering on the bank. The
successful fisher immediately springs on it before its
struggles have again brought it to the water, and carries it off.

When young this animal is as playful as a kitten,
and is not at all particular in the choice of its playfellows. There was a jaguar, a young one, lying

calmly at the mouth of his den, at whom some dogs were sent. The animal, who had just made a hearty meal, and was in great good humour in consequence, instead of annihilating the dogs and springing upon their master, began to play with them in spite of their attacks. The hunter, however, meant to enrich himself with a jaguar skin, so he roused the lazy animal by a bullet in the shoulders. His play was instantaneously changed to rage, and he sprang so quickly upon his assailant, that, although the hunter had a spear ready in rest, the impetus of the animal was so great that it transfixed itself on the weapon, and fairly knocked the man over on the ground. The two rolled on the ground together, and the jaguar all but succeeded in seizing its enemy's throat, when just at the critical moment the fire in the jaguar's eyes went out, and it fell upon the hunter quite dead. Another example of the playfulness of this animal is related by Humboldt.

Near an Indian village on the banks of the Orinoco two native children were sitting, when a jaguar issued from the forest and approached them. He came up to them quietly, playing all manner of tricks like a kitten with a new plaything. At one time he gambolled about them, and then hid among the long grass, and at last began to play with the little boy, patting him on the side of the head. The child felt no fear, and suffered his strange playfellow to continue his pranks, until at last the claws of the jaguar wounded the child and caused the blood to flow. His sister, who also appears to have been equally devoid of fear, took up a branch of a tree that lay near, and began to beat the jaguar, as, in all probability, she had seen her friends beat a dog that had behaved badly, and, curiously enough, the jaguar, betraying no irritation, began to run away, and on the approach of some Indians bounded off into the forest.

PUMA. *

THE puma is another American leopard. It differs
from all its congeners in the colour of its fur, which,
instead of the beautiful variegated spots that decorate
their bodies, presents an uniform silvery grey above,
fading into white on the under parts of the body and
the inside of the limbs, precisely like the " tan " in a
black and tan terrier.   As a rule, all the cat tribe are
brindled, spotted, or striped, except in a very few
instances, such as the lion and puma, and even in
these there are signs of markings in their fur, especially when young, at which time the cubs both of the
lion and puma exhibit markings, those of the lion
being striped, and those of the puma both striped
and spotted.   As the cubs grow older, the spots and
stripes become fainter, and at last disappear entirely,
or at least can only be observed in certain lights and
by very sharp eyes.

The name Puma is said to be a native name ; if so it
is much more euphonous than its other Mexican names,
Gouazuara and Cuguacura, from the latter of which
the term Cougar has been contracted.   This name is
mostly used by the French, the Anglo-American title
being " panther ' (or more familiarly " painter "), by
which name it is very commonly called.   It is extremely powerful, its limbs being very thick, and possesses a strength which the small size of its head
would not lead the observer to suspect.   It is essentially an arboreal animal, and contrives so to assimilate itself to the bark of the branches, that in spite of
its large size it can lie concealed along a branch.
Even in captivity, when the spectator knows that the
creature is in the den, he has often some difficulty in
discovering the puma, as it lies either packed up in
the fork of a branch or stretched along it quite flat,
with its chin resting on its fore-paws, and only an

* *Leopardus concolor.*

occasional blink of the eyelids or twitch of the ears giving signs of life.

The puma is easily tamed, and is very playful. The celebrated actor Edmund Kean possessed a puma which would follow him about like a dog, and was so gentle that it was frequently permitted to appear in a room full of strangers. Its whole life presents a close resemblance to that of Saï, the African leopard already described, even to the circumstances of breaking loose one day. The scene of the leopard's escapade was in a fort, and little damage could have been done, but the puma escaped into the streets of London, and might have done extraordinary mischief, had it been so disposed. A watchman took the playful animal into custody and restored it to its owner.

The flesh of this animal is eaten, and is said to resemble veal. Many a prejudiced Englishman, visiting France with a deeply-rooted British horror of frogs and wooden shoes, has met wooden shoes without recognising them, and been induced to partake heartily of frog without discovering the nature of the dish. In like manner, Mr. Darwin suddenly found out that he had been supping upon puma unawares. Many natives agree in saying that the flesh of the cat is excellent. I can say from personal experience that it is not at all bad, and is not unlike rabbit, being white and dry; but probably my method of cooking was not quite according to Soyer, or it might have turned out quite a superior dish.

Having shown that the cat possesses one agreeable quality, that of making a tolerable roast if necessary, we will try to find some further good qualities.

CAT.*

THE origin of our domestic cat is very uncertain. Some think that the wild cat is the original stock

* *Felis domestica.*

from whence all the varieties of the domesticated mousers sprang. This is very unlikely, if not altogether impossible. In the first place, the tail of the wild cat is short, and very bushy, while that of the tame animal is long and tapering. This peculiarity is not removed by domestication, for many cats of the wild breed that have been tamed, transmitted their peculiar form of tail to their posterity, while tame cats which have got loose into the woods, and have bred there for years, are found still to possess the tapering tails derived from their ancestors. Moreover, the mummies of Egyptian cats are found to possess the elongated tapering tail, which is also represented on their monuments.

The wild cat is rather scarce in England, but is frequently found in wooded places in Scotland. It is a very fierce animal, and displays more aggressive powers than would have been expected from an animal so small. The following account of a "scrimmage" with a wild cat is taken from Mr. St. John's "Highland Sports :"—

"The true wild cat is gradually becoming extirpated, owing to the increasing preservation of game ; and though difficult to hold in a trap, in consequence of its great strength and agility, he is by no means difficult to deceive, taking any bait readily, and not seeming to be as cautious in avoiding danger as many other kinds of vermin. Inhabiting the most lonely and inaccessible ranges of rock and mountain, the wild cat is seldom seen during the daytime ; at night, like its domestic relative, he prowls far and wide, walking with the same deliberate step, making the same regular and even track, and hunting its game in the same tiger-like manner; and yet the difference between the two animals is perfectly clear and visible to the commonest observer. The wild cat has a shorter and more bushy tail, stands higher on her legs in proportion to her size, and has a rounder and coarser look about the head. The strength and ferocity of the wild cat, when hemmed in or hard pressed, are perfectly astonishing. The body when skinned presents quite a mass of sinew and cartilage. I have occasionally, though rarely, fallen in with these animals in the forests and mountains of this country. Once, when grouse shooting, I came suddenly, in a rough and rocky part of the ground, upon a family of two old ones and three half-grown ones. In the hanging birch woods that border some of the Highland streams and rocks, the wild cat is still not uncommon; and I have heard their wild and unearthly cry echo far in the quiet night, as they answer and call to each other. I do not know a more harsh and unpleasant cry than that of the wild cat, or one more likely to be the origin of superstitious fears in the mind of an ignorant Highlander. These animals have great skill in finding their prey, and the damage they do to the game must be very great, owing to the quantity of food which they require. When caught in a trap, they fly, without hesitation, at any person who approaches them, not waiting to be assailed. I have heard many stories of their attacking and severely wounding a man, when their escape has been cut off. Indeed, a wild cat once flew at me in the most determined manner. I was fishing at a river in Sutherlandshire, and in passing from one pool to another had to climb over some rocky and broken kind of ground. In doing so, I sank through some rotten heather and moss up to my knees almost upon a wild cat, who was concealed under it. I was quite as much startled as the animal herself could be, when I saw the wild-looking beast so unexpectedly rush out from between my feet, with every hair on her body standing on end, making her look twice as large as she really was. I had three small Skye terriers with me, who immediately gave chase, and pursued her till she took refuge in a corner of the rocks, where, perched in a kind of recess out of reach of her enemies, she stood with her hair bristled out, and spitting and growling like a common cat. Having no weapon with me, I laid down my rod, cut a good-sized stick, and proceeded to dislodge her. As soon as I was within six or seven feet of the place, she sprang straight at my face, over the dogs' heads. Had I not struck her in mid air as she leaped at me, I should probably have got some severe wound. As it was, she fell with her back half broken amongst the dogs, who, with my assistance, dispatched her. I never saw an animal fight so desperately, or one which was so difficult to kill. If a tame cat has nine lives, a wild cat must have a dozen. Sometimes one of these animals takes up his residence at no great distance from a house, and entering the hen-houses and out-buildings, carries off fowls or even lambs in the most audacious manner. Like other vermin, the wild cat haunts the shores of the lakes and rivers, and it is, therefore, easy to know where to lay a trap for them. Having caught and killed one of the colony, the rest of them are sure to be taken, if the body of their slain relative is left in some place not far from their usual hunting ground, and surrounded with traps, as every wild cat who passes within a considerable distance of the place will to a certainty come to it. The same plan may be adopted successfully in trapping foxes, who also are sure to visit the dead body of any other fox, which they scent during their nightly walk. There is no animal more destructive than a common house cat, when she takes to hunting in the woods. In this case they should always be destroyed, as when once they have learnt to prefer hares and rabbits to rats and mice, they are sure to hunt the larger animals only. I believe, however, that by cropping their ears close to the head, cats may be kept from hunting, as they cannot bear the dew or rain to enter these sensitive organs. Tame cats, who have once taken to the woods, soon get shy and wild, and then produce their young in rabbit-holes, decayed trees, and other quiet places, thus laying the foundation of a half-wild

race. It is worthy of notice, that whatever colour the
parents of these semi-wild cats may have been, those
bred out of them are almost invariably of the same
beautiful brindled grey colour as the wild cats. A shepherd, whose cat had come to an untimely end—by trap
or gun, I forget which—in lamenting her death to me,
said it was a great pity so valuable an animal should
be killed, as she brought him every day in the year
either a grouse, a young hare, or some other head of
game. Another man told me that his cat brought to
the house during the whole winter a woodcock or a
snipe almost every night, showing a propensity for
hunting in the swamps and wet places near which
the cottage was situated, and where these birds were
in the habit of feeding during the night. A favourite
cat of my own once took to bringing home rabbits
and hares, but never winged game. Though constantly caught in traps, she could never be cured of
her hunting propensities. When caught in an iron
trap, instead of springing about and struggling, and
by this means breaking or injuring her legs, she used
to sit quietly down and wait to be let out. There is a
cat at the farm now, who is caught at least twice a
week; but from adopting the same plan of waiting
quietly and patiently to be liberated she seldom gets
her foot much hurt."

The domestic cat will excite our sympathies much
more than the wild one, however interesting the latter
animal may be in a zoological point of view. Accounts of the natural instincts of animals are very
valuable; but it is even more interesting to see how
that portion of reason implanted in animals can overcome their natural instincts whenever the occasion
requires.

While I was at college as an undergraduate, the
bakehouse cat attached herself to me, and was invariably in the habit of coming to my rooms morning and
evening for her breakfast and supper. She seemed
really to partake more of the nature of the dog than

of the cat, for she would suffer me to take from her
the mice which she had caught, even while they were
alive. She was on remarkably good terms with my
dog Rory, who was quite a character in his way, and
would use him as a convenient cushion to lie upon,
and apparently considered that his ears were made as
playthings for herself and her kittens. The only
thing that disturbed her equanimity was when Rory
chose to partake of her saucer of milk. She evidently
perceived that the division was not a fair one, and
remonstrated most vigorously, but even then never
got angry. Her first family of kittens was a source
of great pride to her, and was announced to me in
rather a singular manner. The cat had absented
herself from my table for several days, nor was she to
be seen about the college. This was so unusual a
circumstance, that I began to get uneasy about her,
fearing that she might have shared the tragical fate of
her predecessor. One evening, however, about her
usual time of appearing, she scratched at the door as
usual, and came in. When I sat down, she jumped
on my knee, put a tiny blind kitten into my hand,
and paced about the floor in a decidedly majestic way,
every now and then uttering a short mew. Nothing
would induce her to take her offspring back again, so
I took it to its brothers and sisters myself, its mother
walking before me with her tail held quite perpendicularly. That same evening, when I went into my bed-
room, I found a small black kitten fast asleep on the
bed.

Her predecessor was equally attached to me, but
met with an untimely end. I missed it from its accustomed post at my table, and inquired from the
servant where it was. " Cat, sir," he replied, with all
the nonchalance in the world; " the cat, sir; it's been
baked these three days, sir." I was naturally rather
astonished at this circumstance, and thought that
possibly some enthusiastic reader of Chinese manners
might have had the cat cooked as an experiment. The

poor animal, however, had escaped that danger, but had been accessary to its own destruction in another manner. It had been induced, by the warmth of the oven, to creep into one of the corners, and there had, in all probability, fallen asleep. There, however, it was found, coiled up in a corner, and completely baked. It must have died from suffocation, as it did not move while the oven was being newly heated, and was probably dead before the oven was opened for that purpose ; at all events, its attitude was that which a sleeping cat assumes.

After these lines had been printed, an account was sent to me of another cat, who had met with its death in a similar manner. The owner of the poor animal, wishing to show to his friends that the cat must have probably died without pain, learnedly remarked, that before the creature died, " skumfification " must have taken place.

The fondness of cats for certain scents is well known. Their taste in this respect is rather singular, valerian being their favourite perfume. It is a very unsafe experiment for any one who cares about the appearance of his garden to suffer a single plant of this herb to be placed in it, for every cat in the neighbourhood will inevitably discover it, assemble in troops, and roll over it and the adjacent beds until not a vestige of the plant is left. A waggish individual, who was plagued by the incessant mewing and quarrelling of a colony of cats belonging to an old lady next door, contrived to revenge himself through the medium of her pets. The lady in question had two hobbies, her cats and her garden. Accordingly, after the annoyance had become quite unbearable, her neighbour proceeded to the market, and procured a quantity of valerian. This he brought home, steeped it in boiling water to make it give out the whole of its odour, and scattered it over the garden. Next morning, when the old lady descended into her garden, she found it in most admired disorder. Not a flower was left, the earth from the beds was torn up, and scattered about the gravel. The beautifully smooth lawn was also scratched up in a hundred places, and could hardly have presented a worse appearance had a body of cavalry been exercising upon it. Horrified at the appearance of her garden, the poor lady sought refuge in the house, and consolation from her cats. Alas! her pets were in a worse state than her garden. Covered with mud, with downcast looks, and still savouring powerfully of valerian, those of her cats who could be found at all presented themselves. And worse than this was to come, for the cats, half maddened with excitement at the smell of valerian, had been fighting with each other for the pieces, and, in consequence, her pampered favourites had been worsted in the encounters, and came home with torn ears. scratched noses, and ragged bodies.

I heard lately of a cat who exhibited a penchant for spirits, not in the refined form of perfumes, but in the more vulgar form of brandy. She belongs to one of my friends, and has lately displayed qualities which would have called down the indignation of Father Mathew, and inevitably caused her ejection from a consistent temperance family. Her master had just taken his supper one night, when the cat, as hungry cats generally do, placed her fore paws on his knee. and gently patted his arm. He naturally imagining that pussy intended this as a gentle hint that she would like some supper also, offered her a piece of bread, which she repudiated. He then, intending to play the cat a trick, dipped the bread into some brandy and water which he had just compounded, and again offered it to the cat. To his astonishment, she immediately disposed of the soaked bread, and became very impatient for more. She ate several pieces of this bread, and finished by eating a piece. dipped in *pure brandy.*

If this circumstance had taken place some two hundred years since, in all probability there would

have been a cry of witchcraft, and a call for Matthew
Hopkins, who would inevitably have identified the cat
with a neighbouring dowager celebrated for her devo-
tion to tipsy cake.

Every one must have noticed the love of a cat for her
kittens, and the manner in which she brings them up,
teaching them their lessons, as it were, and exercising
their limbs and eyes by all manner of gambols. Unlike many animals, when her young arrive at years of
discretion, and are able to gain their own living without her maternal care, she does not drive them away,
but still keeps up a kindly feeling for them, although it
is not so strong as when they were little and helpless.
At such a time, she devotes her whole existence to her
young, and if they are in danger, thinks her own life
as nothing when compared with their safety. Some time
since, while a number of kittens were playing about
in the straw near a barn door, a large hawk swooped
down upon them, and seized one of the kittens in his
claws. Being encumbered by the weight, it could not
rise very quickly, and gave the mother time to spring
to the rescue of her offspring. She immediately flew
at the hawk, who in self-defence was forced to drop
the kitten. A regular pitched battle then took place,
the hawk at first gaining the advantage, in consequence of his power of flight. After some time, the
cat, after losing an eye and getting her ears torn to
ribbons, succeeded in breaking the wing of her adversary. Stimulated by this success, she sprang on the
maimed hawk with renewed fury; and after a protracted struggle, made one decisive effort, and laid
him dead at her feet. She spent but one moment in
making sure of her conquest by tearing the head of
her vanquished foe to pieces, and then turned to
her kitten, licked its bleeding wounds, and began to
purr as if she had not received the slightest injury
herself.

The reasoning powers of the cat have been very
much underrated. The intellect of a cat does not

H

come very far behind that of a dog; but as it is
almost always exerted for selfish purposes, comparatively little notice is taken of it.   In the following
anecdotes, the reasoning powers appear to be by no
means small, and in one instance were exerted in a
very singular manner.

Four cats, belonging to one of my friends, had
taught themselves the art of begging like a dog.
They had frequently seen the dog practise that accomplishment at table, and had observed that he
generally obtained a reward for so doing.   By a process of inductive reasoning they decided that, if they
possessed the same accomplishment, they would in all
probability receive the same reward.   Acting on this
opinion, they waited until they saw the dog sit up in
the begging position, and immediately assumed the
same attitude with imperturbable gravity.   Of course
their ingenuity was not suffered to pass unrewarded,
and they always found that their newly-discovered accomplishment was an unfailing source of supplies for
them.

Two cats had taken up their residence in a barn, and
were remarkable for their friendship towards each other.
It so happened that both of the cats were favoured with
kittens about the same time, and of course were very
proud and careful of their young families.   After a few
days the little kittens began to run about; and at last,
both families contrived to stray into a pathway where
they might possibly be injured.   One of the mothers,
seeing this, took up her own offspring, one by one,
and carried them into a place of safety; but there was
then left one kitten belonging to her friend.   This
she would not touch, but went in search of its mother,
brought it with her to the kitten, and waited until it
also had been placed in safety.

The idea of comparative size is in no way above
the comprehension of a cat, as will be seen from the
following anecdote.   There was a remarkably fine cat,
who lived in a house that contained every luxury that

a cat could wish for. The fare was plentiful, the milk unlimited, no lack of mice, and plenty of black beetles for evening amusement. Besides these comforts, there was a very pleasant garden attached to the house, where sparrows, robins, and other little birds were to be caught occasionally. There was but one drawback—the envy of a neighbour. A few doors distant lived a very large tom-cat, who looked with envious eyes upon the prosperity of his neighbour; and, very naturally, from envying her good fortune, he came to hate herself. Accordingly, he lost no opportunity of teasing her, and used to look out for her while she was quietly sleeping in the garden; at such times he would pounce down, give her a blow on the head, and chase her out of the garden. This was treatment to which she never would have submitted, had she been at all equal to her persecutor in strength and size, but as she was decidedly inferior in both respects, she converted her weakness into an instrument of safety. In the garden stood an iron roller, having its ends filled up with scroll-work. The cat being imbued with that spirit of curiosity so strongly implanted in the feline race, had discovered that she could just squeeze through the openings and sit inside the roller. Soon after she had made this discovery, the envious cat again insulted her. This time she did not take the trouble of escaping out of the garden; but ran at once to the roller, crawled in, and sat there watching with perfect equanimity the struggles of her persecutor to force himself through the opening. Ever after that time the roller became her camp of refuge.

Cats are almost as inquisitive as monkeys. If the slightest change is made in the furniture of a room, they find it out at once, and never rest until they have thoroughly surveyed the alterations. My college cat was, as usual, sitting on my hearth-rug in the evening, when a friend came in. Pussy did not at all approve of strangers, and walked round him several times, evidently unsatisfied. This led to some conversation on the curiosity evinced by cats, and various instances were adduced. I had that day been making a large cage for rearing butterflies and moths from the egg. The top was covered with wire gauze, and would lift up, for the convenience of removing and changing the plants on which caterpillars feed. This was very well as long as they remained caterpillars; but it was very evident that when the caterpillars became butterflies, the moment that the top of the cage was opened they would escape, and either get away altogether, or, at all events, batter themselves about sadly before they were recaptured. I therefore cut a small door, about four inches square, in the wooden side of the cage, through which the arm could be passed, and the butterfly caught without the smallest chance of escape. The cat had been seriously perplexed by the appearance of this cage, and had not entirely made up her mind about it; so I told my friend that I would make the cat creep through the little door. He was rather incredulous, as in general cats are not very obedient. I therefore took the cage off its stand and placed it on the ground, at the same time opening the little door. Pussy soon saw this, and began to sniff about it, until she discovered the open door. First she peeped in, then she explored with one paw, and then with the other. At last she found herself unable to resist the temptation, and squeezed herself through the aperture. Directly she was fairly in, I shut and fastened the door. In the meanwhile, pussy examined with great satisfaction; and after she had made herself acquainted with every corner of the cage, she looked for the door at which she had entered, and commenced a tour of discovery, during which she made several dashes at a glass window in the side of the box, about the same dimensions as the door. Finding all her endeavours fruitless, she laid herself down and calmly went to sleep, much to my discomfiture; for I had calculated on hearing her mew piteously for at least a quarter of an hour, and intended the affair as a lesson to pussy not to be inquisitive in future.

Some country friends of mine possess a huge cat, rejoicing in various names, but generally going by the name of Succubus. The great creature is shamefully lazy; and if he is lifted up high in the air, and suffered to fall, he comes down heavily like a lump of clay, and sits down where he fell. Like most cats, he takes great care to make himself comfortable. One spring, his juvenile owners had discovered the nest of a thrush in their garden; they were extremely pleased with the discovery, and took great care not to injure the parent birds. In a few days the nest was completed, and an egg laid. Soon, the full number was completed, and the hen bird began to sit. This was an anxious time for the young ornithologists, who were daily expecting the advent of five little thrushes. Day after day they visited the nest, and found all going on well; but on one unfortunate day, when they went to pay their usual visit, they found Succubus lying curled up in the nest, the eggs broken, and the parent birds gone.

Although the proverb respecting cats and dogs seems to point to an inextinguishable animosity existing between them, no animals can live more comfortably together than do cats and dogs when brought up together. They will even eat together from the same plate without quarrelling, though the dog does get the greater part of the provisions. Sometimes the cat seems to envy the dog's greater powers of mastication, and appears to fancy that she is not well treated. This was most ludicrously exemplified in the case of a very small kitten. The little creature used to consider that the food daily placed for a large Newfoundland dog was so much more than her own allowance, that means ought to be taken to equalise matters. Now kitty, although her estimate of comparative size was rather erroneous with regard to the provisions, was very correct with regard to the dog himself, and she never ventured to make a direct attack, as the Newfoundland could have swallowed her without in the least destroying his appetite for dinner. So she set about her task in a different way. When she saw Neptune at dinner, she would make her appearance, and take a circuit round his kennel, just out of reach of his chain, looking at him in a conciliatory manner. Next circuit would be a little smaller, bringing her within his reach. Neptune, well knowing what she wanted, would lift his nose from the plate and look at her, at which kitty would mew in a very supplicatory manner. This used to be repeated until the kitten had got close to the kennel. When there, she lay down as if perfectly satisfied with making friends with the dog. Soon she began to creep slowly towards his plate, but looking perfectly unconcerned, as if she did not see that any dinner was going on. Having reached the plate, she would watch until Neptune's eye was off her, when she would make a sudden spring across the plate, snatching up a piece of meat in her progress, and dash off as fast as she could scamper.

The cat Succubus mentioned above was frequently used in the light of a musical instrument by his owners. The animal being very fat and lazy, had a great objection to being handled, and was accustomed to resent such treatment by a subdued sleepy kind of a growl. By taking him in the arms as a baby generally lies, and pulling his tail, the growl was always elicited; and by judicious squeezing and pinching his thorax, the growl was changed into a series of sounds sharper or deeper according to the violence of the operation. My own cat, when subjected to that process, gives forth almost a chromatic scale, beginning at a deep note and gradually rising to a very high one, which is apt to degenerate into a hiss if the squeeze is too hard. The animal appears to be perfectly aware of the ludicrous nature of the sounds thus elicited from him.

This is but a feeble imitation of the grand instrument invented by an ingenious musician and mechanist. The musical part of the instrument was entirely composed of cats. The inventor, who, I suppose, in these days, would have dubbed himself professor of Ælurophoneticism, constructed his organ after the following manner. First, he made a number of little boxes, just large enough to hold a cat, with a hole in the lid of each box. The boxes were arranged in a regular scale, each being marked C, C♯, D, D♯, &c. He then sent for a number of cats, and by pinching the tail of each, found out its note, and ticketed it accordingly. When the performance came on, each cat was placed in its proper cell, its tail drawn through the hole in the lid, and fixed in a perpendicular position. To an ordinary set of manuals was attached a piece of mechanism, which, when the performer struck C, pinched the tail of the C-cat; and so on with the remaining keys. A very lively performance then took place, the only drawback being, that sometimes a cat would cry in the wrong place. The inventor found that cats soon got out of tune, and that their notes were too long, a defect which he could not rectify, as dampers were naturally impracticable, so he afterwards substituted pigs, whose notes were more uniform and less sustained.

With regard to the friendship between cats and dogs, I had almost forgotten to mention the curious intimacy that took place between a dog and a cat of my acquaintance. They had been brought up together from childhood, and had formed a Benedict and Beatrice kind of affection for each other, always quarrelling in a humorous kind of way when together, and always miserable when apart. If they were by any chance separated, they never rested until they had joined company. Each knowing this, was accustomed to slip away from the other, and lie in ambush. In such a case, the dog would rush out on the cat, and tumble her over with his nose, or the cat would sit with her right paw ready lifted, and deal her friend a sound box on the ear, immediately escaping up a tree, when he would bark, and she would spit, for a minute or two, when she would come down and engage in a game of romps with him. One day she had hidden herself behind a door-scraper, her paw ready lifted for a blow, and her eyes glowing with eagerness, as she heard the dog's step just behind her. Prince just at that moment caught a glimpse of puss, and made a great spring past her, setting off along the gravel path as fast as his legs would carry him. Pussy made a spiteful blow at him as he passed, but missed her aim; and instantly commenced a pursuit on three legs, holding her right paw in the air, lest it should lose any of its strength, and detract from the force of the blow with which she intended to greet Prince when she caught him.

A little Skye terrier, belonging to one of my friends, was lately blessed with a small family of two. During the time that her puppies were dependent upon her for subsistence, Jip was changed from a good-natured caressing little animal into a savage wild beast. No one, except her master, was permitted to enter the shed where the puppies lay, without being immediately attacked by their mother, who flew at the intruders with the utmost fury, barking until it was a wonder that her throat was not torn to pieces. In due time the puppies grew up, and Jip grew amenable, suffering them to be handled without remonstrance; and when they were a few months old, one of them was given away, and the other died, Jip treating both misfortunes in a very philosophical manner. About the time that the puppy died, a little kitten arrived at the house, and, finding the inhabitants behaved kindly to it, took up its residence there. There was already one kitten in the house, who was a fast friend to Jip, and was accustomed to romp with her continually; but when kitten number two arrived, Jip treated it just as if it were one of her own puppies.

Soon after its arrival, I was passing by the kitchen door, when Jip flew out, barking and growling just as she had done during the childhood of her puppies, and as I persisted in entering the kitchen to see what was the matter, she retreated to the hearth-rug, where lay a little tabby kitten curled up fast asleep. Jip lay down by it, put her paws on each side of it as if to defend the little animal, and set up a savage snarl, changing to a bark at the slightest movement. The kitten still lay quite unmoved at all the noises proceeding from its guardian's throat, and did not even appear to awake.

Cats can use very expressive acting when they wish to make themselves understood; and can render themselves intelligible not only to their own species, but to mankind. My own cat constantly summons me down stairs to open the cellar door; and if he is desirous of a game at play, he waits until he has drawn my attention, and commences a series of antics, just as if I were already playing with him. Sometimes he gets up at the window, just as was related of Saï, puts his fore-legs on the back of a chair, and surveys the street. We can always tell by his demeanour what kind of objects are passing. Nothing takes his fancy so much as a large dog. Directly such an animal appears, his ears prick forward, his neck is stretched to double its usual length, and he does not resume his accustomed placidity until the dog is entirely out of sight. Once a couple of bears came by. Their appearance upset him dreadfully; but he stood his ground until they began to dance, when he sprang from his chair and hid himself under the hangings of a great arm-chair, from which he did not venture for some time.

There are few places where a cat cannot gain admittance either by cunning or activity. My cat is constantly put in the cellar while meals are going on; but he is sure to be back again in a very few minutes. There is a stair going down to the cellars which projects a little. Under this he hides; and when the

servant has reached the top of the stairs, he walks
softly behind, and the moment the dining-room door
is opened, leaps in with a great spring, and takes up
his post as near the carver as possible.   Another cat,
who was on very friendly terms with me during my
residence in the country, was accustomed to make her
way to my room, even when she was fastened out of the
house. There was an espalier pear-tree nailed against
the gable.   Up this she would climb, and from thence
scramble in through a defective loft window.   This
gave her access to the stairs, down which she came;
and by scratching and mewing at my door, always
contrived to be admitted.   She was a very good-tempered cat, and I never knew her discomposed except
on one occasion, when I put her kitten into a large
glass jar.

This cat was ingenious enough, but not quite so
ingenious as one belonging to one of my friends, who
had learned an art beyond that of scratching for admittance, for she had taught herself to open the latch
of a door by springing up to it, and striking it with
her paw.

Some cats, if well treated, will obey the command
of their master like a dog.   I have known of several
instances of this amiable conduct.   One cat belonged
to a schoolboy, who was accustomed to take it out with
him in the fields when he went out for a walk, and had
trained it to run up any tree that he pointed out.
Another cat used always to follow her master when he
rode out, and kept up with his horse for long distances.   Once her master was riding across country,
and came to a brook, over which he leaped his horse.
Pussy stood on the bank, shivering and looking dismayed, but when she saw her master disappearing in
the distance, she sprang into the brook, and scrambled
over.   Her fidelity met with a poor reward, for she
was almost immediately seized with a fit, and died in
a day or two afterwards.

There is a cat now living in Oxford, which is accustomed to catch fish for herself, as they pass under a

wharf on which she sits. She will not touch little fish, and disdains to enter the water for any fish less than a herring.

The cat who resented the temporary imprisonment of her kitten in a bottle, was very much attached to the servants, and used to follow them about the house. One day they had to visit a village about a mile and a half distant, and set off accordingly. When they had reached the village, they saw the people laughing at them, and on turning round to search for the cause, they found the cat, accompanied by her kitten, trotting complacently behind them. So the cats were picked up and carried into the village to keep them from the dogs; when they returned, the two cats were again carried until the danger of canine jaws was passed, and being replaced on the ground, they accompanied the servants home.

The last circumstance of this nature occurred very lately. A lady, on reaching the church door, found that her cat had followed her. It was useless to send pussy back, and, of course, it would have been cruel to shut her out. She, therefore was permitted to enter the church. She then lay down under the seat, and remained quite quiet until service was over, at which time she got up and walked home again.

HYÆNA.

THERE are several species of hyænas, all of them possessing certain peculiarities which distinguish them at once from all other animals, the principal marks being the length of their fore-legs, and the enormous power of their jaws. Their fore-legs are so much longer than their hinder, that the animal moves with a kind of shambling shuffle, that gives it a sneaking appearance, too well borne out by its character. The expression of its countenance is that of untameable, ill-natured ferocity, and its voice resembles an exulting demoniacal laugh. Altogether, it is about as unprepossessing an animal as can well be imagined. Its habits are such

as to deepen the unfavourable impression which its
personal appearance never fails to create, for it mostly
derives its food from dead bodies of men and animals,
for the one, robbing the cemeteries, for the other,
scouring the streets, if it lives near mankind, or following the track of the lion and other beasts, if it
lives in the desert, and disputing the prey with them.
If the body of any departed friend is intended to rest
in peace, the survivors are forced to fence in and pro-
teet the grave by a strong fortress of thorns and
prickly shrubs, as the hyænas very soon scrape away
the earth of a newly-made grave.

The jaws of these creatures are more powerful than
those of any other animal, and to give them this
power, the top of the skull is surmounted with an
enormous bony ridge, serving for the support of the
immense muscles that move the jaws. The lions and
tigers possess tolerably powerful jaws, and have, accordingly, a large ridge on their head; but they sink
into insignificance when placed beside the skull of a
hyæna. The object of this enormous power of jaw
is evident. The hyænas are intended as scavengers,
to remove from the face of the earth those substances
which would otherwise putrefy and pollute the air.
Among these substances may be placed the dead carcasses of large animals, which, in the countries where
the hyæna lives, are frequently seen thrown down un-
heeded, and, if the hyænas and vultures did not remove them, would be suffered to remain there until
they had wasted away by putrefaction. It is, therefore, with a view to this end, that the jaws of the
hyæna have been made so powerful. When they dis·
cover a dead animal, it soon vanishes, for the hyænas
leave nothing but the horns, hoofs, and skull, even
the very bones being devoured. Between the teeth
of a hyæna the leg-bone of an ox is broken up as
easily as a schoolboy cracks a nut; and not only does
the animal break up the bones for the sake of the
marrow, but devours bones and all. Dr. Buckland,
who made several experiments on the strength of

hyænas' jaws, compared them to a crushing mill, or those enormous shears used in foundries to cut up rolls of iron and copper.*

The neck of these animals is also exceedingly strong, and when the skin is taken off, looks like a fleshy cable, and with such force are these muscles endued, that, according to Cuvier, the joints of the vertebræ sometimes become anchylosed, or rendered immoveable by the strain of the muscles. The neck, therefore, becomes quite stiff, and leads many people to imagine that the neck of the hyæna has only one joint.

The hyænas are confined to Africa and part of Asia.

It can hardly be expected that an animal, so singular in its appearance and habits, could escape without considerable vilification at the hands of the earlier naturalists. One of them details an accomplishment possessed by the hyæna, which clearly proves that Electro-biology can be practised by quadrupeds as well as by men.

"If a man meet with this beast, he must not set upon it on the right hand, but on the left, for it hath been often seen, that when in haste it did run by the

---

* These experiments were made in order to clear up a doubt respecting some broken bones found in Kirkdale Cave. Dr. Buckland asserted that they were the bones of certain animals cracked by the hyænas, whose skeletons lay near. The power of jaw required for such a feat appeared so improbable that Dr. Buckland commenced a series of experiments, with a view to ascertaining the point. He therefore presented the leg-bones of oxen to a living hyæna, who instantly broke them between his jaws, and began to swallow the smaller pieces. Dr. Buckland then took away the crushed ends of the bones, and compared them with those found in Kirkdale Cave. As he had imagined, they corresponded so closely that there was no longer any doubt on the subject.

Specimens of the recent and fossil bones broken by the hyæna's jaws were afterwards placed in the Geological Museum at Oxford, where they may now be seen. So closely do they correspond, that, save for their antiquity, the fossil bones might be passed off as those broken by the hyæna only a few years since.

hunter on the right hand, he presently fell off from
his horse senseless; and, therefore, they that secure
themselves from this beast must be careful to receive
him on the left side, that so he may with more facility
be taken, especially (saith Pliny) if the cords wherein
he is to be ensnared be fastened with seven knots.
Ælianus reporteth of them, that one of these coming
to a man asleep in a sheep-cot, by laying her left
hand or fore foot to his mouth, made or cast him into
a deep sleep, and afterward digged about him such a
hole like a grave, as she covered all his body over
with earth, except his throat and head, whereupon
she sat until she suffocated and stifled him; yet
Philes attributeth this to her right foot. The like is
attributed to a sea-calf and the fish hyæna, and therefore the old magicians, by reason of this examinating
property, did not a little glory in these beasts, as if
they had been taught by them to exercise diabolical
and præstigious incantation whereby they deprived
men of sense, motion, and reason."

Although the hyæna has been called an untameable
animal, there have been several tame hyænas known,
which have domesticated themselves like dogs, and appeared quite as much attached to their masters.

The hyæna is a shockingly cowardly animal, and
never attacks those creatures from whom it fears any
resistance, but directs its efforts toward carrying off
their young. Curiously enough it is much more successful in the chase of healthy animals than those
which are weakened by disease, for this reason: the
hyæna has no notion of opposing any animal that
boldly resists him; but if he can put to flight any
creature, he pursues it with all the courage imaginable. When, therefore, he is about to attack any
living animal, he first sets up a tremendous howl, and
gnashes his teeth. At this sound, those animals who are
in health trust to their speed, and scamper off, while
those who are deprived of their speed by illness turn
round and boldly face him, whereat he prudently
leaves them, and chases the fugitives. So, fearing

man, but having a liking for human flesh, the hyæna comes silently by night, and steals away sleeping children from the very arms of their mothers, and that so quietly, that the unfortunate parent is often unconscious of her loss until roused by the cries of her infant as the nocturnal depredator is carrying it off.

I have before mentioned the enormous strength of the hyæna's neck, and will now give an instance where the creature exhibited his powers of neck in a very singular manner. The flooring of a hyæna's den wanted repairing. The carpenter had been working at it for some time, and completed his work by nailing down a stout oak plank about seven feet in length. The plank was fastened down by a dozen or so nails of the description called "tenpenny," being rather longer than a man's middle finger, and proportionately stout. When the plank was nailed down, the carpenter discovered that, at one end, there was a small piece of wood standing out a little higher than the rest. He sought for his chisel, to take off the offending projection, but not finding it, he left the den in order to bring one from his shop. During his absence, some visitors came, and the hyæna was admitted into his den for a time. With the usual curiosity of hyænas, he instantly began an examination of the alterations that had been made, and on discovering the projecting piece of wood, he fastened his teeth into it, and wrenched up the plank in spite of the nails.

The curiosity with which these animals are so strongly imbued often acts as a preservative against danger. They are very suspicious, and if they meet with any object to which they are unaccustomed, they fear it as a trap, and retreat immediately. The farmers, whose flocks and herds had suffered from the attacks of these ravenous animals, were accustomed to place spring-guns in their way, so managed, that when the animal presses against certain leathern thongs stretched across the path, the trigger of the gun is pulled, and the charge lodged in the hyæna. This plan answered tolerably at first; but the crafty animals soon learned to distrust leathern thongs, and the farmers were obliged to substitute the stems of creepers. These the hyænas did not fear, and consequently lost no small number of their forces.

The cowardice of the hyæna has been before mentioned, but, like other cowards, when fairly driven to bay, they fight in the most desperate manner; and then are foes not to be despised, as if they do contrive to get a 'hold on their adversary with their powerful jaws, they seldom loose their hold until they have lost their head, and, at all events, do considerable injury. A hyæna that had ventured to attack Bruce, the African traveller, in his tent, afforded a fair example of the hyænine character, craftiness, cowardice, impudence, and ferocity. He writes as follows:—

" These creatures were a general scourge to Abyssinia in every situation, both of the city and the field, and they seem to surpass even the sheep in number. From evening till the dawn of day, the town of Gondar was full of them. Here they sought the different pieces of slaughtered carcasses which this cruel and unclean people were accustomed to expose in the streets without burial. Many a time in the night, when the king had kept me late in the palace, on going across the square from the king's house, I have been apprehensive lest they should bite me on the leg. They grunted in great numbers around me, although I was surrounded with several armed men, who seldom passed a night without wounding or slaughtering some of them. One night in Maitsha, being very intent on an observation, I heard something pass behind me towards the bed, but on looking round, could perceive nothing. Having finished what I was then about, I went out of my tent, resolving directly to return; this I immediately did, and in so doing, perceived two large blue eyes glaring at me in the dark. I called my servant to bring a light, and we found a hyæna standing near the head of the bed, with two or three large bunches of candles in his mouth. To have fired at him, would have been at the risk of breaking my quadrant or other furniture, and he seemed, by keeping the candles steadily in his mouth, to wish at that time for no other prey. As his mouth was full, and he had no claws to tear with, I was not afraid of him, and, with a pike, struck him as near the heart as I could. It was not until I had done this that he showed any signs of fierceness; but, upon feeling his wound, he dropped the candles, and endeavoured to run up the shaft of the spear to arrive at me, so that I was obliged to draw a pistol from my girdle and shoot him, and nearly at the same time my servant cleft his skull with a battle-axe. In a word, the hyænas were the plague of our lives, the terror of our night walks, and the destruction of our mules and asses, which, above everything else, are their favourite food."

I conclude the accounts of this animal with an extract from Topsell of

The Medicines of the Hyæna.

" There is for the biting of a ravenous dog an excellent remedy, which is this : first to anoint the place so bitten with the fat or grease of a sea-calf, or else to give it in drink; and then, to make the operation more effectual, mingle the marrow of an *hyæna*, and oyl that cometh from the Mastick tree, and wax together, and being so applyed and anointed upon the sore, it will presently cure the same.

" The gall of an *hyæna* being mingled with hony, and anointed upon the eyes, doth sharpen and clear the eyesight, and expel and drive away all blemishes and small skins which cover the sight of the eye; as also the pain in the eyes called the pin and the web. But *Apollonius Pitaneus* doth say, that the gall of a dog, being used in the aforesaid manner, is better to cure the sight of the eyes than the gall of an *hyæna*.

But *Pliny*, whom I think best to follow, and worthyest to be believed, doth best allow of the *hyæna's* gall for the aforesaid purposes, and also for the expelling of certain white spots in the eye, which do hinder the sight thereof.

"The gall of a *bear* and of an *hyæna* being dryed and beaten to powder, and so mixed with the best hony which is possible to be had, and then stirred up and downe a long time together, doth help them on to their eyesight which are stark blinde, if that it be daily anointed and spread upon the eyes for a reasonable space together. The gall of an *hyæna* being baked in a cruse of Athenian hony, and mingled with the crooked herb *crocis*, and so anointed upon the brows or forehead of them which are purblinde, doth speedily help them; it doth also cure them which are troubled with the water or rheume which falleth in the eyes. *Democritus* doth also affirm, that if the brow of either man or woman be anointed with the gall of an *hyæna* only, it will drive away all darkenings and blemishes in the eyes, and expel the water or rheume thereof, and also asswage the pain and grief which may come or happen in them, whatsoever it be."

We will now leave the Hyænas, and turn to the

WEASELS.

THE weasel tribe contains many species, all being more or less destructive, and many being the pests of the places where they live. They, as well as the cat tribe, are digitigrade, that is, they walk on their toes, while the bear and other similar animals walk on the entire foot, and are, therefore, called plantigrade. They all have long, slender bodies, and very short legs, enabling them to penetrate into very small openings, a property necessary to them, as they mostly live on those animals whose residence is in holes. We will here depart a little from the regular order, and take first the common English weasel. This is a very tiny animal, but particularly destructive to mice, rats, and such small deer, although it sometimes ventures on nobler prey, such as a hare, rabbit or partridge. This propensity for mouse-hunting makes it an invaluable assistant to the farmer, who not unfrequently repays its benefits by nailing it on his barn. When prey is very abundant, it does not trouble itself to eat the carcase of the creature it has slain, but contents itself with eating the brain only. This habit, of course, renders the weasels still more useful in farms, as they therefore kill more mice than they would, if they always devoured the entire body. Their plan is usually to kill a mouse, eat the brain, and then hide the body in some place, to which they return if they are hungry. But, when prey is plentiful, they kill so many, that they forget the hiding places, and, therefore, are forced to kill more prey. They destroy the animals which they attack, by a single bite on the back of the head, driving their long, sharp little teeth into the brain, producing instantaneous death. At the moment of inflicting the bite, they generally throw their bodies upon the animal, in order to prevent its escape, should the first bite not prove mortal.

This little quadruped hunts by scent as well as any hound, and if thrown out, quarters its ground in the most business-like manner imaginable, until it hits off the scent, when it starts off again with untiring perseverance. Woe to the unfortunate rat, mouse, or rabbit, whose track is ever taken up by a weasel. Its superior swiftness is of no avail, for its diminutive pursuer continues its hunt slowly but surely, and is certain to catch it at last. Sometimes the persecuted quarry takes to the water in hope of escape, but the weasel plunges in also without hesitation, and unless the animal hunted be a water-rat, is sure to catch it.

Although an useful ally to the farmer, it is especially detested by the gamekeeper, who accuses it, with some reason, of destroying the hares, rabbits, and partridges. This accusation is but too well founded, as the weasel is an inveterate devourer of eggs, even climbing trees to get at them, and is, therefore, very likely to devour those which, like the eggs of the partridge and pheasant, are laid on the ground. Still the weasel is not so guilty in this matter as the stoat, upon whose shoulders the accusation should principally rest. Neither is it likely to resist the temptation of a newly-hatched pheasant or partridge, if it can find no mice at hand, and it certainly does occasionally abstract a chicken or two from the farm-yard; but, on the whole, the good that it does by the destruction of rats and mice more than counterbalances its delinquencies in the matter of ducklings and chickens, and ought to entitle it to our protection.

The weasel is popularly reputed to kill snakes, but this notion is contradicted by Mr. Bell, who placed a snake and a weasel in the same cage, and found that after several hours' confinement the weasel did no further harm to the snake than biting it three or four times on the nose, probably because it disliked its company. The snake was, therefore, removed, and a mouse substituted. As if to show that its forbearance did not proceed from indolence, the weasel's indifference immediately vanished; he sprang from his box, and laid the mouse dead with a bite on the head.

The weasel generally makes its nest of dry leaves and grass, and places it in some sheltered spot, such as the root of an old tree, a dry ditch, or an old well. Sometimes the weasels remain so long in one place, that there is quite a colony of them. At all times the weasel is greatly attached to its young, and will boldly fly at any object which it fancies may injure its property, and at such times, although so small, it can do no little injury by its sharp teeth and indomitable perseverance. But when a colony takes a fancy to attack any object, be it man or beast, the attack then becomes exceedingly dangerous. Some time since, a person riding by an old wall, saw a gentleman flinging his arms about, leaping up and down, and altogether acting in a manner that caused the rider to fancy him mad. He accordingly got off his horse to examine the matter, and see if he could render any assistance. When he arrived, he saw that these extraordinary gestures were caused by the attack of a number of weasels, which were running up the gentleman's body, and striving instinctively to reach his throat. His arms were so occupied with tearing them off and throwing them away, that he had no time for killing any of his foes. A few strokes from the whip of the new performer in the scene killed as many weasels, and the rest, seeing that a reinforcement had arrived, took to flight. The help came only just in time, for the gentleman said that he was all but exhansted with fatigue, and could not have held out much longer. The cause of the attack was this: He had been passing near the old wall, when he saw a weasel running about. He began to tease the animal, which, finding itself unable to escape, uttered a scream, at which about fifteen other weasels issued from the crannies of the wall, and commenced an attack, which, had it not been for the timely succour, would, in all probability, have cost him his life. There are several similar anecdotes on record.

The impudence and self-possession of this little animal is almost unequalled. During my first initiation into the mysteries of shooting, in my school days, I was engaged in the noble sport of tom-tit shooting, when a small animal ran along the bottom of a hedge. I instantly fired, but missed the little creature, which turned out to be a weasel, who ran out of the hedge into the middle of a footpath not ten paces distant, sat up on its hind legs, put its fore paws on its nose, and looked at me with a kind of air that seemed to say, " Fire away if you like, *I* don't care." There it sat until I went towards it, when it very leisurely took its departure.

That incident occurred a long time ago, but another

incident showing quite as much coolness took place recently. Service was being celebrated in one of the Oxford churches, when a weasel made its appearance at the priest's door in the chancel; it walked leisurely into the middle of the floor, and surveyed the scene with great composure. It then left the church, but in a few minutes returned, bringing with it a frog, which it deliberately ate in the church. This is more extraordinary, as the service is choral, and the weasel might have been expected to feel some terror at such unwonted sounds. He had probably just caught the frog in the churchyard, where they abound.

The weasel is not only a determined hunter, as has been before related, but also a most crafty one. In some cases, it bands with other weasels, and the whole pack hunt some devoted animal, which rarely escapes from a band of such bloodthirsty and persevering foes.

As long as it is engaged in the pursuit of land animals, such as rats and mice, the affair is simple enough, as the animal has only to persevere, and its acuteness of scent is tolerably certain to lead it to its prey. But when it comes to pursuing birds, who could escape by a single effort, the matter is very different. How the weasel succeeds in such cases is told by Mr. St John, who actually saw a bird caught by a weasel. In a stubble field was a certain thistle. Several buntings were flying about the field, and occasionally settling on this thistle. Presently, a weasel made its appearance, and hid itself at the foot of the thistle. He thought at first that the weasel had gone into a hole, but as he suspected, from the little animal's manner that it was after some mischief, he waited to see the result. Presently, a bunting came and perched on the thistle, but no sooner had it settled, than the weasel sprang up the thistle, and ran off with the bird in its mouth.

In general, the weasel is not to be tamed, although there are records of tame weasels, and in one case the animal appeared thoroughly domesticated, and would leap into the hand of its mistress from a considerable distance.

The female weasel is rather smaller than the male, and of a deeper red. Many persons have taken it for a distinct animal, and in some parts of England it is called a "cane."

STOAT.

THIS animal is not unfrequently confused with the weasel, why, it is difficult to say, as the size of the two animals is so very different, the stoat being considerably larger than the weasel. The stoat is also known under the name of the Ermine, whose beautiful fur is in such universal request. The fur of the stoat changes, during the winter, from its usual brown tint to a beautiful white, with the exception of the tail, which retains its blackness, and adds so much to the beauty of its fur. A very low degree of cold is required to produce this change in the fur; and the rapidity of the change appears to be in proportion to the severity of the cold. In one of the Arctic expeditions, a rather cruel experiment was tried upon a Lemming. It was placed upon deck, and exposed to the full severity of the temperature, at that time about 30 degrees below zero. By the next morning, a patch on each of its shoulders had become white, together with its cheeks. Day after day, the white patches continued to enlarge, until, at the end of a week, the whole of the fur had become white, with the exception of a dark band extending across the shoulders and down part of the back.

This experiment, showing that in some cases the hair itself changed colour, of course led to other experiments of the same nature. Their results showed that sometimes the hair itself did change colour, but that in most cases the fur was actually changed, the white hairs supplanting the brown at the beginning of winter, and again giving place to the brown hairs, when the warm weather commenced. Probably, if a very violent change in the weather or temperature takes place, the colour of the existing hairs may change, but if the temperature alters gradually, the hairs may be renewed.

The cold which is necessary to produce this change is so severe, that in the southern parts of England the stoat is very seldom found in its wintry garments, while even in the more northern parts the fur never assumes that snowy whiteness which renders it so valuable, but retains a general dinginess that very much mars its effect. The greater number of those furs used in this country are imported from Russia, Norway, Siberia, and Lapland. In those countries the ermine is eagerly sought after; and as it cannot be shot, lest the fur should be damaged, there have been many ways invented for taking it without injuring its coat. Some hunters take the ermine in traps, which, by letting a heavy log fall on the animal, kill it without injury to its fur, and some prefer shooting it with blunted arrows that stun without piercing.

So much for the ermine, under which name it must be considered a foreign animal, while under the title of the stoat, it is British. It is very common in almost every part of England, and does a great part of the mischief usually attributed to the weasel— such as killing the cocks and hens, and breaking the eggs. Yet, in spite of these injuries, it kills so many rats and mice that it is doubtful policy to destroy it. The farmers always do destroy it whenever they have a chance; but farmers in general are not particularly reasonable. They see it carrying off a chicken, and in consequence endeavour to exterminate the whole race of stoats; they see some birds pecking off the buds of their fruit-trees, and accordingly provide themselves with a gun, put in a tobacco-pipe bowl full of powder, and ditto of shot, fire into the tree, knocking off the offending bird, together with innumerable buds which are struck off by the spare shot. Whereupon the farmer picks up the bird, ties it to a -stick, sets the stick in the ground, and goes home rejoicing that he has saved his buds. Now, O man of science! is your time for urging conviction on the farmer. Pick up all the buds knocked off by the shot; take a penknife and open the bird's craw, take out all the buds found therein, and lay them by the side of those knocked off the tree; and show the farmer that his shots are less discriminating than the bird; for every bud picked by the bird will have a little maggot in it, that would not only have destroyed that bud, but would have been the parent of hundreds more; while the buds shot off the tree are mostly quite sound. Then take him into the garden, and make him examine the tree cut up by the shot, how many twigs are hanging down, struck through by missiles intended for the bird, and which would have produced buds next year had they lived; let him see the furrows made by the shot in the bark, which will spend the energy of the tree in repairing damages, instead of producing fruit; and when you have summed up the whole affair, of course you have converted him. Hear his answer: "I dwont care for your fine words and your science, I dwont. If I sees any bridlings a yeatin' of my buds, I'll shee-yute un, I will." And he keeps his word. *Moral.* Don't try to feed swine with pearls.

Now, although it is strongly inculcated upon the farmer that he ought to preserve the stoat, it would be an utterly hopeless task to endeavour to impress the same notion on the minds of boys. There is hardly any sport so exciting to boys as a stoat-hunt, whose fascinations even surpass those of rat-hunting. I well recollect many an afternoon spent in stoat-hunting, during which time, I must be allowed to say, that the time was spent most innocently, for we never killed the stoat. The last hunt of that nature in which I was personally engaged was a very exciting one, accompanied by no small fatigue, for the animal led us an astonishing chase from one hedge to the other, under a constant fire of "cockshys," *i. e.* short stout clubs, about eighteen inches long and as

thick as a man's wrist. Nothing seemed to disturb
the equanimity of the stoat, who evidently thoroughly
despised the whole affair, until a missile of a more
formidable nature came crashing through the bushes,
close by his head. This was a very heavy geological
hammer, having the pick-axe part flattened out for the
convenience of digging in frosty ground. After this
intimation, he redoubled his speed, and after some
time, at last got cleverly away.

As an example of the absorbing interest of a stoat-
hunt, I will only mention that a dignitary of the Uni
versity and a surgeon of the city were seen rushing
down the Broad Walk in full chase of a stoat, having
left behind them some ladies, with whom they had
previously been walking, to wait until they returned.
The stoat escaped.

The stoat hunts its prey by scent, just as has been
already related of the weasel. A very interesting
hunt was seen in the forest of Bere. A hare came
out into the road, and from its appearance seemed to
be listening in fear for something behind her. The
spectator naturally imagined that the hare was pursued by a dog; but as he did not hear any sounds,
he determined to wait and see the cause of her fear.
Soon, a small red and white stoat came in the track
of the hare, hunting her footsteps with the utmost
accuracy. As it seemed rather remarkable that an
animal so small, and so inferior in speed to the hare,
should have a chance of catching it, he concealed
himself in a bush close by, and determined to see
the conclusion of the adventure. For two hours he
was a witness to this extraordinary hunt, during
which time he saw both pursuer and pursued more
than forty times. They were often out of sight for
five or ten minutes; but the hare constantly returned
to the same place, and as constantly her inveterate
pursuer came on her track. At last the hare began
to be fatigued, and endeavoured to escape by dashing
into the thickest coverts she could find; but all in
vain, as the lithe agile body of the stoat pierced the

thickets with less exertion than the hare required. It is well known that, before a hare is taken by dogs, she utters a scream. The concealed spectator now heard her beginning to cry as if she were quite in despair; but she was still evidently endeavouring to escape. At last, as the cries continued to come from one point, he concluded that the stoat had at last caught the hare; and on° going to the spot, he found the hare lying dead, and the stoat fastened on her neck with such eagerness that it did not hear his approach. With his stick, he killed the stoat, and brought both animals away with him.

It seems very remarkable that the hare should not have started off in a straight line, and trusted entirely to her speed; as, had she done so, no stoat could have tracked her for many miles, and a run of four or five miles would have been but a trifling exertion to her. The poor creature appeared to have lost all its faculties, and to have been weakened by absolute terror. I think my readers will agree with me, that the gentleman who had amused himself for two hours with this hunt, ought to have suffered the stoat to enjoy the meal which he had worked so hard to procure.

ICHNEUMON.

Of the Ichneumon there is little to be said. The fabulous histories of this creature are tolerably well known, that is, most people know that the ichneumon was accused of destroying crocodiles by getting down their throats; but very few have seen the original words in which the accusation was made. I therefore insert it here.

" Now there is in Egypt a certain bird called cro-chillus, whose nature is to wait upon the crocodile, and, with her beak and claws, gently and with a kinde of delight, to pull out the remnants of the meat sticking in the crocodile's teeth; wherewithal, the crocodile being pleased, openeth his mouth wide to be thus cleansed by this bird, and so, falling fast asleep gaping, watched all the while by the vigilant eye of the ichneumon; perceiving him to be deeply plunged into a senseless security, goeth presently and walloweth in sand and dirt, and with a singular confidence entereth into the gate of death, that is, the crocodile's mouth, and suddenly pierceth like an arrow through the monster's wide throat, down into his belly.

"The crocodile, feeling this unlooked-for evil, awaketh out of sleep, and in a rage, or madness, void of counsel, runneth to and fro, far and wide, plunging himself into the bottom of the river, where finding no ease, returneth to land again, and there breatheth out his intolerable poyson, beating himself with all his power, striving to be delivered from this insufferable evil. But the ichneumon careth not for all this; sitting close upon the liver of the crocodile, and feeding full sweetly upon his entrails, until, at last, being satisfied, eateth out her own passage through the belly of her hoast. The self-same thing is related by Plutarch; but I wonder for what cause the beast should rowl herself in sand and dirt to enter into the crocodile's belly. For, first of all, if, after her rolling in dirt, she dry herself in the sun, yet will not that hard crust be any sufficient armour of proof to defend her small body from the violence of the crocodile's teeth; and, besides, it increaseth the quantity of her body, making her more unfit to slide down through the crocodile's narrow throat; and, therefore, the authors cannot be but deceived in ascribing this quality to her when she is to enter into the crocodile, but rather, I believe, she useth this defence against the asp, as Aristotle saith; and, therefore, the author, seeing her so covered with mud, might easily be mistaken in her purpose. For it is true, indeed, that when she seeth the asp upon the land, she calleth her fellows, who arm themselves as before said before the combat, by which means they are safely preserved from the bitings of their enemies; or, if it be true that they wallow themselves in the mud, they do not dry themselves in the sun, but while their bodies are moist, slide down more easily into the crocodile's belly."

OTTER.

THE Otter is another of our persecuted animals, whose approaching extirpation is a reproach to England. Careful as the English are to lose no opportunity for increasing the weight of their pockets, and ingenious as they are in turning everything to some useful purpose, it does seem most extraordinary that an animal which might be rendered so useful has been hunted and persecuted until it is almost entirely driven out of England. If the trace of one poor stray otter should be discovered, all the neighbouring population are up with guns and hay-forks, and dogs, enough to withstand a French invasion; and after searching the place near which it was seen, they succeed in killing it between them, and bring it home with as much triumphant demonstration as if they had killed a tiger at least.

Why should it be killed? Why should we not use the natural instinct of the otter in our service? "*Sic vos non vobis*," said Virgil, many years before these days: the bees make honey—for us; the birds ·lay eggs—for us; the sheep give their wool—for us; the oxen plough the fields—for us. Why then should we not make the otter take fish—for us? We tame the lightning and make it our messenger; can we not tame the otter: we can walk unharmed beneath the water; why should we not train the otter a very little, and make him bring out the fish that he takes below the surface? Surely we are not less intelligent than the Hindoos, and they employ otters regularly in their service. Moreover, the otter has more than once been tamed in England, and taught to catch fish for its owner. The Hindoos have a regular system of training for these animals. Of course they commence their instructions at a very tender age; and the first lesson

learned is, that the otter must give up eating fish.
This is managed by mixing bread and milk with the
fish, and gradually diminishing the quantity of the
fish, until, at last, the otter feeds on bread and milk
alone.   Having reached this step, the otter is then
taught to fetch and carry like a dog; and when it has
attained a certain proficiency in that art, a leathern
model of a fish is thrown into the water, and the
otter taught to bring it out.   By degrees dead fish
are substituted for the model, the otter being always
chastised if it attempts to eat, or even tear, them.
At last, it is permitted to go in after living fish, which
by this time, it has learned to carry in its mouth without hurting them.

When in its native state, it kills and carries away
many more fish than it can eat, merely biting off the
flakes of flesh at the back of the neck.   This trait of
epicurism is very valuable to the poor people who
live near the rivers where otters dwell, as they often
find fine fish on the banks very little injured.   In one
place in Scotland, the otters invariably left a fine salmon every morning lying on a particular spot, much
to the gratification of the poor people living near, who
used to find the otters excellent purveyors, and did
not object to eating the fish, because the otters had
bitten out a piece for themselves.

The whole body of this animal is admirably adapted
for the aquatic life which it leads.   Its body is long and
much flattened; the tail is also flattened, and from
its length and shape is admirably adapted as a rud-
der.   The feet are broad and webbed; and the legs
are so loosely articulated, that they can be turned in
any direction while the animal is swimming.   Aided
by these advantages, the movements of the otter while
in the water are most graceful and easy, and appear to
be executed without the smallest effort.   The animal
slips into the water quite as noiselessly as if it were oil,
and emerges in the same easy manner, hardly leaving a ripple on the surface.   Not the least extraordinary part of its aquatic performance is the man-

ner in which it turns a summersault below the surface
of the water without appearing to check its speed.
I have more than once seen an otter in pursuit of a
fish pass under its prey, and then by a quick stroke of
its tail, turn completely over, seizing the fish in the
course of the manœuvre. In order to retain the slip-
pery prey when it has caught them, the teeth of the
otter are very long, sharp, and pointed; even the back
teeth being furnished with sharp points.

The chase of the otter is very exciting, and affords
no small degree of sport. Dogs are generally trained
for this especial purpose, as well they may be, for it
requires a dog of no ordinary skill and courage; first,
to turn an otter out of its camp of refuge, and afterwards to attack it. Even putting aside the difficulty
of getting hold of an animal which is able to pursue
and capture fish in their native element, the otter is
not easily secured when it is seized. Its jaws are so
powerful, and its teeth so strong, that it has been
seen to break the leg of a stout terrier at a single
bite. Its own fur, too, is very thick, and in some
measure defends it from the bites of its enemies.
The only way to get at the otter is to watch it when
it dives, and the moment it raises its head above the
surface to make it dive again, and so on, until the
poor animal is thoroughly exhausted, and crawls out
upon the bank. Even then may the otter bear the
motto, "*Nemo me impunè lacesserit*," for it greets every
foe with the most severe bites, fighting with violent
pertinacity to the very last. It is also very tenacious
of life, and even when it has been struck through with
an otter-spear, after being baited for several hours, it
has been known to inflict the most severe bites on the
staff of the spear.

Many persons have succeeded in taming otters,
who would attach themselves to their masters like a
dog, fawning upon them, and accompanying them in
their walks. One of these tame otters so far followed the nature of a dog as to display a great predilection for gooseberries, and would play with the

feet of its owner like a young puppy. Another person possessed a tame otter, which used to fish for its own living, always returning to its master. One day the animal was taken to the river by his master's son. It entered the water as usual; but when called it refused to obey the command, and remained in the water. Some time afterwards, the owner of the animal, who had been away from home, returned, and upon hearing of the loss of his pet, went to the river-bank and gave the accustomed call. To his great joy, the otter responded to the call, and came crawling out of the water to his feet.

An otter, belonging to a man of the name of Campbell, was so extremely tame, that, whenever it was alarmed by strange dogs, it would endeavour to spring into its master's arms for protection. This animal was accustomed to catch eight or ten salmon in a day. When it caught them, it always tried to break the fish between the last fin and the tail; and if the fish were taken away, it instantly dived in search of more. It was equally expert in the sea, where it caught numbers of cod-fish. It would hunt in this manner until it was tired, when it refused to enter the water again. Its master would then feed it; and after it had taken as much food as it wished, it was accustomed to go to sleep on the spot, and was generally carried home sleeping.

An account of an otter almost equally tame has been forwarded to me. The account is useful, as it exhibits the sagacity of the animal in starting and catching the fish.

It used to be taken to a deep rivulet, into which it instantly jumped, and, keeping close by the banks, dived against the course of the stream, and disturbed the fish with blows of its tail. When the fish, thus disturbed, kept close to the bank, the otter did not notice them; but if one of them darted before its pursuer, it was instantly seized, brought to the surface of the water, probably to lessen the power of its struggles. The otter caught several fish in this manner, and brought them to shore, but resigned its prey with great reluctance, uttering a kind of whining remonstrance. The animal probably swam against the stream, because fish always lie with their heads in that direction, and would not be so likely to be alarmed by their pursuer, as if it had approached them from the front.

Mr. Richardson gives a very interesting description of an otter that had been for some time in his possession. " When I first obtained the animal, there was no water sufficiently near to where I lived, in which I could give her an occasional bath, and being apprehensive that, if entirely deprived of an element in which nature had designed her to pass so considerable a portion of her existence, she would languish and die, I allowed her a tub as a substitute for her native river, and in this she plunged and swam with much apparent delight. It was in this manner that I became acquainted with the curious fact, that the otter, when passing along, beneath the surface of the water, does not usually accomplish its object by swimming, but by walking along the bottom, which it can do as securely and with as much rapidity as it can run on dry ground. After having had my otter about a year I changed my residence to another quarter of the town, where a stream flowed past the rear of the house. The creature being by this time so tame as to be allowed perfect liberty, I took it down one evening to the river, and permitted it to disport itself for the first time since its capture in a deep and open stream. The animal was delighted with the new and refreshing enjoyment, and I found that a daily swim in the river greatly conduced to its health and happiness. I would sometimes walk for nearly a mile along the bank, and the happy and frolicsome creature would accompany me by water, and that, too, so rapidly, that I could not, even by very smart walking, keep pace with it. On some occasions it caught small fish, such as minnows, eels, and occasionally a trout of no inconsiderable size. When

K

it was only a minnow or small eel which it caught, it
would devour it in the water, putting its head, for that
purpose, above the water; when, however, it had made
a trout its prey, it would come to shore and devour it
more at leisure. I strove very assiduously to train
this otter to fish for me, as I had heard they have been
many times taught to do, but I never could succeed in
this attempt, nor could I ever prevail upon the animal
to give me up at any time the fish which she had
taken; the moment I approached her to do so, as if suspecting my intention, she would at once take to the
water, and crossing to the other side of the stream,
devour her prey in security. The difficulty in training I impute to the animal's want of an individual
affection for me, for it was not affection, but her
own pleasure, which induced her to follow me down
the stream, and she would with equal willingness
follow any other person who happened to release
her from her box. This absence of affection was,
probably, nothing more than peculiarity of disposition in this individual, there being numerous instances of a contrary nature upon record.

" Although this otter failed to exhibit those affectionate traits of character which have displayed themselves -in other individuals of her tribe towards the
human species, she was by no means of a cold or un-
social disposition towards some of my smaller domestic
animals. With an Angora cat, she, soon after I got
her, formed a very close friendship, and when in the
house was unhappy when not in the company of her
friend. I had one day an opportunity of witnessing a
singular display of attachment evinced by this otter
towards the cat. A little terrier dog attacked the
latter as she lay by the fire, and driving her thence,
pursued her under the table, spitting and setting up
her back in defiance; at this instant, the otter entered
the apartment, and no sooner did she perceive what
was going on, than she flew with much fury and bitter-
ness upon the dog, seized him by the face with her

teeth, and would, doubtless, have inflicted a severe chastisement upon him had not I hastened to the rescue, and, separating the combatants, expelled the terrier from the room.

" When permitted to wander in the garden, this otter would search for grubs, worms, and snails, which she would eat with much apparent relish, detaching the latter from their shell with surprising quickness and dexterity. She would likewise mount upon the chairs at the window, and catch and eat flies, a practice that I have not hitherto seen noticed by any naturalist."

DOG.

From what source we derived our domestic Dog is not known, nor is the question a subject for these pages. The original stock is by some supposed to be found in the Dingo, or Australian dog, but as no proofs have been brought forward on either side of the question, we may be content to let the matter rest until proofs are found.

All the wild dogs possess pointed ears, and carry with them a general wolf-like appearance, which gradually vanishes as they are subjected to the influence of civilisation. None would be likely to trace much resemblance between the gaunt, hungry, weird-like dingo, and the sleek King Charles, with its long silken hair, its rounded muzzle, and hanging ears. Those dogs which belong to only partially civilised nations always retain their wolfish look, although in other respects they may be altered. The Esquimaux dog, for example, although it is furnished with long hair and a bushy tail, has still the lupine character of countenance strongly impressed. Certainly, they are not treated particularly well by their masters, as the following extract from the accounts of a recent voyager to the Arctic regions will prove. The ac-

K 2

count is given in the " Tents of the Tuski," by Mr.
Hooper.

" Some curious but cruel modes of punishing the
dogs were witnessed, which one could scarcely suppose would ever be invented as a punishment. The
dogs turn very sulky and obstinate sometimes; I
have frequently seen them stop short in a most determined manner, either offended with their fellows,
the road, or the driver, and scarcely any amount of
punishment in the regular way will then induce
them to budge. If the whip is applied, they throw
themselves down on the snow, howl vigorously at
first, their cries gradually subsiding into a short
moan at each blow. Occasionally a good whipping
has the desired effect, and the dog resumes its
labour; but the struggle for supremacy between the
master and beast is often protracted and severe.
I have seen men who knew the temper of the dog
they were about to punish deliberately dispose themselves to the task, place one foot upon the sledge, and
throwing back their arms to clear their dress, rain
down blow after blow upon the wretched creature,
sometimes for ten minutes or a quarter of an hour
continuously; it is seldom this treatment fails of
success, and the beast, if subdued, becomes tractable
enough for a long time; but, on one occasion,
a man of a particularly cold-blooded and savage
nature, being displeased with the conduct of one
of his dogs, quietly drew his knife, stabbed the
dog in two places, unharnessed it, wiped the blade
of his knife on his coat, and proceeded on his visit
to the ship without the least concern. When ordinary modes of chastisement have failed, the proceedings then instituted are very curious indeed.
The driver gets off his sledge, seizes the dog which
has misconducted itself, and makes a nice little
hole in the snow, in which he arranges the unfortunate wretch's nose with the greatest care and at-

tention to its suitable position. Having thus made due preparation, he pounds away at the snout of his victim with the butt end of his whip, which is generally a piece of heavy flat ivory, in the most remorseless manner. I used, particularly on first viewing this novel punishment, to be under great fear that the noses of the poor beasts must inevitably be broken or crushed, but no such consequence ensued, nor had our remonstrances any effect; punishment had been determined on, and it was certainly administered without wavering. If the snow was too soft for the purpose, the man's foot was often put as a support for the victims. This punishment must be dreadful. The dogs know perfectly well what is coming the instant their master touches them, and tremble in every limb. They do not attempt to howl loudly, and when released, only make an occasional short yell as they run; the most stubborn tempers are subdued in this way. No more trouble will be given in the day's drive, one may be quite assured. It is a most summary way of inducing submission."

The same lupine expression of countenance is also seen in the dogs belonging to the American tribes. These creatures are put to much the same uses as they are in the Esquimaux country, and are treated with very little less consideration than the wolves that prowl round the skirts of the village. The poor animals hover round the tents, and pick up whatever scraps they can snatch away, as the idea of regularly feeding any living thing but himself never enters an Indian's head. He does not even feed his wife, and can hardly be. expected to feed his dog. Moreover, he not unfrequently makes his dog feed him. Dog is considered a delicacy, and is always a prominent dish in their solemn feasts, or when the Indians wish to show themselves particularly hospitable. On such occasions, the Indian slaughters his faithful companion without the slightest remorse. There are several ways in which these dog-feasts are conducted. First,.

there is the dog-dance, in which the liver of the dog
is suspended to a pole, just as it is taken out of the
animal.   The Indians then dress themselves in all
their paraphernalia of feathers, scalps, and such like
ornaments, and commence a slow dance round the
pole, each as he passes it biting off a piece of the
liver suspended on the pole, until it is entirely consumed.   Then there is another most singular feast,
in which dog-meat takes a prominent part.   There is
a very peculiar god of the Indians, who is always hot
when the weather is cold, and cold when the weather is
hot. He then has to be worshipped in his own peculiar
manner.   The worshippers dress themselves in long
pointed caps, not unlike those worn by the unfortunate
wretches under the power of the Inquisition.   They
then kindle a large fire, and hang over it a cauldron
containing dog-meat. While the water is boiling, they
perform a mystic dance, and when it is bubbling up
most furiously, each, as he passes, dips his hand in the
boiling water, and exclaims, " How cold it is."   The
next time that the circuit is completed, the same process is repeated, but this time each throws the boiling
water over his naked shoulders, again exclaiming,
" How cold it is."   After some time consumed in
these ceremonies, the meat is supposed to be thoroughly boiled.   Each then takes a piece of the scalding meat out of the pot and swallows it, again exclaiming. " How cold it is."

The European hunters, who have penetrated into
the country occupied by the savage tribes, and have
become familiarised with those tribes that still retain
their customs, after conquering their first repugnance
at eating dog's flesh, have found it very excellent.

The heads of dogs that infest the streets of Oriental
cities also possess the wolfish look, and no small
amount of wolfish ferocity.   It is very unsafe for any
one to injure one of these dogs, as it will call its
comrades to its assistance by howling; and in that
case the only method of escape is to retreat slowly

down one óf the narrow courts in order to escape
being surrounded, always keeping the face to the foe,
and then to wait until some one comes to drive them
away.   Not long ago, a traveller, who was well accustomed to the East, was rather in a hurry, and took a
short cut through some byways.   As usually happens,
the short cut proved a very long one, for a number of
these dogs, resenting the intrusion of a stranger on
their particular territories, immediately assaulted him.
He was forced to stand at bay with his back against
a wall, exerting all his energies to the discomfiture of
the leader of the pack, a ferocious-looking cur, scarred
in all parts of his body by the numerous battles in
which he had been engaged.   In this position he patiently waited until help arrived, and took this as a
warning never to go by a short cut in an Oriental
city.   These dogs always divide the city into depart-
ments, no dog venturirfg to leave his own department,
as if he were ever seen past the boundary, he would
inevitably be killed and eaten by those into whose
grounds he had trespassed.

Dogs are generally used for drawing carriages or
sledges, and although they do not appear to be formed
for that description of labour, they can draw very
heavy weights with some swiftness.   Before an Act of
Parliament forbade the practice, it was quite a common event to see a couple of dogs drawing a small
cart, heavily loaded, and not unfrequently drawing
the additional weight of a heavy man seated on the
cart.   The Esquimaux dogs possess equal strength
and more speed, as from some experiments that were
tried, it was found that three of these dogs could
draw a sledge weighing a hundred pounds, and containing a man, at the rate of ten miles an hour. When
the dogs are very tired, a ruse is practised, not unlike that said to have been invented by an ingenious
chimney-sweep, who was engaged in a donkey race.
Knowing that blows will often only cause donkeys to

go backwards instead of forwards, he tied a bunch of
greens to a stick, and, mounting on the animal's back,
held the greens about a foot before its nose. The
donkey immediately pushed forward to gain the prize,
and the sweep (who would have made an excellent
schoolmaster) won his race. In a similar manner,
when the poor dogs are tired with dragging heavy
sledges behind them, they send a woman in front,
who dangles a fur mitten in her hand. The dogs
think that the mitten is meat, and press forward accordingly. It would be of no use to send a man in
front, as the dogs are so ill treated by the male part
of the population that they would never believe that
any man would feed them, or, indeed, treat them
kindly in any way. So the labour of catching, training, and getting the dogs to move, falls upon the
women. Indeed, the kind treatment of women and
dogs appears to be the natural accompaniment of civilisation. In spite of all the ill treatment, the Esquimaux dog is very faithful, and shows great attachment
to its master.

The courage of many of the races of dogs is well
known. The bull-dog, for example, as long as life is
left in him, will attack his enemy, and grasp so firmly,
that his hold is not always loosened by death. One
brutal fellow, the owner of a bull-dog, laid a wager
that his dog should attack a bull, and that after he
had lost a foot, he would again attack the animal.
The experiment was tried, and the courageous animal
deprived of a foot True to his instinct, he flew at
the bull, hopping along on three feet. Another foot
was cut off, and again he attacked his foe. In short,
the poor animal lost all his feet in succession, and in
that mutilated state dragged himself forward towards
the bull.

Some dogs are trained expressly for lion-hunting.
They do not injure the lion much, but are extremely
useful for hunting him out from the places where he lies

concealed. There is a story well known, of a combat between certain mastiffs and a lion. I here give the story in the original words :—

" Of this kinde were the dogs given to Alexander by the King of Albania, when he was going into India, and presented by an Indian, whom Alexander admired, and being desirous to try what vertue was contained in so great a body, caused a bore and a hart to be turned out to him; and when he would not so much as stir at them, he turned bears unto him, which likewise he disdained, and rose not from his kennel; wherewithal the King being moved, commanded the heavy and dull beast (for so he termed him) to be hanged up. His keeper, the Indian, informed the King that the dog respected not such beasts, but if he would turn out to him a lyon, he should see what he would do.

" Immediately, a lyon was put unto him, at the first sight whereof he rose with speed (as if never before he saw his match or adversary worthy his strength), and bristling at him, made force upon him, and the lyon likewise at the dog; but at the last, the dog took the chaps or snowt of the lyon into his mouth, where he held him by main strength, untill he strangled him, do the lyon what he could to the contrary. The King, desirous to save the lyon's life, willed the dog should be pulled off; but the labour of men, and all their strength, was too little to loosen those ireful and deep-biting teeth which he had fastened. Then the Indian informed the King, that except some violence were done unto the dog to put him to extream pain, he would sooner dye than let go his hold; whereupon it was commanded to cut off a piece of the dog's tail; but the dog would not remove his teeth for that hurt; then one of his legs were likeways severed from his body, whereat the dog seemed not apalled. After that another leg, and so consequently all four, whereby the trunck of his body fell to the ground, still holding the lyon's snowt within his mouth, and, like the spirit of some malicious man, chusing rather to dye than to spare his enemy. At the last, it was commanded to cut his head from the body, all which the angry beast endured, and so left his bodiless head hanging fast to the lyon's jaws, whereat the King was wonderfully moved, and sorrowfully repented his rashness in destroying a beast of so noble a spirit, which could not be daunted with the presence of the king of beasts, chusing rather to leave his life then depart from the true strength and magnanimity of minde. Which thing the Indian perceiving in the King, to mitigate the King's sorrow, presented unto him four other dogs, of the same quality and nature, by the gift whereof he put away his passion, and received reward with such a recompence as well beseemed the dignity of such a King, and also the quality of such a present."

The dogs that are trained to hunt the bear seem to take the most enthusiastic delight in the sport, although a bear is hardly ever killed without first sacrificing several of his foes, or at least inflicting severe wounds. Few bear-dogs can boast of many battles, and yet show an unscathed skin. The chief danger to a bear-dog is in its first few battles, as it is apt to rush too fiercely on the bear, and thereby exposes itself to the terrific " hug" which will often squeeze all the breath out of the unfortunate dog subjected to it. When, however, the dog has assisted in the demolition of a few bears, and has probably gained several scars in the encounter, he learns wisdom, and displays the greatest ingenuity in keeping out of the reach of the bear's claws and teeth. He soon learns to hang on the animal's flanks, and harass it in the rear until it is struck by a bullet, or otherwise wounded, when he instantly springs on the back of the wounded bear, and keeps him employed until another wound can be inflicted.

Although dogs can be thus trained to the most useful purposes, it is much to be regretted that these faith-

ful animals are sometimes used for purposes the very
opposites of good and right. I do not mean to allude
here to those animals who are born and bred merely to
afford their masters some gratification, by seeing them
tear each other to pieces, or cruelly mangle a harmless
and useful animal; neither do I advert to those dogs
which are trained to assist their masters in poaching
of game; but to those used for poaching on the re-
venues, in other words, the smuggling dogs. For it
is true that there exists, or did exist, a regular force
of smuggling dogs, by whose help large amounts of
contraband goods evaded the Custom-house.

The manner in which they were employed was as
follows:—The smugglers, finding that the vigilance
of the revenue-officers was too strict for them, decided
on employing other means. They accordingly trained
a force of dogs, who were taught to travel by night
from station to station, creeping under every ine-
quality of ground, and always keeping in the shade
if the moon was out. They were then taught how
to evade the search of men disguised as revenue-officers, and who punished the dogs if they could catch
them. Having taught the dogs to avoid detection,
they then fastened the contraband goods on their
backs, and trusted to the sagacity of the dog to take
them to the appointed station, while they themselves
remained quiet and possibly unsuspected at their
homes. So cleverly did the dogs manage, that the
stratagem had been employed for some time before it
was discovered, and even when it had become known,
the revenue-officers had no means of detecting the
canine smugglers except by a counter-force of dogs,
trained to find out those of the smugglers.

Dogs have not unfrequently been used to convey
dispatches of importance concealed in their collars,
and have sometimes been employed as postmen on a
small scale, comprising in their own persons the
various offices of letter-box, post-office, and letter-
carrier.

It is well known that dogs are fond of certain fruits. I have good cause to remember that dogs eat gooseberries. While I was at school, the master had missed much of his fruit, especially his gooseberries, and naturally enough supposed that the thief was to be found among the boys. I was unfortunately pitched upon as the victim, principally because I had been seen eating gooseberries during the week, a weakness which was certainly shared by the whole of my school-fellows, any of whom might have been selected upon precisely the same grounds. In consequence, I have still the most vivid recollection of a very severe castigation for the supposed crime of gooseberry-stealing. Only a few days afterwards the master's pet dog was discovered to be the delinquent.

The same dog was also accustomed to rob the hen-roosts. He used to take out the eggs without breaking them with his teeth, and carry them into a back yard. When there, he would break them by a blow from his paw, and lick up every particle of the egg as it flowed out. The little King Charles' dog Prince, whose friendship with a cat has been before narrated, was greatly given to robbing the nests of the black-birds and thrushes that built in the grounds. His first plan was to insert his paw into the nest, and scrape out the eggs, but he soon found that he broke the eggs, and lost the contents, which rapidly soaked into the substance of the nest. He therefore changed his tactics, and by biting a hole in the bottom of the nest, he got at the eggs without breaking them.

Prince was a wonderful dog in his way, and especially exulted in playing at a game called by boys "tigg" or "tick," the game in question being a kind of puss in the corner without any corners, the player enacting the part of "tigg" being a kind of perpetual puss, who can only be released from his position by touching one of the others, who immediately takes his place, and becomes a kind-of Pariah, whose touch is contamination. The dog had learned this game

capitally, and, to incite him to play, it was only necessary to touch him on the back and run away, when
the intelligent little animal would set up a prepos-
terous barking, and rush after his human playfellow,
never resting until he had seized part of his or her dress
in his mouth. He would then avoid being touched with
as much skill as he had before displayed, and, indeed,
never would have been caught at all were it not that
he was very venturesome, and used to jump about his
playfellow in defiance.

Although Prince was one of those unfortunate animals used as lap-dogs, old Topsell would hardly have
ventured to launch at him the caustic anathemas
hurled so freely on these useless creatures.

" These dogs are little, prety, proper, and fine and
saught for to satisfie the delicateness of dainty dames
and wanton women's wils; instruments of folly for them
to play and dally withal, to trifle away the treasure of
time, to withdraw their mindes from more commend-
able exercises, and to content their corrupted concu-
piscences with vain disport (a silly shift to shun
irksome idleness). These puppies, the smaller they
be, the more pleasure they provoke, as more meet
playfellowes for minsing mistresses to bear in their
bosomes, to keep company withal in their chambers,
to succour with sleep in bed, and nourish with meat
at bord, to lay in their laps, and lick their lips as they
ride in their waggons; and good reason it should be
so, for coarseness with fineness hath no fellowship, but
featness with neatness hath neighbourhood enough.
That plausible proverb verified upon a tyrant, namely,
that he loved his sow better than his son, may well be
applyed to these kind of people, who delight more in
dogs that are deprived of all possibility of reason,
than they do in children that be capable of wisdom
and judgment. But this abuse, peradventure, reign-
eth where there hath been long lack of issue, or else
where barrenness is the best blossom of beauty."

Not the least remarkable point in this delightfully

quaint passage, is the manner in which alliteration
has lent her artful aid to the invectives lavished so
freely upon the " dainty dames " who indulged in the
luxury of lap-dogs.

A dog belonging to one of my friends was in the
habit of accompanying his master in his expeditions;
and on such occasions, where the walk had been particularly fatiguing, was in the habit of acting as pillow to his master when he rested. On one of these
occasions, master and servant had both fallen asleep,
and were enjoying their siesta when my friend was
awakened by a succession of short whines from his
dog. He at first thought that the poor creature must
have been injured in some way; but on looking
round, he saw a rat moving about at some thirty yards
distant, offering a sad temptation to the dog, who, not
daring to move lest he should awake his master, was
watching the rat in a state of intense tantalisation.
His master, however, taking compassion upon him,
raised his head, when his canine pillow instantly
dashed off in pursuit of the rat, who fled for refuge
into a ditch full of nettles. In went the dog, and
soon returned triumphantly, having put an end to the
rat. As, however, the dog was entirely disguised
with black mud and stinging nettles, he was not particularly fitted to act the part of pillow again.

Some years ago, while I was in the latter end of
the caterpillar state of Undergraduate at Oxford, and
during the earlier portion of the chrysalis or transi-
tion state of Bachelor, a dog, called Rory, in honour
of Rory O'More, was in my possession. He was
not my own property, but chose to attach himself to
me, utterly discarding his proper master. He was a
large rough black terrier, with hair falling over his
eyes, and completely blinding him when wet; his
ears were partly cocked, but drooping at their extremities; and his general black tints were relieved by
a white patch on his breast, like a shirt-front appearing through a black waistcoat, and another white spot

appeared on the end of his tail. Add to this, a general comicality of aspect, a pair of brilliant eyes, and a tendency to execute a jig whenever looked at, and you will have a good idea of Rory. He was an Irishman by birth, and seemed to have inherited the Irish love of fun to no small extent, fully appreciating a practical joke. For example: he would sometimes pick out some man going quietly along the street, and would charge at him open-mouthed, looking as if he meant to eat him up, at the very least; but when he got within a few yards, he would shoot off suddenly to one side, utter a loud sharp bark, and walk off in a very sedate manner, as if he had been doing nothing at all.

During term time, I never had to feed him, for he was accustomed to wait at the kitchen door every morning, watch for the kitchen boys taking up their breakfasts, and by erecting himself on his hind legs and walking gravely by their side, mostly succeeded in extracting a piece of waste meat. His gift of biped walking was very great: I have often known him walk the whole length of a street upon two legs, merely for his own amusement. Once he did so under rather peculiar circumstances. Rory had few antipathies; but of those few, beggars and fat lap-dogs, perhaps, had the predominance. Indeed, a fat lap-dog was not to be resisted; and if one came in Rory's way, it was sure to be upset and rolled about until it howled for mercy. One day, just as he had started for a walk, he caught a glimpse of a very fat lap-dog, waddling and wheezing along the street and accompanied by a lady, who seemed to be the model on which her dog had formed itself. This was much too tempting an opportunity to be resisted, so Rory dashed off at once, and, with the impetus of the shock, sent the little lap-dog rolling over and over in the mud. He then turned it over with his nose, patted it, danced round, and barked at it in ecstasy, until its mistress, summoning up courage, snatched up her pet and put it on her muff.

This was no defence against Rory; for he immediately got up on his hind legs, and walked by her side, making little jumps and snatches at the poor little dog, which was scarcely less terrified than its mistress, who, at last, hoping to drive Rory away, struck at him with the end of her boa. This was great fun for the dog, who, imagining that the old lady wanted to play with him, seized her boa in his mouth, dragged it off her neck, and dashed off down the street with the boa dangling from his mouth; and occasionally getting his feet on it and tumbling head over heels, at which misfortune he gave the boa a shake, and set off with redoubled energy. He was so occupied in his fun that he did not hear me call; but when he was sufficiently recovered from his excitement, and heard the well-known whistle, the sense of his impropriety seemed to strike him, and he returned in the most penitent manner imaginable, decreasing his pace as he approached me, and casting an occasional glance at my stick, while the boa being held at one extremity, was slowly trailing in the mud behind him. He was not quite a year old at that time, so that his conduct was partly exensable on account of the exuberance of his youthful spirits. Nevertheless, I was forced to administer some punishment, or nothing in the shape of a lap-dog or a boa would have been safe. The whole affair did not occupy more than a minute, so that I was unable to rescue either lap-dog or boa until both had suffered.

The greatest treat that Rory could have, was to run along the banks of the river while I was in a boat. Once or twice in the interminable long vacation, a fellow-student and myself were accustomed to pull to Nuneham, a place about seven miles from Oxford by water, taking with us guns and provisions for the day. On these occasions, Rory used to run along the banks, exterminating rats by the way, and making a practice of swimming across the river every time he heard a shot. This he evidently considered to be his duty; but he never fetched out a wounded bird, merely contenting himself with barking at it, and then wagging his tail. On one of these excursions, Rory got himself into what may literally be called an unpleasant scrape. We had landed from the boat, tied it up, arranged our picnic under a shady bush, having fastened the dog to a stake, to prevent him from making too close an acquaintance with sundry moor hens in the distance, whom we did not wish to be disturbed. We had just arranged ourselves, when Rory began to whine most piteously. Naturally imagining his distress to proceed from the fact that a cold fowl was in the act of disappearing without his assistance, we did not trouble ourselves about him. The whine, however, soon changed to short yelps of such evident distress, that we got up and went to see what was the matter. On reaching the place where he was tied up, the mystery was explained. The poor animal had scraped up an ant's nest, which had attracted his notice, probably from the busy state of the hillock; and as he had investigated proceedings after the manner of terriers, by poking his nose into the nest and grubbing among the ants, the enraged insects had completely covered his face; and as the nose is about the most sensitive part of a dog, he was driven almost frantic with their repeated stings. It was really no small work to brush off the multitudes of ants which had congregated on his nose, or had got entangled in the thick masses of hair hanging about his countenance.

A dog belonging to Mr. Smee met with an accident something of the same nature; but more severe in its effects, inasmuch as the enemies, although belonging to the same order of insects, were very much more powerful than those which disturbed the peace of my dog.

" Last summer, I was walking with my children in

a lane near Tottenham, and we were accompanied by a small spaniel dog. A wasp's nest had been dug out on one side of the road; and the parties who disturbed it had not destroyed the creatures, but left the comb exposed. A young gentleman who accompanied us threw a stone at the wasps, and the dog, who delighted to run after a stone, dashed headlong after it into the enemy's camp. The wasps rose in a cloud, and the screams of the dog soon indicated that he had been stung. I called and whistled, and, at last, induced the dog to run; but still numbers of the irritated creatures kept about him. After he had run about fifty yards, he dropped down apparently lifeless; and after we had beaten off the wasps, and killed those adhering to the skin, I could neither feel nor hear the heart's action. The New River was near at hand, and it occurred to me that a sudden plunge into the water might rouse him. I dipped him suddenly twice, and we were well pleased to witness signs of returning animation. We carried him home, rubbed him dry, and placed him before the fire; but it was several days before he recovered."

When Rory first attached himself to me, he was quite a puppy, only numbering about six months; and, of course, occasionally gave way to many youthful frolics which had to be corrected; but as his days increased in number, so did his wisdom, and at the expiration of two years, he was the most obedient pupil I ever had, always giving the most ready and willing obedience, even if he were told to do anything contrary to his own wishes. He had learned all the usual feats of dogs, and had superadded many others; some being entirely of his own invention. He was on very good terms with the cat—that is, after they had settled their quarrels consequent on his first entrance into the house, and would lie very comfortably on the hearth-rug, while pussy played with his ears. When pussy was not wanted, we used to tell Rory to put her down stairs; whereupon, he pushed her before him by means of his fore-paws, until he reached the cellar stairs; and when there, he pushed her down stair by stair, until he saw her safely deposited at the bottom, when he would return, and again lie down before the fire.

The cat had very good reason to deplore Rory's first entrance. She had a very comfortable bed in the cellar, composed of a large armful of hay in a box. This Rory found out, and coolly usurped the cat's place, to her great discomfiture. Finding, however, that Rory only wanted to find a comfortable bed for himself, and had no wish to turn her out, she overcame her fear, and crept back again; for the box was so large that there was plenty of room for both. After that time, they both used to sleep there.

Rory took possession of this place in a very curious manner. When he first came, there was an edict against any living animal inhabiting the cellar except the cat; and, accordingly, every evening Rory was turned out of the cellar, and put out of doors, nominally to go to his master. But it was rather a curious circumstance that, although he was turned out of doors, and even locked out, with perfect regularity, he was as regularly found in the cellar next morning before the doors were opened. How he managed to escape the vigilance of the servants, and get into the cellar, was beyond our comprehension; for the servants, whenever interrogated, always asserted that he had been carefully locked out overnight. However, there he always was found; and we gave up the practice of turning him out as useless. For several months, the mystery remained unexplained, until one Sunday, as the family were returning from church, they saw the dog in the very act of entering—perhaps I should say, that they saw part of him entering. Our house is a corner house, and as the cellarage extends under the entire house and half-way across

one of the streets, it is of course lighted by windows
in both streets.   In the smaller of the two streets is
a wooden trap-door, through which coals are shot.
One of the boards had become damaged; and the
cunning animal had actually been in the habit of
pulling up the defective board, and letting himself
drop into the cellar.   On Sunday, the dog had been
out to breakfast with a friend, and on his return
found the doors shut.   He, therefore, went round
the corner, and put in practice his old manœuvre.
Just as he was disappearing through the aperture,
the family came by from church, just in time to see
a black tail with a white tip whisking about, and a
pair of black legs struggling violently in the air, and
then descend through the trap-door.   The defective
board was immediately repaired; but Rory was al
lowed free lodgings on account of his sagacity.

How he escaped without injury in performing this
feat I never could tell.   In the first place, the board
was a very narrow one, fixed at one end and loose
at the other, and must have pinched him sorely.   In
the second place, after he had forced himself through,
he had a clear drop of about eight feet on a heap of
coals, whose corners might be supposed to injure him
as he fell.   But he never appeared hurt in the least
by his tumble.

After this discovery, Rory found where all the family
went on Sundays, and instead of getting into the
cellar, was accustomed to wait about the streets until
service was over, when he would walk to the church
door, and accompany the family home.

I have just mentioned that Rory had gone out to
breakfast with a friend.   That seems rather an extraordinary thing to say of a dog, and requires explana-
tion.   The fact is, that he had attained such a command over himself, that he would sit on a chair, with
his fore-paws resting on the table, and remain perfectly
unmoved, even when the leg of a fowl, or some such
dainty, was placed on his plate.   He had often exe-

cuted this feat at my breakfast-table, and had been frequently invested with a cap and gown, in which venerable raiment he used to sit with corresponding gravity, occasionally looking in a very imploring manner at us if a particularly fine bone were placed on his plate; but he never touched it until he had obtained leave. When his habits became known, he was often regularly asked to breakfast by the collegians, and being decorated with cap and gown in a manner similar to that adopted much about the same time by Tiglath Pileser, the Christchurch bear, was accustomed to parade the room on his hind legs with the most laudable gravity, and afterwards to take his place at the breakfast table with due dignity.

He was also perfectly at home at a wine party, and took his port and filberts with gentlemanly ease. He underwent a long course of instruction in cigar smoking, but could never learn that art. Indeed, although he did not mind the dense clouds of smoke that generally accompany, or rather conceal a college wine party, he never could endure a cigar or pipe near his nose, and, whenever one was put into his mouth, sat blinking and patient until the annoyance was removed.

At last he attained to such a pitch of reason, that he was always looked upon more as a companion than an inferior, and if he required instruction, it was generally sufficient to tell him what to do, while if he had done wrong, a gentle remonstrance would throw him into the greatest depression of spirits, and he would crouch flat on the ground, gradually crawling along like a snake, until he reached my feet, on which he would lay his nose, and wait for a word of forgiveness, when he would start up overjoyed, and appear thoroughly happy.

Of course, a dog of such capabilities might not be supposed to be very safe in a place like Oxford, where the superabundance of dogs produces a correspondent amount of dealers. Several attempts were made to seduce his allegiance. These he indignantly repudiated, while all endeavours to use force he resisted; and his teeth were remarkably sharp. If a dog-stealer offered him a piece of meat, he ate it and waited for more; but if the man's hand approached his neck, for he was so well known as to need no collar, he quietly bit the man in the wrist and ran away.

After being acquainted with Rory, one was led to read the Arabian Nights with much less incredulity, for few transformed princes acted with greater propriety or wisdom than did Rory; always excepting the transformed prince, who, under the shape of an ape, gained an introduction at court by his calligraphy, beat the king at chess, complimented him in extemporaneous verses, and at last, in being re-transformed, destroyed the king's daughter, servant, and palace.

The last time I saw Rory was under rather peculiar circumstances. I had been resident in the country for several months, but was forced to leave Rory behind. One day, I returned to Oxford for a few hours, and was met by Rory, who did not give way to his usual ebullitions of joy, but walked behind me with his nose against my heel until I entered the house, when he lay down before me, put his chin on the ground, and never took his eyes off me the whole time of my stay in the house. When I left, he accompanied me in the same way, not having given utterance to a single sound, or indulged in a single bark.

At the expiration of the first term, after he had taken up his residence with us, his master sought him for the purpose of taking him back to Ireland, but sought in vain, for, at the first sight of the packed trunks, Rory had taken himself off, and was not to be found. After three or four days, when he imagined that his master had left Oxford, he came back again and announced himself, after his usual fashion, viz. by jumping on the sill of the dining-room window, and knocking at the pane with his tail. This plan he adopted for.

several years, but at last was outwitted by his master, who laid violent hands on him a day before any one left college, and sewed him up in a hamper. Poor Rory was then carried off to Ireland, under a promise of restoration when his master should again visit Oxford, at which time he was to become our property. A few months ago his master was seen in Oxford, and we immediately went to claim Rory. Alas! poor Rory had died a month or two before, and great was the grief occasioned by the news. Let this history be his monument.

Most animals have the power of communicating with their fellows, and of imparting their thoughts to them. This power is much developed in the dogs. There are many cases known where dogs have sought mutual assistance against superior foes. For example, a dog who has been assaulted and injured by a dog of superior size and strength, has been known to go and fetch some companions, and, with their aid, avenge himself on his assailant. The power of intercommunication was, perhaps, never better displayed than in the following anecdote, related by Mr. Smee, in his work on " Instinct and Reason:"—

" Three dogs belonging, two to M. G and the other to M. P., of St. Bonnet-sur-Galaune, Canton de St. Valair, department of the Drôme, went to the chase without their masters. Having pursued a rabbit almost to an extremity, which took refuge in a burrow, one of the dogs of M. G., carried forward by eagerness, shoved himself so deeply into this subterraneous asylum, that retreat became utterly impossible. After having scratched to no purpose, in the hope of extricating him, the two companions returned home in such a state of sadness and dejection as to be noticed by their masters, who knew not to what to attribute the cause. The next day came a fresh disappearance of the two dogs, which had found the means of joining each other. They were seen to return in the evening to their respective domiciles, harassed with fatigue, to refuse every sort of nourishment, their paws bloody, and their bodies covered with earth and sweat. At first, no attention was paid to what took place; but the same procedure being repeated the next and on succeeding days, and M. G. not finding his dog return, the absence of which began to make him uneasy, surprised, moreover, at the daily disappearance of his second dog, which only came back at night, and then in the most frightful state, mentioned the circumstance to M. P., who declared to him that his dog had done the same thing for a week. Finally, the day following, M. G. was awakened early in the morning by the cries of several dogs, who scratched at his door. He came down to see what was the matter, and what was his astonishment when he saw his dog, which he thought lost, feeble, languid, and like a mere skeleton, escorted by its two liberators to the residence of its master, and which, seeing it in his care, went to sleep tranquilly on a bundle of straw, scarcely able to move their stiffened limbs. M. G. made researches to discover the place where this touching scene occurred. He found, in fact, that the narrow opening into which his poor dog had forced itself was transformed into a large cavity, the working out of which was evidently due to the intelligence of the two other dogs."

This is a more pleasing example than those given above, as it places the disposition of the dogs in a very agreeable light, inasmuch as they exercise their reasoning powers, not for revenge, but for the better purpose of mutual assistance.

There are no guardians so faithful as dogs. Let any one go into the fields at haymaking time, and venture to touch a jacket or basket guarded by a dog. The animal, generally a very small one, immediately sets up a ferocious growl in order to intimidate the intruder, and if that does not succeed, flies at him, and would rather lose its life than suffer the property committed to its charge to be touched. During my school days, there lived a great dog called Nelson, a breed between a bloodhound and mastiff. He used to follow us to the cake shops, and wait at the door for any fragments that might be spared for him. He was very good-natured, and would stand any amount of bullying, a quality necessary in a dog who attaches himself to a number of schoolboys. In the summer months we were accustomed to bathe in that most beautiful Derbyshire river, the Dove. On one such occasion our clothes had been stolen as they lay on the bank, and we had to chase the thief. As we were entirely unencumbered with clothing, and the thief being encumbered with our clothes as well as his own, we soon caught him, and, dragging him to the river, tossed him in, and ducked him until he was half dead, when we let him escape, knowing that our clothes were henceforth secure from him.

But as we wished to secure our garments from any further attacks, we thought we would imitate the conduct of the haymakers. So we took Nelson with us, he being the only dog that we knew, and when we had undressed, we put him in charge. He lay down in the most exemplary manner, and, doubtless, would have made an excellent guardian, had he not been disturbed by an unexpected incident. The field was full of cows, and they, seeing a great dog in the field, felt aggrieved, and summoned a council. In a very few minutes, the whole body of cows set up their tails, and charged down upon Nelson. He lay in some perplexity, until one or two almost poked him with their horns, when he lost his calmness of demeanour, and dashed at the nearest cow. His teeth, however, were nearly gone from old age, and the cow easily shook him off. There was then a grand battle, in which our clothes seemed likely to be trodden to pieces, so we were forced to take them up and swim across the river with them, and deposit them on the opposite bank, where there were no cows. We then got Nelson away, and took him over; but we never trusted afterwards in a big dog to take care of our clothes.

This attack of the cows on Nelson reminds me of a feat performed by a terrier named Crab, belonging to one of my friends. He was running along the towing-path that edges the Isis, accompanying his master, who was in a boat. Presently, Crab came to a gate. Now, the gate itself would have proved no impediment, but unfortunately two young bulls were standing by the gate, and when he came near, they put down their heads, and strenuously resisted his further progress. Crab waited for a minute or two in some bewilderment, but suddenly made up his mind as to future proceedings. He dashed at one of the bulls, barking savagely at him. The bull, of course, charged, and Crab ran away. When the bull stopped, Crab made another attack, and the bull again charged. After repeating this manœuvre several times, Crab drew the bull to the other end of the field, when he ran round him, and set to at the other bull. He, of course, charged Crab just as his companion had done; but no sooner had Crab got him away from the gate, than he ran round him, and jumped through the bars of the gate, leaving the bull on the other side quite discomfited.

Crab was a very clever dog, and exhibited amazing sagacity in getting his own way. While his master was away from Oxford, I generally called to take him out for a walk. Sometimes he evidently thought that his walk was not long enough, and after I had brought him back, he contrived to escape from the house, and follow me. It was of no use to shut him in, so I set people to watch the manner of his escape. The house had a garden attached, and at the bottom of the garden is a river. Into this river Crab jumped, and swam against the stream until he reached a landing place communicating with the road. He then got out of the water, and followed my footsteps. He had one failing, that he was *too* faithful, for when his master went to call at any house, he would lie down at the door, and assault every one who attempted to enter, as he had some wild idea in his head that no one could possibly enter the house without felonious intentions. One day, he missed his master, and set off in search after him. Not being able to find him, he went to one of the houses at which he had called with his master, and, by mounting guard at the door, effectually blockaded the house, not letting any one approach. The master of the house came in while he was lying there, and knowing the dog well, stepped over him, whereupon Crab coolly bit him, an act of fidelity which was not altogether appreciated, and gained him a severe stroke or two with that species of stick denominated a " Penang Lawyer."

On the whole, Crab was a good dog, and tolerably sagacious in many things; but he was also, as the preceding anecdote shows, rather obtuse in others. In fact, he was a dog of deep prejudices, and by no means equal to Rory. Probably he would have turned out a better character had he been regularly trained, as Rory was. Among his prejudices was a deeply-rooted one for cats, even extending to those that lived in the same house, with whom he was never on friendly terms, and, indeed, always chased them whenever he saw them, for he never learned self-denial to any extent. One day, while his master was in the garden with Crab, the cat made her appearance, endeavouring to steal behind some of the shrubs out of Crab's sight. In this intention she was frustrated, for the dog caught a glimpse of her, and set off in pursuit. Away went the cat to her usual place of escape, between the bars of an iron grating, through which she generally shot with such rapidity as to leave her pursuer fretting outside the grating to no purpose. On this occasion, however, she did not succeed in slipping between the bars with her usual agility, and was in consequence intercepted by Crab, who came back with a most self-satisfied air, and deposited at his master's feet a considerable portion of the unfortunate cat. To his great astonishment, his exploit was rewarded by a severe kick in the ribs, and a volley of stones, instead of the approbation which he fully thought he had earned. His master then went to see after the poor cat, whom he found lying before the fire in her accustomed place, apparently little hurt by her injuries, which, however, turned out to be of so serious a nature that the most merciful course appeared to be her immediate destruction. Indeed, she could not have lived another day.

When Crab and Rory first met in my rooms, they conducted themselves in the most absurd way, each evidently considering the other as a rival who had no business there. Crab was very cross, and growled considerably, keeping aloof as much as possible; but Rory took upon himself to do the honours, put on an air of gaiety, and tumbling over on his back, invited the other to play with him; but Crab was inexorable for a long time, until the idea seemed to dawn on his mind that Rory was really the owner of the rooms, and then he became reconciled, and had a game accordingly.

I was only bitten once by Crab, an unexampled circumstance among his acquaintance, and that occurred during my first knowledge of him, before the affair that gained his friendship. This was a complete Androcles and lion business. He had been on a college visit, and on leaving the college, he was observed to walk lame. No notice was taken for some time; but as his lameness appeared to increase, I called him, and although standing in some awe of him, for he was a terrible dog to bite without warning, lifted up his lame foot, and found a large pin three-fourths buried in the ball of his foot. As it was drawn out, he gave a slight whine of pain; but after it had been removed, he ran about fifty yards in order to try his foot; came back and licked my hand. Ever after that he allowed me to take any liberties

with him, not even resenting that worst of insults in
his eyes, namely, taking him by the back of the neck.
Why he always resented any attempt to touch that
part, I do not know; but whatever might have been
the reason, none but his master and myself ever
grasped the back of his neck without being bitten.

Want of self-control was the bane of his character.
He was a capital rat-killer, but he always ate the rats
or mice that he killed, and never could be taught to
leave them. Now, Rory was equally clever at catching
rats and mice, but he always threw them on the
ground when dead, and never meddled with them,
except, perhaps, an occasional indulgence in rolling
over them. His method of rabbit-catching was very
singular. He used to dash after the rabbit, and by
the force of his rush, knock the rabbit over, when he
sprang upon it, and holding it down with his fore-
paws, delivered it unhurt into the hands of his master.
Before he came into my possession, his master was
accustomed to exhibit Rory in the performance of this
feat, and for this purpose had procured a rabbit which
was used over and over again for the same purpose.
At last the rabbit did not care a bit for Rory, but
directly it heard its footsteps close behind, would lie
down of its own accord, and wait until the dog
came up.

One of the reasons urged against the reception of
Rory into the house was, that his four dirty feet would
injure the carpets. We, therefore, directly he was
admitted, took him and rubbed his feet on the mat.
After a few days, he learned to do it himself, and
whenever he entered the house, whether the streets
were muddy or dry, he invariably rubbed his feet on
the mat with great perseverance.

Rory was essentially a college dog, and, as such,
recalls recollections of college dogs as a class. I
think that college dogs deserve to be reckoned as a
separate class, like shepherds' dogs, for they, as a
body, have certain peculiarities that distinguish them

from all other dogs.   It is said that almost any breed
of dogs can be trained as shepherds' dogs, and it is
quite certain that there is no living species of dog
that has not led a collegiate life.

In the first place, almost every resident member of
the University possesses a dog, and many possess
several.   Indeed, at my own college it was estimated
that each member of the college had a dog and a
third, while in another college, two dogs and a quarter
was the average.   In the latter college, the authorities,
thinking that the rage for dogs was carried to an un-
pleasantly large extent, issued a peremptory edict that
no dogs were to be allowed in college at all.   So all
the large dogs were immediately turned out, while the
little ones led an unhappy existence in drawers and
hat-boxes, until their impatient barks caused their expulsion, accompanied with a fine levied on the purse
of their masters.   For some time the edict remained
in force, until the undergraduates, finding their existence to pass miserably without the presence of their
beloved dogs, counselled together how they should
procure a repeal of the edict.   Various methods were
promulgated, such as putting a caricature in the print-
shops, petitioning the college, inserting a letter in the
Times; but at last the following brilliant scheme was
decided on :—

It was well known that the venerable individual
who presided over the college was likely to leave the
college gates at a certain hour.   The conspirators accordingly prepared themselves, and as the authority
in question walked through the " quad," he was met
by the whole body of quòndam dog-owners, being
seven-eighths of the entire college, each leading a
very small *kitten* by a blue riband, kittens not being
included in the edict issued against dogs.   There was
no standing this, so the worthy " don" smiled good-
naturedly as he met the phalanx of kittens; and by
some wonderful coincidence of circumstances, every
dog was reinstated that very day.

Now for the character of the college dog in general. The college dog is a very peculiar animal. He is treated as a companion, and conducts himself accordingly, entering into all his master's amusements, ensconcing himself quietly behind the netting in the tennis court, watching his play with the greatest eagerness, sitting at the head of his skiff when he rows, lying at the bottom of his canoe when he paddles, or running about his punt as he poles it up the Cherwell or Isis. In the former case, the punt is usually moored to the river side, and the occupant, stretched at ease on certain "long-cushions" belonging to the punt, and ingeniously composed of carpeting and straw, smokes a pipe with a large bowl to save the trouble of filling, and reads a novel until he goes to sleep. In this case, his dog takes upon himself the care of his sleeping master, and guards him against the various practical jokes that a sleeping dogless man is sure to be subjected to. He accompanies his master to the cricket ground, and contemplates the game; or follows him to the "Weirs," where, if his master is not a skilful shot, he not unfrequently receives part of the charge intended for a pigeon. He is indifferent as to the means used in transporting him from place to place, being perfectly contented to be carried by his tail, or a leg or his ears, or by a handful of skin, or by any way that comes uppermost. A railway journey is nothing to him, and he luxuriates in a sail.

By the way, did any of my readers ever see a shore-dog take his first sail? It is an absurd sight. The dog Crab, mentioned above, had been bred up as a house-dog, and although he was a fearless swimmer, had never been in a boat, until one day, when I determined on taking him with me. So drawing the boat to the bank, I lifted him in. The moment he felt the unsteady movements of the boat, he sprawled about in the most abject way imaginable, and made himself more like a paralytic toad than any animal could be supposed to be. Finding that no amount of sprawling would render him steady, he gave the matter up, and spreading out all his four legs, he laid the side of his head on the bottom of the boat, and looked so thoroughly terrified, that, at the risk of upsetting the boat, I was fain to restore him to his usual spirits by throwing him overboard. The moment that he was in the water, he recovered from his alarm, and swam merrily to the river side. It took a long course of instruction to induce him to enter a boat without compulsion. But a regular college dog is completely at home in a boat, whether rowing, paddling, punting, or sailing, and in the last-named description of boat always ducks at the proper moment when the boom gybes, having gained some experience from having been swept overboard several times as the boat tacked.

To return to the character of a college dog.

He makes acquaintance with out-college dogs when his master is out of the way, but cuts them dead as plebeian when his master is with him. He has a general acquaintance with all the college servants, but prefers those attached to the kitchen department, and has an objection to the scout of his own staircase, as he sometimes receives a sly kick from that gentleman in return for the perquisites eaten by the dog, which otherwise would have gone into his own basket. At breakfast, he conducts himself with great propriety, and at a wine party he sits upright on a bracket by the fireplace, and catches with much dexterity pieces of biscuit thrown to him, or supports in a victimised manner a long pipe put into his mouth, which he abominates, but dare not let fall. When his master rides or drives, he runs unlimited distances after him, and returns home covered with mud, whereupon he is sedulously pumped on by the scout until clean. He has no kennel or sleeping place in particular, but passes his nights on the mat outside the door, or in the wine bin, or on the sofa, or on the hearth-rug, if sufficiently fortunate. But in general he is rather afraid of the hearthrug. For collegians always want everything in a hurry, and whenever they want hot water, they put on the kettle, cover the fire-place with the " blower," a flat piece of iron that only admits the air at the bottom, and consequently raises a tremendous fire, causes the kettle to boil furiously in about three minutes or so, and makes the boiling water spatter all over the hearthrug, directly the blower is removed. On the whole, the college dog prefers the sofa or the easy chair, which latter article is so large that it cannot be got out of the door, and was, probably, brought into the room in detachments, and there put together.

If the dog is born in college, he is, together with his brothers and sisters, put on a tea-tray, and carried about to be inspected by the whole college, in spite of the remonstrances of his mother; and being in his early childhood constantly used in the light of a ball, he becomes habituated to all kinds of ill-usage, and when pitched into one of the gas lamps adorning the quad, he curls himself up and goes to sleep.

In fine, he passes two or three years of unalloyed happiness; but when he leaves college, his prosperity changes. particularly if there are ladies in the house to which he removes. For. as he is seldom such a dog as a lady patronises, he is banished from the house, and forced to live in a kennel at the end of a chain, at which he tugs furiously, and moans piteously all day and most of the night. No more sitting on brackets for him; no more breakfast parties; no more games with canine and human playfellows; so he forgets his accomplishments, and sinks into a common house-dog

It frequently happens that the University men leave their dogs behind them during the shorter vacations, and give them in charge of their scout. There was one dog, named " Bob," who always spent his vacations at college. He had an extraordinary passion for running after any object that moved, and would walk about with a stone in his mouth, lay it at

M

the feet of any one whom he knew, and look imploringly in their face, hoping to have the stone thrown for him to chase. He was so eager in his chase of stones, that, if a pebble were put into a bucket full of water, he would plunge in without the smallest hesitation, trusting that his master would pull him out by the tail before he was suffocated. He used constantly to accompany me in my walks, and had plenty of exercise in running after stones.

Let me here remark that it is a very foolish plan to let a dog run after stones, as his teeth are soon worn away and rendered useless. If a dog must run after something, give him a solid India-rubber ball, which will not hurt his teeth, and which will give him much more exercise than a pebble. However, in those days, I never troubled myself about Bob's teeth, but gave him as many stone hunts as he wished. At last he began to be quite troublesome, for no sooner had he caught the stone, than he came rushing back with it, and was importunate to have it thrown again. One afternoon, he was so very importunate, that I took up a great round pebble, and threw it over the top of a deadset hedge, about seven feet high, and woven so closely that it was not possible to see through it. I then thought that Bob would have enough to occupy him for half an hour at least, in scratching his way through the hedge; for every one who knew him was quite certain that he would fetch the stone if it cost him half a day's work. Bob, however, managed it in quite a different manner. He retreated about forty yards from the hedge, made a great rush, and sprung at it about four feet from the ground, and striking away the branches with a side blow of his fore feet, he shot through like a cannon ball. In about five minutes, he came back in the same way, bearing the pebble in his mouth. He then commenced a dance in the road, and wanted another chase; so I pretended to throw away a milestone that stood near, on which Bob dashed at it, and commenced a savage attack, growling and snarling, and endeavouring in vain to make his mouth wide enough to take in the entire milestone. Leaving him thus occupied, I went on my walk, and on my return, found Bob still at work at the milestone, growling with undiminished vigour, and so intent upon his task, that I was obliged to remove him by force.

It does not appear that dogs have any very correct idea of measurements. A dog will carry a stick across his mouth, and endeavour to pass through a door much too narrow for the stick. One of my friends had a dog who was never happy unless he had a stick in his mouth. The groom was rubbing down a horse in the stable, when the dog came bouncing in over a kind of half door, and looked disconsolate. The groom knew what he came for, and threw a broom at him, which the dog seized in his mouth, and again leaped over the door. But the doorway was much narrower than the length of the broom, and of course struck the door crossways, sending the unfortunate dog on his back into the middle of the stable. He did not attempt to pick up the broom again, but went off to the house, and was diligently employed for several hours in laying his head on the ground, and stroking his mouth with his paws.

There was a large Newfoundland dog named Nelson, who had a similar habit of carrying sticks, and as he was a large dog, and consequently carried large sticks, he was a considerable nuisance. He carried the sticks in a very peculiar manner, always holding them by one end, and letting the whole of the stick stand out horizontally at right angles to his jaws, causing great discomposure to pedestrians, against whom the long stick would strike with a sufficiently severe blow, for the dog was always running or jumping about, and the stick, of course, described all kinds of figures in the air. Like all Newfoundland dogs, Nelson was passionately fond of water, and once leaped over a bridge into a mill-race, running a very great risk of being dashed to pieces by the wheel.

The dog-owner has been already advised not to let his dog run after stones. This caution is more particularly addressed to juvenile dog-owners, who enjoy the sport as much as their four-legged companions. There is another caution that may be given to the owners of dogs. especially terriers, namely, on no account to crop their ears. It is a practice very generally in use, as it is said to improve the beauty of the dog. Now, I cannot see that the beauty of any animal is improved by curtailing it in any of the ornaments given to it by nature. We certainly cannot improve its beauty by adding or altering any part, as is well and humorously noticed by Southey in his poem on a pig :—

> "Again thou sayest
> The pig is ugly. Jacob, look at him !
> Those eyes have taught the lover flattery ;
> Behold his tail, my friend, with curls like that
> The wanton pig marries her stately spouse :
> So, crisp in beauty, Amoretta's hair
> Rings round her lover's soul the chains of love.
> *And what is beauty but the aptitude*
> *Of parts harmonious ?* Give thy fancy scope,
> And thou wilt find that no imagined change
> Can beautify this beast. Place at his end
> The starry glories of the peacock's pride ;
> Give him the swan's white breast ; for his horn hoofs
> Shape such a foot and ankle as the waves
> Crowded in eager rivalry to kiss,
> When Venus from the enamoured sea arose ; . . .
> Jacob, *thou canst but make a monster of him ;*
> All alteration man could think would mar
> His pig perfection."

If, then, we cannot improve nature by supplying any imagined deficiency, much less can we do so by taking away any imagined redundancy. If we think cropped ears are so beautiful, why do we not crop our own? We do pierce them as it is, and hang superfluous jewels in them, and it would be only one step more to trim them into a more fashionable shape, or to cut them off altogether. Indeed, if the reigning power were destitute of ears, in all probability those organs would become unfashionable immediately, and we should all wear gold ears, just as in the last century people shaved their natural hair from their heads and wore wigs. We made some advance in taste as well as humanity when we discontinued the practice of docking our horses' tails, and snipping our horses' ears, until they were sufficiently maimed to be fashionable. Indeed, the human mind, when in its primitive state, always appears to connect beauty with mutilation. For example, the South Sea Islanders scarify their bodies, and leave indelible marks of the wounds, imagining that the beauty of the human face is considerably increased by a series of black concentric circles on the cheeks, and a triangle on the nose. One nation thinks a man no man unless he has knocked out his front teeth; another nation file their teeth to points, making their mouths resemble a double saw. One man chops off his little finger, or, if he wants to be very aristocratic, sacrifices two fingers; another would think himself plebeian were not his head squeezed up into an apex; another flattens his nose by artificial means, and another places his *beau idéal* of female beauty in a foot crippled from infancy, and much more resembling a hoof than the foot of a human being. So in our own country, in late ages, the steps of civilisation have been invariably marked by corresponding steps in humanity, both to man and beast. When men walked about with whalebone coats, shaven heads, and high-heeled shoes, they clipped their horses' ears, cut off his tail, and shaved their poodles. Now men wear their own hair, reasonable boots, and unstiffened coats, give their horses the proper allowance of ears and tail, and permit their dogs to wear as much hair as nature has provided for them. Now they only.

clip their dogs' ears ; and perhaps when they again permit their own beards to grow where nature intended them to be, they may allow their dogs to possess their natural allowance of ear.

With this foolish practice of ear-cropping we may also connect the equally foolish and perhaps more cruel habit of " worming," as it is called. This is the removal of a portion of the tendon from the body of the tongue, which is laid open with the knife, and the tendon extracted. The force used in taking out the sinew is so great that when taken from the tongue it curls about like a dying worm. The object of removing it is to prevent madness, a disease supposed to be caused by the presence of this " worm." The belief is a very ancient one, and is mentioned in a series of Latin poems on dogs, called the " Cynegeticon," in which it is said that there lies at the root of the tongue a little worm,—" mala atque incondita pestis." The operation is always performed while the dog is young.

However, putting aside jest, the custom of clipping a dog's ears is not only unreasonable and cruel, but also injurious, often causing deafness, and thereby depriving the animal of one of its chief characteristics, viz. quickness of hearing.

In no degree is the sagacity of the dog more distinguished than in its willingness to submit to painful operations for the purpose of healing injuries. Most animals require to be bound when any operation is to be performed, not having intelligence enough to infer future ease from present pain. The dog, however, has often been known willingly to submit to considerable pain, and to bear it with a fortitude not often to be found even in human beings. I have already told how a savage bull-terrier permitted me to remove a pin from his foot. A cat in the same condition would not have permitted any one to approach, and if her wounded foot had been touched, would have resisted with all the power of her teeth and claws.

It is related that Chabert, the famous fire-king, had a remarkably fine Siberian dog, who, when harnessed in a light carriage, would draw his master twenty miles a-day. This dog he sold for nearly two hundred pounds. Between the time of the conclusion of the bargain the dog fell and broke one of his legs. His master, who was in great need of money, or he would never have parted with his docile companion, was almost in despair at the idea of losing both dog and money. He brought the dog to see a surgeon by night, and regularly introduced him by making the surgeon pat him, and offer his hand to be licked. He then enacted a little pantomime before the dog, in which he first walked lame, then, after calling the surgeon and allowing him to bandage his leg, he walked in his natural manner. He then signed to the dog that he was to remain there, and left the house. When he was gone the surgeon went to the dog, who laid himself down, submitted to have the fracture reduced and his leg bandaged without a motion, except by once or twice licking the hand of the operator, a kind of mute assurance that he felt confidence in the man who was inflicting pain on him. After the operation he lay quite still, and remained almost motionless until a month had expired, when the limb was found to have healed so completely that the dog did not even limp. He was then sent to the purchaser, who was unable to detect anything in the dog's walk, and, indeed, never discovered that there had been any accident at all.

Those of my readers who have had the misfortune to break a limb, will fully appreciate the firmness of the dog, in permitting that limb to be handled which shrinks instinctively from the slightest approach.

I must here mention two examples of the freedom of the dog from that fear of fire that possesses most animals. One is, of course, the famous fire-dog, Tyke, who owned no particular master, but lived indiscriminately with the firemen, sometimes choosing to live with one and sometimes with another. He was a regular attendant at every fire, and always was seen in the thickest crowd, and where the press was greatest. His enjoyment of a fire was extreme, and he contrived in some mysterious manner to avoid being trodden upon or injured, except by a dash of water from the engine, which he rather enjoyed than otherwise. One day a magistrate happened to hear of the dog, and expressed a wish to see him. A messenger was accordingly dispatched, and Tyke soon made his appearance, borne in the arms of a policeman. He was not easily persuaded to leave his house, and the only way to get him out was to make a fireman run up the street in a hurry. Tyke immediately set out after him, but on seeing the man slacken his pace, he knew that there was no fire, and turned back again indignantly. The messenger found that he could not be induced to go any further, so he was obliged to pick up the dog and carry him. Tyke lived for many years in the pursuit of fires, all the men attached to the fire-brigade being willing to feed and lodge him as long as he chose to remain. Tyke was a rough terrier, of rather a grim and tattered appearance, in consequence of his mode of life. He died only a short while since, and his death was recorded in the papers.

The second fire-loving dog is in existence now. He goes a little further than Tyke in his habits. Tyke when going to a fire was in the habit of mounting on the engine, but this dog makes a constant practice of riding on a locomotive engine making long journeys. He passes a life of constant vibration between two distant places, going and returning every day, and always sitting on the engine. He is a wiser animal than an unfortunate bull, who had formed a very erroneous idea of an engine. The animal had contrived to stray upon the line, and on seeing a train approaching at full speed, conceived that it was an intruder into his domain. He accordingly plunged

forward to assault it, and met the engine with his full
force. As may be imagined, he was dashed to pieces,
portions of his body being flung completely over the
fence that borders the line.

The cur-dog is properly a breed between the sheep-
dog and terrier, but the term is generally applied to a
cross breed between any two varieties. The nonde-
script dogs about the streets are properly mongrels,
but are usually called curs. They present mix-
tures of almost every variety of domestic dog, the
terrier always predominating. Perhaps the most extraordinary mixture of breed is that between the mastiff and greyhound. With the exception of the bull-
dog, it is impossible to imagine two species of dogs
that would present a greater contrast than these. The
greyhound is entirely made for speed, to which purpose all his make is subservient; his head is slender
and pointed; his ears small; his hair close, so as to
present but little resistance to the air; his limbs long,
flexible, and elastic; his chest large and deep, to hold
plenty of air; his hinder quarters are reduced to
the smallest size possible compatible with strength,
and are apparently composed of nothing but bone
and sinew. The mastiff, on the other hand, is a
generally large dog, majestic in his gait, and quiet in
his disposition. His head is large, and furnished
with large drooping ears, while his upper lip hangs
over the lower jaw; his joints are large and powerful,
and in most respects he presents a great contrast to
the greyhound. Yet we have an anecdote of a dog of
this extraordinary breed which indicates that such a
breed might be a very useful one, although rather a
strange one in appearance. Perhaps in this country
the strangeness of look would procure its greatest
recommendation, for a dog always seems to be valued
in proportion to its ugliness. A Scotch terrier is
considered handsome in proportion to the shortness
of its legs, the length of its body and hair, and the

depth to which its eyes are buried in the tufts of hair over its face. If, in addition to these beauties, it barks at everything and everybody, and bites every stranger that enters the house, it is thought a perfect dog, and its master a fortunate man.

The dog in question was born at California, and, by the account of Dana, by whom his memory is preserved, was a great acquisition to the men who were engaged in the very laborious occupation of cleansing, drying, and shipping hides. The father of the dog was a mastiff, and his mother a greyhound. The union of these parents produced a beneficial re-sult, for the dog possessed the speed and agility of his mother, combined with the strength, powerful jaws, and heavy fore-quarters of his father. An English sailor who happened to see him, declared that he was very like the Duke of Wellington, whom he had once seen at the Tower, and in consequence of this remark, he was immediately dignified with the name of " Welly," and became the prime pet of the men, and, in consequence, the tyrant over the other dogs, of whom they had plenty, of almost every breed in the world.

He was particularly fond of chasing the coatis,* and was known to have killed two of these animals in single combat. The coatis afforded fine sport to the sailors when they had finished their day's work, and were only engaged in cutting and carrying wood. If a coati dared to indulge in the smallest bark, or rather yelp, all the pack of dogs were after him in an instant, Welly always taking the lead, and keeping several lengths ahead, followed by the remainder of the pack. It was useless to run after the dogs, and they soon came back after their chase.

Speaking of greyhounds calls to mind the charac-teristics of a good greyhound, as represented in an ancient " Treatise perteynynge to Hawkynge, Hunt-

* Probably the " Coyote," a kind of wolfish dog, or doggish wolf, inhabiting California.

ynge, &c., emprynted at Westmestre by Wynkyn de
Worde, 1496." The qualifications are as follows :—

> " A greyhounde should be headed lyke a snake,
> And neckyd lyke a drake,
> Fotyd lyke a cat,
> Tayled lyke a ratte,
> Sided lyke a teme,
> And chyned lyke a bream.
> The fyrste yere he must learn to fede,
> The second yere to feld him lede,
> The thyrde yere he is felon lyke,
> The fourth yere there is none syke ;
> The fifth yere he is good ynough,
> The syxth yere he shall hold the plough ;
> But when he is come to the ninth yere,
> Have him then to the tannere ;
> For the best hound that ever bytch had,
> At the nynth yere is full bad."

So the poor dog is rewarded for his nine years of
faithful service by giving up his skin as soon as his
limbs lose their speed.

The cross breed with a bull-dog was first adopted
by Lord Orford, towards the latter end of the last
century. He saw that his greyhounds, although they
were very fleet, were yet deficient in courage and perseverance. He therefore procured a cross between a
bull-dog and greyhound, and found that after six or
seven generations, the external peculiarities of the
bull-dog were lost, while his courage and perseverance
were left, the dog never leaving his chase until he
fell from exhaustion. The example thus set, the
practice has been continued to the present day.

The speed of the greyhound is exceedingly great,
as it has been known to try its speed against that of
a race-horse, and was only beaten by a neck, after a
severely contested race. This in an animal with so
much shorter stride than the horse is very remarkable.
Another greyhound performed a feat even more difficult. The speed of a swift dromedary was being
tried : it left all the horses far behind, but a greyhound voluntarily joined it, and kept pace the whole

way, and when it had returned to the starting point,
lay down completely exhausted.

Mr. Youatt, the writer of a very instructive book on
dogs, has recorded the deeds of a pair of greyhounds
in his own possession, showing that this peculiar
kind of dog is by no means inferior in sagacity to
the other dogs. They were especially devoted to
stealing meat, a crime which was doubly injurious,
first, because they robbed him of his meat, and
secondly, because they were likely to make themselves too fat for coursing. They even contrived to
steal meat while actually boiling. There was a boiler
in a room adjoining the kennel, where the meat for
the dogs was cooked. These greyhounds were accustomed to steal into the cooking-room, raise the lid of
the boiler, seize any projecting piece of meat, and
before the heat could injure them they whirled it on
the floor, and waited until it cooled, when they devoured it leisurely. This plan having been discovered,
the lid of the boiler was furnished with an iron rod
passing under the handle and tied to the handle of
the boiler on each side. Only a few days elapsed
before the dogs had learned to gnaw the cord asunder,
and to help themselves as before. Iron chains were
then substituted for the cords, and the meat was
cooked in safety for nearly a week. But the ingenuity
of the dogs was not to be baffled. They continued to
raise themselves on their hind legs, and by applying
their strength at the same moment, pushed the boiler
fairly off the fire, and set it rolling over the floor,
when, although the iron chains prevented them from
getting at the meat, they were enabled to lap up the
broth as it streamed over the floor. At last they were
sent away, to the great relief of the man under whose
care they were placed, for he was afflicted with sundry
fears that they were not beings of this world, or that,
at least, they were possessed by evil spirits.

The faculty of dogs for remembering time is very
singular. There are so many anecdotes of the dog's

capability for distinguishing Sunday from an ordinary
week-day, that I shall scarcely mention the circumstance, only confirming it by two examples. One
was Rory, who never tried to follow us on Sunday,
and if shut out of the house he would sit upon the
door-step, or lie on the window-sill, until the time approached when the service would be concluded. He
then went to the door of the churchyard, and came
home with us. The other is a small dog belonging
to a clergyman, who, not possessing the discrimination
of Rory, *would* follow his master to church, and if
driven away always got in again. The annoyance
was so great that the dog was obliged to be placed in
confinement during church-time. This answered very
well for one Sunday, but on the next the dog was
missing, and his master went to church. Just as he
was about half through his sermon he happened to
cast his eyes downwards, and saw his dog sitting upright in the middle of the church, looking up at him
with the greatest composure.

There are few things more amusing than a dog in
a complete state of perplexity, when he is balanced
equally between two opinions, and cannot make up
his mind as to which he shall follow. Some boys
who were joint owners of a dog—that is, the dog
was the property of their father, and they of course
considered him as theirs—were wont to amuse themselves in the following curious manner:—They put
him in the middle of a yard, and then, each going to
opposite sides, called the dog at the same time. The
poor animal, not knowing which master he ought to
obey, stood turning his head first on one side and
then on the other, until a louder call than usual gave
him a pretext for running to him who had uttered it.
But no sooner had he taken a few steps than a still
more peremptory call was given from the other side,
and the dog came back again. This process was repeated until the perplexed animal sat down in the
middle of the yard, and began to yelp and whine in

a piteous manner, until he was released by being permitted to reach one of his masters without being called back by the other.

This is not intended as a systematic work, and there is, therefore, no particular arrangement observed in treating of the different animals. I shall therefore make no apologies for closing these Doggiana with a few anecdotes, showing certain traits of character as exhibited in different descriptions of dogs.

The greyhound, of which I have spoken before, when improved by an admixture of the bull-dog, is extremely persevering in its pursuit of game, an instance of which is shown in the following anecdote, extracted from a sporting publication:—"A gentleman of Worcester paying a visit to a friend a few miles distant, took with him a brace of greyhounds, for the purpose of a day's coursing. A hare was soon found, which the dogs chased for several miles, and with such speed as to be very soon out of sight of the party who pursued; but after a very considerable search, both the dogs and the hare were found dead within a few yards of each other; nor did it appear that the former had caught the hare, as no marks of violence were discovered upon her. A labouring man whom they passed said he saw the dogs turn her two or three times."

There was a famous greyhound named Snowball, on the *lucus a non lucendo* principle, his colour being a jet black, and singularly glossy. This dog (who, with his brother and sister, was never beaten) was once started after a hare. The chase was so severe, that of the three dogs who took part in it, Snowball was the only one who could endure it. One stopped, when the hare began a second time to ascend a steep hill a mile in length, and the other having fallen from exhaustion, was only saved by immediate bleeding. Snowball kept up the chase by himself, and finally killed the hare in a village. The length of the chase, not counting the various turns, but merely reckoning from point to point, was full foul miles, two miles being run up a steep hill.

The next anecdote exhibits the sense of gratitude in a dog. The animal had been left by its master under the charge of his servants, while he himself went away on a visit. The servants were on board wages, and naturally did not injure the dog by giving him too much to eat. The poor animal, finding board wages anything but agreeable, made friends with the cook belonging to a friend of his master, and received a good meal every day until his master came back. When thus restored to his usual rights, he was not forgetful of the favours which he had received, but still kept up his acquaintance, although standing in no need of assistance. Some days after his master's return, he discovered a lonely duck in the street, and naturally imagining that the duck was public property, snatched it up in his teeth, and carried it off to that kitchen where he had experienced such hospitality. He laid the bird at the cook's feet, with many waggings of his tail, and then set off under the pleasing consciousness of having discharged his debt of gratitude.

The following anecdote places the character of a dog in a much less pleasing light, and this is the more extraordinary, as the particular species of dog is usually characterised by faithfulness and gentleness. The animal in question was a mastiff, and belonged to a butcher, who had reared it from a puppy. From the trade of his master, the dog obtained plenty of nourishment. It was apparently extremely attached to its master, and always accompanied him wherever he went. One day the butcher purchased for the dog a large quantity of horse-flesh, and when the animal had eaten enough, he took up the remainder to put it away for another meal. The dog instantly seized him by the arm, and lacerated it in a frightful manner; it then, not content with this revenge, quitted the hold of his arm, and flew at his

throat, where it hung until some bystanders, who had
in vain endeavoured to make the dog loosen its hold,
tied a rope round its neck in order to strangle it. No
sooner did the dog feel the rope than it let go. The
butcher thought that the unusually large meal of
horse-flesh was the cause of the ferocity of the animal, as it had on all previous occasions conducted
itself in a perfectly quiet and gentle manner. Impressed with this notion, he prevailed on his friends
to preserve the life of his dog, as he considered himself to be equally blamable.

Every one knows by sight those Danish dogs that
follow carriages, plum-pudding dogs, as they are familiarly named, from whose external appearance the
idea of the wafer-spotted toy-horses seems to be
taken.

One of these animals was of a very playful disposition, and particularly rejoiced in chasing sheep, although he never hurt them. He was one day amusing himself in this manner, and making a flock of
sheep scatter in all directions, when a black lamb
turned round, and looked him in the face. The dog
was quite taken aback, and remained irresolute, until
the lamb began to dance about and play with him.
This generosity of disposition quite overcame the
dog, and he slunk away with his tail between his
legs, and appeared thoroughly confused. Presently,
his new-made acquaintance began to challenge him to
a game of play, by cutting all manner of capers about
him. By degrees, the dog regained his composure of
mind, and accepted the challenge. Off they went,
tumbling over each other, and playing like a couple
of kittens. They ran off at such a pace that the
boy who was in charge of the flock began to be
anxious about his lamb, and went to fetch it. The
lamb, however, preferred the company of its new
friend to that of the boy, and refused to come. The
owner of the dog then tried to assist the shepherd by
calling off his dog, but the dog paid no more atten-

tion to his master than the lamb did to the shepherd. For more than a mile and a half did these two strange playfellows continue their sport; and as they described a large circle in so doing, the owner of the dog and the shepherd were enabled to cross a stream, by means of a plank, before the dog and lamb came up. When they came to the bridge, the shepherd, after repelling several attempts, on the part of the lamb, to force the passage, succeeded in securing it with his crook, and prevented its escape by tying it up in his plaid. Finding his companion thus subducted, the dog reluctantly obeyed the commands of his master, and slowly followed him from the spot, while the lamb made every effort to follow the dog, and tried to gain its point by jumping into the stream. This adventure had a rather singular effect on the dog, for he ever afterwards abstained from chasing sheep.

I conclude these anecdotes of dogs with an account given by Mr. Hogg, the famous Ettrick shepherd, of a remarkable dog belonging to him.

"I thought I discovered a sort of sullen intelligence in his countenance; notwithstanding his dejected and forlorn appearance, I gave a drover a guinea for him. He was scarcely a year old, and knew so little of herding that he had never turned a sheep in his life; but as soon as he discovered that it was his duty to do so, and that it obliged me, I can never forget with what eagerness and anxiety he learned his evolutions. He would try every way deliberately till he found out what I wanted him to do; and when I once made him to understand a direction, he never forgot or mistook it again. Well as I knew him, he often astonished me, for when pressed hard in accomplishing the task that he was put to, he had expedients of the moment that bespoke a great share of the reasoning faculty.

"On one occasion about 700 lambs, which were under his care at feeding time, broke up at midnight

and scampered off in three divisions across the neighbouring hills, in spite of all that he and an assistant
could do to keep them together. The night was so
dark, that we could not see Sirrah; but the faithful
animal heard his master lament their absence in
words which, of all others, were sure to set him most
on the alert, and without more ado he silently set off
in quest of the recreant flock. Meanwhile, the shepherd and his companions did not fail to do all in their
power to recover their lost charge. They spent the
whole night in scouring the hills for miles around;
but of neither the lambs or Sirrah could they obtain
the slightest trace. They had nothing for it, day having
dawned, but to return to their master, and inform
him that they had lost the whole flock of lambs, and
knew not what had become of one of them. On our
way home, however, we discovered a lot of lambs at
the bottom of a deep ravine, and the indefatigable
Sirrah standing in front of them looking round for
some relief, but still true to his charge. The sun
was then up, and when we first came in view, we concluded it was one of the divisions, which Sirrah had
been unable to manage till he arrived at that commanding situation. But what was our astonishment
when we discovered that not one lamb of the whole
flock was wanting. How he had got all the divisions
collected in the dark is beyond my comprehension.
The charge was left to himself from midnight until
the rising sun, and if all the shepherds in the forest
had been there to assist him, they could not have
effected it with greater promptitude.'

WOLF.

WE now come to a group of animals which, although differing in species, are much alike in
habits. These animals are the wolves. Few parts
of the world are free from them, neither extreme
cold nor extreme heat being the smallest protection

from them. There is the red wolf (*Canis Alpinus*), inhabiting Siberia; the Abyssinian wolf (*Canis Simensis*); the Landgah (*Canis pallipes*), a wolf inhabiting Nepal and other parts of India; the Prairie wolf (*Canis latrans*), inhabiting the American prairies (pronounced "peroarer" or "perairer"), as its name implies; the Coyote or Cajote (*Canis ochropus*), a small wolf found in California; the American wolf (*Canis occidentalis*); and the Antarctic wolf (*Canis antarcticus*). So we find these animals ranging through every climate, and inhabiting countries of all gradations of temperature, from the burning heat of the tropics, to the everlasting snows of the Antarctic lands. Perhaps the Jackalls should have been added to our list of wolves, and in that case we may increase our list by the black-backed jackall (*Canis mesomelas*), and the common jackall (*Canis aureus*). All of the above-mentioned animals are to be found in the British Museum.

I shall not in these pages attempt to describe one species of wolf more than another, as the character of all wolves is so very similar. They are excellent examples of a truly cowardly nature. When a wolf is supported by plenty of comrades, it is a most daring animal, fearing not to attack foes far superior to itself; but if it is pursued when alone, it instantly becomes a slinking cowardly animal, and often yields the battle easily. Sometimes, however, when it sees no hope of escape, it turns upon its pursuers, and fights with obstinate valour until the very last. In no case is the cowardice of a wolf so conspicuous as when it is taken in a trap. Wolves are at all times very suspicious, and stand in great awe of anything that looks like a trap. There are many authenticated accounts of travellers who, when met by wolves, would have inevitably been devoured had they not terrified their enemies by letting a piece of cord trail behind their carriage. The wolves were so much afraid of this suspicious-looking piece of cord, that they dared not venture to approach it, lest they should be caught. The hunters take advantage of this trait of character, and when they kill a beast too large to carry away, they keep off the wolves by a similar stratagem. Supposing a hunter has shot a bison; he may only want the tongue or a piece of the hump at present; but next day he may want its skin, or wish to make another meal. Now, if he were to leave the carcass as he shot it, very few hours, or even minutes, would elapse, before it would be converted into a skeleton.

In order, then, to preserve his prey for himself, the hunter generally places a stick upright in the ground near the carcass, and to that stick he ties by a loose string the inflated bladder of the slaughtered animal. This so effectually terrifies the wolves that, although they run round it all night, they dare not approach it, on account of the bladder, which is blown about in the wind. Sometimes a strip of skin is fastened to the stick, but anything to which wolves have not been accustomed will answer the hunter's purpose.

The wolves constantly hang on the skirts of the American prairie hunters, and will follow in their track for innumerable miles, subsisting on the offal of the beasts that they kill. There is some reason for this, for in America, as would be the case in all countries where game is so very plentiful, the hunters get very careless, and often slaughter bisons merely for the sake of their hump or tongue, and not unfrequently merely for practice, leaving the carcass to the wolves. Mr. Catlin, the enterprising American traveller, mentions a party of wolves that followed him on his journey across the prairie. They came "loping" after him all day, and at night, when he made himself a camp under the canopy of heaven, the wolves made their camp a few hundred yards away, and waited patiently until next morning. One of his drawings represents the night-camp, with the group of wolves in the background. They did not attempt to attack him or his horse, but remained about the same distance from them during their long toilsome march, and their evening's rest in the desert.

The wolves also hang to the skirts of the herds of bisons, for if one of them becomes weak from illness, or in any way injured, the wolves immediately set at him, and after a brief scuffle of about two minutes in duration, a cloud of hair and dust subsides, and the wolves move slowly away, their abdominal regions looking as round and hard as a cricket-ball. Yet within an hour they will be ready for such another meal.

When, in spite of all precautions, the wolf is taken in a trap, there is no animal so cowardly. A trapped wolf will allow a man to do anything with him, and will not make the smallest attempt at retaliation. The following extract from Audubon's works will give a tolerable idea of the ferocity and chicken-heartedness of the wolf:—

" Two young negroes, who resided near the banks of the Ohio, in the lower part of the State of Kentucky, about twenty-three years ago, had sweethearts living on a plantation ten miles distant. After the labours of the day were over, they frequently visited the fair ladies of their choice, the nearest way to whose dwelling lay directly across a great cane brake. As to the lover every moment is precious, they usually took this route to save time. Winter had commenced, cold, dark, and forbidding, and after sunset scarcely a glimpse of light or glow of warmth, one might imagine, could be found in that dreary swamp, excepting in the eyes and bosoms of the ardent youth, or the hungry wolves that prowled about. The snow covered the earth, and rendered them more easy to be scented from a distance by the famished beasts. Prudent in a certain degree, the young lovers carried their axes on their shoulders, and walked as briskly as the narrow path would allow. Some transient glimpses of light now and then met their eyes, but so faint were

they, that they believed them to be caused by their
faces coming in contact with the slender reeds covered
with snow.   Suddenly, however, a long and frightful
howl burst upon them, and they instantly knew that
it proceeded from a troop of hungry, perhaps desperate wolves. They stopped, and putting themselves
in an attitude of defence, awaited the result.   All
around was dark, save a few feet of snow, and the
silence of night was dismal. Nothing could be done to
better their situation, and after standing a few minutes
in expectation of an attack, they judged it best to resume
their march; but no sooner had they replaced their axes
on their shoulders, and began to move, than the foremost found himself assailed by several foes.   His
legs were held fast as if pressed by a powerful screw,
and the torture inflicted by the fangs of the ravenous
animals was for a moment excruciating.   Several
wolves in the meantime sprang upon the breast of
the other negro, and dragged him to the ground.
Both struggled manfully against their foes ; but in a
short time one of them ceased to move, and the
other, reduced in strength, and perhaps despairing of
maintaining his ground, still more of aiding his unfortunate companion, sprang to the branch of a tree,
and speedily gained a place of safety near the top.
The next morning, the mangled remains of his comrade lay scattered around on the snow, which was
stained with blood.   Three dead wolves lay around,
but the rest of the pack had disappeared, and Scipio,
sliding to the ground, took up the axes, and made
the best of his way home, to relate the sad adventure.

"About two years after this occurrence, as I was travelling, I chanced to stop for the night at a farmer's
house by the side of the road. After putting up my
horse, and refreshing myself, I entered into conversation with mine host, who asked if I should like to
pay a visit to the wolf-pits, which were about a mile

distant. Glad of the opportunity, I accompanied him across the fields to the neighbourhood of a deep wood, and soon saw the engines of destruction. He had three pits within a few hundred yards of each other. They were about eight feet deep, and broader at bottom, so as to render it impossible for the most active animals to escape from them. The aperture was covered with a revolving platform of twigs attached to a central axis. On either surface of the platform was fastened a large piece of putrid venison, with other matters by no means pleasant to my olfactory nerves, although no doubt attractive to the wolves. My companion wished to visit them that evening, merely, as he was in the habit of doing so daily, for the purpose of seeing that all was right. He said that wolves were very abundant that autumn, and had killed nearly the whole of his sheep, and one of his colts, but that he was now 'paying them off in full;' and added that if I would tarry a few hours with him, next morning he would, beyond a doubt, show me some sport rarely seen in those parts. We retired to rest in due time, and were up with the dawn.

" ' I think,' says my host, ' that all's right, for I see the dogs are anxious to get away to the pits; and although they are nothing but curs, their noses are none the worse for that.' As he took up his gun, an axe, and a large knife, the dogs began to howl and bark, and whisked around us as if full of joy. When we reached the first pit, we found the bait all gone, and the platform much injured; but the animal that had been entrapped had scraped a subterranean passage for himself, and so escaped. On peeping into the next, he assured me that ' three famous fellows were safe enough' in it. I also peeped in, and saw the wolves, two black and the other brindled, all of goodly size, sure enough. They lay flat on the earth, their ears laid close over the head, their eyes indicating fear more than anger. 'But how are we to get them out?' 'How, sir,' said the farmer, 'why, by going down, to be sure, and ham-stringing them.' Being a novice in these matters, I begged to be merely a looker on. 'With all my heart,' quoth the farmer; 'stand here, and look at me through the brush.' Whereupon he glided down, taking with him his axe and knife, and leaving his rifle to my care. I was not a little surprised to see the cowardice of the wolves. He pulled out successively their hind legs, and with a side stroke of the knife cut the principal tendon above the joint, exhibiting as little fear as if he had been marking lambs."

The following account by Mr. Lloyd fully corroborates the preceding instance of the cowardice of an ensnared wolf. A peasant, travelling near St. Petersburg, was attacked by eleven wolves, while he was in his sledge:—"At this time he was only about two miles from home, towards which he urged his horse at the very top of his speed. At the entrance of his residence was a gate, which happened to be closed at the time; but the horse dashed this open, and thus his master and himself found refuge in the court-yard. They were followed, however, by nine out of the eleven wolves; but very fortunately, at the very instant these had entered the enclosure, the gate swung back on its hinges, and thus they were caught as in a trap. From being the most ferocious of animals, now that they found escape impossible, they completely changed, and so far from offering molestation to any one, they slunk into holes, and allowed themselves to be slaughtered, almost without making any resistance."

A very interesting account of the marauding propensities of the wolf is given by Major Strickland. He found the wolves sad plagues to him, especially in their mutton-stealing propensities. On one occasion he found six sheep missing from his pen, and on going with a lantern to search for them, five of them were found with their throats cut in a very scientific manner, and the sixth had escaped. This was bad enough, but not so bad as another misfortune that occurred to him, when the entire flock was lost. The sheep were allowed to run at large day and night, as in the hot months they would not feed during the day time, but crept into the bush and under the fences for shade. One morning their owner saw from his house a sheep standing on the opposite bank of the river, and being struck with a circumstance so strange as a sheep being found on the bank of a river, although no farm was within two or three miles, he took a canoe, and paddled over. On going to the river, one of his own sheep was discovered lying mangled and dead, and soon after, ten more were found in the same condition. The sheep on the bank turned out to be one of the same flock, that had ingeniously escaped the attacks of the wolves which had destroyed its companions, by leaping into the water and swimming over. Nine more were lying drowned on a shoal down the river; they had been swept away by the current in endeavouring to avoid the wolves. Next week, the wolves took away the same number of sheep. The worst of the matter was, that as it was in the hot season, the mutton would not keep, and was, therefore, distributed among the neighbours.

The same writer records a singular example of courage in a female. His wife's youngest sister had a pet lamb to which she was much attached. This, when it had passed its lambhood, and arrived at the dignity of sheep, was attacked by a wolf. Just then its mistress saw her favourite in the jaws of an animal which she took to be a large dog. She, therefore, took up a large stick, and began to beat the assailant, who, dropping the sheep, and turning round with a snarl, proved to be a wolf. The animal seemed determined to get the sheep, and again attacked it, but was beaten off a second time by his courageous foe, who actually followed him down a creek, thrashing him and calling for assistance. The assistance now came in the shape of a brother, accompanied by dogs, and bearing a gun. The wolf was not bold enough to withstand this addition to his foes, but ran away with such speed that there was not even time to get a shot at him.

His accounts of the wolves close with the following anecdote, which I must be permitted to give in his own words :—

" A perilous. adventure once befell my brother-in-law, James. He was a bold brave boy, of ten years old at the time, and was on his return home with a pair of oxen, with which he had been assisting a neighbour, residing about six miles from his father's house. His road lay by the river shore, which was dreary enough at the fall of the year, and on the evening hour ; but the child was fearless, and saw the deepening shades sink into night without experiencing anything like apprehension.

"He was trudging on steadily, singing cheerfully as he walked, when a sound came on the night air that sent a shiver through the young pedestrian's frame—the war cry of the wolves. At first he hoped he was not the object of pursuit ; but the hideous uproar came nearer and nearer, and then he knew that he must instantly adopt some plan for his escape.

" His route lay by the river shore, and he could swim well ; but the night was dark, and he might be hurried into the rapids, and to be dashed to pieces on the rocks was scarcely less dreadful than to be mangled and devoured by wolves. In this extremity, the child lifted up his brave young heart to God, and resolved to use the only chance left him of escape. So he mounted Buck the near-ox, making use of his goad, shouting at the same time to the animal to excite him to his utmost speed.

" In most cases, the horned steed would have flung off his rider, and left him for wolves' meat

without hesitation ; but Buck set off with the speed
of a race-horse, as if fully aware of his young rider's
peril. Nor was his companion less tardy. Fast,
however, as the trio fled, still faster came on the
yelling pack behind ; and James could ever hear—

> " Their long hard gallop which could tire
> The hound's deep hate and hunter's fire."

" Fortunately for him, old Buck heard it too, and
galloped on and on ; but still the wolves came nearer
and nearer ; James shouted to keep them off ; the
oxen almost flying ; their chains rattling as they
went. This clanking sound, to which the hateful
pack were unaccustomed, made them pause whenever they came close upon the oxen, whilst the latter
redoubled their speed, till at length these gallant
racers left the wolves behind, and finding themselves
within a short distance of home, never stopped till
they had brought the brave little fellow to his own
door.

" He had felt afraid but once, and that was when
those dismal yells first broke upon his ear, and *never*
lost his presence of mind. He trusted in God, and
used the means within his reach for preservation, and
arrived safe at last.

" Few boys would have displayed so much sense
and spirit, but the boy is almost always the father of
the man ; and what James was then, he is now."

The bite of the wolf is peculiar to the animal, and
consists of a sharp snap. This snap it can repeat
very rapidly, and the strength of its jaws is so great,
that if it bites a man's arm, every tooth pierces to
the bone. Wolves drink in a different manner from
dogs. Dogs, as we all know, drink by lapping with
the tongue, but wolves draw the water into their
mouths after the manner of horses. These peculiarities, together with the obliquity of their eyes,
afford good reasons for separating them from the
true dogs, of which they were once supposed to be
the ancestors.

The chase of the wolf is very exciting, but is also very arduous, for although it starts with a peculiar shambling gallop, and appears half wearied out, it keeps up this pace for a length of time that baffles the endurance of the best horses, much to the dismay of the inexperienced hunter, who finds that the apparently slow gallop is in reality very swift, and that after his horse is thoroughly tired out the wolf continnes his provoking gallop just as if nothing had happened. When wolves run, they carry their heads down, their noses to the ground, their tail held low against their legs, the hair of their head and neck standing erect, and their eyes flashing with a furious light. There is only one thing that wolves seem good for, and that is, that when the hunter is on short commons, wolf venison is by no means a bad thing, and the ribs roasted are thought rather a delicacy than otherwise.

There are innumerable anecdotes of wolves current, but they all resemble each other so closely, that it is a difficult matter to find any that exhibit any peculiar traits in the lupine character. In all we find the same characteristics repeated — ferocity, cowardice and cunning make up the character of the wolf in its native state.

I say in the native state, because wolves have occasionally been taken when young, and tamed. One of these tame wolves, described by F. Cuvier, had been brought up by its master as if it had been a dog, and was treated in the same manner. It, therefore, obeyed its master exactly as a dog would have done, and was perfectly submissive to him. Its master was forced to leave his home for some time, and not being able to take his pet wolf with him, and being doubtful whether the animal would be as submissive to another man, presented it to the Jardin des Plantes. The poor animal always had been distressed at any absence of his master, and it may, therefore, be imagined that when the

confinement of a cage was added to the deprivation
of his master's company, the wolf pined for some
months. At the end of that time, it reconciled
itself to its fate, and made friends with its keepers.
Eighteen months after its admission into the Jardin
des Plantes, its master visited the gardens. At the
first sound of his voice, the wolf recognised him,
and being set at liberty by the keepers, sprung
upon him, caressing and fawning upon him like
a dog. Again master and wolf were separated, and
again did the wolf pine for a time. After the space
of three years, the master again returned, when the
wolf, who had been living happily with a little dog,
recognised him, and uttered the most impatient cries
until it was released from his cage. It immediately
rushed upon its beloved master, placed its fore feet
upon his shoulder, licked his face, and threatened
its keepers, who endeavoured to remove it, and
with whom it had just before been playing. Again
his master left it, and this time it was so grieved at
the separation, that for a long time its life was supposed to be in danger. Gradually its health returned,
but it had then lost all its affectionate dispositions,
and would suffer none but the keepers to approach,
appearing to all strangers an ordinary wild wolf.

I will conclude these anecdotes of wolves with a
tragic tale, related by Mr. Lloyd. A pack of wolves,
roaming about as usual in search of prey, came upon
a sledge containing a woman and three children.
When the woman, who was driving, saw the wolves,
she urged her horse to its utmost speed, and drove
towards her home, which was not far distant. The
hungry energy of the wolves soon enabled them to
gain upon the horse, and before long several wolves
had ranged alongside, and were on the point of
springing upon the occupants of the sledge. The
wretched mother, hoping, by the sacrifice of one life,
to save the lives of the rest of her family, cast one of
the children to the wolves. They instantly ceased

the pursuit, and flew upon the devoted child, permitting the sledge to gain a little on them. But
the delay caused by merely devouring a child was
very small, as may be well imagined, when it is well
known that half a dozen wolves can finish an entire
deer in less than ten minutes. Soon the still-hungry
pack was again by the sledge, and another child was
sacrificed. Once more the tragical scene took place,
the third child was cast to the wolves, and during
their delay, the sledge reached the village, bearing
with it the unhappy mother. Having reached her
home, she related the circumstances, and endeavoured to palliate her conduct by describing the
dreadful alternative to which she had been reduced,
that if the wolves had once sprung upon the sledge,
all four must inevitably have been devoured, and
that she, therefore, hoped to save the survivors each
time that she had sacrificed a child. At the conclusion of this recital, a peasant, who had been standing
by, said that a mother who would sacrifice her children in order to preserve her own life, was not fit to
live at all. Then taking up an axe, he completed
the tragedy by cleaving her skull with a single blow.
The man was seized and committed to prison for
murder, but was afterwards pardoned by the Emperor.

FOX.*

WHAT reader of Æsop's Fables, whether in verse or
prose, can permit the word " fox" to pass through his
mind without a smile either facial or mental? Every
one has read Æsop, and every one sympathises with
the daring rascal who cheats the crow out of her
beautiful piece of cheese by the most barefaced
flattery, who, when bear and donkey had been laid
prostrate by the lion's paw, wheedled himself into
the good graces of the king of beasts, and who, when

* *Vulpes vulgaris.*

he had accidentally lost his tail in a trap from which he had hardly escaped with life ; with the most unparalleled impudence, assembled his friends, and representing the common habit of wearing tails to be plebeian in the extreme, recommended them to follow his example, and sacrifice their tails to fashion.

Then, again, there is the extension of Æsop in the world-wide story of " Reynard the Fox," a story which we should probably have never known had it not been for the cleverly-stuffed animals in the Exhibition of 1851. One of the specimens told the story of that famous fox with great truth and spirit. Since that time, hosts of illustrators have chosen that story for their choicest labours, and some of them, more especially the German artists, have succeeded admirably. There is a book of illustrations by a German artist, which is a model both of skill in engraving, and of power to depict the countenances of brute beasts agitated with human passion. There is one plate in particular, illustrating the moment when the fox is just about to be hung. He is already mounted on the fatal tree, the rope is round his neck, the cat, who is evidently in high glee at the part which he is called on to perform, is busily tying the end of the rope round a branch, while the other animals are exulting over the fall of their crafty rival. The expression of the countenance of the doomed fox is admirable. There is just that expression that one might imagine Uriah Heep's face to wear while he was declaring himself a Numble individual—there is fear, supplication, and, mixed with all, a sort of lingering reliance on his cunning even at the last extremity. Then, as a contrast, the next plate exhibits the fox leaving the royal palace, and walking with haughty tread between a double row of other animals, who are all bowing low to him as he passes. A fruitful subject is master Reynard.

However fabulous Æsop's Fables may be, they go very little beyond the stories prevalent among sportsmen of the sagacity of the fox, more especially in its cunning in escaping from the hounds. There is one story now before me, in which it is told that a fox escaped from the hounds and got among a flock of sheep. The pack, when they came up, could not discover the scent, nor did it appear that the fox had left the field. At last, one of the old dogs sprang upon a sheep that was lying on the ground, and began to pull it about and tear it. The attention of the remainder of the pack was drawn by this singular conduct, and they came to see what was the matter, when the fox sprang up, and was making the best of his way off, but was intercepted and killed by the hounds. On examining the sheep, the huntsmen found that the fox had killed it, and, tearing open its abdomen, *had crept into the interior, and hidden himself there.*

Such tales as this I am not going to impose on any one who may take up this book; but as the greater part of fox stories are taken from the accounts of hunting, it is no easy matter to choose such as are really authorised from the mass of very doubtful tales with which we are constantly presented. A very few anecdotes, therefore, will be related of the fox.

First, as to the characteristics of the fox. As given by a naturalist, in order to distinguish the animal from the dog, they consist of the lengthened and sharp muzzle joined to a round head, erect and triangular ears, the pupil of the eye linear, like that of the cat, and the long bushy tail. But if we ask a sportsman, he will say that the chief characteristics of a fox are its brush, countenance, and pads, by which he means the tail, head, and feet, which are retained by the fortunate huntsmen who are with the hounds at the death of the fox, and exhibited as trophies. Some sportsmen are so very enthusiastic in the matter, that they preserve a foot for the purpose of dipping in their wine to give it a flavour.

The scent of the fox, by which the dogs follow its track, is remarkably unpleasant, and so strong, that even an uneducated human nostril can perceive it. I have detected the track of a fox myself by the scent that the animal left behind it. I had good reason to know the scent, having on one occasion had rather too much of it. One of my pupils had lost nearly the whole of a fine brood of ducklings by the foxes, and was, of course, in a state of great indignation against them. One morning, while we were in school, a strong and most unpleasant scent pervaded the air, for which we could not account. Presently a servant came in, " Please, sir, here's a man got the fox that stole master Herbert's ducks." So we all adjourned to an out-house, where was an old weather-beaten man seated on a sack, round which two gaunt wiry terriers were jumping and barking. The old man got up from his sack, and after quieting the dogs, announced that he had got the fox. We could see no fox, and asked the old man where it was. He then produced the sack on which he had been sitting, and untied the neck amid a tremendous howling of the dogs. After fumbling about for a chain in the interior, he dragged out a large female fox. The moment the fox was out of the sack, the two dogs flew at it, and had to be kicked out of the shed. Taking this as a hint that they were to let the fox alone, they came back very humbly, and sat down. After the fox had been thoroughly inspected, it was dragged from behind a copper, where it had ensconced itself, and being replaced in the sack, the old man resumed his seat upon it, and looked as if he had done his duty.

" How did you catch the fox, my good man ? "

The old fellow gave a kind of scrutinising leer, and then perceiving that none of us were likely to be fox-hunters, gave the following recital :—

" Well, sir, I had a mortal sight o' young chickens and ducks, but somehow they *would* get lost. Fust, I

o

thinks thieves gets 'em, but arterwards—'FAWKSES!"
—says I. Well, sir, I did n't know for a long time
where the fawks lived; but at last Tyke here (good
dog, Tyke), he finds out the hole. So I takes my
spade, and jams it over the hole, and sets Tyke to
watch, while I goes home and fetches a pick and
Pincher here (good dog, Pincher). Well, sir, I digs
and digs, and presently I finds one of my ducklings.
So I digs again, and in goes Pincher, and out he
lugs a fawks' cub. So I digs again, and it was mortal hot, and I should a liked a drop of beer uncommon—almost as hot as to-day, sir. Fawks is a heavy
weight, sir, and I've walked a many miles." Finding
the ruse fail, he continued his tale. "Pincher, he
shakes the cub like a good 'un, and, thinks I, 'You're
ged.' When I dug a lot more, in goes both dogs,
and brings out another cub. I wish they'd a kept
'em alive, I'd a made half-a-crown out of each on 'em.
Well, I digs again, and I hears the old fawks a snarlin
at bottom of hole, but a *wouldn't* come out. So I
calls off dogs, and ties 'em up, and I gets a top of
the bank just over the hole, and waits. Fawks
thinks dogs is gone, and out she comes. So down
I tumbles on her, and how she did kick. Oh! it
makes me thirsty to think on it. I gets holt of her
hind legs, and swings her round till she's as giddy as
a mouse in a churn, and then I claps her into my
sack, and carries her home. Then I puts Tyke's
collar on her, and thinks to myself that I'll take her
round the country, and show her to them what has
lost their ducks and chickens, and perhaps they will
give me summat for ketching the fawks. There's a
many has lost chickens and ducklings, and hens, too,
so I shall make summat of she. Lie still, old woman!
Hot day, sir."

"Have you got anything yet?"

"Well, sir, I has. Muster Jenkins he give me
half-a-crown, he did, and Muster Bradley, he give me
half-a-crown, *and a drink o' beer.* Muster Bradley had

lost a sight o' ducks. Muster Broughton, he give me a shilling, and young Muster Broughton give me a shilling too. More nor a week's wages that, sir."

"Have you taken it to Mr. —— (a gentleman who possessed a pack of hounds), perhaps he would give you something."

"Ah! he'd give me summat, sure enough. He'd give me a horsewhip across my shoulders for killing o' the cubs, he would. No, no! I shan't take her to he. Got anything for a poor man, sir?"

So we gratified him with a small sum of money, and he got off the sack. "Shall take off her skin, sir, when I get home, and make me a waistcoat for winter. Ah, skin make a beautiful waistcoat."

"But you are not going to let her tail hang behind your waistcoat."

"Oh no, sir; I shall sell the tail to some gentleman, sir," said the man with an intelligent side glance, "and he'll stick it over his chimney-piece. Come along, Tyke; Pincher, let the fawks alone."

The man, fox, and dogs departed; but the scent unfortunately, did not go with them, and for more than a week hung about the place, so that we had every opportunity of making acquaintance with the odour of a fox. If such be the flavour communicated to wine by squeezing a "pad" into it, I would rather be excused from drinking it.

There are so many anecdotes of the cunning of the fox when pursued, that space will not permit me to give many of them. Most people have heard of the clever fox, who, when the hounds were just behind him, leaped over a low wall, and lying flat on the opposite side, waited until all the hounds had cleared the wall, and were hurrying onwards in eager pursuit, when he leaped back again, and, retracing his former path, contrived to escape, in spite of the effort of the horsemen.

In the year 1805, a fox was turned out on Pennenden heath, and was released just as a company of

riflemen, who were exercising, had entered the heath.
The animal, being alarmed at their fire, altered his
course, and leaping over a high wall and several
fences, made his way into Duke's court, Maidstone,
and leaping on a water-butt, scrambled upon the roof
of a school-house.   From thence he sprung upon a
chimney, and seeing his pursuers close at hand, he
dropped down it.   The chimney was a double one, and
in one division there was no fire.   Down this the
fox scrambled, and hid himself in a funnel in the
washhouse chimney.   One of the sportsmen dismounted, and finding Reynard in his ignominious
retreat, boldly dragged him out, not without considerable injury to his hands, and with the help of a
friend, forced him into a bag.   It seems rather a
shame that after such a clever device the fox was not
suffered to go in peace; but we must suppose that a
fox-hunter's ardour is not to be restrained by any
question of humanity.   So poor Reynard was carried
to another heath, and again turned off.   This time,
all his cunning availed him little, and he was killed
in the most approved style.

   This is by no means a solitary instance of a fox
taking refuge in a house.   In one case, the animal
surpassed the performances of the chimney-descend-
ing Reynard just mentioned, as the animal let itself
drop down a chimney, at the bottom of which was a
fire, and tumbled into the lap of an old woman who
was seated in the chimney-corner smoking her pipe.
The poor old woman was terrified out of her wits,
and retreated into a corner, followed by the children.
The hounds, chased the fox as far as the chimney-top,
but did not dare to follow it any further, so some of
the sportsmen were obliged to enter the cabin and
capture the fox, much to the relief of the terrified
inhabitants.   This happened in Ireland, where the
roofs of the houses are usually so low that a dog can
easily jump on them, .and the goats, where goats are
kept, feed on the grass that grows there.

Another fox, on being hard-pressed, rushed into a cottage, and sprung into a cradle, from whence a mother had, only a few minutes before, taken her child. The stratagem was clever, but it did not succeed, for the hounds entered the cottage, and soon dragged the intruder from his lurking place.

It must not be imagined that the fox lives entirely on the inhabitants of the farm-yard. Indeed, if he did so, he would not keep himself in very good condition. He catches rabbits in plenty, and occasionally a hare, or should he be in a country where deer live, he is very fond of a young fawn. But should these fail, he has no objection to rats, mice, weasels, frogs, or the larger insects, such as beetles and grasshoppers. Indeed, insects form a considerable portion of the food of even the larger beasts of prey, the lion and tiger not excepted. The fox is also extremely fond of grapes, a fact that is recorded in a well-known fable. He does not only catch rabbits that are wandering from their holes, but digs out the young by the ingenious device of following the scent until he comes nearly above the place where they lie, and he then has only to dig a foot or two perpendicularly, whereas had he begun at the mouth of the burrow, he would have been forced to expend very much more labour. He also watches birdcatchers, or poachers, and comes quietly and robs the snares and limed twigs which have been laid by biped hunters. When he does get into a farm-yard, he makes tremendous havoc, as he silently carries off the poultry one by one, until he is scared by daylight or by sounds as of approaching feet. Sometimes he is so eager, that he is caught, but even in this predicament his presence of mind does not fail him. His usual method is to lie as if he were dead, and then watch his chance of escape. On one occasion, a fox having been surprised in a hen-house, simulated death with such exactness, that the owner of the slaughtered poultry thought that Master Reynard had over-gorged himself, and perished of a surfeit, like

one of our own kings.   Congratulating herself on
the fate of the robber, she picked him up by the tail,
and threw him out of the hen-house, when the fox
picked himself up and scampered off.

Another time, a peasant, finding a fox in a hen-house,
aimed a blow at him, which apparently killed him.
The man then took the fox up by the tail, slung him
over his shoulder, and carried him out of the farm-
yard, intending most probably to decorate his house
with the brush, his barn with the head and paws, and
his person with the skin.   If so, his meditations
were speedily destroyed, for the fox had only
shammed death, and finding his inverted position
uncomfortable, took measures to relieve himself by
administering a severe bite to that part of the man
against which his head was dangling.   The affrighted
peasant immediately dropped the fox, who set off as
fast as he could, leaving his would-be captor in a
state of mingled fright, pain, and fury.

Mr. Lloyd tells us of another fox, who displayed
as much sagacity in getting out of an equally bad
scrape.   The animal had been caught in a pit-fall,
and was lying apparently helpless at the bottom.   A
very stout peasant then brought a ladder, and having
lowered it into the pit, descended slowly, in order to
destroy the fox.   Reynard, however, had not the
slightest intention of being destroyed, so just as the
stout peasant placed his foot on the ground, the fox
sprang on his back, then on his shoulders, and from
thence to the edge of the pit, thereby deferring the
intended execution to an indefinite period, and injuring, in no small degree, the temper of the man by
whose means he had escaped.   How differently does
a fox, in such a predicament, act from a wolf!   The
latter animal would have lain quite still, and suffered
itself to be knocked on the head with the greatest
composure, while the former is ready to seize the
smallest opportunity for escape, and to make a good
use of it.

•, There are several species of foxes inhabiting various countries. Of these, the Arctic fox (*Vulpes Lagopus*) is the most interesting. This animal changes its coat in the winter, and takes a covering of white instead of the brownish grey colour of its summer dress. At the same time, the hair increases in length, and the animal is further defended from the cold by a quantity of wool, like that on the Alpine hare. The long hair about the head and neck is directed backwards, and gives a singularly swollen appearance to the neck. The soles of the feet are covered with a dense layer of whitish woolly hair, like that seen on the foot of the hare. From this peculiarity, the animal derives its name " Lagopus," signifying " hare-footed."

The change of fur takes place in June, at which time the white winter's coat is thrown off. Towards the end of September, the brown colour gradually fades into a grey, and by the middle of October is entirely white, but increases in length and thickness for another month.

The principal food of this animal appears to consist of lemmings of different species; but it also will eat eggs, birds, blubber, and carrion. If it obtains possession of more food than it can consume at one meal, it hides the remainder, generally in the snow, and afterwards smooths the snow with its nose. It carries this habit into confinement, and always endeavours to conceal its food. One that was confined by a chain used to put his meat on the floor, and coiling his chain carefully over it, would press it down just as if it had been snow. Of course, as soon as the fox moved away, he unwound the chain. Finding his food thus uncovered, he would turn back, and repeat the operation, often going through the whole process five or six times, until he got very angry, and was obliged to eat the food at once.

I have seen an Arctic fox go through almost the same manœuvre. He stole a piece of meat, hid it away under a stone, and then tried to look innocent.

This fox has been tamed, and has proved so gentle, that its owners permitted it to go at liberty, and to have free range of their cabins. At meal times, it would come and sit by the table like a dog, waiting for any casual gifts.

The Arctic fox does not drink water, but eats snow, and prepares the snow by rolling it up into small balls, and pressing them with his nose until hard. These little balls adhere to the animal's nose, and are drawn into the mouth with the assistance of the tongue. The flesh of this fox is very frequently eaten, and is considered rather a dainty. The approved method of dressing it is by first par-boiling, and then roasting. This is only when the animal is young, as in after life it becomes very tough, and is so rank, that the water in which it is boiled is sufficiently acrid to excoriate the mouth and tongue.

The same fox, whose unavailing attempts at concealing his food with his chain, have been mentioned, was very clever at managing that same chain. When first caught, he lived in a kennel, and as many people were anxious to look at him, he was constantly drawn out by the chain. Feeling considerably annoyed at this treatment, whenever he retreated into the kennel, he gathered up the chain in his mouth, and drew it entirely within the kennel, so that no one who had any regard for his fingers would attempt to take hold of that end of the chain that was attached to the staple at the entrance of the kennel. This species of fox is free from the unpleasant scent of its European relative.

JACKAL.*

THE name of this animal is a corruption from " Tschakkal," through the French rendering of the

* *Canis aureus.*

same word, " Chacal." The colour of the jackal is a yellowish-grey above, with yellow legs, a fact from which it derives its name " *Canis aureus*," or gold-coloured dog. The yellow fades into white on the under parts of the body.

I mention this animal merely for the sake of introducing two anecdotes, related in " Thirty-six Years of a Seafaring Life." The individual who tells the story was sleeping in a tent about thirty miles from San Francisco. About four in the morning, he was obliged to leave the tent, and go to the village for a light. He very reluctantly left the tent, and issued forth on his errand. He must have looked a very extraordinary figure, for he was wearing an enormous frock over his sailor's clothing. The frock was made of rein-deer's skin, and was long enough to turn up over the feet, and button up at the skirt. To this elegant dress was added a hood composed of the skin of a bear's head, taken off entire, ears and all, so that the person wearing it must have resembled those ancient warriors figured on the monuments of early Greece and Rome. In front depended a square lappel, which at night buttoned behind the ears, leaving only the eyes, nose, and mouth free.

Equipped in this very unique costume, he left the tent. He had only advanced a few steps, when several jackals came up, and were speedily followed by many of their friends, who, forming a circle round him, seemed only waiting for one to set the example, before they ate him. For some time he remained completely terrified, but at last it occurred to him that he had somewhere heard that animals might be frightened away by a man, if he walked backwards on his hands and feet, a description of progression to which they are not accustomed. Acting on this thought, he threw himself on all fours, and keeping his head as near the ground as possible, began to dance about and cut capers never imagined until then, and which would, in all probability, never be repeated.   As he had anticipated, the jackals were astounded, and after a little edging away from the unknown monster, fled in every direction.

One more jackal anecdote from the same source.

The ship was laying in stores of provisions at San Francisco.   Accordingly a large tent was erected on shore for salting purposes.   In this tent the cooper lived as a guardian to all the beef that was hung about, and had slung his hammock at one end.   One day, a large quantity of beef had been killed and hung up in the. tent ready for salting.   The jackals scented out the meat, and that same night they got into the tent, and getting hold of a side of beef, brought it down with a crash, thereby waking the cooper.   That functionary happened to be a very nervous man, and finding himself unexpectedly sur-rounded with wild beasts, whose numbers and size his fright materially increased, he fired off his musket in a hurry, and throwing his arms about in an agony of fear, seized a great piece of beef hanging by his hammock, and was found senseless by those who came to see the cause of the alarm. Although his senses had gone, his hold had not, for he was clasping the beef so tight that he could not be separated from it with-out some trouble.   It is no wonder that the poor man did not recover the effects of the fright for several days.

BEARS.

WE now come to a very different group of animals. The bears are plantigrade animals, that is, they place the whole of their feet upon the ground as they walk.

Most parts of the globe are inhabited by some species of bear.   Even our own island was one of their dwelling places in a time considerably antece-dent to the extirpation of the wolves.

Our general notion of bears is, that they furnish bear's-grease for the hair.   Let none imagine that

they purchase the natural fat of a bear when they
buy a pot of " bear's-grease." In the first place, the
consumption of the so-called bear's-grease is so great
that if all the bears annually killed in every country
were to be devoted to that especial purpose, they
would not even supply England. Now as nearly the
whole of the fat found in a bear is used for culinary
purposes, we may imagine that the amount of real
bear's fat in England is very small. Of course those
few bears that are now and then slaughtered at the
London perfumers are not to be taken into consideration. Moreover, malicious persons *do* say, that the
perfumers keep a bear-skin in the cellar, and that
when they slaughter a "bear," they kill a pig, dress it
in the bear's fur, and hang it up at the door. The
real composition of the " bear's-grease " is clarified
lard, prepared with a few other substances to give it
an agreeable scent.

Let us see what our forefathers thought of the
virtues of bear's-grease.

" The fat of a lyon is most hot and dry, and next
to a lyon's a leopard's; next to a leopard's a bear's,
and next to a bear's a bull's. The later, physicians
use to cure convulsed and distracted parts, spots and
tumours in the body. It also helpeth the pain in the
loyns if the sick part be anoynted therewith, when a
plaister is made thereof with bole-armoric. It is
soveraign against the falling of the hair, compounded
with wilde roses. The Spaniards burn the brain of
bears when they die in any publick sports, holding
them venomous, because being drunk, they drive a
man to be as wilde as a bear; and the like is reported
of the heart of a lyon, and the brain of a cat. The
right eye of a bear dryed to powder and hung about
children's necks in a little bag, driveth away the terror
of dreams, and both the eyes whole, bound to a
man's left arm easeth a quartain ague. The liver of
a sow, a lamb, and a bear, put together, and trod to
powder under one's shooes easeth and defendeth

cripples from inflammation: the gall being preserved
and warmed in water, delivereth the body from cold,
when all other medicine faileth."

The chase of the bear is a very exciting pursuit,
and the more so, as it is attended with some danger.
Before relating any anecdotes of individual bears, let
us see what kind of an amusement bear-hunting is.
The description is taken from Audubon's American
Birds. (Marvel not to see a bear among birds. Audubon was a naturalist as well as an ornithologist.)

" Being one night sleeping in the house of a
friend, I was awákened by a Negro servant bearing a
light, who gave me a note, which he said his master
had just received. I ran my eye over the paper, and
found it to be a communication from a neighbour,
requesting my friend and myself to join him as soon
as possible, and assist in killing some bears at that
moment engaged in destroying his corn. I was not
long in dressing, you may be assured, and, on entering the parlour, found my friend equipped, and only
waiting for some bullets, which a Negro was employed
in casting. The overseer's horn was heard calling up
the Negroes from their different cabins. Some were
already engaged in saddling our horses, whilst others
were gathering all the cur-dogs of the plantation. All
was bustle. Before half an hour had elapsed, four
stout Negro men, armed with axes and knives, and
mounted on strong nags of their own (for you must
know, kind reader, that many of our slaves rear
horses, cattle, pigs, and poultry, which are exclusively
their own property), were following us at a round
gallop through the woods, as we made directly for the
neighbour's plantation, a little more than five miles
off.

" The night was none of the most favourable, a
drizzling rain rendering the atmosphere thick and
rather sultry; but as we were well acquainted with
the course, we soon reached the house, where the
owner was waiting our arrival. There were now

three of us armed with guns, half a dozen servants, and a good pack of dogs of all kinds. We jogged on towards the detached fields, in which the bears were at work. The owner told us, that for some days, several of these animals had visited his corn, and that a Negro who was sent every afternoon to see at what part of the enclosure they entered, had assured him there were at least five in the field that night. A plan of attack was formed: the bars at the usual gap of the fence were to be put down without noise; the men and dogs were to divide, and afterwards proceed so as to surround the bears, when, at the sounding of our horns, every one was to charge towards the centre of the field, and shout as loudly as possible, which it was judged would so intimidate the animals, as to induce them to seek refuge upon the dead trees, with which the field was still partially covered.

" The plan succeeded. The horns sounded, the horses galloped forward, the men shouted, the dogs barked and howled. The shrieks of the Negroes were enough to frighten a legion of bears, and those in the field took to flight, so that by the time we reached the centre, they were heard hurrying towards the tops of the trees. Fires were immediately lighted by the Negroes. The drizzling rain had ceased, the sky cleared, and the glare of the crackling fires proved of great assistance to us. The bears had been so terri-fied, that we now saw several of them crouched at the junction of the larger boughs with the trunks. Two were immediately shot down. They were cubs of no great size, and being already half dead, we left them to the dogs, which quickly dispatched them.

" We were anxious to procure as much sport as possible, and having observed one of the bears, which from its size we conjectured to be the mother, ordered the Negroes to cut down the tree on which it was perched, when it was intended the dogs should have a tug with it, while we should support them, and assist in preventing the bear from escaping by wounding it in one of the hind legs. The surrounding woods now echoed to the blows of the axemen. The tree was large and tough, having been girdled more than two years, and the operation of felling it seemed extremely tedious. However, it began to vibrate at each stroke; a few inches alone now supported it; and in a short time it came crashing to the ground, in so awful a manner that Bruin must doubtless have felt the shock as severe as we should feel a shake of the globe produced by the sudden collision of a comet.

" The dogs rushed to the charge, and harassed the bear on all sides. We had remounted, and now surrounded the poor animal. As its life depended upon its courage and strength, it exercised both in the most energetic manner. Now and then it seized a dog, and killed him by a single stroke. At another time, a well-administered blow of one of its forelegs sent an assailant off yelping so piteously, that he might be looked upon as hors de combat. A cur had daringly ventured to seize the bear by the snout, and was seen hanging to it, covered with blood, whilst a dozen or more scrambled over its back. Now and then, the infuriated animal was seen to cast a revengeful glance at some of the party, and we had already determined to dispatch it, when, to our astonishment, it suddenly shook off all the dogs, and before we could fire, charged upon one of the Negroes, who was mounted on a pied horse. The bear seized the steed with teeth and claws, and clung to its breast. The terrified horse snorted and plunged. The rider, an athletic young man, and a capital horseman, kept his seat, although only saddled on a sheep's skin tightly girthed, and requested his master not to fire at the bear. Notwithstanding his coolness and courage, our anxiety for his safety was raised to the highest pitch, especially.when in a moment we saw rider and horse come to the ground together; but we were instantly relieved on witnessing the masterly manner in which

Scipio dispatched his adversary, by laying open his skull with a single well-directed blow of his axe, when a deep growl announced the death of the bear, and the valorous Negro sprung to his feet unhurt.

" Day dawned and we renewed our search. Two of the remaining bears were soon discovered, lodged in a tree about a hundred yards from the spot where the last one had been overpowered. On approaching them in a circle, we found that they manifested no desire to come down, and we resolved to try smoking. We surrounded the tree with a pile of brushwood and large branches. At length the tree assumed the appearance of a pillar of flame. The bears mounted to the top branches. When they had reached the uppermost, they were seen to totter, and soon after, the branch cracking and snapping across, they came to the ground, bringing with them a mass of broken twigs. They were cubs, and the dogs soon worried them to death. The party returned to the house in triumph. Scipio's horse, being severely wounded, was let loose in the field to repair his strength by eating the corn. A cart was afterwards sent for the game. But before we had left the field, the horses, dogs, and bears, together with the fires, had destroyed more corn, within a few hours, than the poor bear and her cubs had during the whole of their visits."

It appears that the native Americans do not consider the slaughter of the bear to be merely as the destruction of an injurious animal, but they look upon the animal as an almost supernatural being, and after killing it, solemnly propitiate its manes. The following account, taken from Alexander Henry's Travels, gives an excellent description of the ceremonies used on such an occasion.

" In the course of the month of January I happened to observe that the trunk of a very large fine tree was much torn by the claws of a bear, made both in going up and down. On further examination I saw that there was a large opening in the upper part, near which the smaller branches were broken. From these marks, and from the additional circumstance that there were no tracks in the snow, there was reason to believe that a bear lay concealed in the tree.   On returning to the lodge I communicated my discovery, and it was agreed that all the family should go together in the morning to assist in cutting down the tree, the girth of which was not less than three fathoms.   The women at first opposed the undertaking, because our axes, being only of a pound and a half weight were not well adapted to so heavy a labour; but the hope of finding a large bear, and obtaining from its fat a great quantity of oil, an article at the time much wanted, at length prevailed. Accordingly, in the morning, we surrounded the tree, both men and women, as many at a time as could conveniently work at it, and there we toiled like beavers till the sun went down.   This day's work carried us about half way through the trunk, and the next morning we renewed the attack, continuing it until about two o'clock in the afternoon, when the tree fell to the ground.   For a few moments everything remained quiet, and I feared that all our expectations would be disappointed; but as I advanced to the opening, there came out, to the great satisfaction of all our party, a bear of extraordinary size, which I shot.   The bear being dead, all my assistants approached, and all, but particularly my old mother (as I was wont to call her), took the head in their hands, stroking and kissing it several times ; begging a thousand pardons for taking away her life, calling her their relation and grandmother, and requesting her not to lay the fault upon them, as it was truly an Englishman that had put her to death.   This ceremony was not of long duration, and if it was I that killed their grandmother, they were not themselves behindhand in what remained to be performed.   The skin being taken off, we found the fat in several places six inches deep.   This being divided into two

part,
Fros...

... branches were broken.
... the additional circum-
... in the snow, there
... lay concealed in the
... I comunicated my
... that all the family should
... to assist in cutting down
... which was not less than three
... women at ... exposed the under-
... our axes, ... of a pound and
... were not ... to so heavy a
... the hope of ... bear, and
... from its ... of oil, an
... at the time ... prevailed.
Accordingly, in the ... tree,
both men and women ... could
conveniently work ... like
beavers till the sun was down ... work
carried us about half ... and the
next morning we ... continuing it
until about two o'clock ... noon, when the
tree fell to the ground. ... moments everything remained quiet ... that all our
expectations would be ... but as I advanced
to the opening, there ... the great satisfaction of all our party ... of extraordinary size,
which I shot. The ... all my assistants
approached, and ... my old mother
(as I was wont to ... took the head in their
hands, stroking and ... several times; begging
a thousand pardons ... away her life, calling
her their relation ... grandmother, and requesting
her not to lay ... upon them, as it was truly an
Englishman that ... her to death. This ceremony was not ... duration, and if it was I that

THE BEAR. p. 208.

parts loaded two persons, and the flesh parts were as much as four persons could carry. In all, the carcase must have exceeded five hundredweight. As soon as we reached the lodge, the bear's head was adorned with all the trinkets in the possession of the family, such as silver armbands and wristbands, and belts of wampum, and then laid upon a scaffold set up for its reception within the lodge. Near the nose was placed a large quantity of tobacco. The next morning no sooner appeared than preparations were made for a feast to the manes. The lodge was cleaned and swept, and the head of the bear lifted up, and a new Stroud blanket, which had never been used before, spread under it. The pipes were now lit, and Wawatam blew tobacco smoke into the nostrils of the bear, telling me to do the same, and thus appease the anger of the bear, on account of having killed her. I endeavoured to persuade my benefactor and friendly adviser that she no longer had any life, and assured him that I was under no apprehension from her displeasure; but the first proposition obtained no credit, and the second gave but little satisfaction. At length the feast being ready, Wawatam made a speech, resembling, in many things, his address to the manes of his relations and departed companions; but having the peculiarity, that he here deplored the necessity under which men laboured thus to destroy their friends. He represented, however, that the misfortune was unavoidable, since without doing so they could by no means subsist. This speech ended, we all eat heartily of the bear's flesh, and even the head itself, after remaining three days on the scaffold, was put into the kettle."

Why do we always call a rude man a bear? Why do we select the bear as our model of coarse conduct? There is nothing in the ursine nature to warrant such an attack upon its general character. The bear is quite as gentlemanly a quadruped as any other, and if he does occasionally infringe the rules of politeness, it

P

is from the want of instruction, and 'not from any
innate vulgarity.   We should not form our notions of
politeness from an uninstructed being.   Who, for
example, would form any idea of our refined friend,
Mr. Pelham, from an acquaintance with a Wiltshire pig-driver, or a "Bilstone Chap?"   The educated individual is always taken as the criterion by
which we should judge the politeness of a nation:
why then should we choose the uneducated individual
in judging the politeness of a tribe?   Let our bear
only be properly educated, and see what a refined
individual he becomes.   It is very true that few bears
are fortunate enough to obtain an education, that
raises them from their native state of primitive simplicity to the summit of refinement.   For the education of most bears seldom aspires beyond teaching
the animal to stand on its hind legs, and raise each
foot alternately, a performance popularly entitled
"dancing," and said to be inculcated by placing hot
plates under the bear's feet; while a very accomplished
bear wears his master's hat and leans on his stick
while the pence are being collected.

Sometimes the education of a bear is taken up by
more accomplished hands, and then he turns out a
capital pupil, especially in his choice of food.

Such an animal was the renowned Tiglath Pileser,
the gentlemanly Oxford bear   He was one of the
Syrian bears, the animals mentioned in the Book of
Kings, as the destroyers of the children that mocked
Elisha.   The colour of these bears is a yellowish-
white, except when they are young, at which time the
fur is brown.   It is somewhat remarkable, that the
young of a white animal should be dark, while the
young of many dark animals, such as the Agile
Gibbon monkey, or the Hippopotamus, should be
light.   An opposite change of colour takes place in
the young of the lion and puma, whose fur is spotted
or brindled until they attain to maturer years.

But to return to Tiglath Pileser, called, for the

sake of brevity, Tig. He was a contemporary of my dog Rory, and was much such an individual among bears as Rory among dogs, and indeed in many points their taste was identical. The history of Tig has several times been presented to the public, and I shall, therefore, give but a short notice of him.

His entrance into the University was marked by that eccentricity of demeanour which never deserted him through his life. Immediately on escaping from the confinement of the hamper in which he had made a long railway journey, he ran away, and passing down the cloisters with which the rooms of his master communicated, he got into the cathedral just as the first lesson was being read. So unaccountable an intruder caused great discomposure in the mind of the verger, who took refuge in a pew, and fastened the door. The bear derived his name from this exploit, as the name of Tiglath Pileser happened to be mentioned just when he entered the cathedral. Tig soon escaped from the cathedral, and after a severe chase in " Tom-quad," was captured by means of a gown thrown over him, and was led back to his proper home, walking on his hind legs and sucking one of his master's fingers, an amusement of which he was very fond.

His collegiate life now began, and he conformed him-self admirably to the customs of the University, mean-ing, of course, the undergraduate portion of the Univer-sity. He was decked in cap and gown, and conveyed to wine parties, where he made himself very much at home, and ate ices with great discrimination. By the way, it seems to be an invariable custom with collegians to dress their favourites in full academicals. When the famous dwarf, General Tom Thumb, was in Oxford, he had a little cap and gown made for him, the model of the cap being the tailor's fist, and the gown proportionately small. In these habiliments he went round the colleges to pay his respect to the University as represented by its members.

Tig ought to have lived in a little yard on which

his master's rooms opened, but he made such a noise when left alone at night, that he was brought into the rooms in self-defence. Moreover, in the same yard were an eagle, a tortoise, and a monkey, neither particularly good company for poor Tig, for the monkey used to pull his ears or hair, while the eagle, being unconversational in his habits, stood on the tortoise almost all day, and beguiled the hours by trying to eat it—a proceeding which the tortoise endured with the greatest equanimity.

So Tig's life became that of an undergraduate, and when vacations came he left the college with his master, and lived in a village, where he played sundry pranks. On one occasion he was taken for a ride to a distant village, his hind legs resting on the horse's back, and his fore paws on his master's shoulders. The horse evinced great disapprobation of the claws that Tig wore on his hind feet, and plunged about in order to shake off the incumbrance. But Tig held on quite firmly, and reached his journey's end in safety.

As he grew older his fur became whiter, and he bid fair to become a beautiful specimen of the Syrian bear. The authorities, however, at the college, not being quite so attached to the bear as the junior members, and having for some time exercised considerable forbearance on the subject, at last issued the fatal mandate, and poor Tig's last day at college arrived. In order that he might be properly attended to, he was sent to the Zoological Gardens and put in a den. But the mandate of expulsion was indeed a fatal one, for the poor animal could not be reconciled to the change, and after some time spent in incessantly running up and down his den in vain efforts to escape, he was found dead one morning.

Of all the bear tribe, the Grizzly Bear (*Ursus horribilis* or *ferox*) is the most dangerous. Its ferocity is exceedingly great, and such is its tenacity of life, that it seems to care little for half a dozen bullets or so through its lungs, and has been known to run more

than a hundred yards after a ball had passed through
its heart. Indeed, a ball through the brain or spine
seems to be the only method of bringing this ferocious
animal to the ground at once. The grizzly bear has
rather a peculiar method of approach. When he
sees his foe or his prey, as the case may be, he rises
on his hind legs, surveys the opponent for a few
moments, and then rushes at him with such fury,
that heedless of any mortal wound, he presses forward, and would seize him even if protected by a
body of soldiers.

So formidable is this creature considered by the
American Indians, that a collar composed of its claws
is one of the highest honours that a man can earn,
for none are permitted to wear these trophies, unless
they have killed the bear with their own hand. Even
the much-coveted " scalp " is not prized so highly as
the claws of the grizzly bear. Nor is this to he wondered at, when, in addition to the ferocity of the
animal and its enormous size, we consider that the
claws are five inches in length, and so sharp, that
they cut like so many chisels. No wonder, then, that
a necklace of these fearful claws should be held in
such high estimation. The claws can be moved in-
dependently of each other, like our fingers. An
inquisitive bear has been seen to crumble a clod of
earth to pieces by the mere motion of the claws,
without using the paws at all.

The Indians stand in such awe of this animal, that
when they discover one, they summon as many men as
possible, the whole tribe if they can, and endeavour
to make up by numbers for their want of courage.
So terrified are they at their ursine enemy, that
although they swarm as numerously as the fabulous
bees whose hive was overturned by the fabulous bear,
they often fail in stinging the bear to death.

But the white American hunter knows better.
When he sees a grizzly bear that he thinks is
worth the trouble and danger of shooting, he hides

himself behind a stump or rock, and imitates the
lowing of a young calf. The bear hearing this
welcome sound, runs to the place from whence the
cry proceeded, hoping to make a good supper on
veal, without much trouble in obtaining it. The
hunter then waits until the shaggy monster is quite
close, when he sends a. ball through his head. It is
necessary to inflict an instantaneously fatal wound,
for if that is not done, the enraged beast, although
mortally wounded, has several times been known to
muster sufficient 'strength to overtake and kill his
assailant.

It is said, that in spite of its enormous size,
strength, and ferocity, the grizzly bear stands in
great fear of the smell of man, and that if the
hunter once gets to the windward of the bear, or
" gives him his wind," as it is called, the animal runs
off as fast as he can. One old hunter, it is said, saved
his life by his knowledge of this peculiarity. He was
unarmed, and in that helpless condition, saw a grizzly
bear at some distance. The moment the bear caught
a glimpse of him, it turned and gave chase. The
man, on finding the bear gain on him, tore off a
small portion of wool from his blanket, and threw it
into the air to find the direction of the wind. Having
discovered from which quarter the wind blew, he ran
round until he placed himself between the wind and
the bear. The animal, who was advancing in a
ferocious manner, no sooner caught the scent, than it
turned round, and ran away as fast as it could. I
was, however, informed by an American traveller, who
has resided for several years in the parts infested by
the grizzly bear, and who, therefore, may be supposed
to be a good authority, that the bear is by no means
afraid of the scent of man, but will most certainly
rush at and attack him. Perhaps the bears living on
the outskirts of this country, where they have opportunities of forming an acquaintance with fire-arms,
may, as other beasts certainly have done, learn to

connect the scent of man with the power of his weapons.

This bear, according to my informant, is not to be stopped in his attack by boldly facing it, as is the case with the lion tribe, and some other animals. In fact, " a panther," as my informant said, " if you only know how to work him, has no more harm in him than a squirrel." The " working " consists in keeping a sharp look-out for the animal, never seeming to be afraid of it, and turning round upon it whenever it gets too close.

His reasons for the conduct of the animal under these circumstances, appear to be correct. These beasts of prey, when in pursuit, have but one idea in their minds, that of catching their prey. As they creep closer and closer, the idea becomes so overwhelming, that it banishes every other thought from their minds. This may be often seen in a cat when creeping after a bird. As then, the prey retreats, and the animal gains on it, this one idea completely fills its mind, to the exclusion of every other thought, every faculty being wrought up for that one purpose. If, then, at that time the pursued animal suddenly turns upon the pursuer, the unexpected change of action causes the animal to stop instinctively, or even to retreat a few steps. In either case, the leading idea is suddenly driven from the mind of the animal, and it is completely bewildered. A panther (*i. e.*, a puma), when stopped in this way, often retreats a few steps, and is so perplexed by the action, that it cannot recover itself for some time. A snake also, when it has coiled itself for a spring, will often sink back again, if a stick be struck violently against the earth.

But the grizzly bear is superior to these weaknesses, and is therefore an animal to be avoided. His speed is tolerable, but not equal to that of a horse, so that a mounted man may consider himself in safety. But when a traveller is on foot, he manages in a different way. He takes with him as much meat as he can

carry, and if pursued by one of these bears, he throws
a little piece on the ground, having first scented it
with some material that puzzles the bear exceedingly.
So when the bear comes up, he sees the meat, and
begins sniffing at it.   He is sure to eat it at last, but
not until after a long examination, so that the traveller
has five or six minutes start of him, a space of time
that will suffice to put nearly a mile between himself
and the bear.

Mr. Eaton Stone, the traveller, who gave me this
account of the habit of the animal, was himself chased
nearly thirty miles by one of these bears—in fact, the
creature pursued him to the banks of a large river. He
looked upon the grizzly bear as an animal whose near
acquaintance was always to be declined, if possible.

An adventure with one of these ferocious animals,
fortunately partaking more of the comic than the
tragic, is related by Townshend.   A rash hunter,
whose shooting powers did not seem to be equal to
those of American hunters, whose unerring eye and
hand can use a rifle ball in the light of a hammer,
and drive home a nail while at the distance of fifty
paces, saw a grizzly bear reposing itself under some
willows.   He dropped quietly behind his companions,
approached to within twenty yards of the bear, and
then fired.   Now, a grizzly bear is at all times singularly indifferent to wounds, and will often give fierce
chase even when its body has been riddled by balls.
As, therefore, the hunter only succeeded in wounding
the animal slightly, it may be imagined that its
resentment was likely to be formidable. The moment
that the shot struck it, the bear rushed with an
angry growl upon its opponent, who instantly turned
his horse, and fled.   The horse happened to be a
slow one, and the bear was several times so close to
the terrified animal as to snap at its heels.   During
the race, the rider kept constantly turning toward the
bear, and shrieking, " shoot him—shoot him," in an
agony of fear.   The bear, as may be supposed, had

no*t* the slightest intention of shooting himself, and continued the chase, until he drove the man fairly into the centre of his own party. A detachment rode to his assistance, and when they got within range of the bear, *did* " shoot him." This reminds us of a certain general, who, being chased by a bear, shouted out, " Halt, you rascal, I 'm a general, I 'm a general."

The grizzly bear is generally hunted by several men, who contrive to surround him. One then fires, and is instantly chased by the exasperated bear, but escapes by the blind fury of the animal who, when he feels a fresh wound, turns upon his new assailant, giving the first time to reload. He is thus driven from one to the other in a kind of puss-in-the-corner manner, until he is destroyed. This consummation is not completed without a great expenditure of ammunition, the body being sometimes so pierced with balls, that it is impossible to find four inches square of fur left entire. Every time that this animal receives a ball, he turns round, and begins tearing the wound with his teeth.

" Ephraim," as he is called in mountain phraseology, is at all times an unpleasant animal, and even when quite young, and no larger than a puppy, is so cross, and bites so fiercely, that no one has succeeded in taming it. The hunters have often attempted to rear a young grizzly bear, but have not succeeded, and accordingly every young grizzly bear is mercilessly put to death.

The following narrative is given for several reasons, partly because it exemplifies the ferocity of the grizzly bear, and partly because it shows the courage and endurance of the hunter. Indeed, the sequel of the story is almost incredible, and were it not known from what severe wounds the body of man will recover, when it is not weakened or injured by sloth or luxury, no one would believe that any man who had suffered such injuries could possibly survive. At all events, it shows the perfect health that is given by a life in the wide prairies, where there are no smoky cities to corrupt the air, or close rooms to prevent its circulation; where the body is not inflamed by artificial methods of cookery—and where there are no taxes. There men breathe untaxed air, are visited by untaxed light, ride on untaxed horses, kill untaxed deer with untaxed powder and ball, dress their venison with untaxed fire, cut it with untaxed knives, and, when they have supped, sleep on an untaxed bed, without fear of paying " rates " when they get up.

The tale is told by Mr. Ruxton.

" A trapper named Glass, and a companion, were setting their beaver-traps in a stream to the north of the river Platte, when they saw a large grizzly bear turning up the turf near by, and searching for roots and pig-nuts. The two men crept to the thicket, and fired at him; they wounded, but did not kill him; the beast groaned, jumped on all four legs from the ground, and, snorting with pain and fury, charged towards the place from whence came the smoke of the rifles. The men rushed through the thicket, where the underwood almost impeded their progress; but the beast's weight and strength carried him along so fast, that he soon came up with them. A steep bluff was situated a hundred yards off, with a level plain of grass between it and the thicket; the hunters flew across the latter with the utmost speed, the bear after them. When he reached about half way, Glass stumbled over a stone and fell. He rose, and the bear stood before him on his hind legs. Glass called to his companion to fire, and he himself sent the contents of his pistol into the bear's body. The furious animal, with the blood streaming from his nose and mouth, knocked the pistol away with one paw, while he stuck the claws of the other into the flesh of his antagonist, and rolled with him on the ground. Glass managed to reach his knife, and plunged it several times into the bear, while the latter, with tooth and claw, tore his flesh. At last, blinded with blood and exhaustion, the knife fell from the trapper's hand, and he became insensible. His companion, who thought his turn would come next, did not even think of reloading his rifle, and fled to the camp, where others of his party were resting, to tell the miserable fate of their companion. Assistance was sent, and Glass still breathed, but the bear lay across him quite dead, from three bullets and twenty knife wounds. The man's flesh was torn away in slips, and lumps of it lay upon the ground, his scalp hung bleeding over his face, which was also torn. The men took away the trapper's hunting-shirt, mocassius, and arms, dragged the bear off his body, and left him, declaring, when they rejoined their party, that they had completed his burial."

However, they had not buried him, most probably supposing that the wolves would save them that trouble. Some months afterwards, as some of the same party were taking furs to a trading fort for sale, they were met by a horseman of a singular appearance, whose face was so scarred and disfigured, that his features could not be distinguished. The strange horseman accosted one of the party in the following words :—" Hurrah! Bill, my boy, you thought I was gone under (killed) that time, did you? but hand me over my horse and furs, lad, I'm not dead yet." The individual accosted, who was the man that accompanied Glass in his ill-fated expedition against the bear, was horrified at hearing the voice of one whom he imagined to have died long ago. There he was, however, and proved himself to be alive so completely, that the party at last recovered sufficiently from their astonishment to hear his story. It appeared that he must have lain for some time in a senseless state after they left him. When he recovered himself a little, he tore off the flesh of the dead bear for subsistence, and having loaded himself with as much of this food as he could manage to carry, he crawled down to the river, and set himself to reach the fort, which being between eighty and ninety miles distant, was no small journey for a healthy man, without clothes or arms. Yet this brave fellow, weak, naked, and desperately wounded as he was, contrived to reach his destination at last, having been forced to live on fruits and berries for the greater part of the journey. When he arrived there, he had been properly taken care of, and although disfigured for life by the innumerable wounds that he had received, had perfectly recovered.

His companion must have felt considerably ashamed of himself when addressed by one whom he had forsaken in his need.

The wounded hunter has not recorded his sensations during the time that the bear was inflicting these wounds upon him, but if any of my readers are disposed to derive any particular gratification from ascertaining the precise sensation felt by a man while being torn by a bear, they are recommended to read the following passage, extracted from Mr. Lloyd's interesting work on Scandinavia. He is here relating the history of a bear-hunt, in which he came off less fortunately than usual:—

" Being perfectly prepared, and my gun on the full cock, I, as soon as I caught sight of the beast, levelled at the centre of his skull; but some boughs interfering, which it was to be feared would intercept the ball, caused me to desist from firing; the next instant, however, I took rather a snap shot at the outer side of his head, beyond the boughs in question. But the momentary delay caused by shifting my aim was very unfortunate, for, in the interim, he had seen me, and as I pulled the trigger, he was in the very act of bolting from his couch, and my aim, in consequence, was very uncertain. Indeed, I am inclined to believe I missed him altogether.

" Be that as it may, on the discharge of my gun the beast at once rushed towards me. I had still left my second barrel, with which I ought, no doubt, to have destroyed him; but, owing to his undulating motion, I could not, though I attempted it more than once, catch a satisfactory sight, and it was not till he was within three or four paces that I fired, and then somewhat at random; though my ball, in this or the former instance (for in the one or the other, as subsequently ascertained, it went wide of the mark), wounded him very desperately, it having entered his neck near the shoulder and passed into his body; yet it was not sufficient, unfortunately, to stop his course, for in a second or two he was upon me, not on his hind legs (the way in which it is commonly supposed the bear makes his attack), but on all fours like a dog; and, in spite of a slight blow I gave him on the head with the muzzle of my gun—for I had no time to apply the butt—he at once laid me prostrate.

"Had not the beast been so very near me when I fired the second barrel, it is probable, from his wounded state, I might have got out of his way; but flight on my part, from his near proximity, was then too late, and once in his clutches, and now that my gun was discharged, totally unarmed, the only resource left me was to turn on my face to the snow, that my features might not be mutilated, and to lie motionless, it being a generally-received opinion in Scandinavia, that if the bear supposes his victim to be dead, he the sooner desists from his assaults. In my case, however, though I played the defunct as well as I was able, the beast mangled me somewhat severely about the head in particular; my body also suffered greatly from his ferocious attacks, which extended from the neck and shoulder downwards to the hip. But he did not attempt, in any manner, to hug or embrace me, as we in England seem to imagine his custom to be when carrying on offensive operations: nor did he, seemingly, molest me in any way with his claws. All my wounds were, to the best of my belief, inflicted with his fangs.

"This goes somewhat to corroborate the idea that

commonly prevails in Sweden, that in attacking a
man, and beyond holding him fast, the bear never, in
the manner of the lion or the tiger, strikes with his
paw, which they say is his usual habit when making
an onset on horses and cattle.   If this be true, it is as
well; as otherwise, from the great muscular power of
his arm, annihilation would very probably generally
follow the blow.   But, after all, no inference can fairly
be drawn from my case, as the least forbearance
towards me might have arisen simply from my
remaining quite passive.   Had I, on the contrary,
been on my legs, and offered resistance, I might have
possibly felt not only the weight of his paws, but the
pressure of his embraces.

" Neither at the time of receiving my first fire, nor
whilst making the rush, did the bear, as is usually
the case when enraged, utter his usual half roar, half
growl.   Even when I was lying at his mercy, no
other than a sort of subdued growl, similar to that of
a dog when disturbed while gnawing a bone, was
made by the beast, and so far from coming at me
with open jaws, as one would suppose to be the case
with a wild beast when making his onset, his mouth
at the time was altogether closed.

" The pain I suffered from his long-continued
attacks upon my body was unbearable.   When he had
my limbs in his jaws, it more resembled their being
stuck in a huge vice than anything else; but when
his jaws grasped, as they did, the whole crown of my
head, during which I distinctly felt the fleshy part of
his mouth to overlap my forehead, and his fangs very
deliberately scarify my head, my sufferings were intense.   The sensation of his fangs slowly grating
over the bare skull, was not at all that of a sharp
blow, as is often the case when a wound is inflicted,
but rather, though very much more protracted, the
craunch one feels during the extracting of a tooth.

" From certain circumstances, I have reason to
believe the bear continued to maltreat me for nearly

three minutes. As I perfectly retained my senses the whole time, my feelings, whilst in this horrible situation, are beyond the power of description. But, at length, the incessant attacks of my gallant little dog drew the beast's attention from me, and I had the satisfaction to see him retreat, though at a very slow pace, into the adjoining thicket, where he was at once lost to view.

" Immediately after he left me I arose and applied snow by the handful to my head to stanch the blood, which was flowing from it in streams. I lost a very large quantity, and the bear not a little, so that the snow all around the scene of the conflict was literally deluged in gore.

  * * * * * *

" As it was, I escaped wonderfully: my body, to be sure, was covered with severe contusions, for the skin being only slightly torn, wounds they could hardly be called; two or three days subsequently, indeed, the whole of my left hip, and the adjacent parts, were perfectly black. My right hand and wrist were a good deal hurt, for at the commencement of the affair, how I know not, I got my hand into the mouth, and even partially down the very throat of the beast, where it seemed as if imbedded in saliva. My skull, for a considerable extent, was laid bare in two places, one wound, by the doctor's account on the following day, being eight, the other nine, inches in length, though parts of both were, of course, superficial."

Such being the case with a Scandinavian bear, it may well be imagined that a similar scene enacted by a grizzly bear would be hardly less painful to the sufferer.

The Scandinavian bears appear to be greater plagues than their American congeners. In one year, 1828, a report was made by a committee on the number of animals destroyed by the wild beasts the preceding year, and the returns gave the following rather alarming statistics: 465 horses, 3108 cows, &c.

19,104 sheep and goats, and 2504 pigs. This astonishing number of animals had been destroyed in seventeen provinces in one year by the wild beasts, among which the bear is predominant. In order to destroy the bears, the Scandinavian hunters get up great bear-hunts, or skalls as they are called, and generally return with several slaughtered bears in their train. The bear is generally surrounded by the hunters, and, by their united efforts, killed. Very full and interesting accounts are given of the manner and customs of the bear by Mr. Lloyd, and of all the methods used in killing them, and other wild beasts.

As the snow lies exceedingly deep, the hunters have invented a kind of wooden skates, called " skidor," for the purpose of enabling them to pass over the surface of the snow without sinking, much on the principle of the snow-shoes used in North America. There is, however, a great difference in their construction, for whereas the snow shoes are wide in the middle, and made of strings stretched over a bow,. like a racket, the skidor are narrow strips of fir, of unequal lengths, that for the left foot being about ten or eleven feet long, and that worn on the right about seven or eight. This difference in length is to enable the wearer to turn with more ease. The width of this wooden skate is between two and three inches. In order to prevent the wearer from slipping back while ascending hills, the bottom of the right skate is often covered with fur, the hairs pointing backwards. The wearer's weight being thus distributed over a large space, he is borne over the surface of the snow, while quadrupeds, who have no such artificial supports, sink into it. In this way men are enabled to pursue and overtake the elks, bears, and wolves. Sometimes a substitute for the skidor is used, something resembling an American snow-shoe, but made of wickerwork. This is very clumsy, and does not enable the wearer to go with such speed as he can attain when mounted on skidor.

Sometimes they put their horses upon snow-shoes, in which condition the animals, although they rather straggle in their gait, yet walk with more ease than if they were sinking deep into the snow at every step. The worst kind of snow for the skidor is that which has just begun to thaw, and which, in consequence, adheres to the skates, instead of suffering them to pass over its surface. The skidor are used in two ways, either in a manner somewhat resembling our method of skating, or by the wearer propelling himself by a stick. Each skida weighs about five or six pounds. The principal disadvantage attending them is, that if they are suddenly driven against an object, they are apt to snap in two, and they are, of course, almost useless in thick woods. In some provinces the skidor are made much shorter and considerably wider, but they are not thought so highly of as the long narrow instruments.

The hybernating properties of the bear are well known. The method employed by the animal in thus obtaining a sound winter's sleep, is given by Topsell in the following passage :—

" There was a certain cowherd in the mountains of Helvetia, which coming down a hill with a great cauldron on his back, he saw a bear eating of a root which he had pulled up with his feet; the cowherd stood still till the bear was gone, and afterward came to the place where the beast had eaten the same, and finding more of the same root, did likewise eat it: he had no sooner tasted thereof, but he had such a desire to sleep, that he could not contain himself, but he must needs lie down in the way and there fell asleep, having covered his head with the cauldron, to keep himself from the vehemency of the cold, and there slept all the winter time without harm, and never rose again till the spring time, which fable, if a man will believe, then doubtless this hearb may cause the bears to be sleepers, not for fourteen days, but for fourscore days together."

In the countries where the bears live, there are

always sundry strange stories prevalent respecting
them, their habits, and their cunning. The Norwe-
gians, indeed, declare that the bear has the strength
of ten men and the sense of twelve. They, therefore, never or seldom speak of it by its name, but by
a paraphrase, terming it "the old man with a fur
cloak." This reminds one of the ingenious Jacobite
toast, "the gentleman in the velvet coat, to whom we
are so much indebted," meaning the mole, who had
raised the hill over which William the Third's horse
fell. One most singular opinion respecting the
Scandinavian bear is given by Mr. Lloyd, whose
account is so excellent, that I must be pardoned for
introducing the entire description, together with his
opinion on the subject:—

"Another singular notion also prevalent in parts of
Scandinavia is, that when the bear has received his
death-wound, he, rather than fall into the hands of
his pursuers, will commit self-destruction. If this
strange idea were confined to the lower orders, it
might hardly deserve even a passing notice, but
there are those of the better classes who entertain the
crotchet." The author here quotes the words of another writer:—

" ' That the bear, when mortally wounded, makes
for the *vand* or lake, and there disappears,' says that
gentleman, 'has long been a general belief among the
common people of Norway. But, so far as I am
aware, no certain evidence of the fact could, for a
long time, be obtained, neither could people explain
how the beast could prevent its dead carcase from
rising, at least for a short time, to the surface,
which never happened, and the mystery, therefore,
could not properly be cleared up. Recently, however,
we have not only had convincing proof that the
popular belief is founded in truth, but the manner in
which the body has been kept under water has been
very satisfactorily explained. The discovery took
place in this wise.

" ' Whilst the *Vada*, or drag-net, was being used in a forest lake, situated between Eidsvold and the neighbouring parish of Uurdal, in the near vicinity of which, from olden times to the present, there have been several places where it has been the custom to shoot bears from the *Gäll* (of which presently); a sunken log was drawn up from the bottom, with the skulls of three, if not four, bears, firmly attached to it, the fangs being deeply imbedded in the wood itself. It is not for a moment to be thought of, that these skulls could have been fastened to the tree by the hands of man, and it is not, therefore, beyond the comprehension of human reason to suppose that the beasts, in their death struggles, had thus attached themselves to the solid body, to prevent falling into the hands of their pursuers ; that none of the other bones were found adhering to the skulls, can be easily explained by the influence that water and other causes might, in the course of very many years, have had on the ligaments.'

" In connection with this subject, and in corroboration of what has been stated, I may further add, that a man now living, and a good bear-hunter, had the misfortune, some years ago, to lose a severely-wounded bear in the above manner in the lake in question. After the beast was fired at, and, as was evident from several circumstances, had received his death-wound, his bloody track was observed to lie across the black morass in the immediate vicinity of the vand, and as there was no return track, the only conclusion that could possibly be come to was, that he had thrown himself into the water.

" The circumstance of three to four bears having attached themselves to this particular log, would seem to have arisen from more than mere accident. It is not improbable, if one is permitted to make a surmise, that the several beasts, having crept for some-time unsuccessfully underneath the water, in order to get hold of a solid body, had all, by a strange coincidence, found their way to the same tree.

" That bears in the agonies of death should evade their assailants in the manner mentioned, is not more remarkable than other peculiarities observable with these animals; and to look at the matter in this point of view, it contains no impossibility. We have, besides, quite certain evidence that other animals are endowed with the same instinct.

" Of the fox we know, that after being dangerously wounded, or about to die from other causes, he always attempts to crawl to his den, or to the water, there to terminate his existence. It is also confidently asserted that the otter, when wounded in the water, immediately dives to the bottom, and never comes up again, whereas, on the contrary, when killed outright, he, at least for a short time, floats on the surface; and the like is the case with some of the duck tribe. Speaking generally, it is, therefore, only reasonable to infer that it lies in the nature of all animals, when about to expire, whether from violence or in the common course of nature, to seek as far as may be, the most retired place, thereby to prevent their bodies from being afterwards discovered : were the case otherwise, they would be met with more frequently than they are, which, in fact, happens very rarely. How often, for instance, has the house sparrow, that has died from natural causes, been found ? Seldom or never ! *

" That a bear, when wounded, will frequently take to the water, and that no track leading therefrom can, at times, be found, is perfectly true; but do people properly examine the opposite shore ?

---

* There are many reasons why the bodies of sparrows should never be found, the principal being that a dead sparrow could hardly escape the observation of sundry birds of prey, or even if it did escape their eyes, it would be inevitably interred within twenty-four hours by the burying beetles.

This, is very much to be doubted. On one occasion I was, myself, puzzled to know what had become of a bear under these circumstances. The case was this. A skall on a considerable scale took place under my guidance, at some distance from Ronnum. The Håll was posted across a narrow strip of land, between two extensive lakes, and as the breadth of the lakes near to the pass in question was not considerable, boats were placed at intervals on the water to prevent the quarry from escaping us by swimming. Owing to unforeseen delays, it was all but dark before the Dref reached the spot where the skall was to terminate, by which time the boat parties fancying the hunt at an end, had, contrary to express orders, retired from their several stations. The consequence was, that on our arrival at the margin of the lake, a badly-wounded bear that had for some time been retreating before us, plunged headlong into the water, and though twelve or fourteen random shots were fired at him in the gloom, he, to our great mortification, effected his escape : though on the following morning I narrowly searched the opposite shore of the lake, which was somewhat rocky and hard, no track was to be found of the lost bear, and had I not afterwards waded along the banks of the lake, and examined the mud at the bottom, where I at length discerned his footsteps, I also might have come to the conclusion that he was still in the water. That death should overtake a wounded bear when he thus plunges into a lake or river and is making for the opposite shore, and that he should afterwards sink to the bottom, is very possible; and it is certainly within the bounds of credence, though not of probability, that when decomposition subsequently takes place, the carcase may be so entangled among roots, &c., at the bottom, that it cannot rise again to the surface; but further than this my credulity certainly does not extend." *

* Mr. Lloyd considers that the story of the sunken log and the skulls is a mere hoax.

Among the various methods used for the destruction of the bears, there is one which is almost humorous in its working. The bears are exceedingly fond of honey, and will climb to great heights to get at a supply of their favourite food. Hives, therefore, are manifestly unsafe, and to protect them from the attacks of the bears many plans are adopted. If the hive is fixed at a considerable height in a tree, the ground under the tree is carefully planted with sharpened stakes, the pointed end being upwards. Just below the hive is placed a stout board as a seat on which the bear can rest, while a heavy log of wood is suspended before the entrance of the hive, but not sufficiently close to annoy the bees. The bear, on sniffing the hives, commences an ascent up the tree, and on reaching the hive finds a capital seat ready for him. So he sits down, and tries to poke his paw into the honeyed stores. The log now comes in his way, and he pushes it away with his paws while he endeavours to peep into the hive; but no sooner has he put his nose near the hive than the log returns and hits him on the head. Being naturally exasperated at such treatment, he strikes away the log with his paws, and of course experiences a severer blow than before. Being now thoroughly angry, he engages in a regular fight with the log, which always strikes him on the head, until at last it knocks him fairly off his perch, and throws him on the stakes below, where he remains impaled.

There is one bear which passes its existence in a semi-aquatic manner, living either in the water, on ice, or among snow. This is the white Polar Bear,* whose habitation is found among the eternal frosts of the North Pole. It is a large and powerful animal, although not quite so large or so powerful as represented by some of the earlier Arctic voyagers, one of whom tells us that he and his comrades killed a bear whose skin was twenty-three feet in length; and another relates that the bears frequently carried off

* *Thalarctos maritimus.*

seamen and devoured them within sight of their friends, who were unable to prevent their capture, or to release them afterwards. Yet it is a dangerous opponent, and does not yield its life without a severe struggle.

This bear is almost an historical animal, as Nelson had once nearly lost his life in an attempt to kill a polar bear with an unloaded musket, foolishly imagining that he could knock down the animal with the gunstock. Indeed, had it not been for a wide rift in the ice, England would in all probability have unwittingly lost one of her greatest heroes. Who could have thought at the time that such weighty consequences lay in a blow of a musket, and a stroke from a bear's paw?

The colour of the polar bear is a yellowish white; the fur being short and fine over the back, but lengthening considerably towards the under parts of the body. The feet are particularly bushy, and are also furnished with a plentiful supply of fur on the under surfaces, in order to give the animal a firmer hold on the ice.

The swimming powers of this animal are very great, and, indeed, are required in its chase of fish and seals. The latter animal is, however, so good a swimmer itself, that the bear does not care to chase it in the water, but generally contrives to surprise it when asleep on a piece of ice. When chasing a seal in this way, the bear approaches very stealthily, making long dives, and so manages that at his last dive he comes up directly under the unfortunate seal, who either tumbles into the water in a fright, and is instantly snapped up, or is chased on the ice, where the bear has the advantage in point of speed, and is sure to catch him. But the great banquet of the bear is upon a dead whale, on which, in company with sharks, sea-birds, &c., he feeds, until the carcase is so stripped that the weight of the bones sinks it, and the sharks have it all to themselves.

But the prey which gives the most trouble is the walrus. This enormous seal is often attacked by the bears, but fights with such fury, that it not unfrequently comes off victorious in the struggle. Many a walrus has been killed, bearing on its body scars, the results of battles with the polar bears.* In the absence of large prey, such as whales and seals, the white bear does not disdain fish, sea birds and their eggs, and with an accommodating appetite often feeds on roots and berries.

The tenacity of life in this animal is by no means small, as will be seen from the following account of a bear hunt, taken from Mr. Hooper's interesting work, the " Tents of the Tuski."

" The brute was discovered on a large mass of ice, which with others had grounded at some distance from the beach; one party started in the ' logan ' to cut off his retreat by sea, another, which I joined, made for the summit of the bank which we hoped he would endeavour to ascend. First blood was drawn by our party; a ball from my fowling-piece struck him in the shoulder, and he fell for an instant on the ice and began to suck his paw, which made us think it was there that he had been wounded; speedily rising he ran on along the hummock, taking to the water and climbing the sides of the masses of ice with the utmost indifference and ease. Our hunters (Indians are always excellent marksmen) now paid him some attention; they hit him several times, but did not succeed in turning him; he attempted at last to swim to seaward, and would doubtless have succeeded but for a new opponent. One of the Esquimaux followed the bear, and at close proximity discharged arrow after arrow into his body. This was the most exciting part of the hunt. Each

---

* These scars may possibly be caused by battles between themselves. At certain times in the year, the seal tribes become very pugnacious, and fight with great fury, often inflicting deep and dangerous wounds.

time that an arrow pierced its body the poor animal
seized the missile, if within reach, with its teeth, and
strove to wrench it from the wound, generally, however, breaking it short; then would it turn fiercely on
its persecutor, who, skilfully manœuvring his light
boat, hung at two or three yards distance only in its
rear; so close were they, indeed, that the man deliberately splashed water with his double-bladed paddle
in poor Bruin's face, just backing gently to be clear
of his paws, a single stroke from which would quite
have reversed the fortune of the combat; when, after
a hunt which lasted about four hours, the animal
received its final death stroke by a ball through its
brain; he was stuck all over with arrows, and
looked like a barbacued pig. By the laws of savage
venery first blood always decides the captor, and
the Esquimaux readily recognised the rule in the
present instance. Of course the carcase was divided,
but I stipulated for and obtained the skin, which I
still possess as a trophy. An hour afterwards I ate a
bear steak. The Esquimaux, who had so importantly
contributed to the capture, was rewarded with a large
broad dagger, a very awkward weapon in his hands,
and some other trifling presents, and was delighted
with his good fortune."

The appearance of this poor bear, bristling like the
porcupine with darts, calls to our recollection the
tiger mentioned in a former page, who although
stuck all over with arrows, and having suffered
several arrows to pass completely through his body
without much diminution of his strength or ferocity,
yet sunk lifeless to the ground from the first shot
of a musket.

It is not one of the least wonderful effects of human
reason, that men armed with weapons so insignificant
as those borne by the Esquimaux, and labouring under
such difficulties for want of materials, should dare to
attack, in their own element, animals so powerful as

the whale, or so ferocious as the polar bear, and succeed in destroying both.

There is, however, a still more singular example,
of the ascendancy which man attains over brutes by
the mere power of his mind.

The Esquimaux have a most ingenious plan for the
destruction of this bear without the risk of engaging
in personal combat with so dangerous an enemy.
They take a stout piece of whalebone about two feet
in length, bend it double, and push the two ends into
a piece of blubber. The whalebone thus prepared is
placed in the open air, when the cold immediately
freezes the blubber, and holds the ends of the whalebone fast. The weapon is now complete. Armed
with this singular instrument the Esquimaux sally out
in search of a bear, and on finding one, provoke it to
chase them, a matter of no great difficulty, as " Nen-
nook" generally labours under an infirmity of temper,
and needs but little irritation. So the bear sets off after
the Esquimaux, and the Esquimaux runs away from
the bear as fast as they can, until the animal is in right
earnest. At last the bear gains on them, and is permitted
to come tolerably close, when the fugitives throw the
prepared whalebone at it. The bear sniffs at it, and
finding it to be eatable, swallows it and resumes the
chase. Before very long, however, the heat of its
interior thaws the blubber, and the whalebone being
thus set free, springs open and interferes so materially
with the digestion of the unfortunate animal that it
gives up the chase, and soon dies from the injuries
inflicted.

The history of this singular internal trap seems to
partake in some measure of the devices invented by
Baron Munchausen of miraculous memory, but it is
nevertheless perfectly true.

BADGER.

WITH the exception of the true bears, whose history has just been related, the Badgers are much less carnivorous than the other plantigrade animals. Indeed, in their food, they exhibit a strong resemblance of taste to that of the bears, for they, as well as those animals, feed either on flesh of various kinds, or on vegetable food, such as roots, nuts, and other fruits, and also display a great predilection for honey, which they will devour, regardless of the stings of the bees, whose weapons are useless when opposed to the rough fur and thick hide of their assailants. Even the pugnacious wasps are baffled by the passive resistance offered by the badger's clothing, and see their nests scratched out of the ground, and their young devoured without the power of preventing such devastations.

Like almost all wild animals, the badgers feed much on insects, and also vary their repasts by snails and earthworms; but if they can find the nest of a laying bird, the eggs form a delicious treat, and their contentment is perfect if, at the same time, they can catch the mother, and eat her as well as her eggs.

In days happily gone by, numbers of badgers were captured for the express purpose of being worried by dogs, who were thought to possess great courage, if they could be induced to attack a badger, and drag him out of a barrel in which he had been placed. But this was humanity compared to the method employed to train dogs to this sport, and which, although probably employed by Dandie Dinmont himself with all his varieties of the " Mustard " and " Pepper " breed, was of so cruel a nature, that those who engaged in the sport would have had but their deserts if they had been soundly flogged by a particularly powerful party of drummers, and then pickled afterwards. The poor badger, who was destined to instruct the young dog in the art of badger hunting, was placed in a barrel as usual, his teeth drawn, and half his under-jaw sawn off. In this maimed state the poor animal could of course make but little resistance, and the dog was therefore encouraged by impunity to attack other badgers with their full complement of teeth and jaw.

Dogs are not to be blamed for their unwillingness to encounter this animal in open combat, as its bites are rapid, the strength of its jaws great, and, moreover, the jawbone is so jointed to the skull, that when the animal has closed its mouth, its jaw locks itself into a cavity of the skull, and retains its hold without any exertion on the part of the animal. The great strength of their jaws may be ascertained by a glance at the skull, along the upper frontal surface of which runs a heavy ridge of bone, serving as an attachment for the muscles which move the jaw. Even when the dogs have fastened their teeth in the animal, it cares but little for them, as it is effectually protected by its thick fur and tough hide.

The badger is a fossorial animal, residing in holes, and, like all digging animals, is amazingly strong about the fore-quarters, in proportion to its size. An American badger, which had nearly succeeded in burying its head and shoulders in a hole, resisted the efforts of two powerful men to drag it out of its cave until it had received the contents of a fowling-piece in its body. It is also said to rise up on its hind legs like a bear, and threaten its opponent with its forefeet like that animal.

All these things being considered, it will be seen that it is no easy matter for a dog to pull a badger even out of a cask, but when the dog comes to hunt the badger in the field it is a still harder task. If there is time, the badger makes off for his hole, and if not, he rapidly makes a new one, for he can dive through the earth almost as quickly as a mole. So the dog has a hard job to dig him out again, especially as the badger constantly fills up the passage behind him, by throwing the earth into it, and while the dog is occupied in forcing his way through this new impediment, rises to the surface of the earth and escapes unperceived. But even should the dog drive the badger to bay, the matter is not much mended, for the terrible bites of the badger are tolerably sure to gain the victory, and send the dog yelping away.

The regular house of the badger is a very ingenious domicile, consisting of a suite of chambers, the last of which is round, and well lined with hay. There are also storehouses, where provisions in the shape of round balls of grass are kept, and sinks where all remnants and other offensive substances are deposited.

Although provided with such excellent means of attack as well as defence, the badger is a perfectly harmless creature, and never wittingly attacks any animal (except those on which it feeds), always retreating to its den on the slightest alarm. Mr. St. John was once a witness to a family party of badgers, whose proceedings I will give in his own words.

" I was just then startled from my reverie by a kind of grunt close to me, and the apparition of a small, waddling, grey animal, who was busily employed in hunting about the grass and stones at the edge of the lock; presently another and another appeared in a little grassy glade, which ran down to the water's edge, until at last I saw seven of them busily at work within a few yards of me, all coming from one direction. It at first struck me that they were some farmer's pigs taking a distant ramble; but I shortly saw they were badgers, come from their fastnesses rather earlier than usual, tempted by the evening, and by a heavy summer shower which was just over, and which had brought out an infinity of large black snails and worms, on which the badgers were feeding with good appetite. As I was dressed in grey, and sitting on a grey rock, they did not see me, but waddled about, sometimes close to me, only now and then, as they crossed my track, they showed a slight uneasiness, smelling the ground, and grunting quietly. Presently, a very large one, which I took to be the mother of the rest, stood motionless for a moment, listening with great attention, and then, giving a loud grunt, which seemed perfectly understood by the others, she scuttled away, followed by the whole lot."

Their dispersion was caused by the approach of a servant, whose distant footsteps had been heard by the watchful ears of the badger long before they had been perceived by the duller organs of hearing of the spectator.

The same writer gives us many interesting particulars of the habits of the badger, exonerating it from the serious charges brought against it, whereby a " brock " was always thought to be a kind of land shark, that might be tormented in any way without laying the tormentor open to the charge of unnecessary cruelty, and led such a persecuted life, that to " badger " a man came to be the strongest possible term for irritating, persecuting, and injuring him in every way.

The powerful and disagreeable scent of this animal is, probably, another reason for the dislike with which it is viewed by many. Like many of its congeners, the badger is furnished with a pouch on the lower part of the abdomen, in which is secreted a powerfully-smelling substance. This, although it is of an agreeable nature in such animals as the civet-cat, and is used as a perfume, is so very unpleasant in the badger, that its ill scent has become proverbial. We in England and Scotland, in which latter country it is more commonly found, utterly despise the animal, and would as soon think of eating a centipede as a badger; but in other countries people are more sensible, and eat it with great satisfaction, especially when dressed like hams.

Indeed, it is most singular, that the poor in England will actually starve, while there is round them plenty of good food, which their prejudiced notions consider poisonous. A poor family may see their hovels overrun with mice, but would never dream of eating them, even were they half-starved, and reduced to beggary. Yet mice are remarkably good, as I can testify from actual experience, and not to be distinguished from larks. Frogs, ditto; *i. e* the legs only, omitting the remainder of the body. Why, a capital dinner of frogs and mice, and such small deer, might often be made, at the expense of an hour's search in any field.

Poor people eat oysters, which, on the authority of a well-known writer, always accompany poverty, and yet they will not touch snails, merely on account of early prejudice. The Romans of old knew better, and fed up their snails till they were so big, that one snail was a good supper for one man. There is still a colony of these gigantic snails now living near Oxford, the descendants of a stock introduced by the Romans, when they encamped there and built a snail-fold, just as we should make a sheepfold. Now, I should not like to eat a snail myself, and I dare say my reader would not; but I would venture to say, that a cook might substitute the one mollusc for the other in the dish of scalloped oysters that looks so tempting on the table, without the change being discovered by any one.

Then there are hedgehogs, animals that can be found in plenty in the fields—capital eating, if people only knew it. There are myriads of tiny fish in every brook, which can be scooped out of the water by the bare hand, and which, although individually small, collectively form a dish not to be despised. Indeed, they are but little inferior to whitebait, for which fish, I have reason to suppose, they are often substituted.

In many rivers and brooks there are plenty of lamperns, a kind of very small lamprey, rather larger

than the stem of a clay tobacco-pipe. They are particularly good, and yet no one eats them. Only one
person have I ever heard of who did so, and he was
rather an eccentric old man, who cared not a jot for
the opinion of his friends, but went his own way, and
was generally right. He used to give boys a half-
penny for as many lamperns as would fill a " wisket,"
a basket peculiar to the north of England, somewhat
resembling a very small, very shallow coracle, and
made of broad withs; generally used in collecting
stones off the field, or such-like work. The boys
were only too happy to find such an opportunity of
getting wet through and hunting lamperns, and the
old man made many a savoury dinner for a farthing.
Lamperns are excellent food, closely resembling eels
both in shape and taste, especially when dressed with
their skins.

Then the vegetable productions are innumerable.
The nettles, for example, make an excellent dish
when boiled like greens. They ought either to be
very young, or only the tops should be taken. There
are pignuts to be dug out of the ground; and roots
of the common cuckoo-pint, or lords and ladies, as
it is generally called, abound everywhere, and when
properly dressed, afford a kind of light flour, something resembling arrowroot in its properties Indeed,
in some parts of England, the root is greatly sought
after for that purpose. The common puff ball, or
frog's cheese, is not to be despised, and when dressed
properly, is said to resemble a sweetbread.

So there are plenty of resources, if people would
only take advantage of them, and get the better of
their prejudices.

But to return to our badger. Although its mental
powers are despised, it is by no means a stupid
animal, although it may appear so to be at a casual
glance. One found by Mr. St. John in a trap, suffered
him to release it, and to tie a rope to its hind-leg, by
which he drove it home, as a countryman drives a

pig. This appears very foolish conduct on the part of the badger, but it was not so in reality. Knowing the fossorial properties of the animal, its captor took the precaution of putting it into a paved court, but, when morning came, the badger was gone, having succeeded in displacing a large stone, and then digging a passage under the wall.

Another badger, mentioned by the same author, had gained some experience from age, and could not be caught, as it had a peculiar talent of getting out the baits and springing all the traps without injury to itself. Once it was watched out of its camp of refuge, and traps were placed in all directions round it, but it contrived to regain its hole in safety by jumping over some of the traps, and rolling over others.

The badger is a nocturnal animal, being very seldom seen during the day—a fact which will account for the scarcity of its appearance. It is rather interesting as an inhabitant of this country, as it is the only animal that we have which is allied to the bears, who, in former times, used to inhabit our island in great numbers.

From its very unpleasant odour, it does not appear to be an agreeable animal as a pet. It can, however, be easily tamed if taken young, and displays considerable affection for its master. Probably, when the animal is domesticated, it does not give out the disagreeable scent; for even the skunk can be kept in a house, and is as sweet an animal as a cat. The same may be said of the snake, which has the power of putting forth a most unpleasant odour, if alarmed or roughly handled; but if tamed, will permit all kinds of liberties to be taken without resenting them. I have had a tame snake for many months. The reptile was constantly getting out of its box, and wandering about the room, and when recaptured never displayed any anger. Several of my pupils were accustomed to carry snakes about with them in

R

their pockets, and to give them an airing on the Downs, or a bath in a pond, and yet, after the first few days, never experienced any inconvenience from the neighbourhood of their pets.

MOLE.*

WE now come to a group of animals, widely differing from any of their predecessors both in shape and size. These are the insectivorous animals, the moles, the shrews, and the hedgehog, all included in the family *Talpidæ*.

With the common mole all are tolerably familiar, but generally through the medium of a print (none of which have yet properly represented the animal), by the sight of the numerous " molehills " scattered over the fields, or by seeing the moles themselves suspended on the twigs of a tree, where the molecatcher has hung them after he has received his reward for their capture. Why he should hang them on trees, I never could make out, nor could any one inform me. I did once ask an experienced molecatcher, who replied that he " hallers did," but could give no reason for the custom. They cannot be suspended " in terrorem," as moles working under the earth would not be able to see their companions hanging in the trees, even had they the best eyes in the world, instead of being practically blind; whether theoretically or not is yet an open question. Be this as it may, the coleopterist is deeply indebted to the molecatcher, for out of the suspended moles, he often procures rare and beautiful species of beetles.

No one can examine even the external structure of the mole without admiration of the manner in which it is fitted for its subterraneous life; its silky hair, set perpendicularly on its skin, offering no resistance to

* *Talpa Europæa.*

the sides of its galleries, and being incapable of retaining soil that might arrest its progress; its broad shovel-like claws, slightly turned outwards like the mould-board of a plough; its pointed and flexible snout; its little sharp teeth, so well adapted for seizing and securing the worms on which it feeds; its imperceptible eyes, hidden in the depth of its fur;—all these properties are evidently so suitable to the habits of the animal, that we cannot avoid admiring them.

But when we come to remove the skin of the animal, and then to examine its muscular and osteological characteristics, we are even more struck with surprise. The first circumstance that engages our attention on removing the skin of the mole, is the manner in which the whole power of the body is thrown into the fore-quarters, while from the loins backwards, the animal is rather weaker than might be apprehended from its size. The muscles on the shoulders and neck are exceedingly strong, and quite glisten from the tendinous substance surrounding them. The muscles of the fore-legs are perfectly marvellous. They form a mass nearly as large as a man's finger, and are quite hard to the touch, not yielding in the least, but rolling about between the fingers like a hazel-nut.

When we proceed further, and, by removing these muscles, lay the skeleton bare, we again see a most marvellous structure. The shoulder-blade is narrow, thick, and of immense length in proportion to the animal. Indeed, that of the giraffe is proportionably small, when its skeleton is contrasted with that of the mole. This shape gives the muscles a most powerful leverage upon the bones of the leg themselves. These are very short, very much bowed, very thick, and very broad at the joints, which are knit together in the most powerful manner. The joints of the foot or hand are short, and very much flattened, except the last joints, which are nearly as long as the rest of the hand, and bear the long grooved claws. So short are

the leg bones, that the foot scarcely protrudes beyond
the general line of the body, a property required by
the habits of the mole, who would otherwise be
unable to work with the celerity that is required in its
chase of worms, and in escaping from its enemies.

The skin of the animal is very thick and tough,
requiring several cuts from a sharp knife to sever it
properly. There is now lying before me a mole,
whose skin is so tough and thick, that an incision
made into its substance looks as if a deep wound had
been made in its muscular structure. The rustics
often take advantage of this strength of skin, and
make purses from mole-skins, by the simple process
of cutting the animal in half, and stripping the skin
from the hinder parts. The skin, which is turned
inside out by this process, is then well rubbed with
pepper and other substances until dry, when a string
is run round it, and it is pronounced ready for use.
The skin adheres to the body much more strongly
than is found to be the case in most animals.

The colour of the mole is generally a very deep
brownish black, but there are many examples of other
colours. In the British Museum are specimens of
black, brown, grey, and white moles, all taken from
Cobham, in Surrey. I have now before me a white,
or rather cream-coloured, moleskin, taken, I believe,
in Wiltshire.

The character of the mole is of a nature hardly
warranted by its external appearance. Any one, on
seeing the mole, would proclaim it to be a sluggish,
cold-blooded, miserable creature, passing its life in
the earth, without passions to be excited, or objects
to excite them. Yet it is an animal possessed of
fierce passions, easily roused to anger, and when
roused, most vindictive and persevering in its attacks.

Whenever a mole happens to stray into the hunting
grounds of another, it is instantly attacked by the
proprietor if he is within reach, and either one is put
to flight, or a furious battle ensues, and the weaker is

generally slain. Nor does this little animal fear to attack even larger foes, for a boy who had incautiously seized a mole was bitten in the finger, to which the mole held with the tenacity of a bull-dog, and could not be shaken off until it had been, in its turn, seized by the teeth of its captor.

In connection with this ferocity of disposition, an account is given by Geoffroy of the manner in which this animal is said to attack small birds. The mole is described as creeping up slowly, and using every stratagem to get within reach. It then rapidly changes its method of attack, and springing suddenly on the hapless bird, tears it open, and thrusting its muzzle among the intestines, riots in its sanguinary repast. This anecdote, however, so strongly contradicts the evident blindness of the mole, that it may well be left open to doubt. For, although the animal is enabled, by a peculiar apparatus, to bring the eye forward, so as partially to free it from the mass of fur that serves to protect it, yet when it is thus withdrawn, the vision is evidently so imperfect, that it would hardly serve to conduct the mole through a process so delicate as that of surprising a creature, active and wary as a bird always is, and who could withdraw itself from danger with one stroke of its wings.

The food of the mole consists almost entirely of the earthworm, although it may sometimes vary its repast, by eating the grubs of various insects that pass their larval state under the earth. Worms, however, are its principal food, and it is in search of them that it drives those galleries under the earth, whose presence is indicated, sometimes by a slight ridge, showing the course of the gallery, and sometimes by the little mounds with which we are all familiar. The worms, on hearing or feeling the agitation of the earth caused by the mole, make their way to the surface in order to escape their enemy. Taking advantage of this habit, certain birds stamp upon the

ground to delude the worms into the idea that a mole
is coming.   The worms immediately make for the
surface, and are picked up by the crafty bird.   In the
same way, if anglers are in want of worms, they
either stamp on the ground, or work the earth about
with a spade, and capture the worms as they come
out of their holes.

The exertion required for the mole to force its
way through the earth is, of course, considerable, and
as the animal works with the same energy that
characterises all its movements, it requires propor-
tionate rest.   The molecatcher and field labourer tell
us that the mole works and rests at regular intervals
of three hours each.   In burrowing, the snout seems
to be used to pierce the ground first, and the feet are
then used to enlarge the aperture.   Such was the
plan adopted by a mole in my possession, whose
residence was a tub half full of earth.   In the comparatively loose earth of the tub, it buried itself with
such rapidity, that it was hardly possible to see the
method employed, but when it was taken out of the
tub, and suffered to run on a hard gravel path, it
used to run along at a considerable pace, rooting in
the gravel with its snout, evidently seeking for a softer
place.   Such experiments were rather hazardous, as
sometimes it *did* find a softer place, and half buried
itself before we could catch it.   Whenever it succeeded
in so doing, it was no easy matter to pull it out of
the ground again, as it held so firmly with its forefeet, that we feared lest we should pull it asunder, in
our efforts to recapture it.   At last it succeeded in
escaping, for it pulled so hard, that it resisted all
attempts to prevent its escape, and buried itself in
the garden, much to the discomfiture of the gardener,
who prophesied all kinds of evils to happen in consequence.   As, however, it never made its appearance
again, I suppose that it must have burrowed under
the walls of the garden, and made its escape into the

fields beyond. This mole was fed with worms which were put into the tub, and were almost immediately caught and devoured.

The voracity of the animal is astonishing, and, unlike many voracious animals, it cannot bear to abstain from food for any length of time. Indeed, a fast of only six hours is said to be fatal. It also requires a constant supply of water, and if its runs are not near a river or pond, it digs a number of wells, in which water is sure to be found, some of them being filled to the brim. But as animals never labour without necessity, the mole generally contrives to run a gallery to some piece of water, and is not often found in very dry places.

The mole is a good swimmer, for which exercise the peculiar shape of its fore-paws is admirably adapted. Taking advantage of its proficiency, it does not hesitate to cross a river of considerable width in order to obtain a wider scope for its chase, and has been known to rescue its young when their nest has been inundated by a sudden flood.

The traps employed to catch the mole are of various kinds. Some are box traps, that catch the creature alive. This is rather a cruel plan, as, if several moles are caught together, they are apt to fight, and their contests are so sanguinary, that all the combatants are sure to be wounded, and some of them actually killed. Another trap is made of a steel fork, something like a pair of sugar-tongs, but with the blades crossing each other. The blades are kept separate by a piece of iron, and the trap placed in a " run " where the mole is likely to make its appearance. The mole, in its progress, thrusts away the iron trigger, and the blades immediately spring together, enclosing the mole in their fatal embrace. It seems rather strange that the animal should be killed by means apparently so inadequate, but it must be borne in mind that the mole is killed very easily indeed, particularly by pressure. The common mole-trap is, perhaps, as simple and efficacious as any. It consists of a small flat piece of wood about five inches long, and two inches broad. At each end is inserted a bent willow twig, so as to make two arches, under which the mole must go. The interior of these twigs is hollowed, and within the hollow is hidden a loop of whipcord, passing through the board, and fastened to the end of a supple willow or ash stick. The trap is now buried in the run of a mole, the arches being downwards, and the thick end of the ash stick planted in the ground close by. The stick is now bent, the string being so fastened down, that it is only withheld by a wooden catch from springing up, and the trap is set. When the mole comes by, it disturbs the catch, and is immediately caught by the whipcord, and squeezed against the wooden trap until dead. Mostly the stick is so strong, that it breaks the whole affair, trap, mole and all out of the ground, and leaves them dangling at the end of the string.

Armed with that trap which he approves most, the practised molecatcher will take an incredible number of moles in one season. A Cornish molecatcher took twelve hundred in six winter months, while Le Court, to whom we owe most of our knowledge of this animal, took six thousand in five months. Only experienced hunters can be so successful, as a minute acquaintance with the habits of the animal is required, as well as a general knowledge of the situation of their runs. These are so complicated, that a somewhat detailed description will be necessary.

The habitation of the mole is made in a heap of earth raised by the inhabitant itself. This is not, however, one of the numerous molehills so profusely scattered about the fields, but a very much larger heap raised for the purpose of containing the nest, and generally carefully hidden where it will not readily draw attention. It is usually raised at the foot of a tree, in the centre of a thick bush, or in some place where it is well defended. Here is the mole's dwelling-house, its castle, from whence all its forces are directed, and to which it retreats if threatened with any danger. It has the thorough robber's horror for a house with only one way of escape, and accordingly constructs its habitation in so ingenious a manner that it can escape in almost any direction.

The first operation in constructing a nest is to heap up a mound of earth, very compactly beaten together, as in the mound a variety of passages have to be made, and the earth must, therefore, be very compact, to prevent the soil from falling in. Proceedings having been thus commenced, the four-footed excavator runs a circular gallery near the summit of the mound, and another near the bottom. These galleries are then connected by five short passages. It then works its way into the very centre of the mound, and digs a spherical hole, which it connects with the lower gallery by three passages. A very large passage, called the mole's high road, is then dug outside the nest, and is connected with the spherical hole by a gallery dipping under the circular galleries, and entering the lower part of the spherical hole. Lastly, the mole drives a great number of runs radiating from the nest in all directions, and all opening into the lower circular gallery. It will be seen from this description that if a mole is surprised in its nest, it can either dive through its central chamber and so reach the high road at once, or it can slip through either of the short galleries, and so escape into any of the numerous radiating runs.

In the central spherical chamber the mole places a quantity of grass or leaves, and uses this as its bed-chamber, in which it passes hours of deep repose, so that after it has finished its work in quarrying, it betakes itself to the middle chamber, and there receives its wages in the form of sleep. This complicated house is not used in the summer months, as during that time the mole commonly resides in one of the ordinary molehills.

Mention has been made of the "high road." This is so important a portion of the habitation, that it cannot be passed over without further mention. By the high road the mole travels to the various portions of its hunting grounds, and into the high road all the smaller runs open. It is much larger than either of the other galleries, and is made very hard and smooth in the interior, by the constant friction of the mole's body. The method of construction differs from that of the other galleries. They are made by excavation, the earth being thrown up every now and then, and forming the well-known molehills, but the high road is made principally by the pressure of the mole's body, just as a stake makes a hole if driven into the earth. Indeed, the two kinds of galleries may be compared to two kinds of mines made by engineers in besieging a city, the one being made by digging out the earth, and the other by exploding small quantities of gunpowder so as to force the earth away on every side. The great size of the passage is partly to be accounted for by the constant passage of the mole to and from its fortification.

The passage, although large for a single mole, is not sufficiently large to accommodate two, so that if two moles do happen to meet, the weaker always retreats into one of the side passages that open into the high road, and permits the other to pass. This is not an unfrequent occurrence, for although two moles do not use the same hunting grounds, yet several often make use of the same high road.

During the warmer months of the year the labours of this curious animal are comparatively light, as the earthworms lie mostly near the surface, but when the cold winter months have frozen the surface of the earth and driven the worms far below, then its work really becomes laborious. In order to get at the haunts of worms, the mole is forced to commence its labours by sinking a perpendicular well until it arrives at the yet unfrozen soil. When there, it has to work quite as continuously as in the summer months, for from' the nature of its food it cannot lay up provisions for the winter, and its constitution is of such a nature that a very short fast proves fatal. So work it must, if it desires to live at all, and it does work, although the ground is naturally much more hard and unmanageable than the upper portions. The lightest labour of the mole is in the summer months after a moderate shower. The worms are then all at the surface of the ground, and the mole pursues them by digging a shallow trench, not even deep enough to bury its own body. But this work is principally confined to the females.

The speed of a mole even on the surface is far from inconsiderable, but when the animal is placed in its own high road, it can run with speed equal, as Le Court says, to that of a horse at full trot. He tried the experiment in a very ingenious way. Having discovered that the mole was busy at one extremity of the high road, he fixed a number of straws in the earth, the ends of which penetrated into the passage, while to their tops were slightly fastened small paper flags. He then went to the place where the mole was at work, and by a discordant blast of a horn introduced into the passage, he caused the mole to set off at full speed towards its fortress. In so doing the paper flags were thrown off in succession, as the mole in its course struck against the ends of the straw that penetrated the passage, and from the time taken in passing along the gallery, Le Court calculated the speed of the animal.

The habitation thus described belongs to the mole himself, while his wife lives in a distinct edifice, generally situated at some distance from the fortress, and constructed at the point where two or more runs intersect each other. The earth being thrown out forms a hill much larger than the ordinary mounds, and nearly equalling that in which the fortress is constructed. The bed is formed of a mass of herbage of various kinds, generally roots and dried grass, although, on one occasion, upwards of two hundred blades of green wheat were found to have formed the bed. In this chamber, the mother mole generally bears from three to six young, which remain with their parent until they are nearly half grown.

These domiciles are inhabited by the moles from the autumn until the spring, at which time they are deserted, the mole living in one of the ordinary mounds, while a field mouse generally takes possession of the vacant habitation.

Opinions appear to vary respecting the good or harm done by the mole. It certainly does some good, by establishing a system of subsoil drainage, such as no farmer could carry out, and considerably lightens the soil, by the earth thrown to the surface. The agriculturists, on the other hand, object that the crops are injured by the mole coming in contact with the roots, or that they are actually dug up by the shallow furrows which have been before mentioned. The soil also, they say, is rendered too dry, and the moles not unfrequently devour, together with the worms, the roots of corn and grass among which they have entangled themselves. At all events, such roots have been found in their stomachs, and it is difficult to account for their presence in any other way. The farmers, too, are very angry with the mole, because its deserted habitation forms a place of refuge for the field mouse. As it is always easier to accuse than to defend, the accusers gain the day, and multitudes of moles are annually slain, whether to any good purpose or not, it is difficult to say. except, perhaps, that an industrious man can thereby obtain a tolerable subsistence without much outlay of capital; a spud, a few dozen willow or ash sticks, and some string, being all the stock in trade required.

In some parts of England, people talk of a " water-mole," but according to Mr. Jenyns, this animal is nothing but a black variety of the common water-rat.

The mole goes by various names in different parts of England, the principal being the " want," a name probably corrupted from the Danish " wand." In Scotland it is called, " moudie-warp," which name is derived from the Anglo-Saxon words, " molde," mould, or soil, and " weorpan," to turn up. From the first part of the word we get our word "mole."

HEDGEHOG.*

WERE we to say that the fur of the mole is as soft as velvet, we should be decrying the beautiful softness of the fur—we should rather say that velvet is as soft as a mole's fur. Widely different, however, is the covering of the animal that stands next to the mole in the zoological series. In the hedgehog, the fur is supplanted by innumerable sharp spines, acutely pointed at their extremities, swelling in the middle, and decreasing in size towards the skin. The method in which these spines are fastened into the skin is very remarkable. The end that stands outwards is very sharp, but the other is terminated by a round knob, and the spine is, apparently, thrust through the skin, until it is stopped by the knob, by which it is held much in the same way that a pin would be held if thrust through a piece of leather. By the way, we can form an excellent method of comprehending the setting of the spines through the medium of a piece of leather and a few pins.

Take a piece of tolerably stout leather, and push a dozen pins through it, up to the very head. Now bend all the pins so that their points will form an angle of about 45° with the leather. That is the way in which the spines are fixed in the skin, but if we wish to see how the hedgehog is enabled to raise these spines, we must do something more. Take a piece of linen, and lay it against the inner side of

* *Erinaceus Europæus.*

the leather, fastening all the heads of the pins to it.
Now, if you draw the linen towards the direction in
which the points of the pins lie, you will find that
all the pins will stand upright, the pins forming
levers, of which the skin is the fulcrum. The linen
will represent that extraordinary muscle which lies
under the skin of most animals, and is developed to
such an extent in the hedgehog.

By means of this muscle, the hedgehog is enabled
to maintain its position when it has curled itself into
a ball. The muscle is not so very powerful on the
back, but is enormously large along the sides. When,
therefore, the hedgehog fears an enemy, it tucks its
head under its breast, at the same time drawing its
legs within the scope of this muscle, which, by
its contraction, forms a complete rope round the
body, binding it together with such force that the
animal cannot be opened without rending asunder
this muscle. However, there are no animals who
would attempt such a feat, for at the same time that
the animal curls round, the contraction of the muscle
draws all the spines upright, and offers a chevaux-de-
frise which few wish to encounter.

Hedgehogs are considered very good provender,
mostly, however, by those roving tribes who wander
from town to town all their lives, and, having a whole-
some horror of streets where policemen live, encamp
in the open air. The scientific method of preparing
this dainty is, after knocking the animal on the head,
to look out for some good clay. The hedgehog is
then placed on a fire, where it is rolled about until
all the bristles are singed off. It is then well rubbed
to clear away the ashes, and then, being wrapped up
in the clay, the whole mass is placed on the fire, and
kept carefully covered with the ashes. After a time,
the clay cracks, and the hedgehog is pronounced to
be properly cooked. The clay is then broken, and
the hedgehog extracted, having been baked in a
manner not to be equalled by any oven. It is not

necessary to clean the animal before putting it on the fire, as when it is opened the whole of the inside falls out in a hard mass.

But there are other animals besides man who fully appreciate the value of the hedgehog, but who, not being possessed of reason, are not so well able to gratify their wishes. For the array of spines forms a barricade which none, except a very well-trained dog, or a very hungry fox, will take the trouble to oppose. The dog attacks it boldly, and after a struggle, during which he is wounded in numerous places by the sharp spines, succeeds in tearing it to pieces. The fox, however, is said to employ stratagem, and to roll the poor creature into a pool of water, if one be near, and when it puts out its head, to snap it up in an instant.

This bristly armour exists only on the upper surface of the body, all the under parts being clothed with long thick fur. Indeed, if the lower surface were covered with prickles, the poor creature would not feel particularly comfortable when rolled up. Many of my readers will remember that admirable simile of an envious man, who lived

> " . . . . Like a hedgehog rolled up the wrong way,
> Tormenting himself with his bristles."

These bristles, sometimes, are made to serve a rather unexpected use. Mr. Bell has recorded a feat of a tame hedgehog in his own possession. The little animal was in the habit of fearlessly throwing itself off a wall, of nearly fourteen feet in height, trusting to the elasticity of its spines to save it from injury. It made no stop or hesitation, but threw itself over at once, contracting into a ball as it fell, and after it reached the ground, it would lie quiet for a few moments, and then unfold itself, and run off.

The hedgehog has been accused of being a thief in many matters, especially in the matter of milk and apples. The one it was said to suck from the cows, and the other to steal by rolling over them until its spines were covered, and then running away home with a load of apples on its back. Some said, that it got up the tree first and knocked the apples down, and others affirmed that it carried off eggs also by rolling upon them and fixing them on its back. As to the first of these attacks it is almost too absurd to need refutation, as the mouth of the creature is too small for any such operation, and even if that were not the case, its spines would cause the cow to keep it away. There may, however, be some ground for the farmers' complaint, as I have seen ordinary pigs suck the cows while they were lying on the ground, and the farmers may probably have supposed that hedge pigs and bacon pigs were much the same kind of animal. As to the second accusation, it is almost as unfounded as the first. Not that hedgehogs do not occasionally walk about with apples on their spines, for I have been told so by an eye-witness to the fact, a man who was rather given to the study of natural history, and who had been much struck with the circumstance. But although they may be seen with an apple or so sticking on their backs, yet the apples most probably came there accidentally. It is a very common thing to find a hedgehog covered with leaves through which its spines are thrust, but we do not, therefore, accuse it of eating leaves. In all probability, the creature had been alarmed, and had hastily rolled itself up in a spot where apples were lying, and in that case, some of them would be nearly certain to adhere to the spines. As to the eggs—we wonder how many pins a man could stick into a hen's egg without breaking it.

The usual food of hedgehogs is insects of various kinds, and earthworms, together with some vegetable substances. White tells us that some in his garden were very fond of the root of the common plantain, and that they contrived to bore under the plant, so as to eat the root, leaving the stem and leaves untouched. There is an interesting account by the Rev. L. Jenyns, of the manner in which the hedgehog feeds upon worms:—

" Hedgehogs are still about, and on the alert for food. I fell in with one to-day in my walks, in a sheltered part of the garden, which I was enabled to watch unobserved, and which afforded me an opportunity of seeing a little into their habits and mode of feeding. It was creeping up and down a grass walk, apparently in busy search for worms. It carried its snout very low, insinuating it among the roots of the herbage, and snuffing about under the dead leaves which lay about. After a time, it commenced scratching at a particular spot, to which it seemed directed by the scent, and drew out a very large worm from just beneath the surface of the ground. This it immediately began to devour, taking it into the mouth by one extremity, and gradually eating its way to the other,—an operation which lasted some time, and was attended by an incessant action of the teeth, which grated upon each other with a peculiar noise. After the worm was all gone, as I thought, I was surprised to see the whole put out of the mouth again, and from the appearance of the cast, I was led to believe that it had only been subjected to the action of the teeth for the purpose of being bruised, and squeezing out the soft internal parts of the body, which alone were eaten in the first instance. The skin itself, however, was shortly retaken into the mouth, and the whole clean devoured.

" From the above observation it is probable that worms form no inconsiderable part of the food of the hedgehog, and that they are enabled to detect them by the smell, and to extract them from the ground with their snout, after the same manner that the hog uses his in searching for buried food. In the above instance no attempt was made to kill the worm before eating it, but that part of the poor creature which was still out of the mouth of the hedgehog kept up a continual writhing as the nibbling of its other extremity proceeded."

And no wonder either!

The hedgehog can be domesticated very easily, and is an useful resident in a kitchen, from whence it speedily eradicates all the cockroaches and black beetles that abound to such an unpleasant extent in some houses. I have possessed several hedgehogs, mostly for this purpose, but they all contrived to make their escape from the kitchen into the garden, where they doubtless found food more congenial to their taste than cockroaches and black beetles, even although a saucer of milk was placed for their use every night. One of my prickly favourites committed suicide in a rather curious manner. It always preferred to live in an outhouse in which were piled a large number of bean sticks, and among these sticks it delighted to hide itself. As we kept the animal for the express purpose of eating cockroaches, it was necessary to take it away from the bean sticks, and restore it to the kitchen. On one of these occasions, we found the poor hedgehog hanging quite dead, its neck being firmly fixed in a forked stick. We conjectured that it must have been clambering among the sticks, that it must have slipped from some height, and have been caught by the throat in its fall, as its neck was fixed so firmly in the fork that it required rather a strong pull to extricate it.

My hedgehogs had a great talent for hiding themselves during the day; and so well did they manage it, that even when their haunts were known, it was not at all easy to see them, and their hiding places had generally to be explored by the hand.

The stomach and digestive organs in general of this animal are of wonderful power. It seems invulnerable to poison. Hydrocyanic acid has no effect on it, neither have cantharides (the beetles of which blisters are made), nor has corrosive sublimate. Here, however, the hedgehog has a companion in endurance, namely, the horse, whose coat is actually improved in sleekness by a dose of corrosive sublimate administered internally.

External poisons appear to have as little effect on the hedgehog as those administered internally, for the animal is said to engage in battle with the viper, and when bitten, to suffer no more inconvenience than would naturally be occasioned by a wound from sharp teeth. This may really be the case; for Dr. Buckland, having reason to suspect that hedgehogs occasionally preyed on snakes, determined to ascertain whether they did so or not. He, therefore, placed a hedgehog and a common snake in the same box, and watched their proceedings. For some time the hedgehog remained in its contracted state, and did not appear to see the snake, which was slowly creeping round the box. The hedgehog was then laid upon the snake, and as the reptile began to crawl, it partially opened its body, and, for the first time, caught a glimpse of the snake. It then gave the snake a severe bite, and resumed its rolled-up condition. Three times it repeated this operation, and at the third bite broke the snake's back. Having thus rendered its opponent powerless, it proceeded to treat the helpless snake in precisely the same manner as was related above, of its treatment of the worm. The body of the snake was passed slowly through its jaws, the bones being, by repeated bites, broken at intervals of about half an inch. The hedgehog then began at the tail, and commenced eating the snake until half of it had been devoured and by the next morning had completely finished it.

The hedgehog is a nocturnal animal, being very rarely found in the daytime, but very common at night. I once took a hedgehog in a pit about four feet in depth, that had been dug to receive a large pole. The little animal had been wandering about in search of food, and fallen inadvertently into the pit.

There is no British animal that hybernates so completely as does the hedgehog. Even the dormouse awakens at intervals during the winter months, and partakes of its store of nuts or grain before falling again into slumber; but the hedgehog makes no provision for the winter, and when once curled up asleep in its snug nest, remains there in a state of deep slumber until the warm spring weather rouses it from its long sleep. Its nest is admirably adapted for such a habit, being invariably built in some sheltered situation, generally under the naked roots of some large tree, in a hole of a rock, under large stones, or some such secure place, and rendered very warm and comfortable by a large mass of moss and leaves, among which the hedgehog rolls itself, and there remains, secured from cold by the thickness of its bed, and from rain both by the substances under whose shelter it is placed, and by the admirably-constructed roof, which is so compact, that even were it exposed to the fury of the weather. the rain would be thrown off, and the interior kept dry.

OPOSSUM.*

THE next animal to which our attention is drawn is the Opossum. This animal is one of that strange tribe, who carry their little ones in their pocket, like the old nurse in the fantoccini, and if their young are in danger, put them in their pocket, and run away with them. To the same family belong the kangaroos, &c. The following account, taken from Audubon, is so animated a picture of the habits of this animal, that I can do no better than insert the passage unmutilated :—

" Methinks I see one at this moment slowly and cautiously trudging over the melting snows by the side of an unfrequented pond, nosing as it goes for the fare its ravenous appetite prefers. Now it has

* *Didelphys Virginiana.*

come upon the fresh track of a grouse or hare, and it raises its snout and sniffs the pure air. At length it has decided on its course, and it speeds onwards at the rate of a man's ordinary walk. It stops and seems at a loss in what direction to go, for the object of its pursuit has either taken a considerable leap, or has cut backwards before the opossum entered its track. It raises itself up, stands for a while on its hind feet, looks around, snuffs the air again, and then proceeds; but now, at the foot of a noble tree, it comes to a full stand. It walks round the base of the large trunk, over the snow-covered roots, and among them finds an aperture, which it at once enters. Several minutes elapse, when it re-appears, dragging along a squirrel already deprived of life, with which in its mouth it begins to ascend the tree. Slowly it climbs. The first fork does not seem to suit it, for perhaps it thinks it might there be too openly exposed to the view of some wily foe, and so it proceeds, until it gains a cluster of branches, intertwined with grape-vines, and there composing itself, it twists its tail round one of the twigs, and with its sharp teeth demolishes the unlucky squirrel, which it holds all the while with its fore-paws.

" The pleasant days of spring have arrived, and the trees vigorously shoot forth their leaves; but the opossum is almost bare, and seems nearly exhausted by hunger. It visits the margin of creeks, and is pleased to see the young frogs, which afford it a tolerable repast. Gradually the poke-berry and the nettle shoot up, and on their tender and juicy stems it gladly feeds. The matin calls of the wild turkey-cock delight the ear of the cunning creature, for it well knows that it will soon hear the female, and trace her to her nest, when it will suck the eggs with delight. Travelling through the woods, perhaps on the ground, perhaps aloft, from tree to tree, it hears a cock crow, and its heart swells as it remembers the savoury food on which it regaled itself last summer in the neighbouring farm-yard. With great care, however, it advances, and at last conceals itself in the very hen-house.

" Honest farmer! why did you kill so many crows last winter? aye, and ravens too? Well, you have had your own way of it; but now, hie to the village and procure a store of ammunition, clean your rusty gun, set your traps, and teach your lazy curs to watch the opossum. There it comes! The sun is scarcely down, but the appetite of the prowler is here; hear the screams of one of your best chickens that has been seized by him! The cunning beast is off with it, and nothing now can be done, unless you stand there to watch the fox or the owl, now exulting on the thought that you have killed their enemy and your own friend, the poor crow. That precious hen under which you last week placed a dozen eggs or so, is now deprived of them. The opossum, notwithstanding her angry outcries and ruffled feathers, has consumed them one by one; and now, look at the poor bird as she moves across your yard; if not mad, she is at least stupid, for she scratches here and there, calling to her chickens all the while. All this comes from your shooting crows. Had you been more merciful or more prudent, the opossum might have been kept within the woods, where it would have been satisfied with a squirrel, a young hare, the eggs of a turkey, or the grapes that so profusely adorn the boughs of our forest trees. But I talk to you in vain.

. " But suppose the farmer has surprised an opossum in the act of killing one of his best fowls. His angry feelings urge him to kick the poor beast, which, conscious of its inability to resist, rolls off like a ball. The more the farmer rages, the more reluctant is the animal to manifest resentment; at last there it lies, not dead, but exhausted, its jaws open, its tongue extended, its eyes dimmed; and there it would lie until the bottle-fly should come to deposit its eggs, did not its tormentor walk off. ' Surely,' says he to

himself, ' the beast must be dead.' But no, reader,
it' is only ' 'possuming,' and no sooner has his enemy
withdrawn, than it gradually gets on its legs, and
once more makes for the woods."

RAT.*

OMITTING all the mammalia that are comprehended
under the names of seals, dolphins, and whales, we
arrive at a group of animals easily distinguished by
their external characteristics. These are the rodents,
or gnawing animals. All these creatures may be
readily discovered by a glance at the formation of the
mouth, which even externally is easily distinguished
from that of the carnivorous, insectivorous, or rumi-
nant animals. The only exception is the largest of
the group, the Capybara, which, at a first glance, so
closely resembles a hog, that many have been deceived
by its shape and bristly hide; but even this animal
may be at once set down as a rodent, if the observer
can only obtain a clear view of its mouth.

The principal characteristic of the rodents is the
formation of the teeth. These organs are made in a
very singular manner. All the rodents are much
given to gnawing, as their name implies, and in many
cases, such as the beaver, or even the common rat,
the teeth are used so often and so vigorously that they
would soon be worn away were they formed like those
of other animals.

In order to obviate this difficulty, their teeth have
a very peculiar construction. Their edges are sharp
and chisel-like, enabling the animal to cut its way
through woody substances with great rapidity. Teeth,
however, partake of the nature of every earthly material, and wear away by constant friction, even against
a softer substance. To supply the place of the substance thus lost, the tooth is perpetually pushed
forward by a deposition at its root, so that as fast as

* *Mus decumanus.*

the cutting edge of the tooth is worn away, the tooth is pushed forward by the new substance at its root. This augmentation is constantly going on, and although in general it is so beneficial in its effects, yet it sometimes becomes not only a source of annoyance, but also a cause of destruction to the poor animal. It sometimes happens that the incisor teeth are twisted aside, or that one projects a little further than is correct. In such a case, the animal is unable to gnaw, and the tooth, not being worn away in front, yet receiving fresh accession of substance from behind, continually increases in length until the poor animal is unable even to close its mouth, and eventually dies of starvation. Such an event is not uncommon among rabbits, both wild and tame. There are few museums where there are not several examples of such distorted teeth. There are some remarkable specimens in the museum of the College of Surgeons, in London, and one or two good examples in the Anatomical Museum at Oxford.

The incisor teeth being intended for cutting away woody fibre, must needs have a cutting edge kept always sharp. This object is attained in a manner equally wonderful and simple. A carpenter's chisel is made by fixing a thin strip of steel to a larger blade of iron, and an axe is formed by enclosing a very thin steel plate between two thick iron blades. In the rodents the teeth are formed on the chisel principle, only the anterior surface of the tooth being covered with a thin coat of enamel, the remainder being formed of the comparatively soft substance that forms the body of the tooth. By the necessary friction of the tooth against the corresponding tooth in the opposite jaw, as well as by its constant employment in eating or nibbling, the softer substance is soon worn away, leaving the enamel to produce and preserve a sharp edge.

It must be understood that the whole of the preceding description refers only to the incisor teeth, as the other teeth are formed like those of other animals, excepting in their number. The rodents have no canine teeth at all, a considerable gap being left between the incisors and the molars. Of the molar teeth there are but few, as many teeth would not be required. The incisors are always four in number, two in each jaw, if we except the hares and rabbits, in whose jaws a very small tooth rises behind the large permanent incisors.

The upper lip in these animals is divided, a structure probably intended for the proper management of food, in its passage between the two incisor teeth. For the further attainment of that purpose, the lips are slightly prehensile, as may be seen by watching a rabbit eat a cabbage-leaf or a sprig of parsley.

All, however, are not strictly herbivorous, as there are some who not only eat animal and vegetable matters indifferently, but even appear to prefer the animal. Of this number is the rat, who finds a high place among the rodents in the Catalogue of the British Museum, and must therefore take precedence of more interesting and agreeable animals.

We can accustom ourselves to mice, and can at last even like the little bright-eyed, soft-furred, slender-limbed, long-tailed creatures; but very few persons have succeeded in habituating themselves to rats. In fact, the nearer acquaintance we make with rats, the more we seem to detest them. Not that they are ugly animals, for they yield not in beauty to the mice, but they are such disgusting animals in their habits, and so fierce when assaulted, that it is almost impossible for even the most ardent lover of natural history to reconcile himself to their presence.

There seems to be no part of a house that the rats will not get into, if they have taken up their residence in it. Doors are useless defences, as the little sharp teeth rapidly cut a hole under the door, through which whole tribes of rats pass and repass. So eager are they in the pursuit of food, that they will burrow considerable distances, suffering nothing short of stone or iron to stop them; and they have even been seen to reach a ship by climbing up a rope that had been used to warp the vessel out of dock, and had been inadvertently suffered to remain still attached to the shore.   A slight strip of brass or iron, fastened at the bottom of each door, is, however, an obstacle that not even a rat's teeth can penetrate.   Lead they seem to bite easily enough.   I lately saw a piece of a very thick leaden pipe that had been gnawed through in several places by the rats, in order that they might get at the water which was passing through the pipe. The lead was grooved in numerous places with their teeth, and in some places it was gnawed through. The sagacity of the animal must have been of no mean order to enable it to discover the presence of water in a strong leaden pipe.

Rats can climb capitally, and generally choose the angle of a wall for the display of that particular kind of agility, when they wish to reach a shelf or a closet raised above the floor.

The worst of rats is, that their habits are so un- cleanly.   They are very fond of drains and sewers, and the more filthy the drain is, the more fascinating it seems to be to the rats.   Then after spending several hours in a drain, they will emerge, make their way into the larder, run over everything eatable that they can find, eat what they prefer, and leave everything that they reject, in a hopeless state.   Virgil must have borrowed his idea of the harpies from a recol- lection of a visit from a host of rats.

The rat that we generally find in our houses is the brown or Norway rat,* it having driven out and sup- planted the real English rat, the Black rat,† much in the same way that the cockroach ‡ has succeeded in usurping possession of our kitchens.   The Black rat is now exceedingly scarce, and, in all probability, will be extinct in a very short time, being persecuted to death

* *Mus decumanus.*   † *Mus rattus.*   ‡ *Blatta orientalis.*

by its brown rival. The Black rat is not nearly so large as the Norway rat, and was, in consequence, easily overpowered by it. Some years ago, Mr. Waterton considered the sight of a Black rat a very uncommon one, and predicted its speedy extirpation from British soil; a circumstance for which he appears to blame William III. more than the Hanoverian rat.

The same author, being led on partly by his hatred of the Hanoverian rats, as Hanoverian, and partly by his objection to the noise that they made, and to their filthy habits, waged a successful war of extirpation, at the end of which he was enabled to boast that there was not a Hanoverian in his house. On finding that the rats were accustomed to enjoy their sports behind his wainscotings, he tried many ways to force them to leave his premises, but in vain. He tried poison, but as the rats would contumeliously die behind the wainscoting, the consequences were so disastrous, that the room was unoccupied for several months.

This reminds me of a plan adopted by a naturalist of an inventive genius, for discovering the exact position of a dead rat, the scent of which filled the entire room, and could not be traced to any particular spot. He closed the doors and windows of the room, caught half a dozen blue-bottle flies, and liberated them in the tainted room. Led by their instinct, they instantly flew to the spot where was lying the carcase of the rat, and by settling on the boards, indicated the exact spot where the dead rat lay.

Being so annoyed by the rats, Mr. Waterton invented another plan. Having one day caught a rat in a box trap, he dipped its hinder parts into warm tar, and suffered it to escape. Its friends, disliking the smell of the tar, and fearing that they might be subjected to the same treatment, ran away, and for some months did not return. It was found afterwards on removing a hollow plinth behind which the rats used to make the most noise, that they had gnawed away the corner of a very hard brick, which happened to obstruct their thoroughfare.

This device, although giving temporary relief, was not likely to free the house from the rats altogether. The experiment was, therefore, followed up by a rigorous inspection of every place suspected to be haunted by a rat. The drains were examined, their ends carefully barred, all cracks stopped with cement, until the rats were forced to own themselves mastered, and to abandon the premises as untenable. Mr. Waterton's hatred of the noisy animals is by no means surprising to those who have experienced the same annoyance. No one who has not been pestered with these plagues can have any idea of the extraordinary noises they will make. I have a most vivid recollection of many sleepless hours during my younger days, occasioned solely by the gambols of rats overhead. My room was separated from the rest of the house by a small flight of three stairs, and was the highest room in the house, there being no garrets, and the roof being used as a lumber-room. Night after night there came over my head a heavy measured step, passing regularly from one end of the room to the other. This used to be continued for hours, never changing, but always that slow uniform step, passing and repassing, until I fell asleep. I was told that the rats occasioned it. It may have been so, but I have my doubts still.

Be this as it may, the rats used to make most unmistakable sounds. First there would be a rumbling behind the panels, then a scuffling, then a squeaking, and lastly a furious race terminated the proceedings until they reassembled.

It is said that the best method of expelling rats, without actually destroying them, is by mixing meal with jalap, and placing it in their haunts. This the rats eat, but it gives them such pains in their interiors, that they never return to the spot from whence their sufferings originated. Phosphorus mixed with lard is said to be an excellent poison, and to delay its full effects until the rats have reached water, whither the effects of the phosphorus causes them to repair as soon as possible. The danger of their death in the house is thus avoided. I have never tried either plan, so cannot recommend them from experience.

The ferocity of the rat is sometimes very great, and were its strength equal to its courage, it would soon master those foes before whom it now flies. I was once attacked in the most determined way by a rat that had been taken in a box trap. The trap was one intended for mice, and the rat being large in proportion to the size of the trap, had left his tail hanging out of the entrance where the door came down, and as the door descended with a spring, the tail remained fixed in the same position. Wishing to transfer the animal to a cage in order to keep it, and endeavour to tame it, I attached a piece of string to its tail, and opened the door of the trap. The animal was at first unwilling to come out, and had to be startled out by a stick pushed between the bars. The moment that it had left the cage, it sprang at my hand, and as I raised it from the table to prevent it from springing, it curled itself round, ran up the string, and had just reached my hand, when a blow from a pair of iron forceps that were lying by, laid it senseless on the table.

The rat is a very prolific animal, and were not its number kept down by many foes, it would soon overrun the land. The enormous increase in their numbers, where only a few have gained admission into a house or cornstack, shows the necessity for such foes. Of these the stoat family is the worst, as from their little slender body and short legs, they are able to penetrate every passage which the rat has made, and to destroy it in its own fastnesses. The ratcatchers turn this power to their advantage, by using the ferret for the purpose of assisting them in their occupation The ferret is first muzzled (in days happily gone by, its mouth was sewn up), or it would never return to its master, but would take possession of the barn or stack, and live on the rats. The greater number of the holes are then stopped, the trained dogs are set to watch the others, and the spectators being armed with sticks, the ferret is placed in one of the open holes. Down it glides, and before long is heard a scuffling and squeaking within the holes. In a minute or two numbers of rats and mice, great and small, come leaping out of their holes, and are either snapped up by the dogs, who have been taught to kill them with a single rapid bite, or are knocked down by the sticks of the human hunters.

The dogs display great sagacity on these occasions. They take the greatest delight in the sport, and watch the holes with their ears perched forward, their eyes sparkling, and their whole frame ready prepared for a spring upon any rat who dare show his nose outside the hole. To one ratcatcher belonged a dog who used to lame the rats by a blow from his paw as they sprang from the hole. He was once standing on the watch, with his paw ready lifted for a blow, when a rustling was heard, a head presented itself, and down came his paw. He, however, arrested the blow before it could do any harm, for the head belonged to the ferret, who had reached the mouth of the hole in pursuit of its prey.

These same ferrets are rather dangerous animals to handle, as they cannot really be rendered sufficiently tame to be trusted. I once saw a ferret, a beautiful white one with pink eyes, which had become, as its master boasted, quite tame, and would run about his person, and caress his face. One evening, as he was exhibiting the animal, and showing how it would kiss him, the ferret seized both his lips between its teeth, and bit them quite through, making four cuts as clean as if done with a knife. It was never allowed to kiss its master again.

The following description of rat-catching, without

DOGS WATCHING FOR RATS.   p. 270.

traps, is extracted from Richardson's " Pests of the Farm." The ingenious method of turning the tails of the rats into instruments of their own destruction is very amusing :—

" Mr. John Russel, an extensive bacon merchant in Limerick, who kills between forty and fifty thousand pigs in a season, has adopted the following successful method of destroying the rats which abound on his premises. He has erected a quadrangular stone building, eleven feet long and seven feet wide, with a wall three feet high, having flags laid flat upon the top, but projecting a little over the inside of the wall. All round the wall inside, at the base, are numerous holes, like pigeon-holes, which do not go quite through, except a few to allow a free passage to the little animals. Outside the barrack is a plentiful supply of water and food, such as bones and useless offal. The interior of the walls is occupied by boards, lumber, and straw, just such concealment as these animals are known to prefer, and the whole is covered by a movable wooden roof. When it is judged proper to destroy the vermin, the passages are stopped at the outside, the roof is lifted off, and the boards are taken out. The frightened animals run up the wall, but their escape is impossible, for they strike against the projecting flags, and fall back again. They then run into the small holes below, but these are only just large enough to admit their bodies, whilst the tails remain sticking out, a secure prize to the men, who go in over the wall, and by this unlucky appendage they suddenly drag them out, and fling them to a posse of anxious dogs outside the fortress, or into a barrel of water, where they are soon destroyed. As there are not holes enough in the wall inside, the noise and uproar soon frightens another division of rats into the vacated openings, and these being treated in the same unceremonious manner, the whole garrison is thus speedily destroyed. As many as seven or eight hundred have been killed at one clearing. Rats being fond of straw, they become very numerous in the lofts where the article is kept, to be used for singeing bacon, and they cut it into short pieces with their teeth, which makes it useless for this purpose. The proprietor tried the effect of putting a pet fox to mount guard on the lofts, and it was found that he killed such quantities of the rats, that three or four were procured to garrison the place instead of one. When we visited this extraordinary establishment some time ago, the additional foxes had not been procured, but we saw the first, which was looking fat, contented, and happy with its new occupation."

Among other qualifications of the rat we must mention its proficiency in the art of swimming. Even a stream of considerable width is insufficient to restrain their ravages. The Zoological Gardens in the Regent's Park are, as is well known, surrounded by a canal. Over this there pass nightly myriads of rats, who search among the dens, &c., to look after food of any kind that may have been left by the animals. The rats are too crafty to remain in the gardens all day, so they cross over at night, and before daybreak return to their usual haunts.

This conduct is sufficiently clever, but it is equalled, if not surpassed, by the ingenuity exhibited by a tribe of rats who had fixed their residence near the kennel where a pack of hounds resided. The food for the dogs was poured into long narrow troughs, and the rats, finding this out, were accustomed to sally out and coolly partake of dinner with the dogs, who, trained to the chase of foxes, disdained such insignificant animals. Insignificant as they were in point of size, they were by no means so in point of numbers, and they devoured so much of the dinner that ought to have gone to the dogs, that the keeper determined to extirpate the marauders. He, therefore, bored a hole in the wall at each end of each trough, and placed a heavily-loaded gun in the aperture, so as completely to rake each trough with the shot. He then, at the usual dinner hour, stationed assistants at the different guns, and after carefully locking up the dogs in their dormitories, gave the accustomed call, poured the food into the troughs, retired from the kennel, and determined to wait until the rats, having all the food to themselves, should have filled the trough, in order that he might almost exterminate them with a single discharge.

So he waited very patiently, but not a rat made its appearance. After leaving the food for an hour or so without finding any rats, he released the dogs, who immediately ran to their dinner. Scarcely had they fairly begun, than the rats also made *their* appearance, and as if conscious that they were guarded by the dogs, resumed their usual places at the feeding trough, and made their dinner in safety.

MOUSE.*

MANY people, who have a great objection to a rat, rather admire a mouse, and overlook its depredations for the sake of its elegant form, its graceful movement, and its timid curiosity—its curiosity leading it to come out of its hole and examine every object in the room, and its timidity causing it to dart off at the slightest movement.

Mice can be easily tamed, particularly if taken when young, but they can also be taught to approach with confidence, and to gambol about the room without running off to their holes. I have had several tame mice, one of which used to sit on my hand, and permit me to carry it about so seated, or it would hide itself under a fold of my coat, or creep up the sleeve for the sake of the warmth. In general, brown mice are easier to tame than their white relations. I have seen a common short-tailed field-mouse come to the bars of its cage, and take a grain of wheat from the finger. The best way to tame them, is to inflict a forced fast of a day or so, and then to feed them from

* *Mus musculus.*

the hand, always taking care to accompany the operation with the sound intended to be the call. They
will soon learn to connect the sound and the food,
and will come to the side of their cage the moment
that they hear it. So if any one wishes to possess
tame mice, I would recommend him to save himself
the expense of purchasing white mice, which are also
more difficult to preserve in health than the brown
mice, and to try his hand on a few common brown
mice, only a few weeks old.

But whatever description of mice is kept, the
greatest care should be taken to have the cage
thoroughly clean. The most effectual mode of so
doing, is to have a double set of cage bottoms, so that
one set can be in use, while the other set is getting dry
after washing. It is also necessary to be careful of
the substances used as bedding. White cotton wool
is, perhaps, the best substance that can be used for
that purpose; but black cotton wool, or black wadding as it is generally called, should be scrupulously
avoided. I once lost a whole cage of newly-tamed
mice, by supplying them with black wadding. It
was placed in their cage at night, and by the next
morning all the mice were dead.

With proper care, however, mice may be easily
reared, and converted into amusing little pets. But
however amusing they may be as pets, in most other
respects mice are provoking little creatures. They
contrive to make a lodgment in almost every conceivable place, frequently choosing localities which
would be thought most unlikely. An organ does not
appear a very promising residence for these animals,
yet every one who has busied himself about organs is
fully acquainted with the mischief done to the instrument by the colonies of mice who seem to be drawn
to it by some strange attraction. They frequently
scramble to the mouths of the pipes, fall in, and are
never able to get out again. On cleaning an organ,
it is seldom that most of the large metal open pipes

are not tenanted by sundry skeletons of mice, bats, and even small birds, which do not seem to be able to use their wings in that confined space, and perish miserably. Mice always appear to have a strange penchant for musical instruments. There was a certain closet, one of the shelves of which had long been devoted to filberts. In another part of the closet an old disused harmonicon had been placed, and been forgotten. On turning out the contents of the closet, with a view to a thorough sweeping, the harmonicon was discovered, apparently in the same state in which it had been placed there, even the hammers retaining their original position. The glasses, however, when struck, gave forth a singularly dull sound, and, on moving the instrument about, a strange rattling sound was heard in the interior. On removing the glasses, the instrument was found to be entirely filled with the husks and shells of the filberts, the kernels having been scooped out as neatly as could be done even by an accomplished squirrel. It is difficult to imagine the object for which all these shells were deposited in so singular a place, as mice always make their nests of very soft materials, such as rags, or scraps of paper, and are far too observant of their own comfort to make their beds of sharp, hard nutshells.

The number of traps invented for the purpose of taking mice is beyond the power of statistics to give. There are ingenious boards placed on shelves, which tilt the mouse into a basin of water below, where it swims about for many minutes, and at last sinks through sheer exhaustion. Struggling for life and fighting for breath to the last moment of its little life, it continues its vain efforts even while slowly sinking below the surface. This is generally applauded as a merciful trap. Then there is a spring trap, that drives a steel spike through the mouse's brain, causing instantaneous death. This is generally stigmatised (especially by ladies) as a cruel trap. There is another 'merciful' trap, the box trap, that shuts it in without hurting it, and affords it a piece of cheese to eat, and a view from between the bars until it is shaken out of the trap and carried off by the cat, who picks it up and takes it to her kittens, who practise upon it; the art of mouse-catching and tormenting, which they hope soon to begin on their own account. There is the garotte trap, which strangles the mouse, and the arithmetical 4 trap, which mashes it flat. But there is still extant an account of a trap that, from the elaborate description, must be a most valuable one, and which the describer has wisely prevented from being too common, by enveloping his account in such a mist of impenetrable language, that no one whom I have met has been able to form the least idea of the description of trap intended—what may be its form, how the mouse is to be caught, or what catches it.

In sheer despair, I present the account to my readers, together with a hope, that one of them may be able to make a trap by means of the description, and that, if so, he will kindly forward to me a sketch.

" And again he telleth of another manner of catching of mice, which is as great as the first, and it is after this manner:—Take two smooth boards about the lenth of thy arm, and in breadth half thy arm, but joyn it so together, that they may be distant from the lower part in lenth some four fingers, or little less, with two small spindles or clefts, which must be at every end one, and fasten paper under them, and put a piece of paste therein, being cut overthwart in the middle, but you must not fasten it nigh the middle, and let it be so bound, that it may easily be lifted up betwixt the spindles, that if by slipping it should be altered, it might be brought again to the same form. But the two spindles spoken of before, ought to be joyned together in the ends above, and beyond them another small spindle to be made, which may hold in the middle a crooked wedge or butten, upon the which may be hanged a piece of hog-skin, so that one of them may be easily turned upside down with the skin, and put thou thereunto a little piece of earth or stick, that the mice may easily come to it: So that how many mice soever shall come thereto, and to the meat, shall be taken, always by rouling the paper into his wonted place."

The fecundity of the mouse is as great as that of the rat, for it breeds at all times of the year, and frequently produces three families in the course of one year, each family numbering from four to six. In a fortnight the young are able to obtain their own living, and in a few weeks more, become parents themselves. An experiment on the fecundity of this animal was made so long ago as the time of Aristotle. He placed in a closed box well stored with grain one female mouse who was about to become a mother, and kept the box closed for some time. When the box was opened, he found an hundred and twenty mice, all sprung from one parent.

If any one wishes to repeat the experiment, he must be very careful about a plentiful supply of food, or his mice may come to the same untimely end that befel a company of mice whom a boy had put in a box and forgotten for some time. When he remembered his neglect, he hastened to open his box, and found there only one great mouse, sitting in solitary misery among the relics of his companions, of whom he was the sole survivor, hunger having compelled them to kill and eat one another.

It is not so easy to clear a house of mice as many people imagine, particularly if traps are used as the means of destruction. Many will be caught when the traps are first set, but the numbers fall off, and at last cease altogether, when the householder flatters himself that the mice are all gone. But the fact is that the little creatures have learned caution, and have only avoided entering the trap, while they still continue their depredations. They not only take warning from seeing their fellows caught, but if one that has been captured has been suffered to make its escape, the trap may as well be removed, for no more mice will be caught. After a month or two, it may again be used with success.

During my residence in college, the mice had been a fertile source of annoyance. They nibbled my candles in two, so that they would not stand upright; they drank my milk; they pattered with their little feet over my butter; they raced about between the papered canvas and the stone wall, until the wall was riddled with holes made by a toasting-fork thrust through the paper, in the vain hope of spearing them; they would run across my carpet in the most undisguised manner, until I determined to extirpate them. So I got a double trap, baited it very temptingly, and placed it in the closet. Scarcely had the door been closed, when two smart blows told of the capture of two mice. They were speedily immolated, and the trap again set. During the first two or three days, the trap was constantly going off, until I was tired of going and taking out the mice. The others, however, took warning, and came more and more sparingly, until it was a rare thing to catch one young mouse in a day, and after a week or so, none were caught at all, although the trap was baited with most savoury toasted cheese, and my candles suffered as before. I then bethought me of changing the bait, so, after suffering the trap to be well aired, and the scent of the cheese to evaporate, I substituted a piece of tallow with great success, for the mice came nearly as fast as ever. When they had begun to dread the latter, a piece of bacon was used as the bait, and by systematically changing the bait, great numbers were caught. At last, however, the mice seemed to comprehend that the trap was in fault, and not the bait, and I had to substitute a 4 trap, to which they again came in multitudes, and as the descending weight was a very large book, several often perished at once.

Mr. Smee relates an instance of the sagacity of the mouse in refusing to be caught a second time:—

" Many years ago, I caught a common mouse in a trap, and, instead of consigning it to the usual watery grave, or to the unmerciful claws of the cat, I determined to keep it a prisoner. After a short time, the little mouse made its escape in a room attached to my father's residence in the Bank of England. I did not desire the presence of a wild mouse in the room, and, therefore, adopted means to secure him. The room was paved with stone, and inclosed with solid walls. There was no hope for him that he would ultimately escape, although there were abundant opportunities for hiding. I set the trap and baited it with a savoury morsel; but day after day no mouse entered. The poor little thing gave unequivocal signs of extreme hunger, by gnawing the bladder from some of my chemical bottles. I gradually removed everything from the room that he could possibly eat, but still the old proverb of ' Once caught, twice shy' so far applied, that he would not enter my trap. After many days, on visiting the apartment one morning, the trap was down, the mouse was caught; the pangs of hunger were more intolerable than the terror of imprisonment. He did not, however, will the unpleasant alternative of entering the trap, until he was so nearly starved that his bones almost protruded through his skin; and he freely took bits of food from my fingers through the bars of the cage."

I once made an experiment on a mouse of rather a singular description. At that time Galvanism had become rather a fashionable study among the members of the University; and numerous were the experiments that were tried, from firing gunpowder under water, to knocking down a scout with an electric shock. I happened to have an excellent home-made battery, only a small single-cell one, but one which would cause an electro-magnet to sustain a weight of forty pounds, and, when connected with a coil, would give a tolerably severe shock. A mouse happened to be caught, and the wires were thrust into the trap, as much in jest as in earnest. The mouse, seeing the wires, and, being enraged at its incarceration, dashed at them, and happened to place its feet upon one at the moment that it seized the other in its mouth. I thought that it seemed singularly indifferent to the battery, and withdrew the wire on finding that no effect had been produced. The mouse, however, remained in exactly the same position; and, upon a close examination, proved to be quite dead. On opening the trap and inclining it, the mouse slid out as if it had been carved in wood. All its limbs were rigidly stiff, and its neck stretched out in exactly the same position in which it had bitten at the wire. It is impossible to imagine any death more sudden than this must have been; for it was so instantaneous, that no perceptible sign appeared to mark the moment when the life left the body.

The proverb is well known that speaks of rats deserting a falling house. Topsell gives a circumstantial account of such a proceeding in the following lines :—

" It is also very certain that mice which live in a house, if they perceive by the age of it, it be ready to fall down, or subject to any other ruin, they foreknow it, and depart out of it, as may appear by this notable story, which happened in a town called Helice, in Greece, wherein the inhabitants committed this abominable act against their neighbours the Greeks. For they slew them, and sacrificed them upon their altars. Whereupon followed the ruine of the city, which was premonstrated by this prodigious event. For five days before the destruction thereof, all the mice, weesils, and serpents, and other reptile creatures, went out of the same in the presence of the' inhabitants, every one assembling to his own rank and company; whereat the people wondered much, for they could not conceive any true cause of their departure, and no marvail. For God which had appointed to take vengeance on them for their wickedness, did not give them so much knowledge, nor make them so wise as the beasts, to avoid his judgement and their own destruction; and, therefore, mark what followed. For these beasts were no sooner out of the city, but suddenly in the night-time came such a lamentable earthquake and strong tempest, that all the houses did not only fall down, and not one of them stood upright, to the slaughter of men, women, and children contained in them, but lest any of them should escape the strokes of the timber and housetops, God sent also such a great floud of waters, by reason of the tempestuous winde, which drove the waters out of the sea upon the town, that swept them all away, leaving no more behind than naked and bare significations of former build-ings. And not only the city and citizens perished, but also there was ten ships of the Lacedemonians, in their port, all drowned at that instant."

In another part of his voluminous work, he enu-merates some of the qualities of "Yᵉ vulgar little mouse," among which he numbers its capability of domestication, and gives the following account of a very tame mouse.

"Albertus writeth, that he saw in Upper Germany a mouse hold a burning candle in her feet, at the commandment of her master, all the time his guests were at supper."

Most people have heard of the famous "singing mouse," whose musical performances attracted so much attention some years ago. Many sceptical individuals classed the animal with the "whistling oyster," and undisguisedly expressed their incredulity. However, the little animal certainly did produce mu-sical sounds, although they did not, as was asserted,

rival the notes of the canary and nightingale, either
in volume, strength, or sweetness.

The field-mice* are extremely injurious when
they exist in great numbers, as they are very partial to
the young shoots of various plants, and by nibbling
them off, prevent the plant from attaining its full
growth. They are very difficult to find, as they hide
themselves so carefully, that, even in fields where
they swarm, it is by no means an easy matter to
catch a sight of them. There is a meadow in Wiltshire, where, by carefully watching almost any square
yard of grass, a short-tailed field-mouse is nearly sure
to be found. Yet that field had been used for
cricket, hockey, football, and many other games, for
a long time before any one discerned a single
mouse. If a field-mouse is caught and put down on
the grass of even a newly-mown field, it glides so
neatly under the grass, pressing close to the ground,
and scarcely permitting the slightest motion of a
single blade to betray its pressure, that if the eye is
taken off for a moment, it is almost impossible to
catch sight of it again.

But concealed as the mice are from human eye, the
vision of the owl or kestrel soon detects them. Woe
to the unfortunate field-mouse that dare show its
nose above ground if a kestrel is hovering about; for
down comes the sharp-eyed bird, and flies away with
the mouse in its talons. At night, too, the large
eyes of the owl soon descry its movements, and the
soft-plumed bird, floating over with its noiseless
flight, strikes its talons into the unsuspecting mouse,
and either swallows it whole on the spot, or carries it
off to its nest, where the young owls are expecting
their parent. Indeed, were it not for the exertions
of the hawks and owls, who pounce on them from
above, and the weasels and stoats, who chase them
on the ground, we might fare little better than Bishop
Hatto, whose tragical story is related by various

* *Arvicola arvalis.*

authors, and among these, by Coryat, in his "Crudities."

"Here followeth the history of HATTO, Archbishop of Mentz. It happened in the year 914, that there was an exceeding great famine in Germany, at what time Otho, surnamed the Great, was emperor, and one Hatto, an abbot of Fulda, was Archbishop of Mentz, of the Bishops after Crescens and Crescentius, the two and thirtieth, of the Archbishops after Saint Bonifacius the thirteenth. This Hatto in the time of this great famine aforementioned, when he saw the poor people of the country exceedingly oppressed with famine, assembled a great company of them into a barn, and like a most accursed and mercilesse caitiffe, burnt up those poor innocent souls, that were so far from doubting any such matter, that they rather hoped to receive some comfort and relief at his hands.

"The reason that moved the prelate to commit that execrable impiety was, because he thought the famine would the sooner cease, if those unprofitable beggars that consumed more bread than they were worthy to eat, were dispatched out of this world. For he said that these poor folks were like to mice, that were good for nothing but to devour corne. But God Almighty, the just avenger of the poor folks' quarrell, did not long suffer this hainous tyranny, this most detestable fact, unpunished. For he mustered up an army of mice against the archbishop, and sent them to persecute him as his furious Alastors, so that they afflicted him both day and night, and would not suffer him to take his rest in any place. Whereupon, the prelat, thinking that he should be secure from the injury of mice, if he were in a certain tower that standeth in the Rhine, near to the towne, betook himself unto the said tower as safe refuge and sanctuary from his enemies, and locked himself in. But the innumerable troopes of mice chased him continually very eagerly, and swamme unto him upon the top of the water, to execute the

just judgement of God ; and so at last he was most
miserably devoured by those sillie creatures, who
pursued him with such bitter hostility, that it is recorded they scraped and knawed out his very name
from the walls and tapestry wherein it was written, after
they had so cruelly devoured his body.   Wherefore the
tower wherein he was eaten up by the mice is shown to
this day for a perpetual monument to all succeeding
ages of the barbarous and inhuman tyranny of this
impious prelate, being situate in a little green island,
in the midst of the Rhine, near to the towne of Win-
gen, and is commonly called in the German tongue,
the MOWSE-TURN."*

An enterprising traveller, who, with two companions, succeeded in taking a two-oar boat over several
of the German rivers, remarks, that the breed of
mice must have been of a most superior kind, for
their boat could with difficulty make the passage.

If any of my readers should wish to keep tame
mice, I would recommend as large a cage as possible,
with plenty of bars and perches, on which the mice
love to climb.   The wheel-cages should be always
eschewed.   The mice, if taken young, can be trained
to perform several feats, such as drawing carriages,
and other similar performances.   I have already mentioned the extreme care that is required in preserving
their cage in a state of the most perfect cleanliness.
If this is not done, there are hardly any animals so
offensive.   As for feeding, anything will do, from oats
to ortolans, only white mice should not be permitted to
eat cheese, as it is very injurious to them.

BEAVER.†

WE will now take our leave of the mice, and pro-
ceed to the Beavers, almost the largest of all the
Rodentia. The Capybára is, indeed, the largest of the
Rodentia in point of size, but is not near so interest-

---

* " Mause-Thurm."   The Mouse Tower.
† *Castor fiber.*

ing an animal as the Beavers, who may be considered the chief of that division, both from the excellence of that characteristic from which the Rodentia take their name, and from the very perfect manner in which they make use of those tools with which they are supplied.

I have before mentioned the peculiar construction of the four incisor teeth of the gnawing animals, and the manner in which they preserve their edge, by a slight coating of hard enamel upon a comparatively soft substance. In the tooth of the beaver, the enamel is of an orange colour, something like that of an old squirrel, and is so hard that the American Indians were accustomed to fix beaver teeth in wooden handles, and use them as chisels, wherewith to carve their bone and horn weapons, until the use of iron superseded these primitive tools.

Such being the power of the beaver's tooth in the hands of men, it may well be imagined that when such instruments as these are used by their original possessor, they produce no small effect. And so it is, for the beavers can cut through a tree ten inches in diameter, without much difficulty. They sit on their haunches when they set to work at a tree, and by gnawing round it, the tree is gradually cut through, one side being always cut deeper than the other in order to insure its fall in the right direction; when the tree is thus felled, the stump is left of a conical form.

Their houses and dams are built of a mixed mass of wood, stones, and mud; the stones and mud being always carried under the chin, and the sticks shaped by the teeth. It has been the custom to say, that in the construction of their houses, the beavers drive piles into the ground, and then entwine sticks between the piles. This, however, is not correct; neither is it true that beavers first finish building their houses, and then plaster them over with mud, the fact being that they build their houses of a mixed mass of mud, wood, and stones, the sticks being laid transversely, and the mud and stones worked in at the same time. After the houses are finished, they give them an extra coat of mud in the autumn, which, freezing hard when the winter comes on, forms a secure defence against the Wolverene, or Glutton, an animal that is particularly fond of beavers. The same operation is repeated every year, so that at last the walls, and especially the roof of the huts, become exceedingly strong, being sometimes nearly six or seven feet in thickness.

The so-called apartments in a beaver's hut are, in fact, separate houses, having no communication with each other, except by water. There are often several families under one roof, and, except in a very few instances, there is no means of communication between them, unless the beavers first dive under water.

The dams are constructed in order to gain such a depth of water, that the ice may not entirely dry up their little lakes, and are generally built across small creeks. Where, however, the water is tolerably deep, the beavers build no dams, but spend their energies in constructing their houses.

The form of the dam differs according to the form of the stream. If the current runs strongly, the dam is made of a curved form, its convexity towards the stream, so that the fall of water forms a kind of miniature resemblance to the Horseshoe fall of Niagara. But when the stream is but slight, the curve of the dam is proportionately lessened, and the beavers thereby save much time and labour. When it happens that a colony of beavers continue their labours for a course of years, without being exterminated by the ruthless hunters, the dam becomes a large edifice from frequent repairs; a bank forms on it, from the *débris* swept down by the stream, and arrested by the edge of the dam. Seeds of birch and other trees fall on the bank, take root, and spring up, until at last the dam becomes a permanent bank covered with vegetation, and often decorated with willows, poplars, and birch-trees, among whose branches the birds build their nests.

The food of the beaver is vegetable, and consists mostly of the bark of trees, which their chisel-shaped teeth enables them to slice off with great ease; shoots also, and small twigs, form no small portion of their diet, but, perhaps, the greater portion of their subsistence is derived from a kind of water-lily which grows at the bottom of the rivers, and after which they dive. This is their winter diet, but in the summer they vary their repasts by feeding on the green herbage, and the berries of various plants.

The object for which the beavers are hunted is well known, but the fur of the animal is not of so much importance as it was some years ago. In 1808, no less than 126,927 beaver skins were imported into England from Quebec alone, while in 1827, the entire number imported was little more than 50,000. The reason of the decrease is twofold. First, because the hunters, with the usual improvidence of partially-civilised men, destroyed every beaver they could find, taking no care to leave enough to keep up the supply; and secondly, because silk and other materials have almost superseded beaver in the construction of those cylindrical abominations popularly denominated "hats."

The value of each skin is about eighteen or nineteen shillings, and the manner in which the fur is prepared for making hats is very interesting, but would take too much space to describe; I will therefore merely mention that the fur is shaved from the skin by a very sharp knife made for the express purpose. The fur is of two kinds, long stiff hair and soft wool. The wool is the only part used in hat-making, and is separated from the hair by the action of wind, which blows it along a tube, and deposits the light fur at one end, while the hair is left

stationary at the other.   It is, in fact, a kind of win-
nowing, exercised on hair, instead of corn.   The
wool thus separated is then fixed into the felt of the
hat while moist, by kneading them together, when the
peculiar form of the wool causes it to insinuate itself
into the substance of the felt, and to work its way so
firmly that it cannot be again drawn out.   Indeed if
the kneading process is continued, the beaver-fur will
work its way completely through the felt, and appear
on the other side.   Such used to be the method of hat-
making in former times, so that when a gentleman
thought that his hat was getting shabby, he sent it to
the hatter, who turned it inside out, and brought a
completely fresh surface to the exterior.

The beavers are either taken in traps, or by storming their houses in winter.   The method in which
the latter mode of hunting is conducted is as
follows.   The mere storming their houses would be
a simple matter enough, but the beavers have a
number of holes in the banks into which they retreat
when their houses are injured, or when they are
alarmed.   The chief business is, therefore, to find
out these hiding places, and as the water is covered
with thick and hard ice, it is no easy matter to discover them.   This part of the proceeding is always,
taken by the old hunters, who by means of knocking
the ice with an ice-chisel fastened to a staff, discover
by the sound the entrance of the holes below.   As
each man finds a hole, he sticks the branch of a tree
over it, as a sign that it is his property.   He then
cuts a hole in the ice, and waits his opportunity.

In the meanwhile, the inferior hunters and the
women set to work at the huts themselves, which they
break open with some labour; for six or seven feet of
frozen mud and stones is rather a formidable barrier.
The beavers, finding their fortress assailed, abandon
it, and take refuge in their holes, from whence
they are immediately dragged by the expectant hunter.
The poor creatures are sure to be taken, for they can-

not remain under water for any length of time, and they only have the choice of three evils, either to stay under the ice and get drowned, or to stay in their houses and get killed by the women, or to run away to their holes and get killed by the men.

As an example of the manners of the Beaver, I will here give Mr. Broderip's account of a tame beaver in his possession. The reader will not fail to remark how completely the manners of this animal prove that it is instinct and not reason that governs it in all the extraordinary works which it achieves.

" It was the sole survivor of five or six which were shipped at the same time, and it was in a very pitiable condition. Good treatment quickly restored it to health, and kindness soon made it familiar. When called by its name ' Binney,' it generally answered with a little cry, and came to the owner. The hearth-rug was its favourite haunt, and thereon it would lie stretched out, sometimes on its back, sometimes on its side, and sometimes on its belly, but always near its master. The building instinct showed itself immediately it was let out of its cage, and materials were placed in its way, and this before it had been in its new quarters a week. Its strength, even before it was half grown, was great. It would drag along a large sweeping brush, or a warming-pan, grasping the handle with its teeth so that the head came over its shoulder, and advancing in an oblique direction till it arrived at the point where it wished to place it. The long and large materials were always taken first, and two of the largest were generally laid crosswise, with one of the ends of each touching the wall, and the other sides projecting out into the room. The area formed by the cross brushes and the wall he would fill up with hand-brushes, rush-baskets, books, boots, sheets, clothes, dried turf, or anything portable. As the work grew high, he supported himself on his tail, which propped him up admirably, and he would often, after laying more of his building materials, sit up over

U

against it, appearing to consider his work, or as the
country people say, 'judge it.'   This pause was sometimes followed by changing the portion of the material
'judged,' and sometimes it was left in its place.   After
he had piled up his materials in one part of the room
(for he chose the same place), he proceeded to wall up
the space between the feet of the chest of drawers,
which stood at a little distance from it, high enough
on its legs to make the bottom a roof for him, using
for this purpose dried turf and sticks, which he laid
very even, and filling up the interstices with bits of
coal, hay, cloth, or anything he could pick up.   This
last place he seemed to appropriate for his dwelling,
the former works seemed to be intended for a dam.
When he had filled up the space between the feet of
the chest of drawers, he proceeded to carry in sticks,
hay, cotton, and to make a nest; and when he had
done he would sit up under the drawers, and comb
himself with the nails of his hind feet.   In this operation, that which appeared to be a mal-formation was
shown to be a beautiful adaptation to the necessities
of the animal.   The huge webbed hard feet of the
beaver turn in so as to give the appearance of defor-
mity; but if the toes were straight instead of being
incurved, the animal could not use them for the purpose of keeping its fur in order, and cleaning it from
dirt and moisture.   Binney generally carried small
and light articles between his right fore-leg and his
chin, walking on the other three legs; and large
masses which he could not grasp readily with his
teeth, he pushed forward, leaning against them with
his right fore-paw and chin.   He never carried anything on his tail which he liked to dip in water; but
he was not fond of plunging in the whole of his body.
If his tail was kept moist he never cared to drink;
but if it was kept dry it became hot, and the animal
appeared distressed, and would drink a great deal.   It
is not impossible that the tail may have the power of
absorbing water, like the skin of frogs, though it must

be owned that the scaly integument which encrusts that member has not much of the character which generally belongs to absorbing surfaces.

"Bread and milk and sugar formed the principal part of Binney's food, but he was very fond of succulent fruits and roots. He was a most entertaining creature, and some highly comic scenes occurred between the worthy but slow beaver, and a light and airy macauco that was kept in the same apartment."

HARE.*

WE now come to two animals singularly alike in external appearance, but widely different in habits— the one being fossorial, the other a resident of the green fields. These two animals are the hare and the rabbit. Their resemblance is so great that it does not require the conventional ignorance of a cockney to confuse the two animals. I have heard a boy at a country school define a hare as "a little animal what lives in holes." The poor boy had evidently derived his knowledge of hares from two sources—the one from seeing it in connection with currant jelly and made gravy, the other from his spelling-book, which in its list of "words of similar sound, but different import," gives the following—

> "HAIR . . . on the head.
> HARE . . . in the fields."—

The misled juvenile accordingly made use of the latter piece of information, and having seen certain holes in the fields, conjectured that the hares lived therein.

However, there is not much difficulty in the matter, as the black tips to the ears of the hare are so conspicuous, as to distinguish it at once from the rabbit. This characteristic would not have been found useful in determining the species of a hare mentioned by

* *Lepus timidus.*

T 2

Jenyns.   The animal was shot, and was discovered to
be entirely without ears.   It did not appear to have
lost them by accident, but to have been born without
them, as not only were the ears themselves wanting,
but there was no orifice in the skin.

It is well known that the poachers usually capture
these animals by means of snares, cunningly contrived wire nooses placed across their paths, into
which the hares run, and are quickly strangled, as
they plunge about and struggle violently on feeling
the pressure of the wire round their necks.   One
instance is known where the animal was caught by
the middle of the body, and by the vehemence of its
struggles succeeded in breaking the wire from the peg
to which it was fastened.   Some time after its escape,
it was shot, and presented a most extraordinary appearance, looking, as the man who shot it asserted,
as if it had worn stays.   Its waist was still bound
with the wire, which had contracted its body until it
presented quite the appearance of an hour-glass.

My purpose is not to speak of the hare further than
to mention the method of distinguishing it from the
rabbit, to which animal we will now pass.

RABBIT.*

THERE is, perhaps, hardly any animal, the dog excepted, which is so altered by domestication as the
rabbit.   No one would recognise the common brown
rabbit to be the same animal as its domesticated relation, whose long ears sweep the ground as it walks,
whose fur becomes long and silky, whose colour
varies through all shades from black to white, whose
back has risen in an arch, whose legs are become
bandy, and whose throat has developed into a huge
dewlap, as large as three hens' eggs.

Yet there is no doubt that they are the same species.
for, if no other reason were wanting, the lop-eared

* *Lepus cuniculus.*

rabbits are always returning to the state and colour of
their savage forefathers. Indeed, out of every brood
produced by a pair of thorough-bred lop ears, half
are seen to carry their ears upright, and it is very rare
to secure more than one or two really fine animals out
of, a dozen.

Yes, it is even so. The brown little vagabonds that
scamper about the mouths of their burrows, owning
no law but their own pleasure, tumbling over head
and heels in sheer exuberance of delight, nibbling
the herbage, or sitting up on their hind legs to attain
a wider prospect, scuttling back to their holes at the
slightest panic, and now popping their impertinent
little heads out of their burrows, and playing with
fresh energy when satisfied that the coast is clear;
these animals, purchasable at the rate of sixpence a-
piece in the market, are the progenitors of your never-
sufficiently-to-be-praised prize " Lop," that magnificent
animal, rejoicing in bandy legs, monstrous ears,
humped back, dewlapped throat, butterfly smut, and
all the other deformities that constitute beauty according to rabbit fanciers; whose deportment is grave
and solemn, as befits so aristocratical an animal, and
for whom you have refused fifty guineas.

Now, for my part, I don't admire monsters. I infi-
nitely prefer an unsophisticated, unfashionable warren
rabbit to the finest specimen of " oar," " horn," or
" full " lop that ever issued from a fancier's cage. Of
course I have had lop-eared rabbits—every one has—
and they were really first rate animals, but they never
interested us nearly so much as a colony of the common rabbit, which we kept at the same time. By
" we " I mean the juvenile portion of the family, who
had a disused stable given them for the use of the
rabbits.

We began with three, and in a very short time the
3 took an 0 after it, but could never be changed into
·4· It was a singular fact that although we repeatedly
had thirty-nine rabbits at one time, we never could

reach forty. (A short time ago, I found that William Howitt had experienced precisely the same disappointment.) Not that there was any want of rabbits, but that forty were never in the stable at once, some being cooked, some dead, and some stolen. As to the latter part of the business, we met with rather an adventure.

We had been told that cats were the delinquents— a very reasonable suggestion, as the stable stood in a garden where cats swarmed at night,—and we therefore determined to take summary vengeance on the first cat that entered the stable. We had been lately reading an account of the first French Revolution, and had been greatly impressed with the description of the guillotine. A self-acting guillotine was consequently determined on as the best method of punishing the thief. So we carefully closed every entrance to the stable, merely leaving a hole in the window shutter, about six inches square. Above this we suspended a bill-hook, to the back of which was attached a brick and some pieces of iron, the hook being retained in its place by a slender stick that crossed the aperture. When the stick was moved, the bill-hook descended with great force, forming an arc of a circle, passing over the square aperture. On the whole it was not a bad piece of workmanship for three children, the eldest being ten years of age. The trap was accordingly set, and we retired for the night, in great expectation of discovering next morning a decapitated cat outside the window, and a detruncated head within.

Morning came, and we remained long in anxious expectation of the permission to rise. This given, we scampered off as fast as possible to the stable, where we found the trap down, several drops of blood, but no cat. On entering the stable, appearances were more mysterious, for the bill-hook was covered with blood, and a considerable amount of blood had run down the wall, but still no cat. However, the rabbits were all safe, and the cats never stole any more. The only circumstance that seemed to explain the mystery was, that a lad who had taken some pains about our rabbits, and who used to advise us as to the best method of fastening the stable at night, wore his arm in a sling for several weeks afterwards.

The rabbits themselves were well worth our care. I can easily understand how a shepherd knows every sheep by name, and is acquainted with the peculiar disposition of every member of the flock. We knew all our rabbits, and could distinguish any one by name at some distance. Our nomenclature was certainly limited, and strongly resembled Dandie Dinmont's. There was the big blue, the middle blue, and the little blue—blue meaning that slaty kind of tint which is so often seen in domesticated warren rabbits—these were derived from their comparative size when named, although the " little blue," soon became equal to the " big blue " in that respect. Then some received their name from that of the parent, such as ' Snowdrop's brownie." There were also a few miscellaneous names, such as " Charlie," in honour of the rocking-horse, at that time reduced to the state of the famous Trojan horse, and going on wheels, which the rabbit was supposed to resemble in colour. But pre-eminent over all, was a lovely little rabbit, unanimously called " Beauty."

This pretty creature was always tame. It would come when called, and take parsley from our hands, so that we used to let it run about the grass-plot, or give it an occasional grazing among the carrot-tops. We used to carry it about in our arms and use it like a baby (I mean of course, as *we* should have used a baby), giving it milk to drink, and all kinds of things to eat. I rather fancy that we gave it too many things to eat, for it died at the age of four months. Our grief was exceeding at our loss, and we consoled ourselves by celebrating its obsequies in the most sumptuous manner possible. We put all its family into mourning by tying a black collar round the neck of each; we built a, vault with brickbats and tiles; we

made a coffin out of an old hat-box; we buried the
poor rabbit with great pomp, and put up a monument,
on which was inscribed a truer epitaph than is usually
seen, emblazoned in gold, and engraved on a marble
tablet upheld by four sentimental cherubims, each
with a substantial pear-shaped tear on its inner cheek.

The rain soon washed away the inscription; the
wooden monument fell to decay; but we have not
forgotten our buried pet. The house has long since
passed into other hands; the rabbit stable is desecrated
by horses; the grass-plot is gravelled; but Beauty's
bones lie still in their vault under the apple-tree in
the garden.

It is the fashion to say that only the regular domesticated rabbits can be tamed; but the preceding narrative proves that such is not the case. Moreover,
there is no reason why the wild hare, an animal certainly as timid, should be capable of being tamed,
and rabbits should not. In further corroboration I
cite an interesting account sent by a lady to Mr.
Jesse.

" One evening last spring my dog barked at something behind a flower-pot that stood in the door-porch.
I thought a toad was there, but it proved to be a very
young rabbit, a wild one. The poor thing was in a
state of great exhaustion as if it had been chased, and
had been a long while without food. It was quiet in
the hand, and allowed a little warm milk to be put
into its mouth. Upon being wrapped in flannel and
placed in a basket by the fire, it soon went to sleep.
When it awoke, more milk was offered in a small
spoon, which this time was sucked with right good
will; and the little creature continued to take the milk
in this way for several days, until strong enough to
help itself out of a cup. It appeared to become tame
immediately, soon learnt its name, and I never saw a
happier or merrier little pet. Its gambols on the carpet were full of fun. When tired with play, it would
feed on the green food, and nice bits placed there for

it, and when satisfied. it used to climb up the skirt of
the dress, nestle in the lap or under the arm, and go
to sleep. If this indulgence could not be permitted,
then Bunny (as we called it) would spring into my
work-basket, and take a nap there. At midday it liked
to sit in the sun on the window seat, then it would
clean its fur and long ears, each being separately
drawn down. and held by one foot while brushed by
the other. This duty performed, it would stretch at
full length, and basking in the sun-beams, fall asleep.
Strange to tell, all this was going on with the dog in
the room, who had been made to understand that the
rabbit was not to be touched ; stranger still, the rabbit
ceased to show any fear of the dog, but, on the contrary, delighted in jumping on the dog's back, and
running after his tail. These liberties, however, were
not pleasing to Jewel; they were evidently only endured in obedience to the commands of his mistress.
Not approving of one favourite being made happy at
the other's expense, I was obliged to interfere on these
occasions, and call Bunny to order.

" Being frequently told that a wild rabbit could not
be so thoroughly domesticated, but that it would return to the woods if it regained its liberty, I feared
that if mine got loose it would certainly run away.
Yet I wished it should be sometimes in the garden to
feed upon such green food as it liked best; for this
purpose I fastened it with a collar and small chain,
and, thus secured, led it about. One evening the chain
unfortunately broke, and Bunny was free! At first
we saw it running from place to place with wild delight, but after a little while we could not see it, and
we hunted in vain under the shrubs, calling it by name
until it became dark ; we then ceased to search any
longer, and I concluded my pretty pet was gone.

" Before retiring for the night, I gave a last look
out of the window, in the hope I might chance to see
it once more. The moon was then shining brightly,
and I distinctly saw my little rabbit sitting at the door

with head and ears erect, as if listening for its friends within, anxious, perhaps, for its accustomed nice supper, and soft warm bed. I hastened down stairs to let it in, calling it by name, when, the moment I opened the door, a strange cat darted forward, seized it by the neck, and bore it screaming away! Of course every effort of mine was useless to overtake the cat.

"I feel convinced that this fond little creature would not have left us, to return to the wood. That it did not come when called was the effect of excessive joy for its newly-found freedom, which must have been doubly delightful while we were near, as no doubt it saw us when we could not see it, and was only quietly feeding when we thought it was gone away.

"Four months must have been the extent of poor Bunny's short life."

I mentioned before the probability that our pet rabbit died on account of the strange food that we gave to it. This was no solitary instance, as all our rabbits were subjected to much the same treatment, under much the same circumstances that induced Sterne to give a macaroni to a donkey, namely, out of curiosity to see whether they would eat the unaccustomed food. Certainly it was of a most miscellaneous nature, tallow candles, toffy, Albert-rock, and other such substances. However, the rabbits rather liked the tallow candles than otherwise, and were really fond of toffy. But the toffy was not very easy to eat, for the long incisor teeth of the rabbits stuck firmly in the saccharine compound, and could not be released until the toffy had dissolved in the ordinary course of things. The rabbits used to undergo great struggles, in endeavouring to free their imprisoned teeth, and shook their heads about just as a terrier shakes a rat.

Well would it be did rabbits confine their perverted appetites to such harmless things as Albert-rock and tallow candles. I must, however, state with regret that they not unfrequently eat their own offspring. This

strange habit they possess in common with several
other animals—mice among the number. The reasons for so doing are not very evident; but the fact is
well known. It is a comparatively common event
for the father to devour his offspring, but that the
mother should do so appears a perversion of the
animal instinct for which we cannot account. Sometimes a mother rabbit seems to be driven to the act by
the pangs of hunger, if she is left without food for
several days, but the usual cause appears to be the
disturbance occasioned if her young are inspected too
early. It is always dangerous to examine the young
of a tame rabbit, until they are brought forward by
their mother; as, if disturbed, she is very likely to eat
them, and if she has once done so, she will probably
repeat the offence without any provocation.

In connection with this custom, a curious circumstance occurred in my rabbitry. The mother of a very
young family was displeased at the curiosity evinced
by several children respecting her little ones, who were
very comfortably lying in the day-room. She therefore carried them off one by one into the bed-chamber,
picking them up in her teeth. One unfortunate little
creature was seized by one of its ears, and, in the
struggle between its parent and itself, the ear was
fairly pulled off. The mother took the misfortune
very philosophically; she ate the severed ear, and then
seizing her child by the ear that remained, dragged it
into the bedchamber with the rest.

It is possible to keep several mothers together with
their families in one large room, but the bucks must
be kept separate both from the does and from each
other. They are most quarrelsome animals, and are
liable to sudden attacks of fury, without any apparent
cause. When so enraged, they squeak and stamp
with their feet in as threatening a manner as they can
assume. When this anger is exercised towards man,
as not unfrequently happens, it has a very ludicrous
aspect, strongly reminding one of a puddle in a storm.

But to the companions of the rabbit it is no laughing matter, for the animal attacks any rabbit that comes near. The usual method of attack is by leaping over the object of dislike, and giving it a violent kick as they pass over its back; in this manner they often strike off pieces of fur with a single blow. I once saw a combat between a large buck rabbit and a cat, in which the rabbit came off victorious; the cat was completely puzzled, and after a few rounds, and losing no small amount of fur, left the rabbit conqueror of the field. She would boldly have resisted a dog who attacked her in front, but this method of jumping over her back, and inflicting a severe blow during the leap was too much for her.

That stamp of the foot is also used for other purposes besides that of attack; it serves as a mode of communicating alarm. If a number of rabbits are feeding quietly, and one of them takes fright, it stamps violently on the ground, and all the others scuttle into their holes.

I lately heard of a rabbit that inhabited a house in one of the back streets of Oxford. It especially favoured the shop, because greens and vegetables were sold there. The little animal was accustomed to discharge the part of a house-dog, and would run after and bite any intruder. Men rather laughed at the rabbit, but it was no laughing matter to the softer sex, whose unprotected ankles suffered wofully.

Much more might be said on the subject of rabbits, but as many more animals still remain to be illustrated, we must pass over them and turn to another group of animals.

OXEN.

It needs but a glance at this group to distinguish them from any of those that have been already described. Perhaps the point that shows itself more obviously than any other is the character of the skin

But to the .... of the rabbit it is no laughing matter .... any rabbit that comes near. .... attack is by leaping over the .... it a violent kick as they pass but .... this manner they often strike .... a single blow. I once saw a .... between a rabbit and a cat, in which the rabbit .... ; the cat was .... pricked .... wounds, and losing .... rabbit conqueror of the .... resisted a dog who attacked her .... method of jumping over her .... blow during the leap was .... her.

That .... of the foot is .... other purposes besides that of attack; .... a mode of communicating alarm. If a .... rabbits are feeding quietly, and one of .... fright, it stamps violently on the ground .... all the others scuttle into their holes.

I lately heard of a rabbit .... a house in one of the back streets of Oxford .... specially favoured the shop, because .... tables were sold there. The little animal was .... to discharge the part of a .... and would run after and bite any intruder. .... at the rabbit, but it was no laughing matter .... softer sex, whose unprotected .... suffered ....

Much more .... be said .... the subject of rabbits, but as many .... animals .... remain to be illustrated, we must .... over them and turn to another group of animals.

OXEN.

It needs but a glance at this group .... distinguish them from any of those that have been already .... scribed. Perhaps the point that shows it .... obviously than any other is the character ....

THE RABBIT AND CAT. p. 300.

—the dermal characteristics, as we should say if we wished to speak learnedly. All the animals contained in this group have very thick skins, and are therefore called "Pachydermata," a word which means literally "thick skins." The oxen, elephants, horses, deer, and such like animals, are all Pachydermata. In short, under that name are ranged all those animals whose skins are called "hides." The beasts of prey, the rodents, &c., are covered with "fur," while we must call the covering of the monkey tribes "skins."

I am afraid that if we ask under what name to place our own skins, they must be placed under the denomination of "hides." At all events, human skin tans beautifully in a primary and not in a secondary sense. There is in the museum of the College of Surgeons in London, a piece of tanned human skin, which might be imagined to have come from the sole of a shoe. Moreover, we have heard of the revengeful man, who covered his saddle with the skin of a slain enemy—a substitute for the "pig-skin," which is supposed to form the covering of saddles in general. There is no escape : we wear hides. Now most persons will not believe this, and will, perhaps, back their assertions by exhibiting a particle of what they are pleased to call "skin" displaced from an injured hand. But most people don't know what their skins are. They chafe their hand against a wall, and imagine that the silver-paper-looking substance that they have rubbed off is their skin. They would feel very uncomfortable were their skin no thicker than the slight external covering which has been removed. The skin is, in fact, very thick, the fingers being composed of little but skin, tendon, and bone.

Having thus slightly glanced at the relative qualities of "skin," "fur," and "hide," we will at once proceed to one of the animals whose skin is a hide. The first of these is the common ox.*

* *Bos taurus.*

I am not going to intrude upon the provinces of the spelling-books by enumerating the qualities of the cow, nor upon that of agricultural works, by descanting on the difference between the terms, " bull," " ox," " cow," " heifer," " quey," " beast," &c. Neither shall I discuss the various merits of long or short horns, Alderney, Devonshire, Hereford, or other breeds; but merely give examples of the character of the ox tribe.

The character of the bull is anything but pleasing. As a general fact, the whole of the bovine race are deficient in intellect and capricious in temper. Even the gentlest inhabitant of a farm-yard is apt to break out into fits of ill-temper for no assignable cause, and to kick or butt at those to whom she had been most mild. This characteristic is developed stronger, as the cow increases in years.

But, as may be expected from the usual characters of animals, the bull possesses more of the disagreeable qualities than the cow, and fewer of the amiable. Indeed, the bull is always rather a dangerous animal to approach, as the fits of ill-temper that sometimes possess the cow are exaggerated in the bull into the most ungovernable gusts of fury, during which the animal is perfectly blind to every object except his enemy. It is rather fortunate that the animal is thus blinded to external objects, as the attacked party is often able to escape by suddenly shifting to one side, and permitting the infuriated animal to pass by. It is said, that if a bull displays an inclination to charge, the best method is to get to a tree, if possible, or to any such obstacle, and then to stand *before* it, facing the bull. The animal will close its eyes, drop its head, and charge. By slipping on one side, the shock of the animal will be avoided, and, moreover, it will come with such violence against the tree, as to stun it for a short time, during which the person assaulted can make his escape good. Not very long since, a gentleman contrived to reach a park wall at a considerable distance, by. irritating the bull until it charged. He then leaped aside, and before the animal could check its headlong course, had gained some ground. The bull then made another charge, and was received in the same manner. By thus pursuing a zig-zag kind of course, the gentleman led the bull on until he reached the park wall. On placing his back against the wall, the bull, maddened with its former futile attempts, charged with double vehemence, and dashed its head with such vehemence against the wall, that it lay prostrate at the feet of its intended victim.

It is, however, pleasing to find that even the savage nature of a bull is susceptible of some better feelings, as will be seen in the following anecdote, extracted from a work by Mr. Egan.

" Mr. Benson, a gentleman whose veracity may be depended upon, informed us, that he was spending a month, a few years since, at the house of a farmer in the north of England, who had a bull so wild and ferocious that he was kept constantly chained, except when led to water, &c., at which he was never suffered to be out of the hands of a trusty person. This animal seemed to have conceived a particular antipathy towards Mr. Benson, who being young and daring, had probably at some time irritated him. He never saw him approach the open shed in which he was kept, without being heard to bellow most dreadfully, which he continued when the object of dislike was in view, at the same time tearing up the earth with his horns, and giving every symptom of the utmost aversion. On two occasions, while leading to water, he very cunningly watched an opportunity, and endeavoured to make a sudden spring out of the hands of his attendant, at Mr. Benson, who was standing in the yard. But during the time Mr. Benson sojourned at the house of the farmer, a most tremendous storm of thunder and lightning occurred ; and though Mr. Benson has often been in tropical storms, he declares, for about ten minutes, he never witnessed anything more awful. The lightning re-

sembled sheets of fire, and each flash was instantly
succeeded by a thunder-clap, as loud as if a volley of
ten thousand of cannon had been discharged. But
what most affected him was the piteous roarings of
the poor bull, which, exposed in its open shed to all
the fury of the elements, sent forth every instant a
yell of terror beyond description hideous. Imagining
that it was the lightning that caused alarm to the
animal, Mr. Benson proposed to the men-servants
to remove it to the barn; but in vain. They were
one praying in one corner, and another in another, as
much terrified as the bull, whose roarings made no
impression on them. He then said, "Well, then, I
will go myself; the poor creature will be tame enough
now." He accordingly put on his coat, and went
into the yard. The moment he approached the bull,
which was lying on its back, and had almost torn its
chain through the gristle of its nose in its efforts to
get loose, it rose, and by its fawning actions expressed
how delighted it was at the sight of anything human
amidst such a scene of horror. Like Roderick Dhu's
bull, in the "Lady of the Lake." when it had been
pricked on some scores of miles by the lances of a
troop of Highland foragers, its ferocity was gone, and
with the utmost quietness it suffered my friend to un-
tie it and lead it into the barn.

"The next morning, on crossing the farm-yard,
Mr. Benson remarked that his friend, who had regained his shed, no longer saluted him with his accustomed bellow. He thought that the animal might
remember his last night's kindness. He accordingly
ventured by degrees to approach it, and found that now,
so far from showing any ill-will towards him, it, with the
utmost gentleness, suffered him to scratch its head;
and from that day became to him as tame as a lamb,
suffering him to play all kinds of tricks with it,
which no person about the farm durst venture to attempt, and even seeming to take pleasure in being
noticed by him.

The colour of scarlet irritates a bull in an extra-

ordinary manner, and is certain to provoke an attack.
Whether a bull would attack a regiment of soldiers, I
do not know; but should rather imagine that it would
not, as the simultaneous movements of a body of men
cast cattle into the most abject state of terror. This I
can state from actual experience. During the six months
that I commanded a drill on a small scale, the manœuvres were carried on in a field of no very great
dimensions, so small, indeed, that the whole company once disappeared into a ditch, because the luck-
less commander called out " front," instead of " rear."
In this field were placed several cows, after the drill
had been going on for some time. When the squad
began to march, the cows congregated in an angle of
the field, and apparently determined to make a rush
through the line that was steadily approaching them.
When they neared the line, they changed their minds,
and dashed round the flanks with every mark of fear.
The opportunity was too tempting to be resisted, so
the pace was changed from " slow" to " double," and
the unfortunate cows were chased all over the field,
the squad continually extending, contracting, wheeling, and turning, so as to cut them off from every
hope of escape. The poor animals displayed scarcely
less fear than did a company of rustics who had
crowded into the field to see the performances, and
upon whom we suddenly came with fixed bayonets.
I never saw three cows so active before, or so large
a number of human beings get over a stile in so short
a time. Yet, be it confessed, if a bull had been
among the cows, we should have been very shy of
charging *him*, in spite of our bayonets.

It sometimes, however, happens, that the bull employs this combative quality in an useful manner. A
herd of buffalo bulls have been known to destroy a
tiger that had sprung upon their master; and there is
an account extant of the valour displayed by a bull in
defence of his wife. A jaguar had killed a cow, but
not without great resistance from the bull, who, as his

x

horns had been blunted in consequence of his ferocity, had suffered severely in the contest, and had not been able to prevent the jaguar from killing the cow. The owners of the slaughtered animal, knowing that the jaguar would be certain to return to his prey, plastered up the bull's wounds, re-sharpened his horns, and suffered him to go at liberty.

As had been expected, the jaguar came next night to feast on the body of the cow. The bull found it engaged in its repast, and attacked it with such fury, that it was found next morning lying dead by the side of the cow, its body having been completely transfixed by the bull's horns. Again and again did the bull return to his prostrate enemy, even though he had again received some severe wounds. The double combat had so heightened his ferocity, that his owners were again forced to blunt his horns.

A more extraordinary combat is related by Mr. Palliser, between a bison bull, and a thorough bred domestic bull of one of the long-horned breeds. The combat, as he tells us, must have been quite Homeric.

"About three months previous to my arrival in Fort Union, and in the height of the buffalo-breeding season, when their bulls are sometimes very fierce, Joe was taking the Fort Union bull with a cart into a point of the river, above the fort, in order to draw home a load of wood which had been previously cut and piled ready for transportation the day before, when a very large old bison bull stood right in the cart-track, pawing up the earth and roaring, ready to dispute the passage with him. On a nearer approach, instead of flying at the sight of the man that accompanied the cart, the bison made a headlong charge. Joe had hardly time to remove his bull's headstall, and escape up a tree, being utterly unable to assist his four-footed friend, whom he left to his own resources. Bison and bull, now in mortal combat, met midway with a shock that made the earth tremble. Our previously docile, gentle animal suddenly became transformed into a furious beast, springing from side to side, whirling round as the buffalo attempted to take him in the flank, alternately upsetting and righting the cart again; which he banged from side to side, and whirled round as if it had been a band-box. Joe, safe out of harm's way, looked down from the tree at his champion's proceedings, at first deploring the apparent disadvantage he laboured under from being harnessed to a cart; but when the fight had lasted long and furious, and it was evident that one or the other must fall, his eyes were opened to the value of the protection afforded by the harness, and especially by the thick strong shafts of the cart against the short horns of the bison, who, although he bore him over and over again down on his haunches, could not wound him severely. On the other hand, the long sharp horns of the brave Fort Union bull began to tell on the furrowed sides of his antagonist, until the final charge brought the bison, with a furious bound, dead under our hero's feet, whose long fine-drawn horn was deep driven into his adversary's heart. With a cheer that made the woods ring again, down clambered Joe, and while triumphantly caressing, also carefully examined his chivalrous companion, who, although bruised, blown, and covered with foam, had escaped uninjured. It required all Joe's nigger eloquence to persuade the bull to leave the slain antagonist, over whom he long stood watching, evidently expecting him to get up again to renew the combat; Joe all the while coaxing him with ' Him dear bull, him go home now, and do no more work to-day,' which prospect ' black Joe,' in common with all his sable brethren, considered as the acme of sublunary felicity."

The noble animal, who performed this feat, met with an untimely end. He was one day seen to walk across the river, and make his way to the Fort. He then sank bleeding on the ground, and expired at the foot of the flag-staff. He had been shot by a couple of rascally Sioux Indians, who with their arrows had also severely wounded nearly half of the milch cows, and had actually killed several of them.

I have already recorded the sugar and sweetmeat eating propensities of some rabbits, and must now record a similar perversion of taste on the part of a bull. The animal in question contrived to get at one of the pans into which maple sugar is poured to cool, and began to help himself to the contents. The sugar had just been poured into the pans in a boiling state, so that the unfortunate animal had reason to repent of his gluttony. On discovering his mistake, he set off at full speed, with his tail in the air, and with a considerable amount of the scalding stuff adhering to his nose.

When cows are young, they are often very tame and gentle. There were two cows to whom I was much attached, having known them from their birth. Their names were " Star" and " Primrose." They were exceedingly fond of the mangel-wurzel, and probably based their attachment to me on the grounds of my ability to procure for them the expected dainty. They were even troublesome in their affection, for it was impossible to walk through the yard without having them capering behind, and occasionally butting with their heads in order to claim attention. On one occasion they kept me prisoner for some little time. There was a very narrow shed, at the extremity of which was a pile of mangel-wurzels. I had gone in one day, in order to procure some of the roots for the cows, when the place became suddenly darkened. The cause of the sudden eclipse was the appearance of the two cows, who had come to the half door that closed the shed, and were pressing against it, hoping to obtain admission. They remained there, and ate the slices of root that were given them, but did not relax their pressure on the door, nor could they be removed without a stratagem.

These two creatures were very tame, and would come when called, suffer almost any liberty to be taken with them, even submitting to be used as couches if the grass were not quite dry. They were very playful, and used to get up sham fights, until one of them knocked off one of her playfellow's horns. The horn was replaced and bandaged, but it failed to unite, and its place was taken by a new horn, very shapeless, and very thick. The bleeding was quite alarming when the accident took place.

These two animals gave me the first opportunity of observing that strange etiquette which is so prevalent among cows. With them, if a number of cows have been brought up together, the eldest always takes the lead, and indeed will not stir until she can do so. If a new cow is introduced into a yard, she struggles with the others until she finds her place. So tenacious are the cows of this their privilege, that a senior cow has been known to refuse to enter the shed because the junior cows had gone in first, and actually to wait until they were all turned out again. She then walked in at the head of the procession in conscious dignity.

The author of " Eöthen " avers that in the East, to be respected is not a mere title, but conveys with it a clear right to take your neighbour's cattle, or fruit, or milk, or any part of his property, his wife only ex cepted. Such seems to be the case among cows. The senior cow considers herself to have a right to the best stall, the best fodder-rack, and the best place everywhere. So she exercises her right. When the cows are fed, she generally inspects the food of all the cows, and if, as is generally the case, she sees one of them with a better or larger share of food than her own, she butts the rightful owner away, and takes possession.

" Star " and " Primrose " were mere calves when first placed among the cows, and were shamefully treated by them. The weakest often literally went to the wall, being shoved against it by an elder cow, who wished to inspect the state of the fodder-rack. But as the calves grew older, their dignity increased, and they seemed to be impressed with the same notions as a small fag at a public school who submits patiently to his present ill treatment, fully intending to make up for it when he is a big boy and has a fag of his own. In two years these calves were the seniors of the yard, the others having been sold or killed, and they in their turn bullied the younger cows, pushed them about, and robbed their racks, precisely as they had been bullied, pushed about, and robbed themselves.

It did not seem possible that anything could add to their dignity, but it was even so. One of them was a mother, and became twice as proud. She nearly killed her calf by poking at it with her nose and turning it over. She watched anxiously for every one who entered the yard, and was uneasy until they had paid her a visit and admired her baby. Her behaviour when she and her little one went out was very amusing. She could not bear any one to pass her calf without caressing it, but at the same time, her maternal fears were so great, that she was continually interposing herself, and pressing away the very person whom she had endeavoured to attract.

I conclude this account of the domestic cow with two extracts from Topsell, wherein he teaches us the benefit to be expected from the bull's hide, and also some of the medicinal properties of the same animal.

" Out of the hides of buls, especially their ears and necks, is most excellent glew confected, but for the most part is corrupted by seething with it old leather of shooes or boots; but that of Rhodes is, without all fraud, fit for physitians and painters, and evermore the whiter the better, for that which is black is good for nothing; wherefore that which is made out of bulls' hides is so white that it sendeth forth a brightness, whose vertuous conjunction in conglutination is so powerful, that it is easier to break a whole piece of wood than any part so glewed together therewith; and for this invention we are (saith Pliny) indebted to Dædalus, the first author thereof. They used it in instruments of musick and such other tender and pretious actions."

He then gives us several recipes for complaints, but forgets to state whether he is practically acquainted with them or not. " The fat of a Dormouse, of a Hen, and the marrow of a bul melted together, and poured warm into the ears, easeth their pain very much, and if the liver of a bul be broyled on a soft fire, and put into one's mouth that hath the tooth ach, the pain will go away so soon as ever the teeth touch it. The gall of a bull is sharper than an ox's, and it is mingled with Hony for a wound-plaister, and in all outward remidies against poyson. It hath also a quality to gnaw the deadness or corruption out of Wounds, and with the juyce of leeks and the milk of women, it is applyed against the Swine-pox; but the gall alone rubbed upon the biting of an ape, cureth that malady."

BISON.*

PASSING over the buffaloes, we come to an animal that is often, but erroneously, spoken of as a buffalo, the bison of North America.

The Americans appear to have a great propensity for giving old-world names to new-world objects. The bison, for example, is spoken of as a buffalo, and the puma is called a panther. This propensity is further exemplified by the names of their towns and lakes, many of which have old-world names, but distinguished by the prefix of the word " new." It is much to be regretted that in so many cases they should have abolished the really euphonious native name, and substituted some insignificant European word. This does not apply to the names given by the " Voyageurs," who

* *Bison Americanus.*

continue to affix appellations to the various localities, which are, at all events, appropriate, if not euphonious.

There is not much difficulty in distinguishing a bison from an ox even at first sight, but if we were placed before a skeleton of each we should doubtless be perplexed; just as, although it is easy enough to tell a lion from a tiger when we see it, none but an expert anatomist can distinguish between the skeletons. It does not, however, require any very deep anatomical knowledge to distinguish between the skeleton of a bison and an ox, as the ox has but thirteen ribs on each side, while the American bison has fifteen, the European bison, or auroch, possessing fourteen pairs of ribs.

The bison, by which name we only understand the American species, is only found in the northern parts of America, never appearing south of lat. 33°.

The whole appearance of the animal is most singular, the bull bison being a perfectly unique animal. Its shoulders and 'hump' are covered with a profusion of long hairs, something like a lion's mane, which sometimes sweeps the ground. This mass of hair and wool extends over the whole head, which is enveloped by it, in the same manner as we see the head of a Skye terrier buried in hair. The animal is further furnished with a thick black beard. In the winter months the entire body is covered with thick woolly hair: from this circumstance the skin is more valuable when the animal is killed in winter, than if the hide is taken in the summer, as in the hot months a very large portion of the warm woolly covering disappears.

The enormous mass of shaggy hair and mane gives the animal a most ferocious appearance, which is by no means borne out by its general character. Usually the bison is a quiet and timid animal, and it is only at certain times of the year, or when it is driven to bay, that it is really dangerous.

The enormous size of the fore quarters of the animal, gives its legs an appearance of being too small for the body, an opinion which is the more strengthened by the comparatively small size of its hind legs, which are bent in a manner that strongly reminds the spectator of the hyæna. Indeed a bison is not at at all unlike a vaccine hyæna, if such an animal can be imagined.

But these apparently weak legs can carry the huge animal with perfect ease over places that horses dare not attempt. In activity the bull is not equal to the cow, her lighter body enabling her to surpass the. bull in speed.

The flesh of the bison is remarkably good, and is said to possess the agreeable quality of not surfeiting those who indulge in it even to an unwarrantable extent. The fat is said by some to resemble that of turtle, and the very finest ox beef that our tables can boast is said to be unworthy of comparison with the "hump" of the bison. Indeed, on one occasion, the experiment was tried, and some excellent beef sent to table as a great treat. But the guests soon left their beef, and returned to their "hump." An Indian declared that the beef was coarse and insipid, and that the fat would make one sick.

Through the agency of Cooper's works, the delicious properties of a bison's 'hump' have become as well, or perhaps better, known in England than the similar qualities of venison and turtle. Now let us see how the hunters procure this celebrated hump. When a bison is killed, it is first raised from its prostrate position and placed on its knees, as if lying down. A longitudinal incision is then made from the part of the hump nearest the head, and continued backwards to the loins; a large piece of skin is then removed from each side, and laid on the ground, the hairy side next the earth, and upon them the 'fleeces,' as they are called, are laid, as they are taken from the animal. The 'fleeces' comprise all the flesh that lies at each side of the vertical processes of the shoulder, and, if taken from a full-grown animal, weigh about a hundred pounds. So delicate is this part of the animal, and so common are the bisons, that hundreds are slaughtered, merely for the sake of their hump and tongue, the remainder of the huge animal being left to the wolves and birds. From the peculiar nature of their pursuits, the hunters are singularly improvident, and seem to partake of the nature of the predacious beasts and birds, at one time gorging themselves with the most delicate parts of their prey, while at others, they are worn to the bone with famine and privation, merely through their improvidence in neglecting to cure some little part of the vast quantities of good food left to fester in the desert.

An animal that possesses such qualities as these is not likely to obtain much rest in the vicinity of man. When we see men spending whole days in galloping after a little red animal, of whom they frequently do not even get a glimpse until the end of the hunt, and possibly not then, it can hardly be expected that man will not hunt an animal, which furnishes him with provisions and warm clothing, and which not only affords him a most exciting amusement, but which may be hunted over hundreds of miles without an apparition of a farmer mounting guard with a pitchfork over the gate of a corn-field, where trespassers are warned that they will be "punished with the utmost rigour of the law."

There are many methods of hunting this animal, but that in most request is the chase on horseback. This amusement requires good horsemanship, no small amount of nerve, and a steady hand. The weapon used by the white hunters is generally the rifle, but the native Indians prefer the bow and arrow, which weapons they wield with astonishing skill. They are not good at a long shot, but when mounted, and armed with their favourite weapons, bow, arrow, and spear, they are unmatched. , The bow, used by them for hunting purposes, is a weapon that looks more like a child's toy than an instrument of destruction. It is barely a yard long, and very slight in construction, deriving its power from the sinews of animals, dexterously worked into its back. With one of these bows an Indian has been known to send an arrow completely through the body of a bison. With such dexterity and rapidity are these weapons used, that if white and red hunters go in the same chase, the red men usually kill more game than the white. But that the reason for this circumstance may be understood, we must first see how the bisons are hunted.

The animals generally live in great droves, or herds, one herd often containing upwards of 15,000 individuals. The hunters contrive to separate the best and fattest animals from the herd, and, having succeeded in getting alongside, inflict the fatal wound just behind the shoulder. The horses are so well trained to the work, that they will almost spontaneously place themselves on the animal's left side, and sheer off directly the shot has been fired. It will now be seen why the Indians prefer the bow and arrow to the rifle, as an Indian will discharge half a dozen arrows in the same time that would be occupied in loading and firing a rifle once.

In order to overcome this difficulty, the huntsmen now prefer the smooth bore gun, carrying balls of about sixteen or twenty to the pound. Provided with this weapon, the hunter can fire nearly as fast as the Indian can shoot, and therefore has the advantage over him, as a bullet always does more execution than an arrow. There is no need of ramrod, patches, powder-flasks, copper caps, bullet pouch, or any other impediment. The powder is carried loose in the pockets, and a quantity taken at a guess, and poured down the barrel. The bullet is taken from the mouth, where a stock of balls is always kept, in readiness, as milliners keep their pins, and upholsterers their tacks, and dropped wet into the barrel. The gun is furnished with a self-priming flint lock, and needs no cap.

The gun is not loaded until the moment before it is discharged.   The powder is poured in, the wet bullet dropped upon the powder, the barrel lowered to the charge, and the shot fired, the angle being calculated by the eye, and therefore the act of raising to the shoulder being rendered unnecessary.   The wet state of the bullet prevents it from rolling out of the gun during the short time that the barrel is lowered. A very accurate aim is not requisite at such very close quarters, and the amount of powder is of no particular consequence.

The Indians have various methods of killing the bison.   Sometimes they make a kind of a fold, and drive a number of the beasts into it, where they can be leisurely slaughtered.   Sometimes they form a semicircle round a herd, and by shouts and gestures drive them all over a precipice, those behind forcing forward those in front.   But the greatest ingenuity is shown by the solitary hunter, who, not unfrequently, returns laden with the spoils of six or seven victims. One very favourite method of attack is, by putting on the skin of a bison calf.   The hunter is thus enabled to penetrate into the centre of a herd, and to pick out the choicest animals, whom he soon lays low, as the unsuspecting creatures hear no sound to terrify them, and view their prostrate comrades with indifference. Sometimes the hunter puts on the skin of a wolf, and in that guise crawls near enough to plant his deadly weapon in the heart of any animal that he chooses. For the bisons, when in health, do not care for the wolves, and permit them to walk among the herd unmolested, knowing full well that the wolves will not dare to attack them while they are in the enjoyment of health and strength.   Many a sickly or wounded bison falls to the wolf's lot, but it never ventures to show its teeth to a healthy animal, when protected by the presence of its companions.

In all cases the hunter must beware lest he gives

the animal his wind, for the bison is very acute of
scent, and, on feeling the dreaded presence of man,
instantly makes off at the top of its speed.

The singularly heavy mass of hair, wool, and fur,
that covers the head and shoulders of the bull bison,
has already been mentioned, as well as the usefulness
of the thick fur in forming a winter cloak. But on
one occasion, this woolliness proved useful to the
hunter in rather an unexpected manner. Mr. Palliser
is the narrator of the following story.

"One beautiful, clear, cold morning in January, I
started to shoot some prairie fowl. I had not been
long out, when an Indian overtook me, and said in
Sioux, 'Ho, my friend! I saw the track of your long
foot in the snow.' He wanted me to help him in
stalking up three buffalo bulls that were feeding in
some willows at a little distance. I accordingly
started off with him, and we came within about a
third of a mile from the spot. I went carefully
round to leeward, and directed the Indian to go and
give them his wind, by approaching on the other
side, so soon as he thought I had reached my intended post, whither I knew they would make in
order to pass through to the open plain. So accu-
rately had the Indian calculated time and distance,
that I was hardly at my place, when a huge bull
thundered headlong by me, and received a shot low
and close behind the shoulders as he passed. He
stumbled on for about ten paces, and lay quietly
down. I waited to re-load; and on going up, found
him stone-dead. The Indian then joined me, and
said that the other two bulls had not gone far, but
had taken different directions; so we agreed that he
should pursue one and I the other. I soon came in
sight of mine. He was standing a little way off on
the open plain. But the skirting willows and brushwood afforded me cover within eighty yards of him,
profiting by which I crept up, and taking deliberate

aim, fired. The bull gave a convulsive start, moved
off a little, and turned his broadside again to me. I
fired again, over a hundred yards this time. but he did
not move. I loaded and fired the third time, whereupon he turned and faced me, as if about to show
fight. As I was loading for a fourth shot, he tottered
forward a step or two, and I thought he was about to
fall. So I waited for a little while ; but as he did not
come down, I determined to go up and finish him.
Walking up, therefore, to within thirty paces of him,
till I could actually see his eyes rolling, I fired for
the fourth time directly at the region of the heart, as
I thought ; but to my utter amazement, up went
his tail and down went his head, and with a speed I
thought him little capable of, he was upon me in a
twinkling. I ran hard for it ; but he rapidly overhauled me, and my situation was becoming anything
but pleasant. Thinking he might, like our own
bulls, shut his eyes in making a charge, I moved
suddenly to one side to escape the shock ; but to my
horror, I failed in dodging him, for he bolted round
quicker than I did, and affording me barely time to
protect my stomach with the stock of my rifle, and to
turn myself sideways, as I sustained the charge in the
hope of getting between his horns, he came plump
upon me with a shock like an earthquake. My rifle
stock was shivered to pieces by one horn, my clothes
torn by the other. I flew into mid-air, scattering my
prairie-fowl and rabbits, which had hitherto hung
dangling by leather thongs, in all directions, till,
landing at last, I fell unhurt in the snow, and almost
over me, fortunately not quite, rolled my infuriated
antagonist, and subsided in a snow-drift. I was
luckily not the least injured, the force of the blow
having been perfectly deadened by the enormous
mass of fur, wool, and hair that clothed his shaggy
head-piece."

In reading this account, we cannot but admire the

ready presence of mind which seems to be engendered by a length of time spent in chasing dangerous animals.

The importance of the bison to the Indians cannot be overrated, as it furnishes them with almost every necessary of life. But their improvidence, which is the usual characteristic of man in a savage state, often causes them to be for many days without a morsel of meat. A grand bison-dance is then determined upon by the sages of the tribe. For this dance, every Indian is forced to furnish himself with a grotesque mask, made of the head of a bison, dressed so as to retain the whole of the bushy mane, and further adorned by a long strip of hide taken along the spine of the animal, to the end of which is attached the tail. It is, in fact, a continuous strip of hide, terminating at one extremity by the animal's head, and at the other by its tail. Several excellent specimens of these masks may be seen at Catlin's Exhibition.

When a sufficient number of dancers are assembled, they form themselves into a ring, and keep up a strange movement, intended to resemble the movements of the bison. As the gestures are rather laborious, the dancer is fatigued in a short time. When he finds himself beginning to feel tired, he stoops down and places himself in front of one of the other dancers, who shoots him with a blunted arrow, with which they are all provided. The dancer then falls down, counterfeits the struggles of a wounded bison, and after simulating its death, is entitled to leave the ring and rest himself.

The Indians are very proud of this dance, and boast that it never fails of bringing bisons—an assertion which is strictly true, inasmuch as they never leave off dancing until the bisons have appeared.

The hide of the bison is also used by the Indians in making their shields. For this purpose, a carefully-chosen hide is stretched on the ground, and sur-

rounded with pegs, in order to prevent one part from
contracting more than another. The hide is then
subjected to the dressing-process, the principal part
of which consists in embuing it with glue; and the
pegs being gradually and carefully removed, it shrinks
into barely half its former dimensions, and nearly
doubles its thickness. It is then cut and trimmed
into shape; and when it has seen some service is
fringed with scalps and such like ornaments. Although the shield retains a considerable portion of
flexibility, it is proof against an arrow; but is of little
use against a rifle-ball. The quality of the shield depends materially on the skill of the maker, some
Indians being celebrated for the excellency of their
manufacture. The Indians are most skilful in leather making, if we may call untanned skins leather.
They have a method of preparing the skins of deer
in such a way that they always retain their flexibility,
and, even if saturated with water, do not become stiff
and hard when dry, as is the case with leather in
general.

The flesh of the bison is used extensively in the
manufacture of the hard composition known by the
name of " dried meat " and " pemmican." The dried
meat is very correctly so termed; for it is very dry
indeed, and looks like portions of old rope saturated
with tar; and the pemmican, which is, as it were, the
butter, the dried meat forming the bread, is undisguisedly tallow and sawdust mixed in equal proportions. The pemmican, it may be observed, is considered to be rather a delicacy; and only a small piece
is served out with every pound of dried meat.

I would not recommend any one who can get anything else to try their teeth upon dried meat, even
with the addition of pemmican. I have tried it myself; and on displaying unmitigated disgust, was
told by a sailor, that if I had been three or four days
without anything to eat, it would have been delicious,
particularly if the pemmican had been made into

broth, and the dried meat dipped into it. Broth!
Fancy a " broth" composed of a piece of tallow about
the size of a lady's thimble, immersed in a pint of
boiling water, and you will have a very correct idea of
the broth mentioned with such approbation.

The bison cows are always chosen in preference to
the bulls, for conversion into pemmican and dried
meat, their flesh being much more tender than that
of the male animal. When prepared, I suppose the
difference to the palate would be as great as between
old ropes and old whipcord. The animal does not
only furnish meat for the hunter, but also drink; for
the hunters sometimes relieve their thirst in a
manner similar to that employed by the camel-
drivers—namely, by piercing the stomach of the
slaughtered animal, and collecting the liquid therein
contained. Mr. Townsend, who has related several
" buffalo" hunts with some spirit, on seeing this plan
pursued by some of the hunters, was so disgusted
that, although tormented with burning thirst, he put
aside the cup politely offered him by his companions,
who only indulged in a hearty laugh at such squeam-
ishness, and drained the tin pan with every mark of
approval. He soon, however, so far laid aside his
civilised feelings of disgust, as to quench his thirst by
a method that proves the ancient mode of suicide
by drinking bull's blood to be very apocryphal; for no
harm happened to him after indulging in a lengthened draught from the heart of the bison.

During many months of the year, the prairie is
deeply covered with snow, under which is buried the
herbage on which the bison feeds. The hungry animals do not scrape away the snow with their feet, as
might be supposed, but push it away with their
noses So trying is this duty, that the snow is often
seen stained with blood where they have been feeding, and their noses are found to be quite raw when
they have been shot in winter. In the summer,
however, they fare luxuriously; for many miles of

prairie are often set on fire, sometimes purposely to drive out the lurking animals, sometimes accidentally from the fire left by a hunter. The dry grass is thus burned up, and in its place springs up a large quantity of most delicately tender herbage.

No benefit is without its drawbacks, and the bisons compound for their improved food by their sufferings from the mosquito. To fortify themselves against the attacks of their winged foes, they take every opportunity of rolling themselves in the mud, which, when hardened, forms a defence that even a mosquito cannot pierce. It is not everywhere that the bison can find a mud-hole, so he makes one for himself when the mosquitoes begin to plague him. He looks out for any damp spot, and throwing himself on the ground, whirls himself round and round, until he has made a large hole in the earth. This soon fills with the water that drains into it from the moist earth, and by the continual exertions of the bison's body, is soon made into a large mud-hole. In many places, the ground is quite studded with these holes.

I had forgotten to mention that there is also a preparation called "jerked" meat, made from the bison. The mode of manufacture is remarkable for its simplicity. The flesh is cut from the animal in long, thin, narrow slips, and stuck upon branches of trees, or pegged out on lines erected for the purpose until it is dry and hard. Three days are sufficient for the purpose. Let us hope, for the sake of the consumers, that it is better than dried meat and pemmican.

It may seem rather strange that so conspicuous an animal as the bison should be mistaken for any other creature in existence, especially in its own country. But it is so, and the inexperienced hunter frequently mistakes it for an animal about as unlike the original as can be expected, viz. a *crow*. This is owing to the difficulty of distinguishing distances on the vast expanse of the prairie, when there are no intervening objects to serve as guides for the eye, and therefore, an unaccustomed eye is not aware of the great distance between itself and the little black objects, who are consequently supposed by the novice to be crows. However, to make matters equal, he as frequently takes crows for bisons.

The young of this animal are very affectionate, but by no means discriminating in their affection, as the following extract from Townsend will show :—

" The young buffalo calf is also very often taken, and if removed from the mother and out of sight of the herd, he will follow the camp as steadily as a dog; but his propensity for following close at the horse's heels, often gets him into trouble, as he meets with more kicks than caresses from them. He is considered an interloper, and treated accordingly. The bull calf, of a month or two old, is sometimes rather difficult to manage; he shows no inclination to follow the camp, like the younger ones, and requires to be dragged along by main force. At such times he watches for a good opportunity, and before his captor is at all aware of what is going on, he receives a *butt* from this little brute, which, in most cases, lays him sprawling upon the ground.

" I had an adventure of this sort a few days before we arrived at the rendezvous. I captured a large bull-calf, and, with considerable difficulty, managed to drag him into the camp by means of a rope wound around his neck, and made fast to the high pommel of my saddle. Here I attached him firmly, by a cord, to a stake driven into the ground, and considered him secure. In a few minutes, however, he succeeded in breaking his fastenings, and away he scoured out of the camp. I lost no time in giving chase, and although I fell flat into a ditch, and afforded no little amusement to our people thereby, I soon overtook him, and was about seizing the stunted rope, which was still around his neck, when, to my surprise, the little animal showed fight; he came at me with all his force, and, dashing his head into my breast, bore me

to the ground in a twinkling. I, however, finally succeeded in recapturing him, and led and pushed him
back to the camp; but I could make nothing of him
—his stubbornness would neither yield to severity nor
kindness, and the next morning I loosed him and let
him go."

Mr. Palliser records a similar case of tameness on
the part of a bison calf. He chased it and its mother
for some time, until the mother was at last forced to
leave her offspring. The little animal, who had
scarcely opened its eyes on the world, ran gallantly,
but was at last overhauled. One of its pursuers then
imitated the cry of a bison cow, when the calf turned
round, trotted up to the hunters, and accompanied
them home to the fort, frisking round them the whole
time.

The bison has been successfully tamed, and there
are now several living in Ireland.

DEER.

THE oxen are all more or less clumsy in their shape
and movements, but the deer are almost invariably
both elegant in form and graceful in action. Putting
aside the general shape of the animals, the deer are
distinguished at once from the oxen by the peculiar
formation and shape of their horns. The horns of
the oxen are hollow, permanent, and formed around a
vascular core. They are, moreover, composed of a peculiar substance analogous to the material of which
hoofs and talons are composed.

The horns of all the deer are formed on a very different principle. In the first place, they are solid deposits of bone; in the second, they are deciduous,
being only retained during part of a year; and in the
third place, they are deposited from the exterior instead of the interior. The process of formation is
so singular, that I shall give a short account of the
progress of a horn during its short-lived existence.

We will suppose that a full-grown stag is hiding in
the depths of the forests, in the month of March.
He has no horns of any kind, and is hardly to be distinguished from a doe, but for his superior size. On
his head are two slight prominences, covered with a
kind of velvety skin. In a few days the prominences
become much larger, and in a week or so begin to assume a horn like shape. Now, grasp these budding
horns with your hand, and you will find them quite
hot, considerably hotter than those of the young ox.
They are hot, because this velvety substance, with
which they are covered, is little else than a thick mass
of arteries and veins, through which the blood is
pouring almost with the rapidity of inflammation, depositing with every touch a minute portion of bony
matter. More and more rapidly increases the growth.
The external carotid arteries become enlarged, to
supply a sufficient tide of blood to the horns through
their arteries, whose size can be imagined from the
grooves that they leave on the horn   At this period,
of their growth, the horns can be easily broken off,
and if they are wounded in any way, the blood
pours out with astonishing rapidity. At length the
process is complete, and the noble animal walks
decorated proudly with his enormous mass of horns.
But the horns are at present useless, or worse than
useless to him, for not only does he not use them,
but he fears the slightest touch, because the san-
guineous tide still pours round them. How is this to
be stopped, and how is the velvety covering to be got
rid of?

In a manner no less simple than wonderful. The
arteries, having completed their work in depositing
sufficient matter for the substance of the horn, now
turn their attention to the base. It will be seen that
all the arteries that supply blood to the horns must
necessarily pass up its base. As the bony substance
is deposited, each artery leaves for itself a groove, very
deep at the base, and becoming shallower towards the

tip.   The entire horn being furnished, the base now
becomes enlarged ; the grooves, in which the arteries
lie, are covered by a bony deposit that compresses
the artery within ; the deposit becomes gradually
thicker, and the arteries are in consequence gradually
reduced in size, until at last they are completely obliterated, and the supply of blood cut off entirely.   The
velvet, being thus deprived of its nutriment, soon
dies, and in a few days dries up, when the deer rubs
off the shrivelled fragments against the trees, and is
ready for combat.

Sometimes the deer is so impatient that he rubs off
the velvet before the arteries are entirely obliterated,
and consequently loses some blood.   I have seen a
rein-deer busily engaged in rubbing off the velvet
while the blood was trickling down the horns, and the
velvet hanging in crimson rags, dripping with blood.
The animal presented a most ferocious appearance at
the time.

RED DEER, ETC

WE will commence with the Stag, or Red Deer,* and,
before proceeding with the true account of the animal,
will read an extract from the pages of our friend Topsell.

He here gives us an account of the proceedings
between a hart and a serpent.

"I cannot assent to the opinion of *Ælianus*, that
affirmeth, the serpents follow the breath of a hart
like some philtre or amarous cup ; for seeing that all
authors hold an hostility in natures betwixt them, it
is not probable that the serpent loveth the breath of a
beast, unto whose whole body he is an enemy, with a
perpetual antipathy.   And if any reply that the warm
breath of a hart is acceptable to the cold serpent, and
that therefore she followeth it, as a dog creepeth to the
fire, or as other beasts to the beams of the sun ; I will

* *Cervus Elaphus.*

not greatly gainsay it, seeing by that means it is most clear, that the breath doth not by any secret force, or virtue, extract and draw her out of the den, but rather the concomitant quality of heat, which is not from the secret fire in the bones of the hart's throat (as Pliny hath taught), but rather from her ordinary expiration, inspiration, and respiration. For it cannot be, that seeing all the parts of a serpent are opposite to a hart, that there should be any love to that which killeth her.

" For my opinion, I think that the manner of the hart drawing the serpent out of her den, is not as *Ælianus* and *Pliny* affirmeth by sending into the cave a warm breath which burneth and scorcheth the beast out of her den ; but rather when the hart hath found the serpent's nest, she draweth the air by secret and violent attraction out from the serpent, who to save her life followeth the air out of her den ; as when a vessel is broached or vented, the wine followeth the flying air ; and as a cupping-glass draweth blood out of a scarified place of the body, so the serpent is drawn unwillingly to follow her distroyer, and not willingly as *Ælianus* affirmeth."

This account is wonderful enough, but not so wonderful as the circumstantial relation of the enmity between deer and serpents, and their combats, as given by the same writer in the following lines.

" There is many times strange conflicts betwixt the hart and the serpent thus drawn forth ; for the serpent seeing her adversary, lifteth her neck above the ground, and gnasheth at the hart with her teeth, breathing out very bitter hissings ; on the contrary, the hart, deriding the vain endeavours of his weak adversary, readier to fright than powerful to harm him, suffereth him to embrace both his neck and legs with his long and thin body, but in an instant teareth it into a hundred pieces. But the most strange combats are betwixt the harts and serpents of Lybia, where the hatred is deeper, and the serpents watch the hart when he lyeth asleep on the ground, and being a multitude of them set upon him together, fastening their poysenful teeth in every part of his skin; some on his sides and back, some on his legs, and some do hang upon his belly, biting him with mortal rage, to overthrow their foe.

" The poor hart being thus oppressed with a multitude, and pricked with venomous pains, essayeth to run away, but all in vain, their cold earthly bodies and winding tails, both overcharge his strength, and hinder his pace; he then in a rage, with his teeth, feet, and horns assaileth his enemies, whose spears are entered into his body, tearing some of them in pieces, and beating others asunder; they nevertheless (like men) knowing that now they must dye rather than give over and yield to the pitiless enemy, cleave fast, and keep the hold of their teeth upon his body, although their other parts be mortally wounded, and nothing left but their heads, and therefore will dye together with their foe, seeing if they were asunder no compassion can delay or mitigate their natural unappeasable hatred.

" The hart, having eased himself by the slaughter of some (like an elephant at the sight of the blood), bestirreth himself more busily in the eager battail, and therefore treadeth some under foot in the blood of their fellows, others he pursueth with teeth and horn, until he see them all destroyed; and, whereas the heads hang fast in his skin, for avoiding and pulling them forth (by a divine natural instinct), he flyeth or runneth to the waters where he findeth sea crabs, and of them he maketh a medicine whereby he shaketh off the serpents' heads, cureth their wounds, and avoydeth all their poyson; this valiant courage is in harts against serpents, whereas they are naturally afraid of hares and conies and will not fight with them."

With this extremely probable account, we dismiss imagination and proceed to reality.

The Stag, or Red Deer, is spread throughout the forest lands of Europe and Asia, but only where the climate is temperate. It has been driven out of England, but still finds a refuge among the fastnesses of Scotland. Yet even there the race of rifle-bearing hunters has so materially increased, that the poor stag seems to be in a fair way to be extirpated even from that his last hold.

The stag-hunts of old used to be most magnificent spectacles, many thousand men being gathered together, and great numbers of stags being taken. Now, however, all such meetings are prohibited, as it was found that the chiefs used to make these hunts mere excuses for gathering their followers, and an act of Parliament accordingly prohibited the custom. The act was put forth during the disturbances in Scotland, and although those rebellious days have passed away, the act still remains in force.

Most of the deer that are now slain fall by the hand of the deer-stalker, who creeps with untiring caution over rocks, among thorns, through mud and water, until he can bring his rifle to bear upon the deer, who falls prostrate before the deadly grooved bore.

Considerable judgment is necessary, as to the precise point where the deer ought to be struck, and it not unfrequently happens that an inexperienced hunter actually misses the deer altogether, because he thinks that it is impossible not to hit so big an animal; and sometimes the deer is struck in a place where the ball does not have an immediately mortal effect, but leaves strength enough for the wounded animal to reach some place of refuge, and there lie down and die.

The best place to strike the deer is immediately behind the shoulder, as the ball then must wound the vital organs, either the heart or the lungs, and possibly both. It would seem probable that a ball through either of these important parts would cause instant death, or, at all events, would bring the animal instantly to the ground; such, however, is not the case. If a deer falls

to the shot, it is a sign that the wound is not instantly
mortal, and that the animal will rise in a very short
time and escape; if, then, the deer does so drop, the
hunter must contrive to kill it at once, before it can
rise again.   On one occasion, a huntsman had fired
at a deer which instantly dropped; he, being inexperienced in deer-shooting, ran to the fallen animal,
drew his knife, and standing astride it, was engaged
in contemplating the noble proportions of his prey,
when the deer suddenly rose to its fore feet, and threw
back its head with such violence, that the hunter, who
was carelessly grasping one of its horns, was thrown
completely over the creature's back, and just rose in
time to see the animal at a hopeless distance, galloping as fast as its legs could carry it,

Another hunter had dropped a deer, but he, knowing
the habits of the animal, instantly knelt upon one
horn, and holding down its head with one hand
killed the deer with the other.   "Pithing" is the
method generally employed for this purpose.   The
knife is thrust between the last vertebra and the
head.   The juncture of the spinal cord with the brain
is thus severed, and the animal falls dead as if struck
by lightning.   No force is required, as, if the proper
place is chosen, the knife slips in as easily as into a
sheath.   But to return to our deer.   The animal being
thus killed, its captor naturally enough began to search
for the place where the ball had struck.   Now, a ball
that instantly brings the deer down is usually one
that has ranged too far back, and struck the deer in
the flank.   No wound, however, was to be seen, and
the whole affair looked very mysterious.   At last, a
close inspection brought to view a slight strip of skin
hanging just beneath one of the antlers.   Here the
ball had just glanced, and had stunned the animal for
a short time, but a very few minutes would have set
it on its legs again, when it would have been but little
the worse for the blow.

When the deer is really mortally struck, it only gives

THE RED-DEER AND HIND.   p. 331.

a kind of convulsive shudder, and bounds on with increased speed, but in a very few minutes the hunter finds it lying on the ground. Deer not unfrequently run several hundred yards after a ball has passed through both lungs, and one deer was seen to run a considerable distance after the lower part of its heart had been shot away.

When chased with dogs and brought to bay, it is a dangerous animal, often killing several of the dogs, and putting the life of the hunter in some peril.

The doe of this deer is exceedingly attached to her young, and appears to teach it to be motionless if an enemy is at hand. Of this peculiarity, Mr. St. John gives the following account :—

"I one day, some time ago, was watching a red-deer hind with my glass, whose proceedings I did not understand, till I saw that she was engaged in licking a newly-born calf. I walked up to the place, and as soon as the old deer saw me she gave the young one a slight tap with her hoof. The little creature immediately laid itself down; and when I came up I found it lying with its head flat on the ground, its ears closely laid back, and with all the attempts at concealment that one sees in animals which have passed an apprenticeship to danger of some years, whereas it had evidently not known the world for more than an hour, being unable to run or escape. I lifted up the little creature, being half inclined to carry it home in order to rear it. The mother stood at a distance of two hundred yards, stamping with her foot, exactly as a sheep would have done in a similar situation."

The narrator proceeds to say, that as he would have had to carry it a great distance, and being fearful lest it should be hurt during its transit, he replaced it on the ground. The mother then trotted up with every appearance of joy at the release of her young, and examined it all over, apparently heedless of the presence of man, from whom she would at any other time have fled precipitately.

An account of the maternal love of the fallow deer is preserved in White's " Selborne." It was the custom among the inhabitants of the neighbourhood of Waltham chase to search for young fawns, and to pare their hoofs with a penknife, so that they could not walk even when they were tolerably grown, and the rascally poachers could come and take them whenever they chose. Some of these fellows, accompanied with a dog, went to search after a fawn that they suspected was concealed in a patch of dried fern. Scarcely had they approached the place, when the hind sprung out of a thicket, and coming down on the dog with all its fore feet close together, broke its neck.

Having been thus introduced to the Fallow Deer,* we will say a few words about it. There are few who have not seen this pretty and elegant animal, either couched in parties under the shade of the trees, or wandering at will through the parks in which it lives. The deer are very gentle, except at certain times of the year, when it is even dangerous to come near them, for the bucks are ready to fight with everything that comes in their way, and can charge with such violence, that an unarmed man would stand but little chance against the powerful horns of his active adversary.

At such a time of year, a gentleman, an amateur in landscape-drawing, had ventured into a park heedless of danger, and was engaged in sketching, when a deer saw him, and charged full upon him. Down went his pencils and papers, and he was only too happy to escape the animal's fury, even with the loss of his drawings. The creature's assault had a beneficial effect, for it taught this draughtsman an art of which he had thought himself ignorant. Hearing the animal close behind him he seized a branch that hung overhead, and curled himself into the tree with an activity that could only be expected from one versed in the practice of gymnastics.

The fallow deer are often so tame, that they will

* *Dama vulgaris.*

come and eat from the hand. They are not very discriminating in their appetites, and devour a ham sandwich, mustard and all, with as great appearance of enjoyment as if it had been the most delicate tuft of grass that could be found. There are a few deer kept in the grounds belonging to Magdalen College, Oxford, and it used to be a favourite amusement to the juvenile members of the college to tie a large crust of bread to a string, and angle for the deer out of their windows. The deer would come round the crust, and jostle each other about very roughly to get a bite at it, but when the master deer came by, they silently left the bread to him. It was very curious to see the manner in which the deer would continue to eat a large bread without once letting it fall out of their mouths. The crusts were so large, and the deers' mouths were so small, that they could only take in a very small portion of the bread at once, but by steady and persevering nibbling the crust used to lessen by degrees, and soon disappeared entirely.

Deer are not so agreeable when kept as pets, as when they are permitted to run at large in parks. All pets are proverbially troublesome and presuming in their habits; but a pet deer even exceeds the usual bad behaviour, as will be seen from the account given by Mr. St. John of a pet roebuck.*

" A young roe, when caught unhurt, is not difficult to rear, though their great tenderness and delicacy of limb makes it not easy to handle them without injuring them. They soon become perfectly tame, and attach themselves to their master. When in captivity they will eat almost anything that is offered to them, and from this cause are frequently destroyed, picking up and swallowing some indigestible substance about the house. A tame buck, however, becomes a dangerous pet; for, after attaining to his full strength, he is very apt to make use of it in attacking people whose appearance he does not like. They parti-

* *Capreolus Caprœa.*

cularly single out women and children as their victims, and inflict severe and dangerous wounds with their sharp pointed horns ; and notwithstanding their small size, their strength and activity make them a very unpleasant adversary.   One day, at a kind of public garden near Brighton, I saw a beautiful but small roe-buck in an inclosure fastened with a chain, which seemed strong enough and heavy enough to hold and weigh down an elephant.   Pitying the poor animal, an exile from his native land, I asked what reason they could have for ill using him by putting such a weight of iron about his neck.   The keeper of the place, however, told me that small as the roebuck was the chain was quite necessary, as he had attacked and killed a boy of twelve years old a few days before, stabbing the poor fellow in fifty places with his sharp pointed horns.   Of course I had no more to urge in his behalf."

The red deer has frequently been tamed, and one was brought completely under subjection by a late nobleman, who succeeded in breaking four stags to run in a chariot.   He was naturally very fond of his novel steeds, and was accustomed to drive them to the various sporting localities which he was in the habit of frequenting.

On one of these excursions the whole affair had a very narrow escape of entire destruction.   The noble-man was driving to Newmarket, when the cry of a pack of hounds burst upon his ear.   Unfortunately, the hounds came across the road over which the four stags had just passed.   The hounds immediately changed their course, and set off at full speed after the stags, whose scent was too great a temptation to be resisted.   The stags, on hearing the cry of the dogs, bounded off at their swiftest pace, in spite of the efforts of the driver and the mounted grooms, who always accompanied the equipage.   The pace grew more and more furious on the part of pursuers and pursued, and the driver began to fear for the safety of his vehicle and himself, when he bethought himself of an inn at Newmarket where he had been in the habit of stabling his horned steeds. To this inn he directed all his efforts, and fortunately succeeded in getting his vehicle within the gates. The stags were now overpowered by the force of ostler and stable boys, and the whole affair, stags, vehicle and driver were thrust into a barn and the door shut, just as the hounds entered the inn-yard.

WAPITI.*

THERE is a kind of deer found in North America, called the Wapiti. It is not at all unlike the red deer; but is a large animal, and the shape of the horns is somewhat different. There has risen some confusion regarding this animal, in consequence of the title " elk" being erroneously applied to it by the Canadians. It is a splendid animal; but not likely to be much valued on account of the coarseness of its flesh. The skin is valuable, as it forms very soft leather, and the paws are also extremely useful in their way. The tongue seems to be the only part of the animal worth eating.

The same precautions must be taken in hunting this animal as in the chase of the red deer; and a ball tells upon the two animals in precisely the same manner. It has already been mentioned, that if a red deer drops to the shot, it is likely to rise again and escape, and the same may be said of the wapiti. Not long since, a hunter fired at a wapiti standing on a ledge of rock, overhanging a deep pool, and about thirty feet above the water. Down dropped the deer, and off went the hunter to secure his prey. He drew his knife, grasped it by the horns, and was just about to inflict the fatal wound, when the animal sprang up and commenced a regular attack, striving to drive its assailant into the water. In this it was successful; for it made so powerful a spring at him, that both man

* *Cervus Canadensis.*

and deer toppled over the edge of the rock, and performed a summersault into the pool below.   The
fallen hunter's faculties were absorbed in escaping
from the water, and on gaining the bank, he saw his
deer just disappearing in the distance.   Some months
after this adventure, he shot a deer which, from the
scar of a wound in its neck, he supposed to be his
former adversary, over whom he had at last trium-
phed.

The voice of the wapiti during the breeding season is a curious and highly musical sound, rising a
sixth by a slur, and resembling the tones of an enormous flute.

The deer are very fond of salt, and frequent certain salt marshes called " licks." where the animals
lick the salt away from the soil.   The hunters take
advantage of this predilection, and by concealing themselves near these salt marshes, destroy numbers of
the deer as they pass to and fro.   It appears that
some of these " licks" are frequented exclusively by
the bucks, while the does take possession of other
" licks" for themselves.

The great size of the animal would make it easily
distinguishable at a considerable distance, were it not
that it has the instinct to conceal itself among substances of its own colour, and this it does so effectually, that the eye of a practised hunter is required to
mark it, an inexperienced searcher being unable to
see it even when the exact spot in which it is lying is
pointed out to him.

Although the head is loaded with a large mass of
branching horns, the wapiti can plunge through the
thickets with the greatest ease, so that Æsop's fable
of the stag caught by his horns would not apply to
the wapiti.   So far from being any hindrance to the
passage of the animal through the branches, the
horns are an assistance and a defence ; for as they
form a very acute angle with the line of the back, the
animal, in rushing through a thicket, merely lays the

horns on his back, and thereby defends his skin from the branches.

The Indians hunt the deer after many curious fashions. If a single man goes to hunt the deer, he furnishes himself with the dried head and neck of a stag, and with a branch of a tree. Thus prepared, he creeps as near the deer as he can, and when he finds that they are beginning to take the alarm, he raises and depresses the dried stag's head, so as to delude the animals into the belief that it is only a comrade hiding behind a bush. He is thus enabled to single out the best animal, who is soon laid low by a bullet behind the shoulder. Sometimes a skilful hunter can even attract the deer towards him by imitating their cry.

MOOSE-DEER.*

THE real moose-deer, or elk, is a very different animal, being nearly double the size of the wapiti, and bearing large palmated horns. It is rather a clumsy animal in its movements, and shuffles along in a very awkward way, but with great swiftness. It is an easy animal to tame when it is taken very young; but after it has attained to some age, it is very fierce, as the following anecdote, by Audubon, will show. He is speaking of a young moose-deer that had been captured.

" The moose was so exhausted and fretted, that it offered no opposition to us as we led it to the camp; but in the middle of the night, we were awakened by a great noise in the hovel, and found that, as it had in some measure recovered from its terror and state of exhaustion, it began to think of getting home, and was so much enraged at finding itself so securely imprisoned. We were unable to do anything with it; for if we merely approached our hands to the openings of the hut, it would spring at us with the greatest fury, roaring and erecting its mane in a

* *Alces palmatus.*

z

manner that convinced us of the futility of all attempts to save it alive. We threw to it the skin of a
deer, which it tore to pieces in a moment. This individual was a yearling, and about six feet high."

The moose is generally caught in the winter time
by hunters mounted on snow shoes, which enable
them to skim over the surface of the snow, while the
moose breaks through the snow at every stride and is
soon wearied out. Enterprising individuals have
tried the experiment of taming the moose, and employing it in various kinds of labour; their efforts
have mostly been successful, and the animal is found
to answer very well as a beast of draught. The
mouth is very tender, and the bit must be applied
and removed with great care. The docility of the
young moose is quite on a par with that of the young
horse or mule.

It is rather a remarkable circumstance, that when
the moose is alarmed at a sudden noise, and endeavours to make its escape, it sometimes falls down
suddenly, as if in a fit. The paroxysm only lasts for
a very short time, and the moose leaps up again and
runs as if nothing had happened.

The flesh of the moose is tolerable; but is rather
tougher and coarser than venison is expected to be.
The tongue and nose, however, especially the latter,
are considered great dainties, the nose being said to
resemble marrow.

The skin is mostly used for heavy work, such as
tent-covers and shoe-leather. The hair is very coarse
indeed, brown towards the end, and whitish towards
the base, which is also flattened and rather wavy, presenting an appearance as if it had passed through a
miniature crimping machine.

The pages of Topsell inform us of a curious tradition respecting a chameleonic power said to reside in
the moose.

" The head of this beast is like the head of a hart,
and his horns branched or ragged; his body for the

most part like a wilde oxés; his hair deep and harsh like a bear's; his hide is so hard and thick that of it the Scythians make breast-plates, which no dart can pierce through. His colour, for the most part, like an asses; but when he is hunted or feared, he changeth his hew into whatsoever thing he seeth; as among trees, he is like them; among green boughs, he seemeth green; amongst rocks or stones, he is transmuted into their colour also, as it is generally by most writers affirmed; as Pliny and Solinus among the ancient, Stephanus and Eustathius among the later, writers.

" This, indeed, is the thing that seemeth most incredible; but there are two reasons which draw me to subscribe hereunto : first, because we see that the face of men and beasts through fear, joy, anger, and other passions do quickly change, from ruddy to white, from black to pale, and from pale to ruddy again. Now as this beast hath the head of a hart, so also hath it the fear of a hart, but in a higher degree; and, therefore by secret operation, it may easily alter the colour of their hair, as a passion in a reasonable man, may alter the colour of his face."

GNOO.*

THIS very strange-looking animal has often been asserted to be a mixture of the horse, ox, and stag, deriving its head from the ox, its neck, mane, body, and tail from the horse, and its legs and feet from the stag. Now it is somewhat remarkable, that the gnoo has nothing to do with either of these animals, for it is one of the Antelopes.

The general form of this animal is so like that of a horse, that in the classical caravans of Wombwell it is announced as the " Horned Horse," and a most vivid picture is hoisted over the entrance, representing a number of gnoos in the highest state of friskiness, all bridled and saddled, and ridden by negroes clothed

* *Catoblepas Gnu.*

in the most resplendent habiliments. Wombwell ought to be ashamed of himself for so pandering to the popular ignorance, when he might just as easily teach what is right as what is wrong. The keepers, who go round the interior of the shows and describe each animal, never do so without falling into gross mistakes, which a look into any work on natural history of the present day would rectify. I think that if a keeper were forbidden to tell his hearers that the hyæna had never been tamed, or that "The jackall is the lion's provider," he would be unable to go on with the remainder of his task. The fact is, that the people have heard of the lion's provider, and come on purpose to see it; they hear by tradition that the hyæna is untamable, and are desirous of beholding so dreadful a creature. The keeper's tales are just on a par with the representations of the battle of the Nile usually exhibited at fairs, in which the proprietors find it necessary to introduce the Duke of Wellingtou as a coadjutor to Nelson, as the people are not satisfied with any English battle, unless they see "the Duke" in the thick of the fight. In a similar representation of the battle of Waterloo, considerable effect is always produced by a personal conflict between Napoleon mounted on a white horse, and the Duke of Wellington on a black one, and the spectators are in ecstacies with the next tableau, which represents Napoleon running away as fast as he can, and "The Duke" just at his heels.

Now, having vented our indignation on Wombwell, "et hoc genus omne," for describing the gnoo wrongly, let us see what the animal really is.

It is an antelope, one of the bovine Antelopes. It inhabits the south of Africa, and is always found in large herds, which migrate from part to part, according to the season of the year. It is much hunted, as its flesh is excellent, and its skin valuable for many purposes. It is very wild, and it is no easy matter to get within shot of the herd, as on the first alarm, one animal takes the lead and rushes off, all the rest following in single file.

In hunting expeditions animals are taken in every variety of traps, and by every description of dogs, but few instances can be found like the following, where a gnoo had served as his own dogs and his own trap. " My waggon returned about twelve o'clock that night, carrying the skin of my gemsbok, and also a magnificent old blue wildebeeste (the brindled gnoo), which the Hottentots had obtained in an extraordinary manner. He was found with one of his fore-legs caught over his horns so that he could not run, and they hamstrung him and cut his throat. He had probably managed to get himself into this awkward attitude while fighting with one of his fellows." Those who have noticed the peculiar curve of the gnoo's horn will at once see how difficult it would be for the poor animal, after surmounting the difficulty of getting his leg over his horn at all, to remove it from its unwonted position. Moreover, these kind of animals have not the sagacity necessary for such an operation as releasing the imprisoned limb. They only plunge about in a frantic state, and generally succeed in injuring themselves severely. Those who have seen a horse meet with any entanglement with the harness, such as getting his leg over the traces, will at once understand the position of the poor gnoo. Even a tamed and comparatively intelligent animal exhibits the greatest terror at the entanglement of any of its limbs, and is unable to control its struggles; and the terror that a wild animal was thrown into by finding its leg taken prisoner in so mysterious a manner must have been extreme.

If the creature had only had the sense to put its head down, and lower its horns, the imprisoned limb could have been released without any difficulty, but had it done so, it would have displayed a degree of reasoning greater than is found among the bovine

class of animals, who have but little presence of mind.
It is from want of this presence of mind, that hares
and rabbits are so frequently taken by poachers.
Directly they feel the pressure of the wire on their
necks, they begin dragging at it with such violence,
that they strangle themselves. Indeed, most animals,
if they feel themselves entangled, begin to kick and
plunge, and struggle in a frantic manner, and often
either entangle themselves the more firmly, or break
some of their limbs.

Some of the movements of the gnoo are very grotesque. Mr. Cumming gives the following account of
the gambols of the animal while under the influence
of fright.

"When the hunter approaches the old bulls, they
commence whisking their long white tails in a most
eccentric manner; then springing suddenly into the
air, they begin pawing and capering, and pursue each
other in circles at their utmost speed. Suddenly they
all pull up together to overhaul the intruder, when
some of the bulls will often commence fighting in the
most violent manner, dropping on their knees at every
shock; then quickly wheeling about, they kick up their
heels, whirl their tails with a fantastic flourish, and
scour across the plain, enveloped in a cloud of dust."

The gnoo attacks its enemy in a manner similar to
that practised by the Nyl-ghau, namely, by dropping
on its knees, and springing forward with a sudden
bound, with such rapidity, that considerable activity
is required to escape from the blow.

Mr. Cumming also relates a most peculiar circumstance that happened to a sassayby that he had shot.

"A singular circumstance occurred as I watched
the waters. Having shot a sassayby, he immediately commenced choking from the blood, and his
body began to swell in a most extraordinary manner;
it continued swelling, with the animal still alive, until
it literally resembled a fisherman's float, when the

animal died of suffocation. It was not only his body that swelled in that extraordinary manner, but even his head and legs, down to his knees."

The air must have escaped from the lungs, and been forced by the respiratory powers of the animal between the skin and the flesh, until it had assumed the puffy appearance spoken of. The feelings of the poor animal could have been by no means enviable, as the violent separation of the skin from the muscular tissues must have been attended with very great pain.

The butchers use an analogous plan, to enable them to remove the skin from the body with greater ease. They introduce a tube between the skin and the muscles, and by forcing air between the hide, the skin is separated. The operation is rendered easier by a constant succession of blows upon the skin. The hide is then so loosened, that it is easily taken off.

The skin of most of the antelopes has a very curious property of emitting a delicious perfume of the trees and grass on which the animals have been feeding.

The last of the antelopes that I shall mention is the Spring-bok, a beautiful little animal, chiefly remarkable for the enormous herds in which it congregates. When this antelope migrates, or performs a " trek-bokken," as the Boers call it, the numbers that march together are almost incredible. " For about two hours," says Cumming, " before the day dawned, I had been lying awake in my waggon, listening to the grunting of the bucks within two hundred yards of me, imagining that some large herd of spring-boks was feeding beside my camp; but on my rising when it was clear, and looking about me, I beheld the ground to the northward of my camp, actually covered with a dense living mass of spring-boks, marching slowly and steadily along, extending from an opening in a long range of hills on the west, through which they continued pouring, like the flood of some great river, to a ridge about a mile to the north-

east, over which they disappeared. The breadth
of the ground they covered might have been somewhere about half a mile. I stood upon the fore-chest
of my waggon for nearly two hours, lost in wonder at
the novel and wonderful scene which was passing before me, and had some difficulty in convincing myself
that it was reality which I beheld, and not the wild
and exaggerated picture of a hunter's dream. During
this time, their vast legions continued streaming
through the neck in the hills in one unbroken compact phalanx.".

This antelope derives its name from its unrivalled
powers of leaping, which it exerts sometimes in mere
sport, but mostly when under the influence of alarm.
Its extraordinary leaps are often exhibited when the
animal comes to the track of a man. It is so timid
and fearful, that it dares not walk over the track of a
man, but clears it with a tremendous bound, ten or
twelve feet high, and about fifteen long; during the
leap, the Spring-bok curves its back something like a
cat when she sees a strange dog. It is truly an extraordinary fact that an animal so small should be able
thus to take a leap, which, if it were standing in
the street, would carry it into the first floor-windows.

There is an antelope that inhabits America, and
which is remarkable for the singular way in which it
travels. One animal takes the lead, and the others
follow in single file. with the precision of a line of
soldiers. If the leader turns his head, all the line
turn their heads also, and if the leader springs, all
the line spring too. It is a very inquisitive animal,
although shy, and it is sometimes decoyed within rifle
distance, by a cap or a handkerchief placed on the top
of a stick. The antelopes run round and round this
unknown object, always keeping in single file, until
attracted by their curiosity, they approach so near,
that the hunter who is lying concealed in the grass,
is able to shoot one of them before they take the
alarm.

THe young Indians have a game called the " antelope," something resembling our " hare and hounds." One of the most active of the Indian youths shades and stripes his body with chalk, so as to make it resemble the body of the animal in whose character he is about to appear. He then binds on his head the horns of an antelope, together with a portion of the skin ; at a given signal he starts off, and the other players pursue him among the huts or trees, until, overpowered by superior numbers, the " antelope " is caught.

I suppose that every one has read " Eöthen ; " nevertheless, as there may possibly be some one who has the misfortune not to have accompanied the traveller in his journeys through the lands of the sun, I will conclude the antelopes with an account given by the author of " Eöthen," of a gazelle, as he calls it, that was taken prisoner.

" I saw several creatures of the antelope kind in this part of the desert, and, one day, my Arabs surprised in her sleep a young gazelle (for so I called her), and took the darling prisoner. I carried her before me on the camel for the rest of the day, and kept her in my tent all night: I did all I could to gain her affections, but the trembling beauty refused to touch food, and would not be comforted ; whenever she had a seeming opportunity of escaping, she struggled with a violence so painfully disproportioned to her fine delicate limbs, that I could not go on with the cruel attempt to make her my own. In the morning, therefore, I set her loose, anticipating some pleasure from the joyous bound, with which, as I thought, she would return to her native freedom. She had been so stupified, however, by the exciting events of the preceding day and night, and was so puzzled as to the road she should take, that she went off very deliberately, and with an uncertain step. She was quite sound in limb, but she looked so idiotic that I fancied her intellect might have been really upset. Never,

in all likelihood, had she seen the form of a human
being until the dreadful moment when she woke from
her sleep, and found herself in the gripe of an Arab.
Then her pitching and tossing journey on the back of
a camel, and, lastly, a soiree with me by candle-light.
I should have been glad to know, if I could, that her
heart was not broken."

GOATS, SHEEP, ETC.

THERE are two. genera of animals so similar in their
characteristics, that for many years they were treated
as one genus.   These are " Capra," and Ovis,'" the
one including the goats, and the other the sheep.

There are some goats that look so like sheep, and
some sheep that look so like goats, that the boundary
line was formerly not very clearly distinguished.
There are now, however, a number of distinctions
discovered, which it would be useless to numerate,
and the two genera are rendered perfectly distinct.   One of the principal differences between the
two genera is, that the males of the goat kind are
odorous, while those of the sheep possess no odour
at all.   But the chief distinctions are moral.

Both goats and sheep, when in a wild state, are remarkable for their activity, but the goats far surpass
the sheep in this respect.   Their sure footedness on
elevated pinnacles of rock is as singular as the agility
which enables the goats to reach them.   Frequently
will a goat dash at a perpendicular face of rock the
side of which appears perfectly smooth, and springing
from point to point, will take advantage of the
smallest projection, until it reaches the summit in
safety. Sometimes it is seen perched upon the extreme
apex of a rocky peak, where there appears to be hardly
                                                        closely
together.   Sometimes the animal appears as if stuck
in some wonderful manner against the side of a rock,
and, were it not that the animal jumps about with per-

feet ease, it might be supposed to be nailed there, for no supports for its feet are perceptible.

Some of the goats are very useful to mankind. The celebrated Cashmere shawls are made of the long silky hair of the Thibetian goat. There was once an idea of naturalizing that goat in England for the purpose of shawl manufactures, but it was thought that each goat furnished so little wool, that the expense would have been greater than the gain, especially as the carcass is worthless. The same may be said of the Llama. Moreover, the wool of the Thibet goat would certainly have deteriorated by the change to another climate.

In many countries, large flocks of goats are kept, but in England the goat is generally seen in stable-yards. A few are kept for the sake of their milk, but in general goats are not to be found save in stable-yards and at watering places, in which latter localities they come out in great force, being ribbon-decked as to their horns, and scarlet-robed as to their persons, much to the delight of the juvenility who ride in the miniature carriages to which they are harnessed.

The goat can be rendered very tame, but is always rather apt to give rather a severe blow with its horns in pure play. The kids are very pretty little creatures, as playful as kittens, and quite as graceful in their way. The domesticated goat seems to care little for a dog, but lowers its head if it apprehends an attack, and assumes so determined an air, that few dogs will attack it, and those who venture, generally receive so severe a blow that they are rolled over and over in the mud, and run howling away. A goat seems to hurl itself at a dog, not by making a headlong rush as a sheep does, but by rising on its hind legs, and throwing itself head foremost at its adversary.

The female goat is a very agreeable animal, and so are the kids of both sexes, but when a male kid begins to advance in years, he is by no means so

pleasant. In the first place, he gives forth a powerful odour, which is supposed by grooms to be beneficial to horses, but is, to say the least, very disagreeable
to men; and, in the second place, when he begins to
feel his strength he is much too fond of using it, particularly if he is rather stronger and larger than the
generality of his kind.

The he-goat is a most powerful animal for its size,
and sometimes presumes on its strength in a most
extraordinary manner, tyrannising over every weaker
animal in its way, and not unfrequently boldly opposing
even full-grown men. Of such a nature was the great
overgrown goat, of whose exploits William Howitt
speaks so feelingly. This ferocious animal was the
dread of the whole neighbourhood, particularly when
it happened to break bounds, and chose to play its
pranks in the village. On one of these occasions, it
was seen marching gravely down the village street,
which was immediately deserted by all the pas-
sengers, except a poor old woman, who was too feeble
to get out of his way. Of course, the goat (who
really seems to have been a hircine edition of the
redoubtable Cannon) immediately charged at her, and
knocked her down. The whole population was, of
course, greatly excited. The tailor shook his sleeve-
board at the formidable goat, the blacksmith wished
he had his big hammer at the goat's head, but as the
relator of the anecdote wickedly remarks, never
offered to take it there, all agreed that the brute
ought not be allowed to injure an old woman, but no
one liked to attack him. At last, one, more courageous than the rest, armed himself with a heavy
pole, and dealt the foe such a blow, as would most
certainly have broken the skull of any other animal
but a goat. The goat, however, instantly made such
a spring upon his assailant, that the pole was dashed
out of his hand, he was knocked flat on his back,
and the goat, mounting upon his prostrate foe, looked
round him in defiance. The poor man called loudly

for assistance, as did the old woman, who by this time, had recovered her legs, but no one was bold enough to venture on single combat with a foe of such prowess. The strongest, however, have their weaknesses. The man who rules the world, is sometimes ruled by his wife, and the general, who drove before him a force ten times superior to his own, has fled in dismay before a lady's pet cat. So in this instance, there was one vulnerable point in the goat's constitution. Let but a child grasp his beard, and he became instantly submissive. While he was thus domineering over the whole village, a couple of men arrived in search of the runaway, and one of them taking him by his beard, the redoubtable conqueror was led off, bleating in a most abject and submissive manner. These outbreaks became so frequent, that he was at last complained of as a nuisance, and condemned to be shot.

Far different was the conduct of a beautiful Angora goat, whose acquaintance I made during my childhood. The goat was as tame and gentle as a dog, and would follow its friends about the garden, asking, as plainly as eyes could ask, for the handful of corn which generally fell to its share. It died long ago, and its stuffed skin is now in the Ashmolean Museum, at Oxford.

SHEEP.

I said lately that there were sheep and goats so closely resembling each other, that they were hardly distinguishable. We generally know a sheep by its woolly fleece, If, however, we take one of our horned sheep, carry it into the tropics, and keep it for several years, we shall find that its wool will fall off, and that long straight hair will supply its place, and that, were it not for the curled horns, and the convex forehead, it would certainly be called a goat.

Size is no criterion. We have sheep of all sizes in England, but there is one sheep, the Argali, resident in the mountain-chains of central Asia, which stands four feet high, and measures seven feet nine inches, in length. Its horns are nearly four feet long, and are nineteen inches in circumference at the base. The males are very quarrelsome, and fight with such fury, that even their powerful horns are sometimes broken off, and in their hollow small animals take up their residence.

This animal is not to be confounded with the Rocky Mountain sheep, or " Bighorn," of North America.

Our sheep may be separated into two great divisions, the polled and the horned. These generally inhabit different parts of England, and it not unfrequently happens that a small stream forms the boundary between the two descriptions of sheep, neither pasturing in the grounds occupied by the other.

The principal value in a sheep lies in its wool. Let us then see what the wool is, and what makes it so valuable. Wool consists of a number of fibres, of a peculiar form, and possessing certain properties. The most valuable of the properties is that of " felting," a process said to have been discovered by accident. A man, so it is said, was undertaking a long journey on foot. Wishing, like the celebrated pilgrim, " to walk a little more at ease," he stuffed some wool into his shoes. His walk was not only long, but wet, and when he came to his journey's end, and took the wool out of his shoes, he found that the continual kneading, which it had undergone, together with the oft-repeated saturations which had taken place, during his passage through boggy places, had formed it into a substance like cloth, but without any grain. This accidental invention was followed up, and felt was the result. The substance " felt " is manufactured in a way exactly similar to that employed by its first discoverer, although on a larger scale. The wool is carefully cleansed, placed in water, and kneaded together, until the fibres have united sufficiently. It is then " felt," and can be used for any purpose to which the material is commonly applied. The wool is prevented from felting while on the sheep's back, by the position of the fibres and by the natural grease with which it is furnished, so that careful cleansing is necessary, before the wool will felt. The principal use of felt, is to make hats, which articles of dress are nearly invariably formed of felt as a groundwork, sometimes decked with beaver hair, oftener with that of the rabbit, frequently with silk, and lastly, which is the best of all, are left without any decoration at all, as in those most delightful of hats, the wide-awake, as it is facetiously called, from its want of nap. In order to make hats more impervious to rain, and in order to make them stand stiff on the head, so as to resemble a chimney-pot as nearly as possible, both in colour and shape, the felt is imbued with a solution of lac in spirits of wine; the mixture is insoluble in water, and therefore renders the hat waterproof.

The reason why the wool of the sheep " felts " can be seen by placing a fibre under a good microscope. It will then be seen to resemble a number of thimbles with jagged edges, inserted into one another. The fibres also contract by coming in contact with water. When, then, the oily substances are removed from the wool, water is enabled to act upon it, and when bound together, the fibres contract upon each other, and become so entangled with their jagged edges, that they become a firm mass, which only requires to be properly shaped, to be used for a variety of purposes. This contracting property of wool is the reason why flannel and other woollen substances shrink on first washing.

Felting was supposed to be a comparatively recent invention, but in accordance with the maxim, that there is nothing new under the sun, a large quantity of felt was discovered upon the person of an Egyptian mummy.

The felting property of wool is the reason why cloth never unravels when cut. Almost any other material, when woven, will unravel if cut, but cloth still retains its integrity; even when worn into holes it never unravels, although it is easily torn.

In some parts of the East, it is the custom to kill lambs as soon as they are born, in order to secure a fine material. Sometimes the mother sheep are actually killed before the young is born. The skins thus procured are dressed with the wool, and are extensively used for the lining of winter garments.

The method that we employ to obtain the wool is by shearing, but there was another method employed in days gone by, called "rowing," in plain words, the wool was torn off the backs of the poor animals by the hand, the sheep having been previously starved for several days to make them weaker, in the hope that the wool would come off easier. This barbarous custom was in use in Iceland and the Orkneys, but is now, I believe, discontinued in both countries. The Romans certainly used to employ this method of obtaining wool, as is evident from their word signifying wool, namely, "vellus," viz. a word derived from "vellere," to pluck off. We have also the authority of Pliny for asserting that in many parts of Italy, "rowing," not shearing, was the custom.

In the time of the ancients, it was the custom to preserve the fleeces of the best breeds of sheep by dressing them in leather jackets. Several authorities mention this custom.

The quality of the wool depends materially on the manner in which the sheep is fed, well-fed sheep generally producing good and sound wool, while a half-starved animal is sure to produce a weak and "breachy" fibre. The filaments ought to be uniformly round, brilliant, and properly serrated. In bad wool, there is often an interval of dry, shrivelled material called a "breach." The "breach" cannot bear the operation of the carding-comb, but is sure to snap. Although the real character of the "breach" can only be decided by the microscope, a practised wool-comber will detect wool so affected, without having recourse to any instruments.

We have long been accustomed to look upon the sheep as a model of patience, mildness, and good-temper. That is because we are naturally prone to judge by the exterior. But, mild as the sheep may look, there is a mine of mischief in them, and especially in the rams, who not unfrequently assault the passer-by with the greatest ferocity; and from the thickness of the skull, the onset even of a hornless ram is rather a formidable matter. An instance of this nature occurred not long since, which not only shows the fury and courage of the ram, but also a method of conquering the animal. The story is as follows: "Two gentlemen were fishing in one of the Welsh streams, and in the course of their piscatorial perambulations entered a field where there were some sheep; among them was an enormous ram with a splendid pair of horns. The ram, after examining the intruders for some time, made up his mind that they were to be expelled from the field, and accordingly charged full at one of them, and, when repulsed, made a charge at the other stranger. So furious was he, that the two fishermen, arming themselves with the butt-ends of their rods, separated about ten paces, so that when the ram charged at one, the other belaboured him. This went on for some time, until the ram was covered with blood, and, staggering under the repeated blows that its forelegs had received, yet he undauntedly continued his assaults, until his antagonists could hardly wield their clubs from weariness, and were actually forced to beat a retreat.

"Next day they saw another gentleman going to fish in the same spot, and went to warn him of the ram. When they neared the spot, they heard cries for help, and found the gentleman kneeling on the ground with his rod extended, much as a soldier places himself when ready to resist cavalry. There was the ram, apparently little the worse for his yesterday's encounter, charging with the most determined ferocity. All three then united in attacking the infuriated ram, but with little success, as his fleece protected him from side-blows, and his head was as invulnerable as . that of a brass battering-ram. Presently a farm-servant came up, who told the three combatants to desist from their attacks and he would manage the ram. So saying, he proceeded to cut a slight flexible stick, and walked up to the infuriated animal; while the three fishermen looked on in no small curiosity to see how a single antagonist would vanquish a foe that had driven two enemies out of the field, and could not be overcome by three. The man, however, did not seem troubled by any misgiving on the subject; but put himself in the way of the ram, who instantly charged at his new antagonist. The man stepped aside to let him pass, and as he rushed by, twisted his stick between the horns of the ram, who came to a stop, and seemed completely subdued by this apparently inadequate weapon. His conqueror then led him quietly out of the field, and locked him up.

" In all probability the stick, together with the horns, formed so powerful a leverage on the animal's head that it could not move without incurring some injury."

The foregoing anecdote was communicated to me not long since, and has already appeared in the form of a note to my edition of White's " Selborne."

It is the custom of sheep, when alarmed, to gather themselves into a body, placing the rams in front, and the ewes and lambs behind. It is then rather dangerous for any enemy to approach the phalanx; for the rams will spring forward and dash at their opponent with all their power. The onset of the ram is even more to be feared than that of the goat; for the ram not only springs upon its foe, as does the goat, but rushes at him first, thus adding impetus to weight.

On one occasion, a bull had alarmed a flock of sheep; they immediately formed the rallying square, as a soldier would say, and calmly awaited his attack. The moment that the bull had reached the sheep, and had lowered his head, preparatory for an assault, the fiercest ram sprang forward, with such sledge-hammer force against his skull, taking him just between the horns, that the bull rolled senseless on the ground.

An account of a similar reception is given by Mr. Hall, when he unexpectedly found himself opposed to a flock of hill-sheep.

"I was one day climbing the mountain of Belrennis. On reaching the top, I found myself in a cloud, where I could not distinctly see any object at a distance of more than a few yards. As there was a fine breeze, I hoped that the cloud would disperse; and although I felt exceedingly cold and hungry, I resolved to remain there a little while. While I was walking about to keep myself warm, I perceived something of an uncommon appearance at a little distance from me, and I approached it, not, indeed, without fear. I found it to be a phalanx of sheep drawn up on the top of the hill, and ready to defend themselves against attack. They were arranged in a kind of wedge, presenting its blunt end foremost. In the middle of the line was a large ram, with a black forehead and a tremendous pair of horns. A number of wether-ewes were in the rear, not one of them eating, but looking sternly upon me. I was not at first afraid, knowing them only to be sheep, and yet I was not perfectly easy; for if any fox appeared, they might kill me in chasing him.

"These sheep had been sent into the mountain in April or May, where the owners seldom look after them until October. When they gather themselves together at night, one of them is always placed at a little distance as a sentinel. They never descend into the valley at night, but, even in the most stormy weather, they are on the top of the hill, or on a rising ground; and if they are attacked by foxes or dogs, their assailants rarely fail to pay for their temerity with their lives. Seeing them, however, in this warlike array, I began gradually to feel a little alarm; and, deeming discretion the better part of valour, I slowly retired. ·As the distance between us increased, their line was neither so straight nor compact; but if I stopped and again advanced a few steps towards them, they looked steadily at me, and formed their line with greater precision and coolness; and had I attempted to attack them, I am convinced they would have resisted. I had once a great mind to try; but I confess my courage failed me when I observed them seemingly bending their knees in order to make one simultaneous rush upon me."

Mr. Hall was quite right in his caution, as the attack of a black-faced, big-horned ram would have been anything but agreeable. It is not a very pleasant sensation, when the ribs stop a ball that an expert batsman has hit to "leg;" but the onslaught of a cricket-ball is preferable to that of a ram, for even putting aside the advantages of powerful horns and thick forehead enjoyed by the ram, the cricket-ball can hit but once, while the ram is likely to return to the charge; and the superior weight of the body will more than counterbalance the superior impetus of the ball.

But the ram, although formidable, is not always victorious. There is a story still extant, whether true or not is not quite clear, that a certain well-known sportsman possessed a dog valuable in every respect save one, viz. that he was too fond of mutton, and could not be restrained from chasing and killing sheep. The annoyance at last increased to such an

extent that a death-warrant was issued against him.
Just as the fatal mandate was about to be executed,
a friend came by, who, on hearing the case, recommended a remedy, by whose potent means the dog
could be cured of sheep-murder without losing his
life. The infallible recipe was, that the dog should
be tied by a cord to the horns of an old and savage
ram, and that the two animals should be left in this
position until the ram, by continual huttings, had
effectually cured the dog of his liking for sheep's
flesh.

The experiment was accordingly tried, and a ram
noted for his pugnacity was lovingly coupled with
the dog, and the pair were shut up in a stable. Next
morning the owner went to release his poor dog from
the painful thraldom under which he had groaned all
the night, and was anxious to remove him from the
tyranny of the ram. But on opening the stable-door,
he found that he had indeed been guilty of the error
of enumerating his juvenile poultry before they were
emancipated from the egg-shell, for the dog was lying
very contentedly in the stable, and the ram was lying
down also, but with his throat torn across, and one of
his shoulders missing, which, from all external appearances, might have been discovered in the internal
economy of the dog.

The Oriental shepherds manage their sheep on a
different principle from ours. When we desire to
take a flock from one plain to another, we place ourselves *behind* the flock, and drive them before us. The
Oriental shepherd, on the contrary, walks *before* his
sheep, and leads the way for them.

The business of a shepherd is not so easy as may
be supposed, a fact to which many can bear witness
who have left their counting-house or counter in England to take a sheep-walk in distant lands. One very
necessary qualification of a shepherd is an equable
temper. A hasty man is nearly sure to injure his
stock by his want of patience, and after all will not

do nearly as much work as the quiet, good-tempered man, who walks from point to point, slowly and carefully in order to avoid disturbing the sheep, whose voice is never heard raised in abuse of the poor animals if they happen to stray, and the bark of whose dog is seldom required. "Lend me a bark of your dog," said a bewildered shepherd to another whose flock was pastured near. He would have acted better had he done the work himself, and put the sheep in the right way without terrifying them by the barking of the dog. Not that I depreciate in any way the useful qualities of the shepherd's dog : on the contrary, he is the very best ally that a shepherd can have, and will frequently succeed in keeping the sheep in order while his master would have been helpless; but the custom that some shepherds have of abusing the sheep, and constantly sending the dog to make inroads upon them, cannot be too much reprehended.

In many parts of the East each sheep has its name, and will come when called, like a dog. But when the flock becomes very large, such a proceeding is evidently impracticable, and the shepherd then teaches certain sheep to come when called; when he wishes to move his flock, he walks first, calling his tame sheep. They follow him, and the rest of the flock, according to their instinct, follow their companions.

To this instinct the shepherd can always trust, for it is unfailing in its operation. Wherever the leading sheep may choose to go, there the flock are sure to follow. Of this instinct there are many instances on record, some ludicrous, and some tragic. One flock of sheep suffered the loss of more than a hundred of its members, because one of them chose to leap over a steep bank. This tragic event was only an exhibition of the same instinct that caused a whole flock of sheep to leap over an old man and a broom, with which instrument he was attempting to stop their progress. A shepherd was moving his flock through some streets, and, as may be expected, found considerable difficulty in guiding them through the intricate windings of their urban existence. Finding that the flock were about to turn down a wrong street, he called out to a crossing-sweeper to keep them back. The old man did what he could, running up and down the line, and at last came to a halt before a very obstinate sheep, and finding from its looks that it was meditating a spring, grasped his broom in both hands, and held it over his head. The sheep seems to have taken this attitude as a challenge, for it instantly sprang over the man, without touching his broom, and was followed by the entire flock, the poor man remaining in the same position as if petrified with astonishment. Petrified or not, he appeared to have taken the first step towards that process, for he was covered with mud spattered upon him by the sheep.

The worst foe that the shepherd has to contend against is the snow and cold in the winter months. It is not only the mere snow and cold that is dreaded, although they are formidable enough, but it is the power of the wind that is the shepherd's chief dread. The wind has a doubly injurious effect. In the first place it carries off all the heat from the body, and in fact causes the cold to have a more powerful effect than would have been the case had the thermometer been many degrees lower, provided that the wind had lulled. It is said that even the cold of the Polar regions, where mercury can be cast into bullets merely by pouring it into a mould, and leaving it in the open air, is not felt very severely, as long as there is no wind. But immediately after the rising of the wind, the cold pierces through the body, even though defended by fourfold shields of wool and furs.

The second reason why the wind is so injurious is, that it drives the snow into heaps, and sometimes carries it along in such large masses, that a small party of sheep is soon buried under the cloud of flakes, and even men do not always escape unhurt.

As an example of the effects of a regular snow-storm, I will quote a passage from the writings of Kohl, a German traveller, to whom the account was given by one of the men who were engaged at the time.

"We were once grazing the *ottara* of a rich Bulgarian. It is in the steppé of Otshakoff, and there were seven of us, with two thousand sheep and a hundred and fifty goats. The month was March, and we had just driven out for the first time. The weather seemed mild, and there was some grass already on the ground, so that we deemed of no mishap. In the evening it began to rain, and the wind was bitter cold. Soon the rain turned to snow, and our wet cloaks were frozen as hard as boards. A few hours after sunset we had a regular Siberian *rynaga* (snowdrift), from the north-east, whistling about our ears, till seeing and hearing became equally impossible. We had not got far from home yet, so we tried to find our way back, but it was impossible to make the sheep face the wind; and even the goats, who will face anything but a *vynaga*, were beginning to run before the storm. To keep the flock from scampering away was impossible; all we could attempt was at least to keep them together. In this way we had to race it all night, and in the morning nothing but snow was to be seen around us.

"The *vynaga* raged all that day, and the poor sheep were even more wild and frightened than during the night. Sometimes we gave up all as lost, but then we roused ourselves again, and ran with the scampering, bleating flock, while the oxen trotted after with the waggon, and the dogs came howling behind. The very first day, on which we ran at least fifty versts, the poor goats were all lost or frozen to death; the very next day, on which we ran at least fifty or sixty versts (a verst is about three fourths of an English mile), we left a track of dead sheep behind us the whole way. In the evening the poor beasts ran less wildly, for they were fairly exhausted with hunger and fatigue. We were also knocked up. Two of our party reported themselves sick, and crept under the mats and skins in the waggon, while the rest of us had only time to take a little bread and snow to sustain life.

"Night came on, but no house or home was anywhere to be seen, for the Otshakoff steppe is one of the wildest countries in the world. That night was worse than the first, and as we knew the storm was driving us right upon the coast, we expected every moment to be blown, with all our stupid flock, into the sea. Another of our men fell sick, so we packed him in the waggon along with the rest. We all thought that night would have been our last. Towards morning the wind fortunately shifted about, and drove us towards some houses, that we were able to see through the drifting snow; but though they were not more than thirty feet from us, it was impossible to make the foolish sheep turn aside. On they went right before the wind, in spite of all we could do, and we soon lost sight of the houses; but the good people had heard the howling of our dogs, and guessed what was the matter: they were German colonists, and some fifteen or twenty of them came to our help, and then we managed to stop the sheep, and drive them under the sheds and in the houses.

"We had lost all our goats, and about five hundred of our sheep, but many of the poor things died after we got them under the shelter, for in their fright they kept so close that many of them were smothered. We thanked God and the good Germans for our safety, for half a verst further we should have come to .the coast, rising twenty fathoms high above the sea. The Germans did all they could to make us and our sick men comfortable; but some of us were a long time before we recovered from the effects of the bout."

The adventure was perilous enough, but there are many Scotch shepherds who could narrate incidents

quite as perilous as those described by Kohl. Sometimes several hundred sheep become imbedded in
one drift. The reason is this : the sheep, on feeling the
cold blast, naturally fly for shelter to the first place that
seems likely to guard them from the drifting snow.
Their sheltering-place serves as a defence for some
time, but at last comes a severer blast than usual,
which drives into the air all the snow that had ac-
cumulated on the windward of the sheltering place,
and throws it in a mass on the sheep at the opposite
side, sometimes burying them between eight and
ten feet deep beneath the surface. The sheep are not,
as might be imagined, immediately suffocated, for
the snow is very porous, and admits sufficient air to
support life. The heat of their bodies also seems to
melt the snow round them, and gives them room to
move about a little. When many sheep are thus imprisoned in a snowy dungeon, the united heat that
is given out melts a comparatively large space. wherein
the sheep can even walk. Their locality is much warmer
than any ordinary place of shelter could have been, and
were it not that hunger lays its grasping hand upon
them, and causes them to nibble the wool from their
neighbours' backs, they would have no uncomfortable
residence.

Sheep thus found are frequently rescued by the
owner, and either are discovered by means of dogs
trained purposely, or by means of poles, which they
thrust into each drift. A practised "prodder" will be
able to distinguish the body of a sheep from other substances, even from the heath or mountain moss.

The diseases to which sheep are liable are innumerable, and it requires the greatest care to guard
against them. The quality of the air and the food
are the two principal causes of disease. The foot-rot
is one of the greatest plagues to the shepherd. It is
mostly caused by damp pasturage, which softens the
hoof at the same time that it promotes the growth of
the substance. The unfortunate sheep that is afflicted

with this disease cannot walk, but drags itself along on its knees.

I once saw a lamb thus afflicted that had fallen into a dry ditch, and replaced it in the meadow. After some days the little animal had eaten itself a long passage through the tall grass, just as if a path had been cut. What became of it afterwards I do not know, although its general health was much improved, as when it was first found in the ditch, it had hardly sufficient strength to raise its head from the ground. Sometimes when a sheep is in this state, a companion attaches itself to it, and attends to it during its illness.

There is another evil with which sheep are often afflicted : this is the " turnsick," as the shepherds call it ; in reality it is the presence of hydatids in the brain. Hydatids are singular substances, belonging to the Entozoa. They are certainly living creatures, but their life is of a very restricted kind, for they consist only of a membrane, filled with a watery substance. That which is found in the brain of sheep is called "*Polycephalus ovinus.*" How it gets there no one knows; it is sufficient to know that it does form within the animal's brain. These substances, by pressing against various parts of the brain, according to their situation, disorder its action, and force the afflicted animal to go through the most extraordinary movements.

There is a report in the " Lancet " of a sheep afflicted with this evil, which was brought to a veterinary surgeon. He removed a portion of the skull, in order to extract the hydatid, and after he had done so, he found that almost the whole of the brain was wanting. He was actually able to let down a waxlight into the cavity, and to examine the amount of mischief. The sheep, when released from the operation, got up and fed as usual, but on the fourth day after the operation it died. On examination, it was found that a mere shell of brain remained adhering to the base of the skull, and here and there to the sides,

so that there was not even a perfect shell of brain left.
What say the phrenologists?

These hydatids are found in almost all animals.
I have seen removed from the body of a monkey four
cysts, the smallest as large as a man's fist, and the
largest nearly the size of a child's head. The monkey
was not a large one, and the cysts had usurped the
place of other organs. The two large ones were in
the cavity of the abdomen, and the others in the
cavity of the chest, having pushed the heart quite
out of its place, enveloped the greater part of one
lung, and squeezed the other against the ribs. The
former owner of the monkey thought that the animal
had over-eaten itself, as the abdomen was so dis-
tended and hard; whereas the poor creature, as may
be expected, presented an emaciated appearance.

How the creature could have lived at all under such
a disarrangement of the vital organs is a mystery.
On examination with the microscope, the hydatid was
found to belong to the genus Echinococcus.

The love that a sheep bears to its young is very
great, that is, while they are young; as, in accordance
with that instinct implanted in brute animals, she
casts them off as soon as they are able to provide for
themselves.

Sheep are little inferior to the goats in activity among
rocks and precipitous places. Even in the rocky parts
of Derbyshire, and the steep Wiltshire Downs, they
exhibit their climbing and leaping propensities; but
they are not seen to advantage, except in those countries where shepherds heed them not, and where they
are never confined by the walls of a fold, but wander
where they will from their birth. Such sheep are
well described by Curzon in the following words:—

· "The method employed to hunt this sheep is to
climb to the highest summit of a mountain, and then
cautiously approaching the edges of the cliffs, to peep
down with a telescope into the gorges and ravines below, where, if you have luck, you may see the sheep

capering about on the ledges of the precipices, jumping, standing on a stone on their hind legs to reach
a little tuft of herbage, and playing the most curious
antics, for no perceptible reason, unless it is that they
find their digestion improved by taking a great deal
of exercise. In these gymnastics, the hunter must
participate to a great extent in following the tracks of
the jumpingest creatures (excepting fleas) that he can
ever have to deal with. It requires much activity, and
a good head for looking over a height, to attempt
to come up with them; and many a sad accident
has occurred to the adventurous sportsman in this
pursuit. I myself have been in some awkward situa-
tions—once particularly, having let myself down by
the roots of a kind of juniper, on to the ledge of a
precipice, I found there was no way further down,
and, what was of more consequence, no way up
again; for the roots of the stunted tree were above
my reach. A hunter—a Laz, or a native of Lazistaun—was with me; and when we had done watching
the sheep scampering out of shot below, we looked
at the place we were on, and then in each other's
faces in blank dismay. We were in the same scrape
as the Emperor Maximilian got into in the Tyrol, near
——, only there being no angels about in the mountains of Lazistaun, we had no expectation of being
assisted by a spirited or spiritual goatherd, as he was.

" After a good deal of pantomime, which would have
puzzled any bird who might be wondering at our manœuvres—for we did not understand each other's
language — we took off our boots, all our outer
clothes, and our arms and rifles, and tied them up in
a bundle; then I planted myself firmly with my face
to the wall of the cliff, sticking my rifle into a crevice
to give me more steadiness, and the hunter climbed
carefully up my back on to my shoulders, till he got
hold of the roots of the tree; the tree shook, and
plenty of stones and dirt fell upon my head, while
the hunter scrambled into the trunk, and he was safe.

He sat down awhile to rest, and then hauled up the
clothes and guns with our shawls that we had taken
off from round our waists. A gentle qualm came
over me at this moment, for fear he should be off
with my to him very valuable spoils, and leave me in
peace upon the shelf. But he was a true man, as a
hunter generally is; so after a variety of signs and
gesticulations to each other, as to how it was to be
done, he lugged me up, first by the shawls and then
by hand, until I could reach the roots of the tree.
Here there was only room for one, so he climbed
higher; and after some wonderful positions, struggles,
kicks, and scrambling, I got back amongst the roots,
then up the trunk of the old gnarled juniper, or
whatever it was, and at last upon a slope, partaking
much of that character which, in the States of the
free and independent slave-dealers over the water, is
called slantendicular. Here we both lay down."

I conclude this history of the sheep with an account
of its natural love. Mr. Hogg is the narrator.

A very affecting example of the attachment of
the sheep to its young is told by the Ettrick Shepherd:—" I requested of my master to spare me a lamb
for a ewe which he knew, and which was standing over
a dead lamb in the end of the Hope, about four miles
from the house. He would not let me do it, but bid
me let her stand over her lamb for a day or two, and
perhaps a twin would be forthcoming. I did so; and
faithfully did she stand to her charge. I visited her
every morning and evening for the first eight days,
and never found her above two or three yards from
the lamb, and often as I went my rounds she eyed
me long ere I came near her, and kept stamping with
her foot, and whistling through her nose, to frighten
the dog away. He got a regular chase twice a day,
but, however excited and fierce an ewe may be, she
never offers any resistance to mankind, being perfectly
and meekly passive to them. The weather was fine
and warm, and the dead lamb soon decayed; but still

this affectionate and resolute creature kept hanging over
the poor remains with an attachment that seemed to
be nourished by hopelessness. It often drew tears
from my eyes to see her hanging with such fondness over a few bones, mixed with a small portion of
wool. For the first fortnight she never quitted the
spot, and for another week she visited it every morning and evening, uttering a few kindly and heart-
piercing bleats, till at length every remnant of the
offspring vanished, mixing with the soil, or wafted
away by the winds."

GIRAFFE*.

HAVING wandered from the Pachydermata, let us return
to them again, commencing with one of whose pachy-
dermatousness, if we may coin such a word, there is
no doubt. This is the Giraffe, whose hide is more
than an inch in thickness.

The appearance of the animal is so singular, that
we do not wonder at the sceptics of the last age re-
jecting its very existence, or the still stranger credulity of the earlier ages, when men were not contented
with accepting the accounts of the animal, but also
believed that its father was a leopard, and its mother
a camel. Some men went further, and gave it a more
complicated composition. " The Giraffa, or Camelopardalis," says Leo, " a beast not often seen, yet very
tame, and of a strange composition, mixed of a libard
(leopard), hart, buffe (buffalo), and camell."

But even the present sceptical age, which believes
nothing that it has not seen, is convinced; for there are
many specimens of the animal now alive in England,
and the Giraffe is as familiar to most men as the cow.

Enormous in size as this animal is, it can conceal
itself so effectually by means of the lofty trees among
which it dwells, that none but a practised eye can discern it, and as will be seen from the latter part of the

* *Camelopardalis Giraffa.*

following extract from Cumming, even the eye of the
native is sometimes at a loss. The account of an
eyewitness is always to be preferred to that of one
who has only heard of the object. I shall, therefore,
give the words in which an eyewitness describes the
appearance of this animal in its native wilds.

" These gigantic and exquisitely beautiful animals,
which are admirably formed by Nature to adorn the
forests that clothe the boundless plains of the interior,
are widely distributed throughout the interior of
Southern Africa, but are nowhere to be met with in
great numbers. In countries unmolested by the in-
trusive foot of man, the Giraffe is found generally in
herds varying from twelve to sixteen ; but I have not
unfrequently met with herds containing thirty individuals, and on one occasion I counted forty together ;
this, however, was owing to chance, and about sixteen
may be reckoned as the average number of a herd.
These herds are composed of Giraffes of various
sizes, from the young Giraffe of nine or ten feet in
height, to the dark chestnut-coloured old bull of the
herd, whose exalted head towers above his companions, generally attaining to a height of upwards
of eighteen feet. The females are of lower stature,
and more delicately formed than the males, their
height averaging from sixteen to seventeen feet.

" Some writers have discovered ugliness and a want of
grace in the Giraffe, but I consider that he is one of
the most strikingly beautiful animals in the creation,
and when a herd of them is seen scattered through a
grove of the picturesque parasol-topped acacias which
adorn their native plains, and on whose uppermost
shoots they are enabled to browse by the colossal
height with which Nature has so admirably endowed
them, he must indeed be slow of conception who
fails to discover both grace and dignity in all their
movements. There can be no doubt that every animal is seen to the greatest advantage in the haunts
which nature designed him to adorn, and among the

various living creatures which beautify creation. I
have often traced a remarkable resemblance between
the animal and the general appearance of the locality
in which it is found. *

" In the case of the Giraffe, which is invariably met
with among venerable forests, where innumerable
blasted and weather-beaten trunks and stems occur,
I have repeatedly been in doubt as to the presence of
them until I had recourse to my spy-glass; and on
referring the case to my savage attendants, I have
known even their practised optics to fail, at one time
mistaking their dilapidated trunks for cameleopards,
and again confounding real cameleopards with these
aged veterans of the forest."

The entire structure of the head and its organs is
very singular, and well worthy of notice. The most
conspicuous objects on the head are the two horns,
as they are called. These horns are utterly unlike
those of other animals. They are not hollow, like
those of the oxen and ovine race ; they are not deciduous and bony, like those of the deer, but they are
projections from the skull of the animal, composed of
true bone, and cemented to the skull by distinctly-
marked sutures, which can be easily separated, especially when the animal is young. These horns are
covered with skin, and surrounded with a ring of hair
at their tips, leaving the centre bare. There is also
a third bone, comparatively small, and situated in the
centre of the forehead. Its osteological formation is
exactly the same as that of the other two, but it never
attains any great length, and, being covered by skin,
merely appears like a protuberance on the forehead.
Some writers have considered that this bone is a
proof that the Unicorn may be a real animal after
all, bearing a similar horn on its head.

The eyes are very prominent, and stand out so far
from the head, that the animal can see objects behind
it. It is doubtless endued with this property, to avoid

* See p. 4.

B B

those powerful animals which, together with it, inhabit the African plains.

The tongue answers almost the same purpose as does the trunk of the elephant, for with it the animal can pull down small branches, pluck off leaves, take a piece of bread from the hand, roll up a wisp of grass, or pick up a piece of sugar from the ground. It is said that the Giraffe possesses so complete a power over this organ that it can contract the tip sufficient to pass it into the pipe of an ordinary key. The tongue is not only flexible but powerful, and is sometimes put to rather unexpected uses by tame giraffes.

Professor Owen, who has carefully examined the structure of the tongue, has given the following account, which may be found in the Transactions of the Zoological Society.

" I have observed all the movements of the tongue, which have been described by previous authors. The giraffe, being endowed with an organ so exquisitely formed for prehension, instinctively puts it to use in a variety of ways, while in a state of confinement. The female in the Garden of Plants, at Paris, for example, may frequently be observed to amuse itself by stretching upwards its neck and head, and with the slender tongue pulling out the straws which are planted into the partition separating it from the contiguous compartments of its inclosure. In our own menagerie many a fair lady has been robbed of the artificial flower which adorned her bonnet, by the nimble filching tongue of the object of her admiration. The giraffe seems, indeed, to be guided more by the eye than the nose in the selection of objects of food ; and if we may judge of the apparent satisfaction with which the mock leaves and flowers so obtained are masticated, the tongue would seem by no means to enjoy the sensitive in the same degree as the motive powers. The giraffes have a habit, in captivity at least, of plucking the hairs out of each other's manes and tails, and swallowing them. I know not whether we must attribute to a fondness for epidermic productions, or to the tempting green colour of the parts, the following ludicrous circumstance, which happened to a fine peacock which was kept in the giraffe's paddock. As the bird was spreading his tail in the sunbeams, and curvetting in presence of his mate, one of the giraffes stooped his long neck, and entwining his flexible tongue round a bunch of the gaudy plumes, suddenly lifted the bird into the air, then giving him a shake, disengaged five or six of the tail feathers, when down fluttered the astonished peacock, and scuffled off with the remains of his train dragging humbly after him.'

Those interesting animals, now in the gardens of the Zoological Society, will frequently make use of their tongues to take their favourite dainty, a lump of sugar, from the hands of visitors, who always *will* feed them, in spite of the printed notice to the contrary. When they eat grass they treat it as we do asparagus, viz. they bite off all the soft green part, and reject the tough coarse stem.

Although a blow from the horns would be very severe, as the head would naturally swing violently against any object that is struck, the giraffe does not appear to use these weapons in actual conflict, at all events if it is opposed to dangerous foes, like the lion. When two giraffes fight between themselves they stand side by side, and strike violent blows with their horns, which can tear off the skin when used vigorously; but when the lion comes to attack the giraffe, it is too wise to place its head within the reach of the lion, who with a single blow from his iron-sinewed paw would lay the animal senseless. When, therefore, the giraffe feels itself opposed to such a foe as the lion, its defence consists in rapid kicks, administered with great precision, and with such rapidity, that the eye can scarcely follow them. A blow from limbs which can carry such an enormous weight over rocky passes, would be likely to demolish the lion if it took full effect.

· The lion, according to the accounts of the natives, is not always to be driven off by its formidable kicks, but watches his opportunity to spring on the back of the giraffe, and never relaxes his hold until his prey sinks to the earth from the mingled effect of fear and loss of blood. ·

At first sight the fore-legs of the Giraffe appear to be much longer than the hinder pair. Such, however, is not the case, as the apparent difference is caused by the great length of the shoulder-blades, from which the back of the animal slopes to the haunches. Both pairs of legs are of equal length.

The construction of the giraffe is such that it is forced to straddle widely with its fore legs before it can reach a small object placed on the ground. This characteristic attitude is copied in the Prænestine pavement. This work of art being attributed to Sylla, is a proof that the ancients were aware of the existence of the animal. There is also a figure of the giraffe, copied by Rosellini, found in Egypt, where are represented two men leading a very well-drawn giraffe by cords attached to its fore-legs. Running up the neck of the giraffe is a *lusus naturæ*, in the shape of a monkey of a vivid green colour, agreeably set off by a pink countenance.

Our knowledge of the character of this animal is either derived from tame specimens, or from the account of its behaviour when being hunted. We have already seen something of its character in a state of domestication; let us now peruse an account of the manner in which the animal demeans itself while it is being chased by an unknown foe.

· " It was on the morning of our departure from the residence of his Amazoola Majesty, that I first actually saw the giraffe. Although I had been for weeks on the tip-toe of expectation, we had hitherto succeeded in finding the gigantic footsteps only of the tallest of all quadrupeds upon the earth, but at dawn of that day, a large party of hungry savages, with four of the Hottentots on horseback, having accompanied us across the Mariqua, in search of elands which were reported to be numerous in the neighbourhood, we formed a long line and, having drawn a great extent of country blank, divided into two parties, Richardson keeping to the right, and myself to the left. Beginning at length to despair of success, I had shot a harte-beeste for the savages, when an object, which had repeatedly attracted my eye, but which I had as often persuaded myself was nothing more than the branchless stump of some withered tree, suddenly shifted its position, and the next moment 1 distinctly perceived that singular form, of which the apparition had oftimes visited my slumbers, but upon whose reality I now gazed for the first time.

" Gliding rapidly among the trees, above the topmost branches of many of which its graceful head nodded like some lofty pine, all doubt was in another moment at an end—it was the stately, the long-sought giraffe, and putting spurs to my horse, and directing the Hottentots to follow, I presently found myself half choked with excitement, rattling at the heels of an animal which to me had been a stranger even in its captive state, and which thus to meet free on its native plains has fallen to the lot of but few of the votaries of the chase; sailing before me with incredible velocity, his long swan-like neck keeping time to the eccentric motion of his stilt-like legs—his ample black tail curled above his back, and whisking in ludicrous concert with the rocking of his disproportioned frame,—he glided gallantly along like some tall ship upon the ocean's bosom, and seemed to leave whole leagues behind him at each stride. The ground was of the most treacherous description; a rotten black soil, overgrown with long coarse grass, which concealed from view innumerable gaping fissures, that momentarily threatened to bring down my horse.

"For the first five minutes, I rather lost than gained ground, and despairing, over such a country, of ever diminishing the distance, or improving my acquaintance with this ogre in seven-league boots, I dismounted, and the mottled carcass presenting a fair and inviting mark, I had the satisfaction of hearing two balls tell roundly upon his plank-like stern. But as well might I have fired at a wall; he neither swerved from his course, nor slackened his pace, and pushed on so far ahead during the time I was reloading, that, after remounting, I had some difficulty in even keeping sight of him amongst the trees. Closing again, however, I repeated the dose on the other quarter, and spurred my horse along, ever and anon sinking to his fetlock; the giraffe now flagging at each stride, until, as I was coming up hand over hand, and success seemed certain, the cup was suddenly dashed from my lips, and down I came headlong, my horse having fallen into a pit, and lodged me close to an ostrich's nest, near which two of the old birds were sitting.

"Happily, there were no bones broken, but the violence of the shock had caused the lashings of my previously-broken rifle to give way, and had doubled the stock in half, the barrels only hanging to the wood by the trigger-guard. Nothing dismayed, however, by this heavy calamity, I remounted my jaded beast, and one more effort brought me ahead of my wearied victim, which stood still, and allowed me to approach. In vain did I now attempt to bind my fractured rifle with a pocket-handkerchief, in order to admit of my administering the *coup de grace*. The guard was so contracted, that, as in the tantalising phantasies of a night-mare, the hammer could not by any means be brought down upon the nipple. In vain I looked around for a stone, and sought in every pocket for my knife, with which either to strike the copper cap, and bring about ignition, or hamstring the colossal but harmless animal, by whose towering side I appeared the veriest pigmy in the creation. Alas! I had lent it to the Hottentots to cut off the head of the harte-beeste, and, after a hopeless search in the remotest corners, each hand was withdrawn empty.

" Vainly did I then wait for the tardy and rebellious villains to come to my assistance, making the welkin ring, and my throat tingle with reiterated shouts. Not a soul appeared, and in a few minutes the giraffe, having recovered his wind, and being only slightly wounded on the hind-quarters, shuffled his long legs, twisted his bushy tail over his back, walked a few steps, then broke into a gallop, and diving into the mazes of the forest, presently disappeared from my sight. Disappointed and annoyed at my discomfiture, I returned towards the waggons, now eight miles distant; and on my way overtook the Hottentots, who, pipe in mouth, were leisurely strolling home, with an air of total indifference as to my proceedings, having come to the conclusion that 'Sir could not fung de kameel' (catch the giraffe), for which reason they did not think it worth while to follow me as I had directed."

The preceding account is taken from Harris, whose work on the wild animals of South Africa will repay a careful perusal.

Every one must sympathise with the eager sportsman in his disappointment in losing so magnificent a prey, and especially as the laziness of the servant was probably the cause of the animal actually escaping him. However, his efforts were at last crowned with success, as will be seen from his narrative.

" Notwithstanding that I had taken the field expressly to look for giraffes, and in consequence of several of the remarkable spoors* of these animals

* Footprints.

having been seen on the evening before, had taken
four mounted Hottentots in my suite, all excepting
Piet, who had, as usual, slipped off unperceived in
pursuit of a troop of Koodoos. Our stealthy approach
was soon opposed by an ill-tempered rhinoceros,
which, with her ugly old-fashioned calf, stood directly
in the path, and the twinkling of her bright little eyes,
accompanied by a restless rolling of the body, giving
earnest of her mischievous intentions, I directed Piet
to salute her with a broadside, at the same time putting spurs to my horse.

"At the report of the gun, and sudden clattering of
the hoofs, away bounded the herd in grotesque confusion, clearing the ground by a succession of frog-like
leaps, and leaving me far in their rear. Twice were
their towering forms concealed from view by a park of
trees, which we entered almost at the same moment,
and twice, on emerging from the labyrinth, did I perceive them tilting over an eminence far in advance,
their sloping backs reddening in the sunshine, as with
giant port they lopped the ridges in right gallant style,
a white turban which I wore round my hunting-cap,
being dragged off by a projecting bough, was instantly
charged and trampled under foot by three rhinoceroses, and long afterwards, looking over my
shoulder, I could perceive the ungainly brutes in the
rear fagging themselves to overtake me.

" In the course of a few minutes, the fugitives arrived at a small river, the treacherous sands receiving
their spider legs, their flight was greatly retarded, and
by the time they had floundered to the opposite side,
and scrambled to the top of the bank, I could perceive
that their race was run. Patting the . steaming neck
of my good steed, I urged him again to his utmost,
and instantly found myself by the side of the herd.
The lordly chief being readily distinguishable from
the rest of the herd by his dark chestnut robe, and
superior stature, I applied the muzzle of my rifle
behind his dappled shoulder with my right hand, and

drew both triggers; but he still continued to shuffle along, and being afraid of losing him if I should dismount among the extensive marshes and groves with which the landscape was now obscured, I sat on my saddle, loading and firing behind the elbow, and then placing myself across his path to obstruct his progress.

"Mute, dignified, and majestic, stood the unfortunate victim, occasionally stooping his elastic neck towards his persecutor, the tears trickling from the lashes of his dark humid eye, as broadside after broadside was poured into his brawny front.

> 'His drooping head sinks gradually low,
> And through his side the last drops ebbing flow,
> From the red gash fall heavy one by one,
> Like the first of a thunder shower.'

" Presently a convulsive shivering seized his limbs, his coat stood on end, his lofty frame began to totter, and at the seventeenth discharge from the deadly grooved bore, like a falling minaret, bowing his graceful head from the skies, his proud form was prostrate in the dust. Never shall I forget the intoxicating excitement of that moment! At last, then, the summit of my ambition was actually attained, and the towering giraffe laid low! Tossing my turbanless cap into the air, alone in the wild wood, I burned with bursting exultation, and unsaddling my steed, sank, exhausted with delight, beside the noble prize that I had won.

" While I leisurely contemplated the massive form before me, seeming as though it had been cast in a mould of brass, and wrapped in a hide an inch and a half in thickness, it was no longer matter of astonishment that a bullet discharged from a distance of eighty or ninety yards, should have been attended with little effect before such amazing strength.

" So he did ' fung de kameel ' after all."

Like others of the cervine race, the flesh of the giraffe is scented with the herbage on which it feeds.

When the giraffe is hunted on rocky ground, it springs forward with a succession of frog-like hops; but when at its ease, upon level ground, its usual mode of progression is like that of an ambling horse, that is, it moves both its legs on the same side at one time. The elephant, camel, and one or two other animals use the same step.

I may mention, that it is the opinion of many commentators, that the giraffe is the animal intended by the Hebrew word *zemer*, which our version translates " chamois:" One reason for this belief is, that the chamois was not known so far southward as Egypt and Palestine.

CAMEL.

WE change our scene from the fertile plains and dense forests of Southern Africa, to the desert sands, where no tree or patch of green meets the view, and where water can only be obtained by long journeys through the parched sands. There is no locality, however unpromising, that is not inhabited by some animal; the icy plains of the North Seas afford a resting-place to the seal, and a hunting ground to the polar bear; the mountain fastnesses of Switzerland give pasturage to the chamois, and even the thirsty desert sands themselves are not without inhabitants.

· The " Ships of the desert " pass over these sands, enduring the heat of the sun and the lack of water with a patience that no other animal possesses, for no other animal is fitted with an organisation that enables it to dispense with water, that greatest of necessaries.

Indeed, the entire organisation of the camel is moulded to the one purpose, the formation of an animal whose life is intended to be spent on dry sands. ·Therefore its head is lifted high above the earth to be out of the way of the drifting particles, its nostrils can be closed at will, if the sandy storm is very violent, its foot is elastic and spreading in its form, so that the animal can walk upon the loose sand without sinking into it; the teeth are sharp and powerful, in order that the camel may feed on the dried and stunted shrubs which here and there spring up, and whose thorny branches would defy any palate but that of the camel; and last of its peculiarities, it can drink at one time such an enormous quantity of water, and can retain it so perfectly, that even under the burning sun of Africa, it requires no more drink for several days.

The hump is a peculiarity confined to the camels. The bison and zebu have a kind of a hump, but that is situated on the shoulders, whereas that of the camel is placed on the centre of the back. The Bactrian camel, indeed, has a hump on the shoulders, but it is balanced by another on the hinder quarters. The hump is composed of a fatty secretion, and is supposed to supply nourishment to the animal by absorption, if food is not to be obtained.

The more ancient books of natural history represent the camel as having two humps, and the dromedary only one. Now this is so far right, that some camels have two humps, and no dromedary has more than one; but they are wrong in asserting that all camels have two humps. The Bactrian camel* is so ornamented, while the Arabian camel bears but one hump. The Dromedary† is a finer breed of the Arabian camel, and bears the same relation to the common camel, as a race-horse does to a roadster. The dromedary is used principally for conveying messages across the desert. Its name, which signifies " a runner," is sufficiently indicative of its character.

The camel is found over a large space of country, extending through Arabia, Persia, part of Tartary, part of India, and is also found in the Canary Isles. Many allusions to the camel are found in the Old Testament, where they are spoken of as forming a principal part of the wealth of their owners.

* *Camelus Bactrianus.* † *Camelus Dromedarius*

Some of the habits of the camel are well described in the following account communicated to me by the Rev. J. H. Pollen :—

" My principal experience in camels has been during my travels through the Arabian desert. I followed, after some interval of time, the route of the Hajji—the Mecca pilgrimage.

" The temper of the camel is, in general, not very amiable. It is unwilling, jealous, and revengeful to the last degree. Of this latter quality various tales are told : one which was fully believed by the Arab that narrated it to me was as follows. A certain camel-driver had bitterly insulted (*i. e.* thrashed in some ignominious way) the animal under his charge. The camel showed a disposition to resent, but the driver knowing from the expression of its eye what was passing within, kept on the alert for several days. One night he had retired for safety inside his tent, leaving his striped abbaya or cloak spread over the wooden saddle of the camel outside the tent.

" During the night, he heard the camel approach the object, and after satisfying himself, by smell or otherwise, that it was his master's cloak, and believing that the said master was asleep beneath it, he lay down and rolled backwards and forwards over the cloak, evidently much gratified by the cracking and smashing of the saddle under his weight, and fully persuaded that the bones of his master were broken to pieces. After a time he rose, contemplated with great contentment the disordered mass, still covered by the cloak, and retired.

" Next morning, at the usual hour for loading, the master, who had heard this agreeable process going on, from the interior of his tent, presented himself to the camel. The disappointed animal was in such a rage, said my informant, on seeing his master safe before him, that *he broke his heart, and died on the spot.*

" I had once to cross a very high range of rocks, and we had very great difficulty in getting our camels to face the steeper part of the ascent, though any horse would have made very light of it. All the riders had to dismount, and the laden animals made the bare rocky solitudes ring to the continual and savage growls with which they vented their displeasure. It is well on these occasions to keep out of the reach of their long necks, which they stretch out, and bring their teeth into dangerous proximity to the arm or side of any one but their master.

"While being laden they testify their dislike to any packet which looks unsatisfactory in point of size or weight as it is carried past them; though, when it is once on their backs, they continue to bear it with the patient expression of countenance which I fear passes for more than it is worth. All camels are loaded kneeling, and can go from twenty-four to sixty hours without rest, or more than a few mouthfuls of food, which they can crop off a thorny bush as they pass, or a handful of barley given them by their master. Parts of the desert are strewed with small dry drab-coloured plants, thorny and otherwise, which the camels continue to crop as they walk, jostling the rider not a little. They are very sparing of drinking. I have taken camels for eleven or twelve days without a drop of water. All of them did not drink even when we came to water, nor did any drink a large quantity or seem disturbed by the want of it, though the sun was very powerful and we travelled twelve or thirteen hours daily.

"At first they are difficult to ride. The rider mounts while the animal is kneeling, and sits like a lady, with the right leg over the fore pommel of the saddle. In rising, the camel suddenly straightens its hind legs before moving either of the fore legs, so that if the rider is unprepared, he will be jerked over its ears. It moves the legs of each side alternately, occasioning a long, undulating motion, which sways the rider to and fro from the loins. The motion, however, is soon learned; and when fatigued the rider can change sides, or shift his position in various ways.

"Sometimes a traveller places his whole family, wife and children, in one pannier fastened to the saddle, puts himself in another pannier fastened on the opposite side, and then falls in with a caravan and accompanies it.

"Dromedaries, the finer and better bred camels, have sparer frames and more endurance, and are principally led by the Bedouins of the desert: they also object either to going up or down hill.

"They are fond of kneeling at nights just behind the ring of Arabs who squat round the fire, and they stretch their heads over their masters' shoulders, to snuff up the heat and smoke, which seem to content them vastly.

"Between Cairo and Suez I saw more than one camel dead or dying. They seem very tenacious of life, as they remain unable to rise from a broken limb or any other cause for very many days. I more than once wished to go up and shoot the poor creatures, to put them out of their misery. But the Arabs have superstitious notions on this point, and would not suffer it. I did once find a camel that had been stabbed by its master, and once only. The poor beast had been exhausted, and the long broad dagger struck into his heart. It must have been a very short time before I reached the spot, as the blood was almost fresh.

"The camels at Grand Cairo are extremely powerful, and my informant told me that they are very *proud*, and will only eat their food from their master's hand, preferring to starve rather than receive it from any other source."

The swiftest description of dromedary is that called by the Arabs El Heirie. This animal is equally celebrated for its endurance and its speed. One of these dromedaries has been known to run more than a

hundred miles per diem, and to keep up this pace for
eight days in succession. In absolute speed, also, it
is unrivalled, a swift horse having no chance against
it. This, by the way, is not to be wondered at, if the
animal is possessed of agility to correspond with its
size and length of limb, for it can cover so much
ground at each step, that the horse will have to take
several steps while it takes one.

The camel is not only useful for its power of existing for a time without water, but also for its sagacity
in perceiving water at a distance. If a camel has
been kept without water for a longer period than
usual, it becomes very impatient, and if it perceives
the water at a distance, will sometimes break its
bridle and rush to the welcome fount. We call it
"fount" by courtesy, for if all things went by their
proper names, the desert fount would often be called
a mud puddle.

The camel is very useful in its own country, but
utterly useless in any other place. Their broad
cushiony feet, so admirably adapted to the dry sandy
soil, slip about in a pitiful manner if the ground be
wet; and if the animal gets among rocky ground, it
often injures itself fatally.

Sometimes the camels take their course without
being led at all, one taking the lead, and seeming to
take the right course by a mysterious instinct, the
others following in its track, and never attempting
to pass before it.

The desert is the home of the Arab and his camel,
both master and animal appearing to suffer equally
when brought within the reach of inhabited walls.
In "Eöthen" is a faithful description of the pain
endured by these children of the desert when brought
within the scope of civilisation.

"The want of foresight prevents the Bedouin from
appreciating at a distance of eight or ten days the
amount of the misery which he entails upon himself
at the end of that period. His dread of a city is one

of the most painful mental affections that I have ever
observed, and yet, when the whole breadth of the
desert lies between him and the town you are going to,
he will freely enter into an engagement to land you
in the city for which you are bound. When, however, after many a day of toil, the distant minarets at
length appear, the poor Bedouin relaxes the vigour of
his pace; his steps become faltering and undecided;
every moment his uneasiness increases; and, at length,
he fairly sobs aloud, and embracing your knees, im-
plores, with the most piteous cries and gestures, that
you will dispense with him and his camels, and find
some other means of entering the city. This, of course,
one cannot agree to, and the consequence is, that one
is obliged to witness and resist the most moving ex-
pressions of grief and fond entreaty. I had to go
through a most painful scene . of this kind when I
entered Cairo, and now the horror which these wilder
Arabs felt at the notion of entering Gaza, led to
consequences still more distressing. The dread of
cities results partly from a kind of wild instinct
which has always characterised the descendants of
Ishmael, but partly, too, from a well-founded apprehension of ill-treatment. So often it befalls the poor
Bedouin (when once entrapped between walls) to be
seized by the government authorities for the sake of
his camels, that his innate horror of cities becomes
really justified by results. The Bedouins with whom
I performed this journey were wild fellows of the
desert, and when they found that by the natural ascendancy of Europeans they were gradually brought
down to a state of subserviency to me, or rather to
my attendants, they bitterly repented, I believe, of
having placed themselves under our control. They
were rather difficult fellows to manage, and gave to
Dthemetri a good deal of trouble, but I liked them
all the better for that. Selim, the chief of the party,
and the man to whom all our camels belonged, was a
fine, savage, stately fellow; there were, I think, five

other, Arabs of the party, but when we approached the end of the journey, they, one by one, began to make off towards the neighbouring encampments, and by the time that the minarets of Gaza were in sight, Selim, the owner of the camels, was the only one who remained; he, poor fellow, as we neared the town, began to discover the same terror that my Arabs had shown when I entered Cairo. I could not possibly accede to his entreaties, and consent to let my baggage be laid down on the bare sands without any means of having it brought on into the city. So, at length, when poor Selim had exhausted all his rhetoric of voice, and action, and tears, he fixed his despairing eyes for a minute upon the cherished beasts that were his only wealth, and then suddenly and madly dashed away into the farther desert. I continued my course and reached the city at last, but it was not without immense difficulty that we could constrain the poor camels to pass under the hated shadow of its walls. They were the genuine beasts of the desert, and it was sad and painful to witness the agony they suffered when thus they were forced to encounter the fixed habitations of men; they shrank from the beginning of every high narrow street as though from the entrance of some horrible cave or bottomless pit; they sighed and wept like women. When, at last, we got them within the court-yard of the Khan, they seemed to be quite broken-hearted, and looked round piteously for their loving master, but no Selim came.

"I had imagined that he would enter the town secretly by night, in order to carry off those five fine camels, his only wealth in this world, and seemingly the main objects of his affection. But no—his dread of civilisation was too strong; during the whole of the three days that I remained at Gaza, he failed to show himself, and thus sacrificed, in all probability, not only his camels, but the money which I had stipulated to pay him for the passage of the desert. In order, however, to do all I could towards saving him

from this last misfortune, I resorted to a contrivance
frequently adopted by the Asiatics.   I assembled a
group of grave and worthy Mussulmans in the court-
yard of the Khan, and in their presence paid over the
gold to a Sheik well known in the place and accustomed to communicate with the Arabs of the desert,
when all present solemnly promised that if ever Selim
should come to claim his rights, they would bear true
witness in his favour."

As the chief food of the camel consists of the thorny
bushes which stretch their harsh withered branches
here and there in the desert, the teeth must be of no
small power and sharpness.   This is all very well as
long as the animal employs its teeth for their legitimate
purpose, but when it begins to exercise these same
teeth upon other animals, the case is altered.   Not
only are the cutting teeth of the camel sharp and
strong, but the canines are largely developed, and a
wound inflicted by such weapons as these can be no
trifling matter.   It is not very easy to avoid a camel's
bite, as the animal can twist its long neck about so
rapidly that the object of attack has not time to
escape before it is seized.

At one time of the year camels are quite dangerous,
fighting with each other directly their loads are removed, and sometimes attacking their masters, to
whom they seem rather attached at other times.
One of the camels in the Zoological Gardens took
a fancy to assaulting a goat that lived in an adjoining
enclosure, and which was shaken about rather severely
by the camel, whose long neck was thrust over the
fence that was supposed to separate the animals.

The flesh of the camel is sometimes eaten by the
Arabs, but not very often, as when it is killed the use
generally made of it is to extract the water contained
in its stomach.   Sometimes, after a long and weary
journey, when the water has either been all consumed, or has evaporated from the leathern bags in
which it is kept, the travellers, in approaching the

long·wished-for spring, find it exhausted. All they can do is then to push forward their wearied beasts as fast as possible towards the next spring. But all are perishing of thirst except the camels, whose peculiar organisation enables them to hold out longer than their masters. A camel, therefore, must die, and yield up its liquid stock. This is done, and the travellers sometimes retain sufficient strength, by this painful though necessary sacrifice, to reach another well.

Water thus taken from the stomach of the camel does not appear to be a very tempting draught, but thirst makes all things pleasant that will alleviate its cravings. Nothing is so much to be dreaded as the want of water. Food can in a manner be dispensed with for a long time, but water *must* be had. Moreover, the water thus obtained cannot, in point of fact, be less palatable than that carried with the travellers, and would certainly be cooler, and devoid of a very powerful flavour of old leather with which the water carried in bags is strongly impregnated. It is true also that the water is of a light green colour, but this can hardly be deemed a fault in the eyes of those accustomed to drink water tinted with a reddish coffee-coloured tint. The water is cooler than that contained in the leathern bags, because the rays of the sun are not able to penetrate through the ribs, &c., of the camel, as they do through the leathern sack, and the water, if drunk at once, would not be at a higher temperature than ninety or so of Fahrenheit. It may not be absolutely true that an egg may be boiled in the bag slung on the camel's back, but the water is at all events in a very hot state, and would serve better to compound punch with, than to drink unmixed.

If any one wishes to obtain a tolerably correct idea of the water used in desert travelling, he may do so by taking a very old Wellington boot, and making it water-tight by a dressing of pitch; then let him fill it with water, and place it in front of a hot fire for an hour or two : the boot should be well shaken every now and then, and when about half the contents have evaporated, the remainder will give a tolerable idea of the water which any one aspiring to travel in the desert must make up his mind to drink.

HORSE.*

"Hast thou given the horse strength ? hast thou clothed his neck with thunder ?

"Canst thou make him afraid as a grasshopper ? the glory of his nostrils is terrible.

"He paweth in the valley, and rejoiceth in his strength ; he goeth on to meet the armed men.

"He mocketh at fear and is not affrighted, neither turneth he back from the sword.

"The quiver rattleth against him, the glittering spear and the shield.

"He swalloweth the ground with fierceness and rage, neither believeth he that it is the sound of the trumpet.

"He saith among the trumpets, ha, ha; and he smelleth the battle afar off, the thunder of the captains and the shouting."

THIS magnificent description of the horse can scarcely be applied to the animals that we see in our streets. He who wishes to see the proud horse rejoicing in his strength, must either visit the deserts of Arabia, where the horses are brought up with their masters, or transport himself to the prairies of America, where the horses have no masters at all, and range freely over vast ranges of country.

It is true that our horses are not treated so badly as they once were, but still we are far from managing this beautiful animal properly. We force back his

* *Equus Caballus.*

head ,with bearing reins to make him look more
spirited; we hurt his mouth with an uselessly powerful bit, and we put him on a regulated system of
diet, forgetful of the fact that animals are the best
judges of those matters that concern their health. But
perhaps the horse-owners judge their quadrupeds from
themselves and other bipeds, and think, that as themselves would be apt to run riot if they were placed without restriction in a place where was everything that
could be desired, so would the horses run riot, if they
were permitted to eat and drink at what time and
in what quantities they liked best.

About thirty or forty years ago, the treatment of the
horse was shameful. Among other cruelties inflicted
upon them. by their owners, their ears were cropped
and their tails were docked; many even went further than this; and thinking that the horse ought to
carry his tail high, conceived the barbarous notion of
cutting across the muscles of the lower side of the
tail, and then, when they had thus deprived the animal
of the power of lowering the member, they prevented
the muscles from regaining their power by fastening a
rope to the end of the tail, passing it over a pulley in the
ceiling, and attaching a weight to the cord, by which
the tail was always kept raised, in whatever position
the poor horse placed itself. This custom, called
"nicking," was greatly in fashion about thirty or
forty years ago, and the books of farriery of that period give ample instruction in the art. I remember
seeing in one of these books an engraving of a stable
full of nicked horses. If the appearance of the animals
had not called forth pity, risibility would have been the
prominent impulse on seeing the print. There were
four or five stalls, each occupied by a horse. Some of
the horses were lying down, and some standing up, all
of them had their long tails gathered into a peak, and
standing perpendicularly in the air, as if they had been
submitted to the action of the "gravitation pump." *

When the tortured animal has remained in this man-

* "Story of a Chemist."

ner for some time, the wounds on the tail heal, and the operator has the satisfaction of knowing that the horse is completely deprived of the use of that appendage. The pain suffered during the healing process must be intense. We know that when a cut heals the parts are drawn together, and sometimes with such force as completely to change the appearance of a man's countenance, if he has been wounded in the face. The torture, then, that is experienced by the poor horse, whose wounds are kept open by mechanical force, must indeed be extreme.

It is supposed that the wild horses which scour the plains of Tartary are the originators of our domestic horse, while it is evident that the herds of horses that are found in the American prairies are derived from those animals that were brought into America by the Spaniards in 1535, and whose strange appearance contributed so greatly to their victory over the natives. There is a story that the Americans supposed the rider and his horse to be one animal, and that when they saw a soldier in battle tumble off his steed, they were so terrified at one foe thus becoming two, that although they had gained the ascendancy, they took to flight, fearing lest all their opponents had an unlimited power of doubling their numbers. Now the American Indians ride the horse themselves, and some of the tribes, the Comanches in particular, are unrivalled as horsemen.

We will suppose ourselves among the Comanches. There is a young man who wants a horse, and does not wish to go to the expense of buying one; so he takes a lasso, mounts a swift horse, and sets off in search of a herd of wild horses. These having been found, he begins a chase after them, endeavouring to pen them in by a precipice, or some other obstacle, so that they are forced to rush past him. The herd spring by with the speed of fear, but one animal is devoted. One bound, and he is free as air, another, and he is on his haunches, choking and struggling in vain to free himself from the noose that has tightened round his neck. After he has plunged about until he is wearied, the operation of " choking." down commences. The Indian dismounts, leaving his horse to itself. The animal is trained to remain quiet, and waits patiently until its.master remounts : the Indian, now holding the lasso in his hand, advances cautiously towards the captive animal, going hand over hand, as the sailors say, and choking the horse by a jerk of the lasso, whenever it struggles. At last he reaches the horse and grasps its nostrils, and having succeeded in so doing, he breathes once or twice into the nostrils of the animal, which, as if under the operation of some spell, appears to be tamed by the very action. He then puts a bit into its mouth, and leading it towards his first horse, remounts, and leads the captured animal home. Next day, the newly taken horse is seen doing his work.

The best horses are seldom taken in this manner, as they cannot be overtaken by the mounted Indian ; it is therefore the less speedy that fall victims to the lasso. There is also another method used, called " creasing;" this consists in striking the upper part of the neck with a rifle bullet, so that the horse feels stunned for a few minutes; and when he recovers, finds a bit in his mouth and a man on his back. But this is a method seldom resorted to, as it requires a most practised shot to strike the neck, and avoid injuring the animal; and moreover, the animals so taken are never so spirited as those captured by the lasso. As is usual, when men can obtain horses at a low price, the Indians are cruel masters, and beat their horses unmercifully with a formidable whip, that always hangs at their wrists ready for use. These whips are sometimes used for a different purpose, in a strange method of obtaining horses, called " smoking." Let Mr. Catlin give the account of the custom in his own words.

" When General Street and I arrived at Kee-o-Kuk's village, we were just in time to see the amusing scene in the prairie, a little back of his village

The 'Foxes,' who were making up a war party to go against the 'Sioux,' and had not suitable horses enough by twenty, had sent word to the 'Sacs' the day before, according to ancient custom, that they were coming on that day at a certain time to 'smoke' that number of horses, and they must not fail to have them ready. On that day, and at that hour, the twenty young men who were beggars for horses were on the spot, and seated themselves on the ground in a circle, where they went to smoking. The villagers flocked around them in a dense crowd, and soon after there appeared on the prairie, at half a mile distance, an equal number of young men of the Sac tribe, who had agreed to give each a horse, and who were then galloping them round at full speed; and gradually, as they went around in a circuit, coming nearer to the centre, until they were at last close to the ring of young fellows seated on the ground. Whilst dashing about thus, each one with a heavy whip in his hand, as he came within reach of the group on the ground, selected the one to whom he decided to present his horse; and as he passed, gave him the most tremendous cut with his lash over the naked shoulders; and as he darted around again, he plied the whip as before, and again and again, with a violent crack, until the blood could be seen trickling over his naked shoulders; upon which he instantly dismounted, and placed the bridle and whip in his hands, saying ' Here, you are a beggar, I present you a horse, but you will carry my mark on your back.' In this manner they were all, in a little time, 'whipped up,' and each had a good horse to ride home and into battle. His necessity was such, that he could afford to take the stripes and the scars as the price of the horse, and the giver could afford to make the present for the satisfaction of putting his mark on the other, and of boasting of his liberality."

And a considerable boast he would have made of his liberality when he returned to his own camp, for your

Indian is a most unmitigated boaster ; he seems to act on the principle of the advice given by an experienced writer to one who was about to launch his first work on the world—" If you have only a penny trumpet, blow it."

The " lasso," " creasing," and " smoking," are three very ingenious methods of obtaining horses, but they are not universally employed by the Indians. In the first place, the first two methods require a considerable amount of trouble, and Indians, like all savages, avoid trouble when they have an opportunity. The third method is certainly attended with very little trouble, but it puts the men to great pain; and although an Indian is most heroic in his endurance of pain when inflicted by an enemy, or in accordance with the laws of his peculiar chivalry, he is quite as unwilling to undergo bodily suffering as the most civilised European; so he avoids all difficulties by stealing his horses from some one else who has caught them and trained them. There is not a more inveterate race of horse-stealers in the world than the American Indians. In the pursuit of horses, they are unrivalled for their cunning and boldness in carrying out, and their craft in concealing their measures until the actual blow is struck.

The capture by the lasso is used in other parts of America, and by civilised men. In Chili, the Guachos evince great skill in catching and breaking the wild horse. Two accounts, by Darwin and Head, will illustrate the modes employed in the work. Mr. Darwin's description is as follows :—

" One evening a domidor (subduer of horses) came for the purpose of breaking in some colts. I will describe the preparatory steps, for I believe they have not been mentioned by other travellers. A troop of wild young horses is driven into the corral, or large enclosure of stakes, and the door is shut. We will suppose that one man alone has to catch and mount a horse which as yet had never felt bridle or saddle.

I conceive, except by a Guacho, such a feat would be utterly impracticable. The Guacho picks out a full-grown colt, and, as the beast rushes round the circus, he throws his lasso so as to catch both the front legs: instantly the horse rolls over with a heavy shock, and whilst struggling on the ground, the Guacho holding the lasso tight, makes a circle so as to catch one of the hind legs just beneath the fetlock, and draws it close to the two front; he then hitches the lasso, so that the three legs are bound together; then, sitting on the horse's neck, he fixes a strong bridle, without a bit, to the lower jaw; this he does by passing a narrow thong through the eyeholes at the end of the reins, and several times round both jaw and tongue. The two front legs are now tied closely together with a strong leathern thong, fastened by a slip knot; the lasso which bound the three legs together being then loosed, the horse rises with difficulty. The Guacho, now holding fast the bridle fixed to the lower jaw, leads the horse outside the corral. If a second man is present, (otherwise the trouble is much greater) he holds the animal's head whilst the first puts on the horse cloths and saddle, and girths the whole together. During this operation, the horse, from dread and aston-ishment at being thus bound round the waist, throws himself over and over again on the ground, and, till beaten, is unwilling to rise. At last, when the sad-dling is finished, the poor animal can hardly breathe from fear, and is white with foam and sweat. The man now prepares to mount, by pressing heavily on the stirrup, so that the horse may not lose its balance; and at the moment he throws his legs over the ani-mal's back he pulls the slip-knot, and the beast is free. The horse, wild with dread, gives a few most violent bounds, and then starts off at full gallop: when quite exhausted, the man, by patience, brings him back to the corral, where, reeking hot and scarcely alive, the poor beast is let free."

This, however, is only the preliminary step, as the

horse is not thought to be completely under subjection until it can be checked instantly on a spot when at full speed. A Guacho will ride his horse at full gallop, and stop it at once on a cloak thrown on the ground, or will even charge headlong against a wall, and force the animal to rear up so as to scrape the wall with its hoofs.

But the triumph of horse-training is the feat that Darwin saw performed in Chili. The rider, merely holding the reins betwen his thumb and finger, dashed up to a post, and made the horse wheel round it, while with his outstretched arm he kept one finger on the post. The circuit having been made, the rider executed a demi-volte, and made the circuit of the post in the opposite direction, keeping the finger of his other hand against it.

The horses are thus trained as a preparation for purposes for which they are used. It appears that when a bullock is caught in the lasso, it will often gallop round in a circle at the extent of the rope, and thus, if the horse is not able to wheel within a small space, will catch the rider in the cord, and almost inevitably kill him. Such has frequently been the case, the unfortunate men having had their bodies nearly severed in two.

The description by Capt. Head gives a similar account, and mentions several additional circumstances.

" A man, mounted on a strong steady horse, threw his lasso over the neck of a young horse, and dragged him to the gate. For some time he was very unwilling to leave his comrades, but the moment he was forced from them, his first idea was to gallop away; however, the jerk of the lasso checked him in the most effectual manner. The Peons now ran after him on foot, and threw the lasso over his fore legs just above the fetlocks, and, twitching it, they pulled his legs from under him so suddenly, that I really thought the fall he got had killed him. In an instant a Guacho was seated on his head, and with his long knife, in a few seconds, cut off the whole of the horse's mane, while another cut the hair from the end of the tail. This they told me is a mark that the animal has been once mounted. They then put a piece of hide into his mouth to serve as a bit, and a strong hide halter on his head. The Guacho who was to mount, arranged his spurs, which were unusually long and sharp; and while two men held the animal by his ears, he put on the saddle, which he girthed extremely tight; he then caught hold of the horse's ears, and in an instant vaulted into the saddle, upon which the man who was holding the horse by the halter threw the end of it to the rider, and from that moment no one seemed to take any notice of him. The horse instantly began to jump in a manner which made it very difficult for the rider to keep his seat, and quite different from the kick or plunge of an English horse; however, the Guacho's spurs soon set him going, and off he galloped, doing everything in his power to throw his rider. Another horse was immediately seized, and so quick was the operation that twelve Guachos were mounted in a space which I think hardly exceeded an hour."

Although our own horses cause us no such trouble in taking, they often cause us sufficient trouble in breaking, and even when broken, almost every horse has its peculiar tricks, and after residing for any length of time in one place it gains also peculiar habits. Every one who has had experience in horses can remember numberless instances of the tricks and habits of these creatures.

It is astonishing to see how readily a horse learns to know his way, after he has been a few times on the same journey. There is a horse, now rather aged, whom I have repeatedly driven, who always goes through a regular routine, and completely astonishes those who are not used to him. When harnessed (an operation which he always greatly resents), he sets off at a sharp trot until he comes to a place where three roads meet: here he slackens his pace,

and turns his head round, as if to ask which way he is
to go. This point being settled, he always turns off
sharply at the first by-road which leads to a village
where he is hospitably entertained. To prevent this,
it is necessary to give a decided hint some time before reaching the by-road, that he is expected to go
quietly on and not look for the hospitality of his
friends at the village. After he has received this intimation he does not attempt to turn off, but proceeds
on the high road. The first time that I drove him,
he carried me for some distance down the by-road
before I could persuade him to retrace his steps. He
then proceeds steadily enough, always slackening his
pace in order to cross the railway, and then turns off
to reach the station. Being admonished that the
station is not his destination for that day, he next
makes a bolt for a stable-yard, where he is entertained
if he has to wait any considerable time. It always
requires a steady bearing on the opposite rein, and a
slight application of the whip, to induce him to pass
the stable-yard; but this difficulty being overcome,
he proceeds to the next village, always choosing the
proper turnings, and invariably taking the correct side
of the road, whether he sees a vehicle or rider meeting
him, or hears it from behind. He then, of his own
own accord, crosses the road, and draws up at the
baker's shop from whence the bread of the house is
furnished. If, however, he is told not to stop here,
he goes off to the clergyman's house, and draws up at
the door in the most artistic manner conceivable.
Here he always considers his journey ended, and
when his master again enters the gig, he turns round
and makes the best of his way homewards. Once
when he was driven past this, his last resting-place,
his astonishment and indignation were unbounded.
He started off with great reluctance; and during his
journey was constantly turning his head, and looking
first to one side and then the other, besides making a
few attempts to turn round altogether. His satisfac-

tion, when he was at length suffered to retrace his steps, was very evident, and he set off, shaking his head, ears, and harness with an air that plainly showed his idea that his master had at length discovered his error. He always paid the greatest attention to the conversation taking place behind him, and slackened his pace according to the interest of the discussion, often nearly stopping when he thought his driver too much engaged to notice his pace. His expressive ears, and general way of carrying his head, always demonstrated his perfect knowledge when he himself was the subject of conversation.

The tricks that saddle-horses fall into are often not only vexatious but even dangerous. It is not at all pleasant to be mounted on a horse, who, for no imaginable reason, springs sideways across the road, and leaves his rider on the ground while he is enjoying a solitary gallop. I was once nearly the victim of an eccentric pony. The little animal was one of those which are so commonly used in the Peak of Derbyshire, little hard-mouthed animals, who are perfectly independent of bit and bridle, and generally prefer going on their own course to taking that indicated by their rider. At first the pony objected to move at all, and could only be kept at a respectable pace by one of the party remaining behind him, and paying away at him with a heavy whip. After some miles had been passed in sundry vagaries, he changed his mind, and became very obedient, galloping for more than a mile without requiring the whip once. I was just congratulating myself on having conquered the obstinate animal at last, when I flew up into the air, and on coming down again, found myself seated on the pony's neck, the creature being firmly fixed, with his fore legs planted before him, exactly as he had stopped. I would defy the best trained cavalry horse to have halted more instantaneously.

However, he did not attempt that trick again, for instead of regaining the saddle I rode on his neck for several miles up and down the very hilly roads that exist near Matlock.

Not many months since a startled horse ran away at Oxford, and met with an extraordinary fate. There is a certain very narrow street in Oxford called Bear Lane, in honour of a public-house whose exterior was at that time decorated with a sign representing an animal popularly supposed to be a bear, and wearing an expensive gold chain and collar. The lane opens into another lane crossing it at right angles, and almost entirely composed of colleges. Down this lane a hack was coming gently enough, when, being startled, it dashed suddenly forward, sprang over the rough stones, and not being able to check itself, its fore feet came on the flag pavement of the cross lane, slipped over it, and the animal was hurled with such violence against the stone-wall that it was killed on the spot, the subsequent appliance of a butcher's knife being an unnecessary precaution. The rider most providentially escaped unhurt. I passed by the spot just as the catastrophe had occurred. The poor horse was lying quite dead, half on the pavement and half on the road, and the gutter was crimsoned with its blood. For weeks afterwards the stain remained on the wall where its head had struck.

That horse presented no very pleasing spectacle, but it was not so unearthly hideous as one that I saw lying dead on a country road. It was about six in the morning when I was taking an early walk, that I came unexpectedly upon the body of a horse lying in the road. The animal had evidently been dead some few hours: I was remarking to myself how complete was the difference between a dead and a sleeping horse, and how the energy of every limb seemed to have gone together with the life that had once animated it. The limbs were stretched out, each rib was plainly conspicuous, and the head was thrown back. I moved round to obtain a better view of the head, but found that the rising sun behind threw a shadow exactly on the animal's head. I therefore moved aside in order to permit the sun's rays to stream full upon the fallen animal. As they did so, I started back, for from the eyes of the dead horse there gleamed a ray'of living emerald light that might fitly have flashed from the eye-balls of the pbantom horse that carried Leonora and her spectre bridegroom to their home among the tombs. Or rather it appeared as if a demon had slain the horse and was looking out of its eyes.

That emerald ray haunted me for weeks.

It would have· been a great windfall for Edgar Poe to have witnessed such a sight. Had he done so, there would have been no necessity to manufacture an ideal raven,

> " Whose fiery eyes burned into his bosom's core."

When a horse is left to his own desires, and his senses permitted to remain unblunted, he is a very sagacious animal, and gifted with no small degree of curiosity.

A horse of the common cart-horse breed, that used to work on the railway at Oxford, was always trusted by his master to return home unaccompanied after his day's work was over. The signal for departure was given to him by throwing the end of his chain upon his back. This notice having been given, he invariably walked home very deliberately, never failing to scrutinise every new object on his way with the utmost attention. At one time an epidemic for keeping goats prevailed at Oxford. As the horse was returning home, the unwonted sight of a goat walking about in the street caught his attention, and he immediately walked over to the goat to inspect such an extraordinary animal, nor was. it until he had surveyed it for some time, and gravely driven it before him for a few hundred yards, that his mind seemed set at rest on the subject : afterwards, the sight of goats never disturbed his equanimity. About the same time, a blind horse was accustomed to draw a cart, which duty he performed as well as if he had possessed the use of his eyes.' He directed his course by means of certain indescribable vocal sounds produced by his master, and never failed to change his course at the proper moment when his master's voice was heard.

Now this horse used to be considered as rather a prodigy, and was thought to exhibit a very high degree of reasoning powers. Yet, I am quite sure that nearly every horse would behave in the same manner if it had been treated as well. The fact is, that we are so full of our railroads, power-looms, steam-presses, and other mechanical powers, which are whizzing and twirling throughout the length and breadth of the land, that we are always too apt to endeavour to turn our very servants into machines; and it is not to be expected that the horse is to escape while man suffers.

A soldier, for example, is looked upon by his officer as a machine, principally useful in making " wheels," " drills," " echelons," " squares," and other implements of a like nature. A labourer (from whom, by the way, the soldier is generally manufactured) is set to work so many hours per diem, and expected to turn out a certain amount of carrots, turnips, corn, &c. The same may be said of the mechanic, substituting chairs, tables, and other articles, for carrots and turnips. The doctor is, perhaps, more of a machine than either, for after the day's work has been done, every body feels himself privileged to set the wheels going again—principally through the medium of the night-bell. But perhaps the greatest machine of all is worked by the publishers. The poor author-machine is supposed to be a kind of rotatory, self-acting steam-engine, capable of pouring out an unceasing supply of " copy." Sometimes the safety-valve is soldered down, and double the quantity of blackened paper is expected to be made. This falls very heavily on the machine, for only the head and hands, the boiler and the pistons, can work, and so sometimes the boiler bursts.

So, a man, being himself a machine, is naturally anxious to reduce his horse to the same level, and commences his work by putting blinkers on its head, in order to prevent it from seeing anything at the side of the road which might startle it, or induce it to stop from curiosity. Now as to the first reason, it is no reason at all, for ignorance is always one great cause of fear; and a horse is much more likely to shy at an object which he does not understand, than at one which he has had an opportunity of observing.

From stable to harness, and from harness to stable, is all the experience of life that many a horse obtains. What wonder then, if he starts aside at catching a glimpse of an object which he does not understand, and which he may fancy has some connection with the whip which he has never seen, but whose stinging strokes are always felt on the tenderest parts of his body? Or an unexpected sound may strike his ear, and he naturally starts away from it. Nothing prevents a horse from shying so effectually, as familiarity with the objects which excite his alarm.'

But when left to itself, the horse is anything but a machine, and displays a considerable amount of sagacity. There is an instance of cunning in a horse recorded by Mr. Smee:—

" Some time ago I was stopping at a farm-house, in Wales during harvest time, and I wanted a pony in order that I might take a ride. All the men were in the fields, some distance off, and the females declared that it would be impossible to catch the pony, because it was so uncommonly cunning. However, I thought that I would make an attempt myself, and was surprised to find how easily I could drive it into a close place. To my astonishment, the pony went coolly to the gate, pressed its mouth against the spring, pushed the gate open, and away it ran, with several horses after it, into a field, kicking up its heels and frisking about as much as to say, ' Catch me if you can.' However, I fastened the springs of all the gates but one, tried the manœuvre over again, and captured the little rascal by his opening the gate and entering into the farmyard, intending to go out on the opposite side."

Perhaps this animal was a near relation of the tall quadruped who objected to being mounted by Mr. Winkle, in the disastrous journey from Rochester to Dingley Dell, and who, although not possessed of mathematical powers, succeeded in demonstrating that each point of the circumference of a circle is equally distant from the centre.

The reader will observe, that although this clever little horse was gifted with sufficient reason to deceive one who was not accustomed to his tricks, yet the higher intellect of the man soon overcame that of the animal.

Those resident by the sea-shore almost daily witness a combat between a horse and his rider. The horse is intended to take a sea bath, but the sound of the waves so terrifies him, that he at first dares not come near it. The rider takes him up and down the sands, until he can venture to skirt the waves with tolerable equanimity. Presently the rider urges him on the track of a receding wave, and waits for its return. Back it comes, curling over the horses' feet, and dashing its foam over him. But at this first touch of the many-sounding sea, the affrighted horse springs off, as if Neptune in person were assaulting him with his trident, and takes to flight. He is then brought back again, and the same scene repeated over and over, until he suffers the white-crested waves to break over him with as much indifference as do the draggle-tailed animals who draw the bathing machines.

Patience and an even temper are two requisites for managing a restive horse. Two-thirds of the hard mouths, and evil tempers are caused by pretenders, who are quite as much at home in managing a horse, as a cockney sailor in managing a yacht. Unhappily, the feat of porting the binnacle, or reefing the lee-scupper of the would-be sailors, is not so disastrous as the equestrian exploits of the would-be horsemen, for when they get on board a yacht, they wisely leave its management to the sailors; whereas if they mount a horse, they must manage it themselves.

The memory of the horse is very good, and he will remember, not only persons, but places after an interval of several years. There is an account in the "Penny Magazine," that illustrates the excellent memory of the horse :—

"During my residence on the head-waters of the Susquehanna, I owned a small American horse, of the name of Charlie, that was very remarkable for his attachment to my own person, as well as for his general good qualities. He was a great favourite with all the family; and being a favourite, he was frequently indulged with less work and more to eat than any of the other horses on the farm. At a short distance from the dwelling-house, was a small but luxuriant pasture, where, during the summer, Charlie was often permitted to graze. When this pasture had been originally reclaimed from its wild forest state, about ten years previous to the period of which I am speaking, four or five large trees of the sugar maple species had been left standing when the rest were cut down, and means had afterwards been found to prevent their being scorched by the fire at the time the rest of the timber had been consumed. Though remarkably fine trees of their kind, they were, however, no great ornament, their stems being long and bare, their heads small, and by no means full of leaves—the case generally with trees that have grown up in close contact with each other in the American forests. But if they were no ornament, they might serve as shade-trees. Beneath one of these trees Charlie used to seek shelter, as well from the heat of the meridian sun as from the severe thunder-gusts that occasionally ravage that part of the country. On an occasion of this sort Charlie had taken his stand close to his favourite tree, his tail actually pressing against it, his head and body in an exact line with the course of the wind; apparently understanding the most advantageous position to escape the violence of the storm, and quite at home, as it were, for he had stood in the same place some scores of times. The storm came on, and raged with such violence, that the tree under which the horse had sought shelter, was literally torn up by the roots. I happened to be standing at a window, from whence I witnessed the whole scene. The moment Charlie heard the roots giving way behind him, that is, on the contrary side of the tree from where he stood, and, probably feeling the uprooted tree pressing against his tail, he sprang forward, and barely cleared the ground upon which, at the next moment, the top of the huge forest tree fell with such a force that the crash was tremendous, for every limb and branch were actually riven asunder. I have many a time seen horses alarmed, nay exceedingly frightened; but never in my life did I witness anything of the sort that bore the slightest comparison to Charlie's extreme terror, and yet Charlie, on ordinary occasions, was by no means a coward. He galloped, he reared his mane, and tossed his head, he stopped short, and snorted wildly, and then darted off at the top of his speed in a contrary direction, and then as suddenly stopped and set off in another, until long after the storm had considerably abated, and it was not until after the lapse of some hours that he ventured to reconnoitre —but that at a considerable distance—the scene of his narrow escape. For that day, at least, his appetite had been completely spoiled, for he never offered to stoop his head to the ground while daylight continued. The next day his apprehensions seemed somewhat abated; but his curiosity had been excited to such a pitch, that he kept pacing from place to place, never failing to halt as he passed within a moderate distance of the prostrate tree, gazing thereat in utter bewilderment, as if wholly unable to comprehend the scene he had witnessed the preceding day. After this occurrence took place, I kept this favourite horse several years, and during the summer months he usually enjoyed the benefit of his old pasture. But it was quite clear he never forgot, on any occasion, the narrow escape he had had; for neither the burning rays of the noontide summer sun, nor the furious raging of the thunder-storm, could compel Charlie to seek shelter under one of the trees that still remained standing in his small pasture."

The Horse fights in two ways. One method is by lashing out with the hind legs, but another is by rearing up and striking with the fore feet. The animal strikes very rapidly, and can inflict very severe blows, as, from the formation of the foot, each blow is struck with the end of the hoof. This mode of fighting is generally used in the battles of the horses among each other, or in combating the wolves that hang about the skirts of the wild herds. Mr. Lloyd tells us of a mare that used voluntarily to fight the wolves merely for the fun of the thing. She always waited until she was properly shod, and then trotted off into the woods alone, ready and willing to meet a foe.

The bear is one of the most formidable enemies to the horse, and the inhabitants of Scandinavia say that it leaps on the back of the horse, and while it holds on to its prey with three paws, it endeavours with the other to grasp at the trunks of the trees through which the affrighted animal is dashing; such, they say, is its strength, that it can in this manner stop the horse to which it is clinging; sometimes it grasps too small a tree, and then the tree is torn out of the ground.

The words of his master are perfectly understood by the horse, and it not unfrequently happens that it is unnecessary to direct the animal at all. Every one is familiar with the horses driven in a London omnibus, and has noticed, that they never require to be checked when they have to stop; the "Hold hard" of the conductor being sufficient to bring them to a stop. In like manner the violent slamming of the door, or the blow of the strap buckle on the roof, is all that is required to start them; the one method being used by misanthropical conductors as a convenient way of startling the passenger who happens to sit immediately beneath, and the other employed for the purpose of projecting the passenger who has just entered to the farther end of the vehicle: or in case of a mild conductor, the word "right" suffices.

The cavalry horses all know the words of command as well as their riders, and would go through the manœuvres, even if their riders were asleep. Not long since, during a fox hunt, an officer who made one of the party, thought he recognised some horses in the field, as having formerly been in his own company. Wishing to be quite certain, he suddenly shouted "Halt!" The word was magic. The suspected horses threw themselves back, ploughed up a yard or two of soil with their feet, and when they recovered their position, their riders were lying on the ground, considerably in advance. So at the riding schools, the word of command is given more to the horses than the riders, who being screwed into stiff and unnatural postures by the riding master, are carried along quite at the mercy of the animal.

Before we proceed to that most beautiful of animals, the Arab Horse, I will quote a passage from Acerbi, giving an excellent account of the passage up the frozen Gulf of Bothnia, accompanied by the excitement of a horse chase.

"When a traveller is going to cross over the gulf on the ice to Finland, the peasants always oblige him to engage double the number of horses to what he had upon his arrival at Grioleham. We were forced to take no less than eight sledges, though being only three in company, and two servants. The distance across is forty-three English miles, thirty of which you travel on the ice, without touching on land. This passage of the frozen sea is, doubtless, the most singular and striking spectacle that a traveller from the south can behold. I expected to travel forty-three miles without sight of land, over a vast and uniform plain, and that every successive mile would be in exact unison and monotonous correspondence with those I had already travelled; but my astonishment was greatly increased in proportion as we advanced from our starting post. The sea, at first smooth and even, became more rugged and unequal. It assumed, as we proceeded, an undulating appearance resembling the waves by which it had been agitated. At length we met with masses of ice heaped one upon another, and some of them seemed as if suspended in the air, while others were raised in the form of pyramids. On the whole, they exhibited a picture of the vilest and most savage confusion, that surprised the eye by the novelty of its appearance. It was an immense chaos of icy ruins, presented to view under every possible form, and embellished by superb stalactites, of a blue green colour. Amidst this chaos, it was not without much fatigue and trouble that our horses were able to find and pursue their way; it was necessary to make frequent windings, and sometimes to return in a contrary direction, following that of a frozen wave, in order to avoid a collection of icy mountains. In spite of all our expedients for discovering the evenest paths, our sledges were every moment overturned to the right or the left, and frequently the legs of one or the other of the company raised perpendicularly in the air, served as a signal for the whole caravan to halt. The inconvenience and the danger of our journey were still further increased by the following circumstances. Our horses were made wild and furious both by the sight and smell of our great pelisses, manufactured of the skins of Russian wolves or bears. When any of the sledges were overturned, the horses that belonged to it, or to that next to it, frightened at the sight of what they supposed to be a wolf or a bear rolling on the ice, would set off at full gallop, to the great terror of both passenger and driver. The peasant, apprehensive of losing his horse in the midst of this desert, kept firm hold of his bridle, and suffered the horse to drag his body through masses of ice, of which the sharp points threatened to cut him in pieces. The animal at last wearied out by the constancy of the man, and disheartened by the obstacles continually opposed to his flight, would stop; then we were enabled again to get into our sledges, but not till the driver had blinded the animals' eyes. But one time, one of the wildest and most spirited horses in our train, having taken flight, and completely made his escape, the peasant who conducted him, unable any longer to endure the fatigue and pain of being dragged through the ice, let go his hold of the bridle. The horse, relieved from his weight, and feeling himself at perfect liberty, redoubled his speed, and surmounted every impediment; the sledge, which he made to dance in the air, by alarming his fears, added wings to his flight. When he had fled a considerable distance from us, he appeared, from time to time, as a dark spot, which continued to diminish in the air, and at last totally vanished from our sight. And now the peasant, who was the owner of the fugitive, taking one of the sledges, went in search of him, trying to find him again by following the traces of his flight. As for ourselves, we made the best of our way to one of the isles of Aland, keeping as nearly as we could, in the middle of the same plain, still being repeatedly overturned, and always in danger of losing one or other of our horses, which would have occasioned a very serious embarrassment. During the whole of this journey on the ice, we did not meet with so much as a man, a beast, a bird, or any living creature. These vast solitudes present a desert abandoned, as it were, by nature. The dead silence that reigns is interrupted only by the whistling of the winds against the prominent points of ice, and sometimes by the loud crackings occasioned by their being irresistibly torn from this frozen expanse ; pieces thus forcibly broken off, are frequently blown to a considerable distance. Through the rents produced by these ruptures, you may see the watery abyss below ; and it is sometimes necessary to lay planks across these rents, as bridges, for the sledges to pass over.

"After considerable fatigue, and having refreshed our horses, about half way on the high sea, we at length touched at the small island of Signilskar, about thirty-five English miles distant from where we started ; but from the turnings we were obliged to make, not less than ten miles might be added. All this while, however, we were kept in anxious suspense about the fugitive horse, supposing him lost in the abyss ; we had even prepared to continue our journey, and had put on new horses to the sledges, when, with inexpressible pleasure, we espied the two sledges that went in pursuit, returning with the fugitive. The animal was in the most deplorable condition imaginable ; his body was covered all over with sweat and foam, and was still enveloped in a cloud of smoke. Still we did not dare to come near him ; the excessive fatigue of his violent course had not abated his ferocity ; he was as much alarmed at the sight of our pelisses as before ; he snorted, bounded, and beat the snow and ice with his feet ; nor could the utmost exertions of the peasants to hold him fast have prevented him from once more making his escape if we had not retired to some distance, and removed the sight and scent of our pelisses. From Signilskar, we pursued our journey through the whole of the Isle of Åland, where you meet with post-houses, that is to say, places where you may get horses. You travel partly by land, and partly over the ice of the sea. The distance between some of these islands is not less than eight or ten miles. On the sea, the natives have had the precaution of fixing branches of trees, or putting small pines along the whole route for the guidance of travellers in the night-time, or directing them how to find out the right way after the falls of snow."

. The celebrated Arab horses are indeed models of beauty, fleetness, strength, and docility. The three first qualifications they receive by inheritance, but the last is derived entirely from the kind treatment that the animal meets with at the hand of its master. An Arab horse lives with its master's family, and is treated quite as if it were a member of that family. From its earliest youth it is accustomed to live among the children, who tumble about it, hang on by its ears and tail, and take all kinds of liberties, which are never resented by the gentle creature.

. When a foal is born, it is the custom to assemble a conclave of the chief men, and to draw up a genealogy and account of the new-born horse. This warrantry is generally sewn up in a leathern bag, and fastened about the horse's neck. Here is a specimen of a warrantry given with an Arab horse. The account is taken from the " Court Journal:"—

"This horse, the sire of Rabhamy, equal in power to his son, is of the tribe of Zazzalah, and descends from the uncle of Lahadah, the sire of Alket, is of a fine figure, and fleet as an ostrich; herewith is his tooth, when a colt, in a bag, with his pedigree, which a Caffre may believe. Among the honours of relationship, he reckons Zalwah, the sire of Mahat, who was the sire of Kallak, and the unique Alket, sire of Manasseh, sire of Alsheh, from generation to generation, down from the noble horse Lahalala. And npon him be green herbage in abundance, and the waters of life, with an edifice enclosed with walls, a reward from the tribe of Zoab, for the fire of his race; and let a thousand cypresses shade his body from the hyena of the tombs, from the wolf, and the serpents of the

plain; within the enclosure a festival shall be kept;
and at sunrise thousands shall come, and observers
arrive in troops, whilst the tribe exhibits, under a
canopy of celestial signs, the saddle and the name,
and the place of the tribe of Bek Altabek, in Mesopo-
tamia, and Kulasla of Lutarek, of the inspired tribe
of Zoab. Then shall they strike with a loud noise,
and ask of Heaven, in solemn prayer, immunity for
the tribe from evil and the demon of languor, from
pestilence, from wandering from God, from scabby
camels, from scarcity, from perplexed congregations,
from the spleen, from the fiery dragon, from commixa-
tion, from beating on the feet, from treading out with
the feet, from Heiubnu, or the unknown son of an
unknown father, from lameness at birth, from impost-
humes, from seclusions, and from fascination, from
depression and elevation, from cracks in the feet, from
numerous assemblies, from importunate soothsayers,
from the offspring of prophets and nocturnal travellers, from diviners of good opportunity for a purpose, from relations and degrees of affinity, and from
rash and inordinate riders, deliver this tribe, O Lord,
and secure those who are slow to follow and slow to
advance, who guard the truth and observe it."

With such an animal as this, the Arab is happy
even in the midst of poverty. Riches are nothing to
him, as long as he can keep possession of his beloved
horse. Very many times have Arabs been tempted
to part with their horse for a sum which would have
enriched them for life, but very few, indeed, have
yielded, and purchased wealth by the loss of that animal, that to them was more valuable than wealth.
One Arab, who had been forced, from the pressure
of poverty to do so, was in the habit of coming daily
to see his favourite, and would sit by her and talk to
her for hours at a time.

And well does the noble animal repay such kindness. It follows its master about like a dog, it shields
him from the rays of the sun, is never so happy as when

bearing its master on its back, and it has been known to render him even more valuable service. There is still extant a record of an Arab horse who, with its master, was taken captive by an adverse tribe. During the night the man contrived to drag himself to the place where his favourite animal was picketed, and, bound as he was, to loosen its bonds. He knew full well that the horse would at once return to his own tribe, and that his return without his owner would cause an alarm among the tribe. However, the horse, when free, refused to stir, and not all the whispered commands of his master could induce him to move. He seemed to be quite at a loss to discover why his master did not at once mount on his back, instead of lying helpless on the ground. At last the truth flashed on him. He stooped over his prostrate master, grasped his robe between his teeth, lifted him from the ground, and dashed out of the hostile encampment at full speed; nor did he slacken his speed until he arrived at the encampment of his own tribe. He laid his bound and wounded master at the door of his tent, and then sank lifeless to the ground.

The manner in which a well-bred Arab horse accompanies his master on a journey is well described by Lieutenant Wellstead :—

"The day before Sayyid came into my hands, he had been presented to the Imaum by a Nejd sheikh. Reared in domesticity, and accustomed to share the tent of some Arab family, he possessed in an extraordinary degree, all the gentleness and docility, as well as the fleetness, which distinguish the pure breed of Arabia. To avoid the intense heat and rest their camels, the Bedouins frequently halted during my journey for an hour about mid-day. On these occasions Sayyid would remain perfectly still while I reposed on the sand, screened by the shadow of his body. My noon repast of dates he always looked for and shared. Whenever we halted, after unsaddling him and taking off his bridle with my own hands, he

was permitted to roam about the encampment without
control.   At sunset he came for his corn at the
sound of my voice, and during the night, without
being fastened, he generally took up his quarters at a
few yards from his master.   During my coasting
voyages along the shore, he always accompanied me,
and even in a crazy open boat from Muskat to India.
My health having compelled me to return to England
overland, I could not in consequence bring Sayyid
with me.   In parting with this faithful attached creature, so long the companion of my perils and wanderings, I am not ashamed to acknowledge that I felt an
emotion similar to what is experienced in being separated from a tried and valued friend."

The same animal once saved him from the pursuit
of a number of Arab robbers, on whom he came unexpectedly, and only escaped by the speed of his horse.
Perhaps the beauty of the animal was as much his
preservation as its speed, for the pursuers could easily
have shot the horse at first, but were deterred by their
wish to possess it unhurt.

It is said that when an Arab horse is sold it refuses
to obey its new master until its former owner puts the
bridle, with his own hand, into that of the purchaser,
and formally delivers it over with a speech which the
horse is supposed to understand.

The Arabian horse furnishes one of the most valuable constituents in our present breed of race-horses.
The "Darley Arabian" was the original horse from
which the Arab mixture came.   The animal was imported from Palmyra in the reign of Queen Anne.
Indeed several of our most celebrated racers have been
pure Arabs.   Such were the "Godolphin Arabian,"
and Chillaby, the "Mad Arabian," so called from his
ferocity; for only one groom was permitted by the
animal to approach it; and on one occasion, when its
owner put a stuffed effigy of a man in its way, it rushed
at the image, and tore it to pieces.

One of the most celebrated of our race-horses was

the wonderful "Eclipse." There was not much to recommend it in its outward appearance, for it was a great gaunt, ungainly animal, with an awkward mode of carrying its head, and a bad habit of "roaring." Yet in speed the animal was unrivalled, and at one race, its rider was actually seen to be endeavouring to hold it back, in order that it should not get too far in front of the other horses. It is believed that the animal never did put forth its full speed. "Eclipse" at last died, after a long life, during which he won many races, but latterly was not permitted to run, because he would have been certain of winning. So he staid quietly at home, while the owners of the other horses paid his master large sums to withdraw him from the list. He left behind a numerous progeny of racers, I believe about one hundred and thirty or so. His skeleton is now in the Ashmolean Museum at Oxford. The person who mounted the skeleton has well preserved the very ungainly attitude generally assumed by the horse when living, and many of its peculiarities can be discerned even in the scaffolding of dry bones which remains as the memorial of this wonderful horse.

It is useless to deny the charge of cruelty that is often brought against the custom of racing. It is cruel without a doubt, but yet the horses themselves are actuated with as much desire to win the race as their riders, and have even been known to fight with each other when engaged in a race.

In some parts of the Continent, such as Rome, on the Carnival, there are horse-races managed in rather a singular manner, the horses being without riders. They are urged to the top of their speed by metal balls covered with spikes, which, being suspended to strings on their backs, are flung about with every movement, and goad the poor animals into a state of fury.

I have already mentioned the aptitude of the horse for remembering those places where it has been accustomed to visit. I was once nearly thrown from a gig on account of the memory of a horse. Having occasion to visit a village at some distance, a friend promised to obtain the loan of a horse and gig for the journey. At the appointed time the apparatus arrived, drawn by a sharp-looking pony. He was very unwilling to stop at all, and when requested to move again, he got up on his hind legs, and came down again in precisely the same place. This he repeated several times, until my companion led him at a trot a few yards, and then jumped in, while the vehicle was in motion. Once started, his eccentricities ended, and he went on steadily to the end of his journey. When the evening began to draw on, we set off home again, with the same ceremonies that accompanied our start. The night grew darker and darker, and we were going on very steadily, but not able to see two yards before the pony's head, when the animal gave a sudden lurch to the right, and dashed up a steep bank three or four feet in height, gig and all. How we got to the top I never could tell, but we went down again by a gentle slope which we had passed. It appeared that the pony's owner was of a convivial turn of mind, and had been accustomed to halt and refresh himself and pony at a public-house on the top of the bank.

The most singular use of horses is that in practice near St. Francisco. On Easter-day the inhabitants have a kind of Guy Faux business, the object being Judas Iscariot. They make a puppet to represent the traitor, and, after firing at it with blank cartridge for an hour or so, the following events take place. The account is taken from Gerstäcker's travels :—

" After having first thrown the steed on the ground by means of the lasso, and then blindfolded her, he buckled a strap round her waist, which caused the fiery animal to bound with a shriek of terror ; after which she threw herself down, trying, by rolling herself about and kicking, to get rid of what she mistook for a burden imposed upon her. Yet all her efforts were in vain. Judas Iscariot was cleverly put on her back, notwithstanding all her furious plunging and rearing; and soon the mare, with the new but decently-dressed Mazeppa, ran off like an arrow down the street, and in the direction of the mountains, among the triumphant yells of the multitude, and pursued by the Spaniards, who were now nearly all of them mounted.

"The puppet hung to the back of the snorting animal like a mad hobgoblin, nodding its head and flinging its arms in the most comical manner, whilst the other horsemen, who were racing after it, might be compared to the spectral followers of the wild hunters. The object of this mad pursuit was to cut off the poor animal from its retreat to the mountains, in order that the ladies, watching the sport from the verandah, might not so soon be deprived of their amusement. Valentine distinguished himself here, as well by his nimbleness as by the cruelty with which, catching the mare by the tail, he threw her over, and brought her forcibly back to the place from whence she had started. At last the poor tortured animal, completely worn out by her fright, as well as by the unwonted exertion, was no longer able to keep up. She fell, and neither blows nor other ill-usage made any impression on her."

ASS.*

This very respectable, although hardly aristocratic animal, has suffered much from the mistaken ideas of men, who first ill-treat it in every way, and then abuse it because its temper suffers in consequence of their ill-treatment.

It has been already remarked that the connection between a rude man and a bear is difficult to be traced, and the same difficulty will be found in ascertaining the reason why a stupid man is called an ass.

* *Asinus vulgaris.*

In the first place we must understand that the ass, as we see him in our country, worn down by cruelty and fatigue, ragged from neglect, and gaunt from hunger, his natural spirit gone, and its place supplied by a mixture of obstinacy and cunning, is hardly to be recognised for the swift, spirited animal that roams at large over the plains of Persia, India, and the northern parts of Russia. Michael Armstrong himself, in his worst days, is not a greater contrast with a wild Scotch lad than is the ordinary ass with the khur, or wild ass of Persia. No one who wishes to make a fair calculation of the wealth and intelligence of London would prosecute his researches in Seven Dials or Whitechapel, nor ought we to form an estimate of the intelligence of a race merely from some persecuted individuals of it. Moreover, even did we do so, we should not be quite correct in affixing the brand of stupidity on this animal. Let any one turn an old ass into a field and try to mount and ride him, and after an hour or so the ass will not appear a very stupid animal. Even a party of boys find no small difficulty in achieving the capture, and when they have driven the animal into a corner it is not so easy to mount it, for its hind legs seem to be animated with the spirit of the famous steam leg, and launch volleys of kicks in every direction where an enemy approaches from the rear, while its ready mouth is perfectly capable of defending the front. But even should an adventurous youth succeed in mounting on its back, his triumph is often but short-lived, for the ass generally refuses to stir an inch from its place, or jumps about with such strange contortions, that the rider is left sprawling on the ground, while the animal dashes through its persecutors, taken off their guard by their companion's fall, and regains the open field. Sometimes, on finding that its rider is not to be unseated by such means, it lies down and deliberately rolls over, or puts him to excruciating torture by grinding his leg against a wall or the rough stem of a tree. It has been known, in such cases, to walk into a pool and lie down there, leaving the rider to scramble out as he could.

It is an animal of considerable endurance, although not possessed of swiftness or much strength. In some parts of Ireland asses are used to draw carts from a mine and back again. They leave the mine by day, draw their load, wait while it is discharged, and return again. The drivers, after the load is discharged, start the vehicle in its homeward course, lie down in the cart, and go to sleep, while the ass has to finish the journey by its own sagacity. When the poor animal sleeps is very problematical.

In England the use of the ass as a riding animal is generally confined to the sweeps or dustboys, who perch themselves on the extreme end of the spine, and appear as satisfied with their steed as if it were the handsomest horse in the world.

But in the East, where the ass is comparatively a noble animal, it is used for riding almost exclusively by the rich and great. The Arabian asses are said to be the best, to carry their head gracefully, and to throw out their legs elegantly in walking or galloping. They are valued very highly, and are decorated with rich caparisons by their riders. A variety of this animal is white, and is used only for personages of the highest distinction. This custom is alluded to in the Book of Judges,—" Speak ye that ride on white asses, ye that sit in judgment, and walk by the ways."

The ass is distinguished from the horse by differenees so essential, that Mr. Gray has placed it in a different genus. The principal distinction is the manner in which the hair is set on the tail. The hair of the horse's tail is very abundant, and entirely covers the tail itself, concealing its form, whereas that of the ass is comparatively scanty, and only springs from the extremity of the tail. The mane, too, is different both in length and shape. That of the horse is very long, and hangs down on one side of its neck, but that of the ass is shorter, stubby, and forms a mere ridge down its neck. There is also a black mark running along the spine, and another crossing the shoulders, the two forming a cross. There is a very ancient tradition that this cross was placed upon the ass as a memorial of the time when the Saviour rode upon the ass in his triumphal entry into Jerusalem.

When the ass is properly treated, it is really an intelligent animal, and can be taught to perform many tricks. In the pages of our friend Topsell, there is a circumstantial account of the exploits of a " learned ass :"—

" There was a cunning player in Africa, in a city called Alcair, who taught an asse divers strange tricks or feats, for, in a publick spectacle, turning to his asse (being on a scaffold to shew sport), said, ' The great Sultan proposeth to build him an house, and shall need all the asses of Alcair to fetch and carry wood, stones, lime, and other necessaries for that business.' Presently the asse falleth down, turneth up his heels into the air, groaneth, and shutteth his eyes fast, as if he had been dead; while he lay thus, the player desired the beholders to consider his estate, for his asse was dead; he was a poor man, and, therefore, moved them to give him money to buy another asse. In the meantime, having gotten as much money as he could, he told the people he was not dead, but knowing his master's poverty, counterfeited in that manner, whereby he might get money to buy him provender, and, therefore, he turned again to his asse, and bid him arise, but he stirred not at all; then did he strike and beat him sore (as it seemed) to make him arise, but all in vain,—the asse laid still. Then said the player again, ' Our Sultan hath commanded that to-morrow there be a great triumph without the city, and that all the noble women shall ride thither upon the fairest asses, and this night they must be fed with oates, and have the best water of Nilus to drink.' At the hearing whereof, up

started the asse, snorting and leaping for joy. Then
said the player, 'The Governor of this town hath
desired me to lend him this, my asse, for his old
deformed wife to ride upon,' at which words the asse
hangeth down his ears, and understanding like a
reasonable creature, began to halt as if his legs had
been out of joint. 'Why,' but said the player, 'had
thou lifer carry a fair young woman?' The asse
wagged his head in token of consent to that bargain;
'Go, then,' (said the player,) 'and among all these
fair women, chuse one that thou mayest carry;' then
the asse looketh round about the assembly, and at
last went to a sober woman, and touched her with
his nose, whereat the residue wondered and laughed,
shutting up the sport with crying out, '*An asse's
woman! An asse's woman!*' and so the player went
unto another town."

The racing instinct appears strong in man. Who
has not heard of the famous race of two drops of rain
down a window, and the manner in which it became a
drawn race by the two drops coalescing before they
reached the goal? Small boys race hoops, and whip
tops against each other, while the big boys turn the
little ones into racers for their amusement, the prize
being generally a negative one, viz. to escape being
pelted at thirty paces' distance. Even naval officers,
when they can find no vessel to race against, content
themselves with putting two biscuit maggots against
each other, in a course over a plate. So donkeys are
occasionally metamorphosed into racers, the object
being diametrically opposite to that of horse races,
the last donkey gaining the prize. Each rider mounts
his opponent's donkey, and tries to bring it in before
his own, and thereby to win the "highlows," or the
real beaver hat, brilliant with its many-coloured
ribbons. These amusements are generally carried on
at wakes and fairs, and are supposed to be restricted
to such places. But there are other places where
donkey races are run for hats, the only difference

being that the hat, instead of being beaver berib-boned, is gold bejewelled, and not unfrequently is very hurtful to the head.

As a proof of the real qualities of the ass, if it is treated in a proper manner, we may cite that animal mentioned by Mr. Bell as having being used as a hunter:

"The most remarkable instance, within my own knowledge, was that of an ass in the possession of an ancestor of mine, who, from age and disease, was obliged to give up riding on horseback, and be-take himself to the easier exercise of this animal's more gentle paces. 'General,' for that was the name of the ass in question, was of an unusual stature, at least for those bred in this country; his pace was easy and free, but swift, perhaps, beyond example; and many times before my grandfather obtained him, he had been in at the death, after a tolerably hard fox-chase. Matches had often been made, and asses of unusual power and fleetness had been placed against him, but he never met with a competitor. He was docile also, and gentle; and having survived his master, to the comfort of whose latter days he had essentially contributed, he spent the remainder of his life in ease and idleness, and, at his death, was buried with due honours in his own little paddock."

The sure-footedness of this animal is almost as wonderful as that of the goat, and is applied to a more useful purpose. Asses are employed in the passage over the Alps or Andes; over rough roads that no horseman yet could pass, they continue to make their way, and do so even when having a rider on their back. The "road" on which they have to travel is generally a mere projection from the face of a cliff, the rock rising in a perpendicular wall on the one hand, while the precipice yawns on the other. A hasty step, or even an inadvertent blow against the rocky wall, is sufficient to hurl the traveller over the cliff into the cavern below. This would be sufficiently dangerous, even if the path were level, but, as it is frequently very steep or very narrow, forming declivities of several hundred yards, it becomes a very serious matter to attempt the passage over such a road, which, in addition to these evils, is always winding, and frequently strewed with loose stones. Nothing but their instinct would guide the animals down these terrific passes, and even that instinct is sorely tried. The rider must let the animal have its own way, and suffer the bridle to hang loose, for a check upon the ass while descending one of these paths would be certain to destroy its balance, and to precipitate both ass and rider over the rocks. The mode in which the animal accomplishes its descent is very remarkable. When it arrives at one of these dangerous paths, it stands still for some time, eying the road down which it has to pass, and appears to make up its mind respecting the mode of procedure. Having stood for some time thus ruminating, and occasionally snuffing at the road with its nose, having apparently settled a plan in its head, it places its fore feet forwards, as if it were stopping itself, and puts its hind feet together, placing them also forward. In this attitude it slides down the descent with astonishing swiftness, and contrives, in some mysterious manner, to steer its way through all the windings of the road.

Mules, often used for the same purpose, have apparently derived the art from their asinine ancestors.

The antipathy that exists between the horse and the ass is well known, and has been known for ages, as it forms the basis of one of the fables attributed to Æsop. But the antipathy usually lies on the side of the horse, that animal disdaining the company of so humble a personage as the ass. Possibly this may be the case because a solitary horse is stronger than a solitary ass; at all events, when the latter animal is in power, it fully reciprocates the feeling. In Quito, where there are large herds of asses, a horse is not only not permitted to live among them, but not even to come into their grazing grounds. If an unfortunate horse does happen to stray into the domains of one of their herds, the asses immediately assault him, and cease not from their bites and kicks until they have left him dead on the spot.

These Quito asses are the descendants of those that were imported into America by the Spaniards. They are exceedingly swift, and can pursue their course among rocks and declivities where no horse can follow them. As is the case with the wild horses, they are nominally private property, but in reality can be taken by any one who chooses to take the trouble of catching them, the owner only requiring a small sum for each day's hunt. They are caught with the lasso in the same manner as the wild horse, only they are rather more difficult to manage, on account of the skilful way in which they defend themselves with their teeth and hoofs.

It is rather remarkable, that although these animals are so vicious and spirited, yet, after they have borne their first load, their speed and spirit leave them, and they assume the ordinary asinine look of dullness and stupidity.

There are several species included under the genus 'Asinus.' The Zebra,* the Dauw,† the Quagga,‡ and the Dzigguetai,§ all belong to this genus.

The zebra and the dauw closely resemble each other, the differences of locality being, that the true zebra is found among the mountainous and rocky districts of Southern Africa, while the dauw, or Burchell's zebra, inhabits the plains. There is also a difference in the aspect of the body, as the ears of the dauw are shorter than those of the zebra, and the stripes are of a lighter colour, and are not continued round the body or on the limbs. The zebra has never

---

* *Asinus Zebra.* † *Asinus Burchellii.*
‡ *Asinus Quagga.* § *Asinus Hermionus.*

been•brought under entire subjection to man. Sometimes an individual has been partially trained to bear a saddle, or to draw a carriage, but even these animals are not to be trusted, as their savage nature continually breaks through their superficial civilisation, and renders them rather dangerous. There are, however, mules between the zebra and the common ass, which are powerful animals, and are forced to work as well as can be expected. .

It is rather curious to mark the development of the stripes in the various species of asses. The zebra has the stripes extending over the whole body and limbs, even including the tail and the fetlocks. The dauw is striped like the zebra, only the marks are of a lighter colour, and are confined 'to the upper parts of the body and the head. The quagga is destitute of stripes on the hinder parts, and the limbs, but the face, neck, and shoulders resemble those of the dauw, with the exception that the general colour has a more indistinct appearance; while in the dzigguetai and the common ass the only remnant of the stripes is the black line along the spine and across the shoulders.

The flesh of the dzigguetai is considered a great delicacy by those who inhabit the countries where it is found. From its skin is made the celebrated " shagreen," a well-known substance used for covering instrument cases, boxes, and other articles. The granulated effect is produced in a very ingenious manner. The skin is softened for some time in water and scraped perfectly level, small hard seeds are then strewed upon its surface, and a heavy roller is passed over it, forcing the seeds into its substance. The skin is then dried, leaving the seeds in their places. The next part of the process is to beat out the seeds, and the skin is then subjected to the action of a plane, which cuts away the skin to the level of the depressions made by the seeds. · The hide is then again soaked in water, which causes it to swell, when the places which had been pressed by the seeds, and had therefore escaped the action of the plane, resume their former thickness, and form a series of little knobs all over the skin.

The skin of the back is mostly used for this purpose. Horses, mules, and asses all contribute their skins for this purpose, although the hide of the wild ass is reckoned the best. This shagreen is in great request, as, although it is very hard when dry, it is readily softened in water and works easily. There is an imitation of shagreen in common use, formed from certain fish skins.

There are manufactures of shagreen in Russia, in Poland, and in the Levant; those of Constantinople being reputed the best.

The dzigguetai is supposed to be the same animal as the Khur, or Ghurkhud, of Persia. Supposing such to be the case, we have an excellent example of its swiftness in an account given by Sir R. K. Porter of the chase of one of these animals.

"The sun was just rising over the summits of the eastern mountains, when my greyhound started off in pursuit of an animal which my Persians said, from the glimpse they had of it, was an antelope. I instantly put spurs to my horse, and with my attendants gave chase. After an unrelaxed gallop of three miles, we came up with the dog, who was then within a short stretch of the creature he pursued, and to my surprise, and at first vexation, I saw it to be an ass. Upon a moment's reflection, however, judging from its fleetness it must be a wild one, a creature little known in Europe, but which the Persians prize, above all other animals, as an object of chase, I determined to approach as near to it as the very swift Arab I was on would carry me. But the single instant of checking my horse to consider had given our game such a head of us, that notwithstanding all our speed we could not recover our ground on him. I, however, happened to be considerably before my companions, when at a certain distance the animal in its turn made a pause, and allowed me to approach within pistol shot of him; he then darted off again with the quickness of thought, capering, kicking, and sporting in his flight, as if he was not blown in the least, and the chase was his pastime. When my followers of the country came up, they regretted that I had not shot the creature when he was within my aim, telling me that his flesh is one of the greatest delicacies in Persia. The prodigious swiftness and peculiar manner in which he fled across the plain coincided exactly with the description that Xenophon gives of the same animal in Arabia. But above all, it reminded me of the striking portrait drawn by the author of the book of Job. I was informed by the Mehmender, who had been in the desert when making a pilgrimage to the shrine of Ali, that the wild ass of Irak Arabi differs in nothing from the one I had just seen. He had observed them often for a short time in the possession of the Arabs, who told him the creature was perfectly untameable. A few days after this discussion we saw another of these animals, and, pursuing it determinedly, had the good fortune to kill it."

INDEX.

Woodfall and Kinder, Printers, Angel Court, Skinner Street, London.

10/19/98

Printed by BoD™in Norderstedt, Germany